Robert H. F

M000007155

From Sprawl to Smart Growth

Successful Legal, Planning, and Environmental Systems

ABA

Section of State and Local Government Law
American Bar Association

Book design by Catherine Zaccarine.

03 02 01 00 99   5 4 3 2 1

Freilich, Robert H., 1936-
    From sprawl to smart growth/Robert H. Freilich.
        p. cm.
    Includes bibliographical references and index.
    ISBN 1-57073-719-3
        1. City planning and redevelopment law—United States. 2. Land use—Law and legislation—United States. 3. Environmental law—United States. I. Title.
    KF5692.F74 1999
    346.7304'5—dc21   99-24031
                                                                  CIP

Discounts are available for books ordered in bulk. Special consideration is given to state bars, CLE programs, and other bar-related organizations. Inquire at ABA Publishing, Book Publishing, American Bar Association, 750 North Lake Shore Drive, Chicago, Illinois 60611.

www.abanet.org/abapubs

Dedication

To my most wonderful friend and colleague, Norman Rubinson, who was prematurely taken from us; for his friendship, guidance, brilliance, and loyalty in the countless hours from 1960 to 1968 when we together in the Town of Ramapo, New York, shaped the psychology, politics, administration, law, and planning system that began the growth management, control of urban sprawl, and smart growth movement in America. My loss of Norman has left an enormous void in my life. Without Norman, the world of planning in America today would be vastly different.

Frontispiece

" . . . the present amendments are the product of foresighted planning . . .
Ramapo has utilized its comprehensive plan to implement its timing controls
and coupled with these restrictions provisions for low and moderate income
housing on a large scale. Considered as a whole, it represents both in its inception and implementation a reasonable attempt to provide for the sequential,
orderly development of land. . . ."

Golden v. Planning Board
of the Town of Ramapo
285 N.E.2d 291
(N.Y. Ct. App. 1972)
Scillepi, Judge

"Sprawl has created enormous costs that California can no longer afford. Ironically, unchecked sprawl has shifted from an engine of California's growth to a
force that threatened to inhibit growth and degrade the quality of our life."

Bank of America
Beyond Sprawl: New Patterns
of Growth to Fit the New California
(1995)

Contents

Acknowledgments

In 1968 I left the private practice of law in Rockland County, New York, to become the Hulen Professor of Law in Urban Affairs at the University of Missouri-Kansas City School of Law and Editor of *The Urban Lawyer,* the national journal on state and local government law of the American Bar Association. Prior to leaving the East, I enrolled at Columbia University (1967–68 academic year) for my master's and doctorate in juridical science and published my thesis in 1975 on the timing and sequencing of growth in America. The J.S.D. degree awarded in 1975 thus is the precursor to this book. In 1988 I became Professor Emeritus of Law to continue to work with the nation's cities, counties, regional councils, and states in helping to control sprawl through my firm while continuing to teach land use, write, and consult. My firm, Freilich, Leitner & Carlisle, with offices in Kansas City, Missouri, and Aspen, Colorado, is a planning and law firm—a unique entity in America. We help develop comprehensive plans from initial goals to effective systems of implementing the plans and ultimately defending them, from expert witness to appellate counsel.

In writing such a book as this, I am indebted to so many countless individuals that by naming some I will inevitably unintentionally omit others who deserve mention for their wonderful contributions to the advance of land use planning and law in the United States.

First and foremost to my wife Carole, who has been my guiding inspiration in sparing the hours but especially in encouraging the effort without which it never would have been accomplished. To my children, Amy and Brad, who endured many days of the absence of their father during the thousands of trips from Seattle to the Florida Keys and South Beach Art Deco Redevelopment in Miami; from San Diego to Plymouth Rock and everywhere in between. Amy is now a practicing attorney in Los Angeles and making waves in her own right representing vast public-private development projects from the Kings-Lakers Arena to MTA and MTD corridors and headquarter sites. My son Brad is the gastroenterologist-liver specialist who stayed in Kansas City to treat his dad's anxiety-ridden conditions.

In Ramapo, first to my partners Sidney Schwartz, Frank Kobb, and Joel Scheinert, who encouraged my efforts to work on the public side of land use when their practice lay in real estate and subdivisions. Special mention must go to John McAlevey, the town supervisor who foresaw the utility of controlling sprawl and who with his colleagues on the Ramapo Town Council, Bernard Charles and Ned Siner, supported my endeavors in preparation, adoption, and defense of the system. To Herb Reisman and Morty Baron, chairmen of the Rockland County and Town of Ramapo Democratic Party, who recognized and guided the need for comprehensive planning in the suburbs of New York. To John Keough, who faithfully administered the system, Norman Slovik, chairman of the Planning Commission, and Manny Emanuel, who prepared the comprehensive plan for the town (with state and federal funds). Last to Norman Rubinson, to whom this book is dedicated, who worked with me night and day to shape the strategy, psychology, and politics of getting the plan through.

At Columbia: to Professor Curtis Berger, who guided my J.S.D. thesis from 1967 to 1975 and who added incomparable advice on land use development practices, and to Professor Alan Farnsworth, who guided me to the editorship of *The Urban Lawyer*, which I hold to this day.

At Yale Law School: to Professor Myles McDougal, who introduced me to the wonders of land use planning law; and at the University of Chicago: to Professor William Winslow Crosskey, who allowed a young undergraduate student the glimpse of the fascination of public law and who changed my life.

In Kansas City: to Dean Patrick D. Kelly at UMKC Law School, who enticed me to the midwest and was an ardent supporter; and Deans Pasco Bowman, Robert Popper, and Burnelle Powell (who has revitalized the Master of Laws in Urban Affairs program), who encouraged my endeavors in every way in the writing of this book. To Professor John Ragsdale, who helped me in the writing of the Ramapo briefs and who coauthored with me the leading article for the Minneapolis-St. Paul development guide system. To former students David Greis and Allen Bass, who labored with me on early articles on the Ramapo system.

To the many people in my firm who have been instrumental in working with me on growth management over the years. To my partner Marty Leitner, who has worked with me for twenty-four years from Hawaii and San Diego to our new projects in Prince George County, Maryland; Dana Point, California; and Tampa-Hillsborough County, Florida. Marty has been the driving force in conceptualizing and carrying out the planning process. Dick Carlisle has been my devoted and loyal friend and ever the inspiration and common sense force to my ideas. Our legendary arguments over the years have helped me to reach a higher level of understanding in order to achieve the greatest results. Steve Moore has furnished me with the solid legal framework and devoted friendship. S. Mark White has been coauthor with me since 1990 when we ventured into transportation corridor development in Los Angeles. His work and writing in the fields of concurrency management, affordable housing, and transportation management have taught me much and led him to the heights of his profession. To my former partner Terry Morgan, who enhanced my understanding of fiscal, constitutional, and economic factors, particularly in Reno-Washoe County and Sunnyvale, Texas. To Marlene Dickson, our firm administrator, who for twenty years has organized my working life, managed our firm, and kept me going through thick and thin. I owe her more than can be expressed.

To my secretaries Joan Dwork and Marilyn Odell, who patiently typed the manuscript. To Michael Lauer and Jennifer Barrett, my planning experts at the firm. To Steve Chinn, Neil Shortlidge, Elizabeth Garvin, David Bushek, Brenda Nichols, Wayne Senville, Susan Schoettle, and Bruce Peshoff, who while at the firm, devoted hundreds of hours of dedicated work with me on growth management. To my law clerks: Roxanne Doyle, Eric Stuhler, Linda Davis, Bridget Guth, and Amy Trainer for their assistance with the research, text, and footnotes that were indispensable to publication of the book.

Most especially I am indebted to Leslie Hollmann who single-handedly over a six-month period organized and edited the book. Without Leslie's brilliance the book would still be in limbo.

In the field, to the many people who rose to the challenge of containing urban sprawl: Robert Einsweiler and Ian Ball at the Minneapolis-St. Paul Metropolitan Council; Mayors Pete Wilson and Maureen O'Connor for their political support; John Witt (City Attorney) and Judge Janice Sammantino (Deputy City Attorney) for their legal support and friendship over the years, and Michael Stepner for his insight and guidance in developing the San Diego plan; to Uri Avin, one of America's most insightful planning consultants, for his work as County Planning Director in Howard County, Maryland; to Malcolm Fromberg, Mayor of Miami Beach for engaging me to develop the extraordinary South Beach Art Deco plan; to Jim Duncan for his collaboration with the Hollywood, Florida TDR plan; to my former partner in our Los Angeles office, Katherine Stone, for her efforts in Riverside, Los Angeles, and Ventura Counties; to John Eppling, State Planning Director, and Charles Siemon, coprincipal consultant on the New Jersey State Plan; to Joseph Fernandez and Robert

Banks, County Attorneys on the Palm Beach County corridor right-of-way and comprehensive plan litigation; Doug James, Robert Anderson, Dave Welsher, and Dennis Wilkison for their collaboration on the Sarasota County plan; to Lorenzo Aghemo and Mark Rosch for the Monroe County Florida Keys project; Dale Burch in Lexington Fayette County, for retaining me to plan the preservation of the horse farms; to Antoinette Seymour and David Hamme of Wallace, Roberts and Todd for their work with me on the Baltimore County and New Jersey plans; Edward J. Sullivan for his work in developing the Oregon system and Portland Urban Growth Boundary policy; Steve Del Judice, John Funk, and Tom Tyson for their incisive help with me on the Prince George County, Maryland Plan; Richard Tustian of Montgomery County with respect to financing fees for the County's transportation corriders and Marian McCoy of Anne Arundel and Baltimore Counties for her work with me in introducing growth management in Maryland; and countless others who must remain unnamed. To Associate Dean Patricia Salkin of the Albany Law School, Timothy Tosta of Baker and McKenzie in San Francisco and Dwight Merriam of Robinson & Cole, Hartford, Connecticut, and Professor Arthur Nelson of Georgia Tech for their helpful comments and suggestions on the book. To my law professor colleagues Charles Haar (Harvard), David Callies (Hawaii), Patrick Randolph, Julie Cheslick, Rob Verchick and Doug Lindner (University of Missouri-Kansas City), Dean Janice Griffith, Georgia State, Gideon Kanner (Loyola), Tom Roberts (Wake Forest), Bruce Kramer (Texas Tech), Dan Mandelker (Washington University), Fred Bosselman (Chicago-Kent), Robert Anderson (Syracuse), and the late Donald Hagman (UCLA) for their help over the years. To my colleagues at the American Planning Association, Frank So, Stuart Meck, Sylvia Lewis, and Rodney Cobb; at the Urban Land Institute, Doug Porter, and in the American Bar Association, to the present and immediate past chairmen of the Section, Larry and Sholem Friedman, and to Richard Paszkiet and Amelia Stone of ABA Publishing for their editorial help. To the Lincoln Institute for its financial support in the preparation of the book over the past five years through research grants. To Phil Bennett of the University of Wisconsin, Mark Smith of the Southwest Legal Foundation, and Stuart Meck, Peter Buchsbaum, Larry Smith, and John DeGrove for their help with state land use "smart growth" systems. To my lawyer colleagues at the ALI-ABA for their insight over the years: Frank Schnidman, Mike Berger, Ted Taub, John Delaney, Dwight Merriam, Bob McMurray, Ken Bley, Dan Curtin, and

Stanley Abrams. To Peter Levi and Michael Shultz for their coauthorship of the two editions of the book *Model Subdivision Regulations.*

While all of these people have helped with the book it is I alone who take responsibility for its shortcomings.

About the Author

Robert H. Freilich, professor of law and partner in the nationally recognized law and planning firm of Freilich, Leitner & Carlisle in Kansas City, Missouri and Freilich, Myler, Leitner & Carlisle, Aspen, Colorado, is at the forefront of land use, and taking litigation, and the development of comprehensive plans and implementation including zoning, subdivision, capital improvement programs, impact fees and financing of capital facilities, utilities, economic development and joint public-private development. During his distinguished career, Dr. Freilich has represented more than 200 cities, counties and states, from San Diego to Plymouth, Massachusetts, Seattle/Tacoma to the Florida Keys and has appeared in over 80 briefs and oral arguments in State Supreme Courts, Federal and State Courts of Appeals and the U.S. Supreme Court on all aspects of land use litigation. He has conducted dozens of workshops on developing alternatives for plan implementation before communities engage the firm.

Dr. Freilich received his A.B. degree from the University of Chicago, holds a Juris Doctor from Yale Law School and M.I.A., LL.M. and J.S.D. degrees from Columbia University. In 1968, he became Hulen Professor of Law in Urban Affairs at the University of Missouri-Kansas City School of Law. In addition, he has served as Visiting Professor of Law at Harvard Law School (1984–1985), the London School of Economics, Reading University (1974–1975), and the University of Miami School of Law (1996–1997).

Dr. Freilich is Editor of *The Urban Lawyer,* the national quarterly journal on state and local government law of the American Bar Association; Director of the Annual Planning and Zoning Institute Southwestern Legal Foundation; Immediate Past-Chair of the Planning and Law Division of the American Planning Association; a member of the Federalism Committee of the International Municipal Lawyers Association; Advisory Board of the Land Use and Environment Law Review; and a member of the American Institute of Certified Planners.

Dr. Freilich has appeared as an expert witness in more than 30 land use cases for both public and private clients nationwide and was appointed as Special Master in the U.S. District Court in *United States v. Conservation Chemical Company,* the most complex Superfund case in the nation.

Preface

With accelerating pace in the 1990s and with each gathering year, the nation, the public, states, local governments, scholars, and the courts have come to recognize that sprawl is America's most lethal disease. Smart growth programs battling sprawl have appeared everywhere. The front page of the *New York Times* on June 9, 1998, reports that "half a dozen states are considering ambitious plans to preserve farmland and other open space [and] to curb suburban sprawl. . . ."[1] More recently, Vice President Gore, in announcing the administration's $10 billion Smart Growth Program, stated, "Plan badly, and you have what so many of us suffer from first-hand—gridlock and sprawl."[2] The *Times* reports that sprawl is even devouring Montana, one of our most rural and distant states.[3] From Phoenix and Denver to Maryland and Michigan, containing urban sprawl through smart growth will be the battleground for the 2000 election from city council races to governorships to the U.S. House, says the editor of the *Washington Post Centers Group.*[4]

States like Maryland have made "Smart Growth" public policy, and environmental groups have begun to take the issue nationwide. The Sierra Club has launched a national "Challenge to Sprawl" campaign and has issued a blistering report on the effects of sprawl.[5] Even one of the nation's largest banks has issued a clarion call to address a problem that may devour our nation:

> Sprawl has created enormous costs that California can no longer afford. Ironically, unchecked sprawl has shifted from an engine of California's

---

1. Jennifer Preston, *Battling Sprawl: States Buy Land for Open Space,* N.Y. TIMES, June 9, 1998, at A1, col. 2.

2. Michael Janofsky, *Gore Offers Plan to Control Suburban Sprawl,* N.Y. TIMES, Jan. 12, 1999, at A16, col. 1.

3. Timothy Egan, Montana Journal, *Urban Sprawl Is Home on the Range,* N.Y. TIMES, July 9, 1998, at A13, col. 1.

4. E.J. Dionne, Washington Post, *"Slow Growthers Gaining Clout in Suburbia,"* K.C. STAR, July 19, 1998 at M4 (" . . . testimony to the power of a new issue that is taking hold across the country: opposition to urban sprawl.").

5. The Sierra Club, *The Dark Side of the American Dream: The Costs and Consequences of Urban Sprawl* (1998).

growth to a force that now threatens to inhibit growth and degrade the quality of our life.[6]

What has not fully reached the public consciousness is that many metropolitan areas, states, and local governments (cities and counties) with the ever-increasing support of state legislation and federal and state courts have been successful over the past quarter century in containing sprawl using the growth tier systems that emerged with the *Ramapo* case in 1972. The *Ramapo* system, which I developed from 1965 to 1969 and argued for successfully in the New York Court of Appeals and U.S. Supreme Court in 1972, established the concept of an "urbanizing tier" that assembles growth into effective nonsprawl patterns of timed and sequenced growth related to the adequacy of public facilities. The "urbanizing tier," by creating corridors, mixed-use centers, and urban growth boundaries contiguous to existing built-up areas, prevents sprawl; encourages growth and infill back into cities and inner suburbs; protects rural, agricultural, and environmental resources from urban sprawl development; and significantly enhances real economic development, public-private development opportunities, and growth in corridors and centers.

Every major piece of state legislation, from Florida's and Washington's concurrency management systems, Maryland's "Smart Growth," and Oregon's and Kentucky's urban growth boundary systems, have evolved from the adequate public facility timed and sequenced requirements pioneered in Ramapo. All of the nation's leading urban growth boundary, transportation corridor, and centers approaches to containing sprawl derive from Ramapo's geographical, timed, and sequenced growth management plan.

This book has been exactly thirty years in the making. Having moved from developing the Ramapo Plan, I helped establish the nation's leading examples of nonsprawl systems (Metropolitan Council, Minneapolis-St. Paul; San Diego; Puget Sound (Seattle-Tacoma); Montgomery, Baltimore, and Howard Counties, Maryland; Reno-Washoe County, Nevada; Ventura County, California; Palm Beach, Sarasota, and Monroe Counties (Florida Keys), Florida; Boulder and Grand Junction, Colorado; from the east to west, midwest to the mountain states. All of this has been accompanied by modern state legislation creating the means to control sprawl, from statewide targeting of capital infrastructure to

---

6. BANK OF AMERICA, BEYOND SPRAWL: NEW PATTERNS OF GROWTH TO FIT THE NEW CALIFORNIA (1995).

establishing tools for cities, counties, and regions. I have written this book to show the nation that sprawl can be and has been controlled by governments and communities using the Ramapo Urbanizing Tier Approach and that its use in the twenty-first century will advance the conquest of America's most lethal disease—sprawl.

This is also a book for city-county, rural, suburban, metropolitan, and state governments. It establishes that what you do on the "outside" will have more impact than all the programs since World War II to revitalize cities and older suburbs from the "inside." Each suburban city or county, metropolitan area and state can gain and enhance its own self-interest by controlling sprawl—by making its infrastructure more efficient; avoiding future deficiencies; safeguarding its fiscal revenues; building corridors, centers, and mixed-use developments that enlarge its quality of life and economic development base; and ensure a sustainable environmental, agricultural, and rural way of life. This is not solely a program to revitalize older built-up areas—although that clearly will be one of its major by-products—but to control sprawl on its destructive march to the fringe and beyond of our metropolitan areas. We have the knowledge and the tools to do the job. We know more about economic markets, planning and implementation to effect a sound society, at the same time safeguarding property rights, than we have ever known before. Now it will be a question of whether we have the political will to act.

The book is not an intellectual exercise. By utilizing the self-interest of competing groups in society—from existing built-up areas, suburban taxpayers, environmentalists, farmers, rural and property interest groups, and that most intractable group—the "cappuccino cowboys" who want to recreate the American frontier with a rural lifestyle coupled with an urban income—a sound consensus for antisprawl development patterns can and has been achieved. By reducing the 90 percent of new growth going out in single-family, large-lot sprawl, with only 10 percent locating in existing built-up areas, to even an 80/20 percent division, we can double the amount of investment going back into areas already serviced with capital facilities. That in itself, by creating economic opportunity in bypassed areas, will build further consensus for control of sprawl in suburban America.

Our society places great resources in corporate planning, individual planning (for college, retirement, and death), and even military planning (we call it "intelligence"). We know that planning is not a communist conspiracy nor a

Stalinist five-year plan. It is the use of human intelligence with a little bit of forethought. It is only government that we deprive of the intelligence function and then we call politicians ignorant, avaricious, and short-sighted. Let us give back to our government officials working with our diverse interest groups the ability to make long-term decisions that will help shape a better future life. Let us turn back to creating communities—not sprawling subdivisions.

This book is, to a great extent, semiautobiographical. It traces my thinking and implementing antisprawl solutions for over thirty years. Rather than write in the third person about these incredibly successful experiences, I thought it would be helpful for the reader to see the problems as they lay and, without hindsight, to examine the alternatives that were available and the choices that needed to be made to create the solutions. We do not have a crystal ball to the future; we must take the experiences of the past to our current problems, analyze the techniques, and use a community-building consensus to create the future. The twenty-first century will certainly be an exciting period to live in if we can sustain our environment, our sense of place, and a balance of our felt need for economic development that creates at the same time an enhanced quality of life. To this I have dedicated my life.

CHAPTER ONE

The Emerging Problem of Sprawl

Introduction

Traditionally, the United States has been thought of as a place of seemingly limitless land and resources.[1] Even a cursory study of American history reveals a conscious preoccupation with continuous and ever-increasing growth. From the nineteenth century onward, the federal government actively encouraged population settlement in the vast, largely uninhabited sections of the expanding country.[2] By providing land at little or no cost from the public domain, citizens received incentives to locate in the new territories. At the same time, federal aid to private railroad companies linked developed and undeveloped parts of the country, facilitating economic growth in the new settlements.[3]

Westward expansion became a basic national goal in the nineteenth century —the major national growth policy. "Manifest destiny" provided the justification, and free land provided the impetus, as settlers rushed into the new lands of the frontier. For the new immigrant from the "Old World," the possession of land conferred security, economic freedom, and social status. A great opportunity lay on the frontier where land was free from the vestigial constraints of feudalism. The emphasis was on growth, almost for growth's sake, and the incentives were provided by the disposal of the federal land,[4] and construction of canals, roads, and rails.[5]

The westward surge of population enveloping vast areas of previously undeveloped frontier land went hand-in-hand with a movement in its early stages— the urban movement.[6] Even as the westward migration was beginning, the cities along the Atlantic began to grow. Industrialization, with its promise of wealth and prosperity, began to lure workers and their families to the cities where jobs were plentiful and wages were higher. With the coming of the twentieth century, the rate of urban development in the nation at large began to surpass that of rural development.[7]

Most of America's growth during the twentieth century, and especially in the postwar era, has taken place in the suburban-rural fringes of major metropolitan areas rather than in the central cities themselves. Cities became less desirable places to live because of deterioration, abandonment, high crime, and racially impacted housing and school systems.[8] Numerous "patchwork" federal programs initiated in the post–World War II period to aid cities (urban renewal, "701" planning grants, the war on poverty, and model cities), actually accelerated the suburbanizing process through its various housing, taxation, and transportation policies.[9] Incentives for the construction of low-density, detached single-family housing were provided by federally insured mortgage money and the many tax advantages of home ownership.[10] The interstate highway system provided access to suburban areas where land was cheaper for residential, industrial, and commercial uses. The net effect of these centrifugal forces was to leave the central city with severe housing, educational, and environmental problems while depleting important natural land resources in the path of suburban development. Moreover, the desire for a rural lifestyle—more spacious housing, lavish kitchens, master baths, and "great rooms"—coupled with large lot "ranchettes," but ironically with a demand for urban services, and access to urban income, became the dominant trend in population migration of the new "cappuccino cowboys."[11]

Other causes of suburbanization were the decreasing fiscal ability of central city governments due to cutbacks on federal assistance generally and the recent nationwide property tax revolt. The tremendous out-migration of commerce and industry from the central city and first-ring suburbs,[12] and the spiraling costs of rebuilding existing built-up areas' deficient infrastructure,[13] have resulted in most regions not being able to cope with the trend of modern urban demographics and economics.[14]

Under this pattern of growth, the abundance of our limitless open space is rapidly disappearing because of the extraordinary loss of rural and agricultural land to the encroachment of urban sprawl. It is estimated that 1½ percent of our prime agricultural land is disappearing every year to suburban sprawl.[15] The conversion of agricultural land is producing many serious effects, including: the

diminishment of domestic and export food capacity, the destruction of rural and open space environments, the stimulation of wasteful expenditures of scattered capital improvement with concomitant fiscal inefficiencies and the increase of energy utilization.[16] It is estimated that the gross loss in agricultural acreage is nearly five million each year[17] and is predicted to continue at such a pace well into the twenty-first century.[18]

Traditional Land Use Tools and Their Ineffectiveness to Combat Sprawl

By the turn of the last century, many Americans began to realize that laissez-faire might not be the best means of building spacious, beautiful cities.[19] Some government regulation was necessary if the ruthless exploitation of land and other natural resources was to be effectively curbed. Land use planning in the United States has been traditionally utilized by local governmental units. The states initially defined their primary role in land development regulation as a delegator, by providing local governmental bodies with the power to zone through land-use–enabling legislation. This early abdication of zoning responsibility by the states permitted local governments to dominate land use control and to determine the course of development in terms of their own local self-interest.[20] The problems caused by fractionalized governments and local parochialism translated into a lack of local governments' ability to coordinate necessary planning strategies throughout the region.[21]

Local governments have been particularly unable to deal effectively with the problems that urban sprawl created. In large part, this is a product of a system that allows each community to attempt to solve its own problems without regard to the general needs and wants of the region of which the community is a part.[22] As the Douglas Commission pointed out in 1968:

> Today, a basic problem results because of the delegation of the zoning power from the States to local government of any size. This often results in a type of Balkanization, which is intolerable in large urban areas where local government boundaries rarely reflect the true economic and social watersheds. The present indiscriminate distribution of zoning authority leads to incompatible uses along municipal borders, duplication of public facilities, attempted exclusion of regional facilities.[23]

The reality of this situation is reflected both in uncoordinated development, which has taken place on the suburban fringe, and in the domination of policy programs by local values.

A further barrier to affirmative planning mechanisms has been the collision of planning considerations with traditional notions of property ownership. As one commentator states:

> The conventional concept of "ownership" in land is detrimental to rational land use, obstructive to the development of related environmental policies, and deceptive to those innocent individuals who would trust it for protection.[24]

Americans have traditionally treated land as a commodity—as a consequence, land has been bought and sold much like any other form of property. A strong sense of a private right of ownership in land has resulted. When this is combined with the historical abundance of land in America and the relative disinclination of government to interfere with private land use, it is easy to understand why the tradition of private property has been highly resistant to the imposition of public land use controls.[25]

Recent advocates of private property rights argue that the interests of private landowners are not adequately protected by any level of government.[26] The proproperty rights leaders have led an attack against governmental regulation of land by introducing takings and vested rights legislation in Congress and in every state.[27] In addition to the takings legislation movement, a coalition of local groups who are proproperty rights became known as the wise-use movement. They have sought to undermine the ideological and policy success of mainstream environmentalism. As a part of the wise-use movement, the members have managed to promulgate land use plans across the country, which assert the primacy private property rights of individual landowners.[28] The goal of both private property rights movements is to chill or slow down governmental regulation of land use, but recently there has been a notable lack of success.[29]

Local governments often make planning decisions based upon parochial considerations, which not only fail to take account of the problems of sprawl, but in many instances are detrimental.[30] This is partly a result of local protectionist considerations, but also it reflects a lack of foresight about the need for controlling sprawl and the government's inability to perceive its role to protect

its own self-interests by controlling sprawl. Most local governments lack both administrative and fiscal resources to deal effectively on their own with problems beyond a very limited scope. Without the capacity to plan effectively for solutions of sprawl, local governments cannot deal with the inherent difficulties of modern urban life.

While local government has been unable to control sprawl effectively, non-governmental tools for regulating the use of land—common law nuisance and the private restrictive covenant—have also led to uncoordinated, haphazard development that demonstrate the inadequacies of utilizing economic forces and individual preferences to regulate urban land. Common law nuisance and restrictive covenants are dependent upon private initiative and impose only scattered, unsystematic restraints. This situation continues today with "gated communities" governed by private covenants, which are becoming increasingly hostile to public responsibilities.[31]

The traditional land use and zoning tools in effect since zoning was recognized in the mid-1920s[32] have been ineffective to combat sprawl.[33] The first fifty years of zoning witnessed primarily a two-dimensional system. All areas of a community would be zoned into commercial, industrial, and residential uses capable of being developed at any time and without adequate facilities or proper geographical sequence. To handle rapid growth on the fringe, local communities would have to use two-dimensional methods of either excluding uses or enlarging lot size and building area requirements. The sophisticated techniques of growth management, involving timing and sequencing of development with proper densities and mixes of housing and nonresidential uses without using exclusionary methods,[34] began with the *Ramapo* case in the 1970s.[35] Large lot zoning, while increasing the cost of individual ownership, did not limit development as much as it promoted suburban sprawl and produced secondary racial and economic exclusionary effects.[36] Exclusive industrial zoning, where used to control residential growth, further promoted leapfrog development. Zoning regulations that excluded multiple-family housing encouraged low-density development.[37] The net effect of these zoning tools promoted sprawl and did not effectuate proper growth management techniques.

As a result of techniques that did not work and were simultaneously unfair to developers and lower-income groups, the courts developed a number of limitations on the use of local zoning and planning in the last few decades. The general constitutionality of zoning has been upheld as a valid use of police power.[38] However, it has been established that zoning regulations will be ruled unconstitutional, as applied, if the regulations are so restrictive that they constitute a regulatory taking of property.[39] Overbroad regulations, otherwise known as inverse condemnations, have been ruled as deprivations of property under the Fifth Amendment and invoke liability for compensation under Section 1983 of the Federal Civil Rights Act.[40]

Zoning ordinances prior to *Ramapo* did not deal with urban sprawl problems. On the contrary, they protected owners and occupiers of land from the effects of discordant land uses by segregating different types of uses in separate zones or districts. The ideal, planned community was viewed as "a great patchwork of contrasting zones rigidly segregating incompatible land uses, each zone being furnished with appropriate density, light and air, and open-space regulations, all 'in accordance with a comprehensive plan.' "[41] As a result, planning became a negative mechanism—the object was to separate out different uses—rather than an affirmative vehicle for managing growth and dealing with the problems of the locality and the region.

The *Ramapo* System and the Urbanizing Tier

These challenges, coupled with the absence of state policies and detrimental federal policies, created the need for supplementing the market by organizing development in appropriate directions. The key was to channel development into locations, uses, and densities adequate to support an appropriate urban form, one that discourages low-density sprawl and encourages serviceable densities.[42]

The breakthrough of growth management in the United States came with the landmark decision of *Golden v. Planning Board of the Town of Ramapo*,[43] where the New York high court upheld the timing and sequential control of residential subdivision activity for periods of up to eighteen years. This was the first instance of a state high court and the United States Supreme Court upholding the uncompensated restriction of land development by means of timed and sequential phasing under the Due Process Clause and Taking Clause. In essence, *Ramapo* established the principle of "reasonable use" over a "reasonable period of time," as measured by the life of the comprehensive plan.[44] The principles and techniques upheld in *Ramapo* were the innovative linking of timing and sequencing over an eighteen-year period with capital improve-

ments;[45] tying this to the purchase of development easements to reduce tax assessments;[46] and integrating the development plan, the capital improvement budget, subdivision regulation, affordable housing, and zoning.[47]

Ramapo has been ranked the most significant land use regulation case since the inception of zoning's constitutionality in the *Euclid* case, nearly fifty years before.[48] The leading treatise in the field has the following observation regarding the significance of *Ramapo*:

> The *Ramapo* decision shifted the balance of power from the developer to the land use agencies. The developer no longer has an absolute right to proceed with development, irrespective of whether public facilities can reasonably accommodate the development. Instead the developer can be made to wait a reasonable period to allow public facilities to catch up or be forced to expend funds to ripen the land for development. At the same time, the *Ramapo* case has expanded the judicial view of just what incidental costs affiliated with development may be shifted to the developer. . . . The *Ramapo* decision and rationale also permanently altered the courts' perspective of the land use regulatory process and paved the way for subsequent decisions that have favored public regulation over the developer or landowner's immediate right to develop property (irrespective of the harm such development might inflict upon the public good). . . .[49]

The importance of the *Ramapo* plan is the recognition of the fundamental constitutional principle that techniques to handle growth over the next fifteen to twenty years can be controlled by linking the proposed development with the planned extension of capital improvements over the lifetime of a comprehensive plan.[50] The use of an "Urbanizing Tier" developed from the sophisticated *Ramapo* growth management technique by organizing the fifteen- to twenty-year period of timed and sequenced urbanization within orderly corridors, centers, or urban growth boundaries to prevent sprawl. The use of proper timing and sequencing controls in suburban areas is also the key to correlated urban infill and rural-agricultural preservation.[51]

The "Urbanizing Tier" concept is a far more sophisticated application of the urban growth boundary approach.[52] A principal tenet of the "tier" system involves the geographic and functional division of the planning area into sub-areas ("tiers"). Tier I constitutes the existing central city. Tier II is the first or second ring of built-up suburbs. Tier III constitutes the area where active growth is channeled (the *Ramapo* tier). Tier IV is the rural and agricultural preservation area. The functional planning area concept recognizes that different areas of the community present different problems relating to growth and development. Therefore, the different areas utilize different techniques, such as subsidies in Tier I; code enforcement in Tier II; timing, sequencing, and charging new development with the cost of capital facilities in Tier III; and economic incentives, TDRs, and development easement contribution in Tier IV.

Nevertheless, while individual geographical or functional areas may receive specialized treatment, they must also be viewed in terms of their interrelationships with other areas and with the community as a whole. The tier system divides the community into "growth" and "limited growth" categories and adds the tiers as subdivisions of those general categories.[53] It is the growth category that is typically designated as the "Urbanizing Tier."[54]

The "Urbanizing Tier" consists of those areas that are undergoing active urbanization and served by public facilities. The "Urbanizing Tier" is generally delineated based on many factors, which include:

1. the proximity to existing and planned transportation and transit corridors and corridor centers;
2. the degree of contiguity to already developed areas available for infill;
3. the recognition of planned public capital improvement projects currently served by sewer or logical capital improvement phasing; and
4. the development of mixed-use commercial and neotraditional residential centers.

Management within this tier situates and directs growth, which is vital for helping rehabilitation, infill, and revitalization efforts in already built-up suburban and urban areas. The "Urbanizing Tier" is the place at which planners and developers can control growth to contain sprawl and save agricultural land.

Today states, regions, counties, and cities have begun to take up the quest of halting sprawl. *Ramapo's* novel path of ingenuity has evolved into today's Smart Growth systems. New antisprawl mechanisms culminating under the label of "Smart Growth" starting from the state level have seeped both upward into federal government programs and downward into local governmental bodies.[55] Some have had much success, while others are still in search of that success. It is the legal and planning principles of timing and sequencing that

Ramapo introduced to metropolitan, regional, state, and national thinking within the tier system that Smart Growth has built upon to continue the battle against sprawl.

Endnotes

1. ROBERT FREILICH & ERIC STUHLER, THE LAND USE AWAKENING 32–33 (1981) [hereinafter FREILICH & STUHLER]; *see also* Patrick J. Skelley II, *Defending the Frontier (Again): Rural Communities, Leap-Frog Development, and Reverse Exclusionary Zoning*, 16 VA. ENVTL. L.J. 273 (1997); DAVID L. CALLIES, ROBERT H. FREILICH & THOMAS E. ROBERTS, CASES AND MATERIALS ON LAND USE 555 (West 2d ed. 1994) [hereinafter CALLIES & FREILICH].

2. *See* Barlowe, *Federal Programs for the Direction of Land Use*, 50 IOWA L. REV. 337 (1965).

3. *See* Holland, *National Growth Policy: Notes on the Federal Role*, 1973 URB. LAW. ANN. 59, at 64.

4. Even after the Homestead era, the federal government today owns approximately 740 million acres of land of which 440 million are "disposable" administratively, without congressional approval, except for national parks, forests, and wildlife refuges. *See* BUREAU OF LAND MANAGEMENT, U.S. DEP'T OF INTERIOR, PUBLIC LAND STATISTICS (1980 at 9, 21).

5. *See* James A. Kushner, *The Reagan Urban Policy: Centrifugal Force in the Empire*, 2 UCLA J. ENVTL. L. & POL'Y, 209, 211 (1982).

6. *See* C. GLAAB & A.T. BROWN, A HISTORY OF URBAN AMERICA (1967).

7. In 1790, the vast majority of the American population lived in rural areas. Only 5 percent lived in communities of more than 2,500 people, and only half of those in cities of more than 10,000. *See* UNITED STATES PRESIDENT (NIXON), REPORT ON NATIONAL GROWTH, at 14 (1972). Between 1890 and 1900, the beginnings of a major migration from agricultural to urban areas got under way. By 1900, 40 percent of the population were living in urban areas of 2,500 or more, and more than 60 percent of the economically active population were working outside of agriculture. In 1920, for the first time, the census showed more than half the population living in urban areas and by 1990, 78 percent of the population resided in a metropolitan area. *See* Henry R. Richmond, *From Sea to Shining Sea: Manifest Destiny and the National Land Use Dilemma*, 13 PACE L. REV. 327, 331 (1993); *see also Those Lights in Big Cities Get Brighter, Census Finds*, N.Y. TIMES, December 18, 1991, at A10.

8. DAVID RUSK, CITIES WITHOUT SUBURBS 9 (1993).

9. Shelby D. Green, *The Search for a National Land Use Policy: For the Cities' Sake*, 26 FORDHAM URB. L.J. 69 (1998); *see generally* Chapter 2, *infra*. *See also* Nelson, GROWTH MANAGEMENT PRINCIPLES PRACTICES (American Planning Association, 1995); ERIC H. MONKKONEN, AMERICA BECOMES URBAN: THE DEVELOPMENT OF U.S. CITIES & TOWNS 1780–1980 (1990); AUSCUREL, CITIES & INFRASTRUCTURE (National Academy Press, 1988); Mark Baldassare, THE GROWTH DILEMMA (1981).

10. Robert H. Freilich & Bruce G. Peshoff, *The Social Costs of Sprawl*, 29 URB. LAW. 183, 186–87 (1997). Other causes of the decreasing fiscal ability of municipal governments is due to cutbacks on federal assistance generally, and the recent property tax revolt seen nationwide. James Nicholas, *Paying for Growth: Creative and Innovative Solutions*, GROWTH MANAGEMENT: THE PLANNING CHALLENGE OF THE 1990S (1993). Reviewing these limitations on the fiscal

ability of municipalities in conjunction with the tremendous out-migration of industry from the central city, and the spiraling costs of rebuilding older, built-up core areas, it is easy to see why many municipalities have been unable to cope with the realities of modern urban problems.

11. ROBERT H. FREILICH, TO SPRAWL OR NOT TO SPRAWL: NATIONAL PERSPECTIVES FOR KANSAS CITY (CHARLES KIMBALL LECTURE) p. 10 (Western Historical Manuscript Society 1998).

12. Michael E. Lewyn, *The Urban Crisis: Made in Washington*, 4 J.L. & POL'Y 513, 514 (1996); JOEL GARREAU, EDGE CITY: LIFE ON THE NEW FRONTIER 4 (1991).

13. NANCY RUTLEDGE, REPORT OF PRESIDENT REAGAN'S NATIONAL COUNCIL ON PUBLIC WORKS IMPROVEMENT (1989).

14. Peter Dreier, *The Urban Crisis: The Kerner Commission Report Revisited: America's Urban Crisis: Symptoms, Causes, Solutions*, 71 N.C. L. REV. 1351, 1378 (1993).

15. U.S. DEP'T OF AGRICULTURE AND PRESIDENT'S COUNCIL ON ENVIRONMENTAL QUALITY, THE NATIONAL AGRICULTURE LANDS STUDY (1981).

16. *See generally* FREILICH & STUHLER, *supra* note 1; *see also* CALLIES & FREILICH, *supra* note 1, 555; *see generally* Robert H. Freilich & Linda Kirts Davis, *Saving the Land: The Utilization of Modern Techniques of Growth Management to Preserve Rural and Agricultural America*, 13 URB. LAW. 27, 28 (1981) [hereinafter Freilich & Davis]; Frederick R. Steiner, et al., A DECADE WITH LESA: THE EVOLUTION OF LAND EVALUATION AND SITE ASSESSMENT (1994); Frank Schnidman, et al., RETENTION OF LAND FOR AGRICULTURE: POLICY, PRACTICE AND POTENTIAL IN NEW ENGLAND (Lincoln Institute, 1990) (1990); PLOWING THE URBAN FRINGE: AN ASSESSMENT OF ALTERNATIVE APPROACHES TO FARMLAND PRESERVATION (HAL HIEMSTRA & NANCY BUSHWICK, eds., 1989); *see* Dr. Robert H. Freilich, An Address to Berlin Marshall Fund Workshop on Sustainable Transportation in Urban Areas (Oct. 28, 1997) titled *The Land Use Implications of Transit Oriented Development: Controlling the Demand Side of Transportation Congestion and Urban Sprawl*; James A. Kushner, *Urban Transportation Planning*, 4 URB. L. & POL'Y 161, 173 (1981).

17. *See* Shelby B. Green, *The Search for a National Land Use Policy for the Cities' Sake*, 26 FORDHAM URB. L.J. 69, 80 (1998) *citing* Julian Juergensmeyer, *Farmland Preservation: A Vital Agricultural Issue for the 1980s*, 21 WASHBURN L.J. 443, 444 (1982) (in the twenty-year period from 1954 to 1974, 119 million farmland acres, or nearly six million acres per year, were lost to suburban sprawl).

18. William L. Church, *Farmland Concession: The View from 1986*, 1986 U. ILL. L. REV. 521, 536–37, in which Church predicted cropland losses to continue at an unabated pace to 2020.

19. For a history of development of land use controls in America, *see* Cribbet, *Changing Concepts in the Law of Land Use*, 50 IOWA L. REV. 245 (1965).

20. Note, *State Land Use Control: Why Pending Federal Legislation Will Help*, 25 HASTINGS L.J. 1165, 1167 (1974); Jayne E. Daly, *A Glimpse of the Past, A Vision for the Future, Senator Henry M. Jackson and National Land Use Legislation*, 27 URB. LAW. 1 (1996).

21. John F. Kain, FAILURE IN DIAGNOSIS: A CRITIQUE OF THE NATIONAL URBAN POLICY, 11 URB. LAW. 261–62 (1979) (the irrational placement of governmental entities and geographical jurisdiction makes it inordinately difficult to correct the structural deficiencies).

22. 1995 HUD NATIONAL URBAN GROWTH REP., at 27–28; James H. Wickersham, *The Quiet Revolution Continues: The Emerging New Model for State Growth Management Statutes*, 18 HARV. ENVTL. L. REV. 489 (1994).

23. NATIONAL COMMISSION ON URBAN PROBLEMS, BUILDING THE AMERICAN CITY (1968), at 19.

24. Caldwell, *Rights of Ownership or Rights of Use? The Need for a New Conceptual Basis for Land Use Policy*, 15 WM. & MARY L. REV. 759 (1974).

25. Richmond, *supra* note 7, at 327; Caldwell, *supra* note 24, at 761. *See also* C. MADDEN, LAND AS A NATIONAL RESOURCE, 6–30 (C.L. Harris ed., 1974).

26. *See* R. Miniter, *You Just Can't Take It Anymore: America's Property Rights Revolt*, 70 POL'Y REV. 40–46 (1994); M. Lavell, *The "Property Rights" Revolt*, 15 NAT'L L.J. 36 (1993); H.M. Jacobs & B.W. Ohm, *Statutory Takings Legislation: The National Context, the Wisconsin and Minnesota Proposals*, 2 n.2 WIS. ENVTL. L.J. (Summer 1995).

27. Robert H. Freilich & Roxanne Doyle, *Takings Legislation: Misguided and Dangerous*, 46 LAND USE L. & ZONING DIG. 3 (Oct. 1994).

28. Jacobs & Ohm, *supra* note 26, at 2.

29. Anita Miller, 25 URB. LAW. 827 (Fall 1993); U.S. v Nye County, 920 F. Supp. 1108, (D. Nev. 1996).

30. *See* Patricia E. Salkin, *Statewide Comprehensive Planning: The Next Wave,* in STATE AND REGIONAL COMPREHENSIVE PLANNING: IMPLEMENTING NEW METHODS FOR GROWTH MANAGEMENT, 236 (Peter A. Buchsbaum & Larry J. Smith eds., American Bar Ass'n 1993); Feiler, *Metropolitanization and Land-Use Parochialism: Toward a Judicial Attitude*, 69 MICH. L. REV. 655 (1971); ROBERT L. LINEBERRY & IRA SHARKANSKY, URBAN POLITICS AND PUBLIC POLICY, 154 (3d ed. 1978).

31. For chilling stories of what gated communities might become in the future, *see* Neil Shouse, *The Bifurcation: Class Polarization and Housing Segregation in the Twenty-First Century Metropolis*, 30 URB. LAW. 145 (Winter 1998); Rebecca J. Schwartz, *Public Gated Residential Communities: The Rosemont, Illinois, Approach and Its Constitutional Implications*, 29 URB. LAW. 123 (Winter 1997).

32. Village of Euclid v. Ambler Realty Co., 272 U.S. 365 (1926); Nectow v. City of Cambridge, 277 U.S. 365 (1928).

33. Freilich & Davis, *supra* note 16; *The National Commission on Urban Problems (Douglas Commission)* in BUILDING THE AMERICAN CITY recognized the limitations of traditional zoning techniques in 1968: "At the metropolitan scale, the present techniques of development guidance have not effectively controlled the timing and location of development. Under traditional zoning, jurisdictions are theoretically called upon to determine in advance the sites needed for various types of development. In doing so, however, they have continued to rely on techniques which were never designed as timing devices and which do not function well in controlling timing. The attempt to use large-lot zoning, for example, to control timing has all too often resulted in scattered development on large lots, prematurely establishing the character of much later development—the very effect sought to be avoided. New types of controls are needed if the basic metropolitan scale problems are to be solved."

34. *See* my presentation at the Missouri Association for Social Welfare 71st Annual Conference (Oct. 27–29, 1971) discussing strategies to make cities livable again through public housing initiatives; *see also Cooperation Urged in City Solutions*, K.C. TIMES, Oct. 29, 1971, at 20; Laura Rollins Hockaday, *Cities Need to Disperse the Poor*, quoting Robert Freilich (concentrations of low-income families in the center of the city must be dispersed over the entire metropolitan area, or city problems will continue to worsen. Providing affordable housing in the central city and surrounding areas will help lower-income families to disperse and live in bet-

ter conditions); Jeanne A. Fox, *Bill of Rights Half Empty?*, K.C. STAR, April 25, 1976, at 4; *Lawyer Hits Concentration of Low-Income Families*, MISSOURIAN, Dec. 12, 1969 (to deter bias against low-income subsidized families, "scattered housing" can be available); George McCuitson, *Focus on Growth*, K.C. STAR, May 18, 1971; *Freilich Depicts National Housing Crisis*, Southwestern Ill. Metropolitan Area Planning Comm'n, Oct. 1970 (presenting the various housing alternatives and need to spread adequate housing throughout the region); William D. Tammeus, *Housing Problems 'Critical,'* K.C. TIMES, Dec. 11, 1973 (I recommended dispersal of low-income and minority families to prevent racial segregation; regional approaches to housing so all cities share low- and moderate-income housing; total inner-city neighborhood redevelopment to help attract middle- and upper-income families back into the city; preserving older city neighborhoods; and creation of a unified housing department); E.S. Evans, *Warns of New Rules on Ghetto Citizen Role*, ST. LOUIS POST, Jan. 18, 1970 (I warned that failure to meet the new citizen participation requirements could halt all housing and redevelopment programs in St. Louis).

35. Freilich & Davis, *supra* note 16; *see* IRVING SCHIFFMAN, ALTERNATIVE TECHNIQUES FOR MANAGING GROWTH 17–18 (1989); *see also* James Carberry, *Boon or Bottleneck? Builders Say Governmental Rules Raise Prices*, WALL ST. J., July 10, 1978, at 1 (builders believe "that growth management plans should be judged by whether the public's need for adequate, affordable housing is satisfied"); Herbert G. Lawson, *No Vacancy: Civil Libertarians Join Developers to Oppose Cities' Growth Curbs*, WALL ST. J., Jan. 31, 1975, at 1 (the Ramapo plan includes a provision for low-income housing and subsequent development after the timing and sequencing have been completed with adequate public facilities); *Phased Growth Controls Meeting*, YOUNG LAW., Sept.–Oct., at 3 (ABA 1973).

36. CHARLES M. HAAR, SUBURBS UNDER SIEGE: RACE, SPACE AND AUDACIOUS JUDGES (Princeton Univ. Press 1996); Bruce M. Stave, *Thinking the Unthinkable About Our Cities Thirty Years Later, A Conversation with Charles M. Haar*, 25 J. OF URBAN HISTORY 57, 75 (1998); Report of the National Advisory Commission on Civil Disorders "The Kerner Commission" Report, chs. 1, 2 (New York 1968).

37. For an excellent summary of deficiencies in traditional methods, see Richard W. Cutler, *Legal and Illegal Methods for Controlling Community Growth on the Urban Fringe*, 372 WIS. L. REV. 370 (1961). I was legal counsel for the Kansas City School District and nine individual black school children and commenced litigation to achieve regionwide desegregation and nondiscriminatory integration of the Kansas City Metropolitan Area schools. *Jenkins v. Missouri*, 807 F.2d 657 (8th Cir. 1986), *cert. denied*, 484 U.S. 816 (1987). *See* Letter dated Mar. 16, 1977, to the K.C. STAR from Mildred Clapp; Paul Delaney, *Integration Suit by Kansas City Board Could Open Way to Interstate Schools*, N.Y. TIMES, May 28, 1977, at 8C; Andrew C. Miller, *District Tries Untested Paths to Desegregation*, K.C. STAR, July 29, 1975, at 3; Robert H. Freilich, *Community Cooperation Vital*, K.C. STAR, May 13, 1977, at 1D; Stephen E. Winn, *Desegregation Suit: Districts Raise Ethical Issue*, K.C. STAR, July 19, 1979, at 1; Rosalind C. Truitt, *Desegregation: Economics in School Changes*, K.C. STAR, May 7, 1977, at 4A; Howard S. Goller, *School Forum Draws Believers*, K.C. STAR, May 13, 1977; Andrew C. Miller, *Professor Predicts White Flight*, K.C. STAR, Jan. 14, 1976; *AJC to Discuss School Integration*, K.C. STAR, April 26, 1974, at 14; Robert L. Carroll, *For Area-Wide Integration*, K.C. TIMES, April 12, 1973.

38. Euclid v. Ambler Realty Co., 272 U.S. 365 (1926) *cited in* Freilich & Davis, *supra* note 16 at 31.

39. Agins v. City of Tiburon, 447 U.S. 255 (1980); Penn Cent. Transp. Co. v. City of New

York, 483 U.S. 104 (1978), *rehearing denied,* 439 U.S. 883 (1978); Freilich & Garvin, *Takings After Lucas: Growth Management Planning and Regulatory Implementation Will Work Better Than Before,* 2 STETSON L. REV. 409 (1993).

40. Freilich & Davis, *supra* note 16, at 31; Monell v. Dep't of Soc. Serv. of the City of New York, 436 U.S. 658 (1978); Lake Country Estates, Inc. v. Tahoe Reg. Plan. Agency, 440 U.S. 391 (1979); Lynch v. Household Fin. Corp., 405 U.S. 538 (1972).

41. Roger A. Cunningham, *Land-Use Control—The State and Local Programs,* 50 IOWA L. REV. 367, 382 (1965).

42. Freilich & Davis, *supra* note 16, at 33; Robert H. Freilich & S. Mark White, *Transportation Congestion and Growth Management: Comprehensive Approaches to Resolving America's Major Quality of Life Crisis,* 24 LOY. L.A. L. REV., June 1991, at 915.

43. Golden v. Planning Board of Town of Ramapo, 30 N.Y.2d 359, 285 N.E.2d 291, 334 N.Y.S.2d 138, *appeal dismissed,* 409 U.S. 1003 (1972); ERIC DAMIAN KELLY, MANAGING COMMUNITY GROWTH: POLICIES, TECHNIQUES, AND IMPACTS, at 30.

44. Robert H. Freilich, Elizabeth Garvin & S. Mark White, *Economic Development and Public Transit: Washington Growth Management,* 16 U. PUGET SOUND L. REV. 949, at 952 (1993) [hereinafter Freilich, Garvin & White].

45. Sequencing is "the phasing of development permission consistent with the availability of services, facilities and other infrastructure necessary to accommodate development. . . . " Kushner, at § 2.12 (citing Robert H. Freilich & S. Mark White, *Commentary: Effective Transportation Congestion Management,* 43 LAND USE L. & ZONING DIG. 3 (June 1991)). *See also* David Brower et al., URBAN GROWTH MANAGEMENT THROUGH DEVELOPMENT TIMING (1976); Carol R. Stone, *The Prevention of Urban Sprawl Through Utility Extension Controls,* 14 URB. LAW. 357 (1982), *cited in* Freilich, Garvin & White, *supra* note 43, at 14.

46. *See generally* Robert H. Freilich & John W. Ragsdale, *Timing and Sequential Controls: The Essential Bases for Effective Regional Planning: An Analysis of the New Directions for Land Use Control in the Minneapolis-St. Paul Metropolitan Region,* 58 MINN. L. REV. 1009 (1974), *cited in* Freilich, Garvin & White, *supra* note 43, at 15.

47. *Ramapo* has clearly been determined to be the father of growth management in the United States. *See* Douglas R. Porter, MANAGING GROWTH IN AMERICA'S COMMUNITIES 20, 31, 123 (1997); KELLY, MANAGING COMMUNITY GROWTH 30–32, 78, 79, 185 (1993); Stephen P. Chinn & Elizabeth A. Garvin, *Designing Development Allocation Systems,* LAND USE LAW. 3 (1992); Thomas G. Pelham, *Adequate Public Facilities Requirements: Reflections on Florida's Concurrency System for Managing Growth,* 974 FLA. ST. U. L. REV. 973, 976 (1993); IRVING SCHIFFMAN, ALTERNATIVE TECHNIQUES FOR MANAGING GROWTH 17 (1989); Louise Crago, *Growth Control Planning, Yes—Panic Bans, No,* BOCA RATON SUN-SENTINEL, Feb. 21, 1974, at 1B ("Dr. Freilich was . . . the godfather of the outstandingly successful growth control program in Ramapo, NY"). The many cases that have subsequently cited *Ramapo* are too numerous to cite. A few significant ones follow: Torsoe Brothers Constr. Corp. v. Village of Monroe, 366 N.Y.S.2d 810, 814-15 (N.Y. 1975); Marcus Associates, Inc. v. Town of Huntington, 393 N.Y.S.2d 727 (1977); Robert E. Kurzius, Inc. v. Village of Upper Brookville, 414 N.Y.S.2d 573, 577 (1979); Construction Industry Assoc. of Sonoma County v. City of Petaluma, 522 F.2d 897, 908 (9th Cir. 1975); Schenck v. City of Hudson, 114 F.3d 590 (6th Cir. 1996).

48. DOZIER & HAGMAN, 4 ENVTL. COMMENT 4 (1978) after a nationwide survey of land use professors and practicing land use lawyers and planners.

49. ROHAN, 1 ZONING AND LAND USE CONTROLS § 4.05 (1984) (1997 Supp.).

50. For a history of Ramapo's capital improvement programming as a guide to land use planning, *see* Stuart L. Deutsch, *Capital Improvement Controls as Land Use Devices*, 9 ENVTL. L. REV. 61 (1978).

51. *See* FREILICH, LEITNER & CARLISLE, GROWTH MANAGEMENT APPROACHES FOR THE NEW JERSEY STATE DEVELOPMENT AND REDEVELOPMENT PLAN, TECH. REF. DOC. 87-15, January 1987; FREILICH, LEITNER & CARLISLE, RENO-WASHOE COUNTY REGIONAL PLAN (November 1991). Another example of this approach is found in the Puget Sound, Washington Region, which has divided development into the following land use categories: major urban centers, activity centers, employment areas, and residential neighborhoods. *Bellevue Conference Center, Transit/Land Use Linkages: Making It Work* (July 1993) at 4. Major Urban Centers are areas that contain high concentrations of housing and employment, with direct service by high-capacity transit, and a wide range of other land uses such as retail, recreational, public facilities, parks, and open space. Major Urban Centers are a focus of regional activity and provide services to the general region. Activity Centers are locations that contain many of the same land uses as Activity Centers but tend to be more automobile-oriented because of their physical layout. Low Density/Intensity Employment Areas include office parks, industrial areas, and manufacturing locations that are developed at relatively low densities. These areas are typically automobile-oriented, single-use areas and do not generate a high degree of transit use. Residential Neighborhoods generally include single-family residences with varying degrees of multifamily, depending on location. Commercial services can range from numerous and convenient to non-existent. *See* Freilich, Garvin & White, *supra* note 44.

52. Other "tier systems" have been developed by Freilich, Leitner & Carlisle in San Diego, Los Angeles, Riverside, and Ventura County, California; Baltimore County, Montgomery County, and Howard County, Maryland; Minneapolis-St. Paul region, Minnesota; Lexington-Fayette County, Kentucky; Palm Beach and Sarasota Counties, Florida; Washoe (Reno) and Clark Counties (Las Vegas), Nevada; Pierce County (Tacoma), Washington; and many others. Robert Freilich & S. Mark White, *Transportation Congestion and Growth Management: Comprehensive Approaches to Relieving America's Major Quality of Life Crisis*, 24 LOY. L.A. L. REV. 915 (1991); Robert H. Freilich, A FIVE-TIERED GROWTH MANAGEMENT PROGRAM FOR SAN DIEGO, 2–7 to 2–11 (1976); Freilich & Ragsdale, *supra* note 46; CALLIES & FREILICH, *supra* note 1, at 586.

53. R. Freilich, A FIVE-TIERED GROWTH MANAGEMENT PROGRAM FOR SAN DIEGO (1976).

54. *See* CALLIES & FREILICH, *supra* note 1, at 586. The tiers within the limited growth category would be "Rural/Future Urbanizing," "Agricultural," and "Conservation/Open Space." Each of the tiers has specific geographical boundaries and is capable of being mapped. The Rural/Future Urbanizing area may be a permanent rural density development area or may be a temporary "holding" zone until the growth areas are built out; it generally contains lands that are presently unanswered and that have a lower population density. The Agriculture tier is intended to identify those lands that should be preserved either temporarily or permanently for agricultural production. The Conservation/Open Space tier consists of lands containing natural resources or environmentally sensitive areas.

55. *See* STATE AND REGIONAL COMPREHENSIVE PLANNING: IMPLEMENTING NEW METHODS FOR GROWTH MANAGEMENT (Peter A. Buchsbaum & Larry J. Smith eds., American Bar Ass'n, 1993); Shelby D. Green, *The Search for a National Land Use Policy*, 28 FORDHAM URB. L.J. 69 (1998).

The Need for Smart Growth

The Beginning of Sprawl

Without the timing and sequencing of growth within the Urbanizing Tier, sprawl will continue to deplete existing built-up areas, develop land in suburban areas by leapfrogging beyond adequate public facilities, and destroy agricultural and environmental resources. From the time of America's early colonial settlements, cities, towns, and villages were planned and designed in the European mode to emphasize urban community. Yet the vast majority of people lived in rural and agricultural areas with rural levels of service and facilities. Our transition from an agrarian to an urbanized nation first became noticeable in the 1910 census, as the nation's "urbanizing" population appreciably began to rise. In concert with the burgeoning of the industrializing and urbanizing economy, individual and community expectations changed. Urban planning as a social tool became commonplace, attempting to balance a sense of community founded on rising expectations and aspirations with the rapid physical outward growth of cities emerging in a compact form.[1]

Ironically, as the nation's frontier came to a close in the late nineteenth century, the city began to exhibit its own "frontier" with the exodus from the city scene to suburban "rural" living. This development was not sprawl as it followed contiguous patterns and trolley line corridors. Urban life in the post-industrial age began to exhibit suburban lifestyle tendencies of the growing economic and social class of business owner-managers. Those with the financial capability moved into suburban, semirural developments located at the fringes of cities. Streetcars, trains, and subways were available modes of transportation to and from residential and commercial uses, creating a land use pattern of corridor growth, not sprawl, predating the advent of the automobile.

It was only from the post-World War I years to the 1950s' Interstate Highway System that a pattern of sprawling, low-density residential development began to leapfrog away from the central city—a pattern that in the last forty years has accelerated despite political rhetoric, energy crises, and fiscal distress. While that sprawl seemingly accommodates the greatest amount of growth, it requires significant development of new facilities and services, with accompanying abandonment and underutilization of existing facilities. Sprawl also increases development costs to the suburbs, diminishes the environmental factors needed to sustain viable economic growth, and requires the consumption of the greatest amount of agricultural land, energy, and natural resources.[2]

Sprawl has engendered six major crises for America's major metropolitan regions. These crises are:

1. deterioration of existing built-up areas (cities and first- and second-ring suburbs);
2. environmental degradation—loss of wetlands and sensitive lands, poor air and water quality;
3. overconsumption of gasoline energy;
4. fiscal insolvency, transportation congestion, infrastructure deficiencies, and taxpayer revolts;
5. agricultural land conversion; and
6. unaffordable housing.

Perhaps the most telling definition of "sprawl" has been penned by Richard Moe, President of the National Trust for Historic Preservation, who stated that sprawl is "low-density development on the edges of cities and towns that is poorly planned, land-consumptive, automobile-dependent [and] designed without regard to its surroundings."[3]

The Nationalization of Sprawl

Sprawl has been promoted by social forces, which reflect the desire for a rural lifestyle coupled with an urban income. It is also encouraged by the political power of development interests and supported by legislative mandates that sustain income tax deductions for single-family mortgage interest payments and property taxes and subsidization of new growth being laid upon existing built-up areas because of inadequate development funding of infrastructure, the need

for which is generated by new development.[4] It has become an institutionalized facet of American life.

Suburbanization and sprawl are as ingrained in our national myth as baseball and apple pie once were. Its progenitors are the "cappuccino cowboys" who want jacuzzi baths, great rooms, mammoth kitchens, and five-acre ranchettes to imitate rural life while demanding a full set of urban services. The image of curvilinear streets, cul-de-sacs, ranch houses, station wagons, and gated communities denigrates the urban counterpoint—the value of community represented by open access, neighborhood commercial centers, cultural resources, and pedestrian access to all.[5]

Simultaneously as social infrastructure and fiscal needs escalate in cities and first- and second-ring suburban areas, the property tax base supporting community facilities and services has decreased due to sprawl's outward migration of people and businesses. Government action and inaction have resulted in sprawl, perpetuating a lack of resources in urban areas that are a cancer attacking the region from the inside out and the outside in.[6]

Every twenty years we desperately revolt from this pattern. In the 1950s we talked about "the City of Man."[7] In the 1960s and 1970s we focused on building "new towns" in the suburbs.[8] Today we are trying to build "neo-traditional" areas.[9] Since the 1960s, there has been an increasing awareness that states and local governments have not dealt effectively with problems that are national in scope, yet a national growth policy for guidance is still not in existence. The federal government's attempt to implement scattershot national solutions to problems through attempting dispersal of federally subsidized housing and regional review and coordination[10] has occasioned miserably ineffective results.[11]

Recognizing a need to focus more attention on comprehensive land use planning at the federal level, Congress considered the Land Use Policy and Planning Assistance Act of 1971,[12] introduced by Senator Jackson in January 1971. Section 302 of the Jackson bill would have required that the states must, within three years, develop an administrative basis for comprehensive land use planning.[13] Under this Act, the federal government would have provided funding for up to 90 percent of the total cost to the state. To qualify for the funds, the states would establish a timetable for reports on the progress of the plan. The plan itself would develop in accordance with the timetable. The proposed Act set out very few guidelines about what should be included in the plan or what approach the state should take; it merely required that there be a plan. It did, however, require by the end of a five-year period that the following be developed:

1. a method to control the use of land that is or may be impacted by key facilities;
2. a method to control private large-scale development of more than local impact;
3. a method to control use and development in areas of critical environmental concern; and
4. a method to influence the location of new communities and control surrounding land use.[14]

Although the Jackson bill encouraged the states to develop legislation, it proposed no concrete guidelines by which states could approach the specialized aspects of the problem of sprawl. Nor did it deal with the problem of how to balance effectively and judiciously the development and growth of our society with the preservation of our environment, maintaining the viability of our existing built-up areas, providing effective infrastructure solutions to our growing massive deficiencies, while at the same time conserving or replenishing our depleting energy supplies. The impetus for planning was again on haphazard, piecemeal thinking, with federal funding offered to those states following these standardless federal guidelines. No positive, comprehensive scheme was ever set out, or ever required to be produced. The Jackson bill, S. 268, was passed by the Senate but failed by a few votes to pass the House in 1971.[15]

Without encouragement by the federal government, local governments frequently become their own worst enemies concerning sprawl.[16] Existing urban areas have experienced the effects of diminishing economically viable populations—reacting to but unable to combat effectively, through regional and state policies and strategies, the outward exodus because of the inability to coalesce urban and suburban political interests. Suburban communities have only slowly come to realize that growth requires costly infrastructure and that it is in their own self-interest to establish efficient land use patterns that can control the adverse effects of sprawl eating away at their own stability. Gone are the days when virtually unfettered development and growth was considered a win-win situation. Prior to World War II, property taxes were used to finance state government activities, while local development was required only to finance on-site infrastructure costs. The financial responsibility for off-site community facili-

ties and services was subsidized almost exclusively by the general taxing public through sales and property taxes. Today it is universally recognized that new growth in the suburbs must pay for its own one-time cost of major off-site (arterial highways, regional parks, sewer and water systems, fire and police substations, downstream drainage, and schools) capital infrastructure so that the general fund can be used to cover infrastructure deficiencies, operation, and maintenance; yet suburban communities have failed to make growth pay for needed infrastructure and services, creating instead a current deficiencies gap in excess of trillions of dollars. Effective approaches to these problems have largely remained unused and/or unadopted.

Racial factors have also been powerful influences contributing to sprawl and socioeconomic polarization. The "race card" remains a symbol of sprawl. Housing discrimination is fueled by animosity toward targeted racial and ethnic groups, denying housing opportunities through the use of restrictive zoning, buyer steering, indirect or off-market sales (that is, sales occurring by word of mouth), and unfair lending practices. Moreover, the National Housing Acts of 1934, 1937, and 1949 actually promoted racial discrimination through the creation of urban ghettos, leading to higher concentrations of poverty and failing to promote dispersal of federally subsidized housing into the suburbs.[17] These actions created barriers to a class of persons searching for better housing for their families—some who can afford to leave but find limited opportunities, others who cannot afford to leave and are forced to find "affordable" or subsidized housing in geographically constrained areas.

During the 1960s there was an increasing effort on the part of the federal government to implement a national policy of equal opportunity in housing, especially after the race riots in 1967 and the resulting Kerner Commission Report.[18] This attempt was the result of a realization that previous policies had led to an increasing residential separation within the nation's metropolitan areas.[19] The effort emphasized three areas where legal action was required: (a) protection against discrimination; (b) increases in the supply of lower-income housing; and, most important, (c) dispersal of such housing outside of areas of minority and poverty concentrations.[20] Although federal legislation was enacted to provide for fair housing throughout the United States, the goal of dispersal proved to be elusive.[21]

The Federal Housing Authority was created to spur residential development during the depression era through home mortgages that required lower down payments, lower interest rates, and longer repayment terms. Unfortunately, these federally assisted loan programs were tainted by unfair lending practices. Neighborhoods were rated by the FHA/VA based on socioeconomic variables, including race. Redlining occurred, racial restrictive covenants were required by the FHA limiting investment in the suburbs to whites while encouraging reinvestment in central cities for multiple-family housing for minorities. Federal tax policies were geared in favor of white, single-family home ownership in the suburbs.[22]

The critical goal of dispersal was never reached, for several reasons. First, two of the four federally subsidized housing programs—rent supplements and low-rent public housing—carry statutory provisions that permit a local government to determine whether the programs will operate within its jurisdiction. Under the former program, housing may not be built in any community unless local official approval has been given. This has the effect of allowing suburban communities, through inaction, to exclude rent supplement housing.[23] Second, low-rent public housing has encountered problems in suburbia. Most states' laws place restrictions upon the geographical jurisdiction of local public housing authorities—thus, central city housing authorities are frequently not authorized to provide public housing outside the central city.[24] Federal law also requires that the local governing body of the locality in which public housing is to be located must enter into a cooperative agreement with the local public housing authority under which the locality agrees to exempt the project from taxes and to provide municipal services. By merely failing to take the affirmative step of signing the cooperative agreement, low-rent public housing may be effectively excluded from the community.[25]

In addition, lower-income and public housing has been excluded from suburban communities by conditioning such housing upon prior approval of the electorate, through traditional exclusionary zoning techniques, and by refusing to extend municipal utilities to proposed housing sites.[26] Even where such housing is permitted to be built, other devices are frequently used to confine it to designated parts of the locality and to ensure that occupancy will be on a racially segregated basis.[27] Only where racial discrimination in either motive or effect has been demonstrated have the courts invalidated such techniques.[28] But even where racial discrimination is shown, as long as the ultimate decision to allow or disallow such housing is left to the voters, racial exclusion may be upheld.[29] As a result, with the exception of a few judicial decisions invalidating exclusionary practices because they discriminate on racial grounds, federal efforts to disperse low-income and public housing throughout suburbia have largely failed.[30]

Compounding the failure of federal efforts to achieve a national policy of equal opportunity and dispersal in housing was other federal legislation that led to increased sprawl. The Federal Aid Highway Act provided preferential federal highway expenditures for motor vehicle traffic and discouraged transit or multimodal uses. The new interstates and ring roads were instrumental in linking the country with a usable and dependable interstate highway system, which also resulted in a surge of suburban employment centers. Unfortunately, as many of the interstate highways and federal highways were constructed after residential and commercial areas had already been built up, the process of building the roads resulted in the decimation of thriving but politically powerless neighborhoods. Neighborhoods, many with predominantly minority populations, that were not totally razed were now bisected by highways, prompting a downward cycle of decay. Conversely, previously undeveloped areas were now developable. The irony of the interstate highways is that they became the routes, literally and figuratively, out of the cities.[31]

Despite a federal history of promoting sprawl through piecemeal policies and programs, some changes in federal legislation designed to encourage changes in urban travel from the automobile to public transit, such as the Intermodal Surface Transportation Efficiency Act (ISTEA)[32] and its new 1998 successor, the Clean Air Act Amendments of 1990, and the "brownfields Superfund legislation," are beginning to shift federal policy and are discussed in greater detail in Chapter VII.

The Costs of Sprawl

Sprawl's costs are pronounced, both for those residents remaining in the central city and built-up first-ring and second-ring suburbs, and for the developing suburbs and rural/agricultural areas beyond. Henry Richmond, chairman of the National Growth Management Leadership Project, identified five negative impacts of sprawl:[33]

1. poverty becomes concentrated in existing built-up areas;
2. society resegregates along racial and economic lines;
3. public investment in urban facilities and services becomes unfeasible;

4. increased automobile dependence undermines environmental, agricultural, and energy policies; and

5. social anxiety increases due to financial instability, rising housing costs, and limited employment opportunities.

Community Impact

Sprawl causes and exacerbates the problems of built-up communities as people feel "trapped" living in areas with little growth (or lower growth) potential and limited employment opportunities. Sprawl reinforces segregation, creating a new concept of *separate and unequal*. As noted in *American Apartheid, Segregation and the Making of the Underclass* (Massey and Denton, 1993), sprawl systematically deprives city and first-ring and second-ring suburban residents of opportunities and adequate services, which stimulates the antisocial behavior suburban America rejects but finds itself increasingly facing as in the Columbine High School massacre.[34] Decreasing demographic diversity, geographic separation, and escalating costs due to sprawl-borne social problems minimize the bond of social responsibility that should exist between central cities, suburban communities, and the new expanding exurbia.

The metropolitan area loses its sense of community as families and businesses move away from established neighborhoods into "new" third-, fourth-, and fifth-generation suburban or exurban neighborhoods. Sprawl diminishes community ties, for both suburban and remaining urban populations, as evidenced by reported decreases in volunteerism,[35] a general lack of commitment by individuals to join community-based organizations, and decreases in donations to charities. The economic climate creates the perceived need for two-income families—working urban families typically need two incomes to meet their families' needs; suburban families want two incomes to maintain a desired standard of living. Making time to commit to nonfamily, nonwork functions becomes more difficult.

Newer suburbs lack the types of community institutions available in older, established neighborhoods. There is more political isolation and less political participation. Central city schools, on the other hand, suffer as populations decline from lower budgets (attributed to remaining residents' lower incomes), closed schools, and overcrowded classrooms (as neighborhood-based schools are closed or merged with other schools). Crime, real and perceived (since crime rates in cities have dramatically declined),[36] continues to be a strong issue

driving development outward, and is manifested in the increasing numbers of walled or gated communities in suburban areas, as well as firearms and home security alarms becoming more commonplace in urban and suburban dwellings.

Housing Impact

As discussed previously, the lack of affordable housing is a crisis made worse by sprawl, as suburban development reduces demand for residential and commercial properties in the urban core and first- and second-ring suburbs and the lower densities increase per-unit housing costs for land even if gross acreage costs are lower. Nevertheless, the myths of better housing appreciation in third-ring suburbs versus the central city gentrified or infill areas continue to be spread by an ill-informed real estate brokerage industry. In a plan I developed for San Diego that continues to accelerate infill development, the incentive for sprawl was removed through nonsubsidized pricing of infrastructure on the fringe. Median closer-in, gentrified housing values may actually appreciate more than ex-urban sprawl housing values, a fact that is little known and, if fully appreciated, might make a huge difference in perception.[37]

Employment Impact

Employment has been redistributed by sprawl. The central city and first- and second-ring suburbs have lost a significant share of the job market to the outer suburbs. Entry-level and midlevel jobs that historically have been vehicles of upward mobility similarly have relocated to outer suburban areas. This has led to higher rates of poverty and greater unemployment in the urban core. Decentralization makes middle class employment inaccessible for many urban residents, especially in areas lacking transit, or requiring reverse commutes from the cities to the suburbs.

Businesses similarly are not immune to sprawl, relying on access to qualified workers and the community's (that is, the metropolitan area's) perceived quality of life by employees and other businesses. The competition for development within the metropolitan area also pits communities against one another, making the whole weaker. The effect of "subsidized" sprawl on the overall business climate and the use of excessive tax incentives forces all regional businesses and residents to pay more taxes to maintain a constant level of service and act as a disincentive to stay and contribute to one community.

Fiscal Impact

The fiscal costs of providing services have at least doubled in outlying areas, compared to development located contiguously to existing facilities.[38] A recent study conducted for the Urban Land Institute by James Frank estimated that in the typical three-unit-per-acre development located ten miles from central sewer facilities and employment centers, infrastructure costs would be twice as great per unit as a twelve-unit-per-acre development closer in with an equal mix of townhouses, garden apartments, and single-family detached homes, a "premium" of $48,000 per unit.[39] Housing costs are inflated, attributable to new development occurring in "leapfrogged" areas that exhibit scattered, inefficient development patterns of low density, with concomitant loss of scale economies. New Jersey's plan for managed growth will save the state $700 million in road costs, $562 million in sewer and water costs, $178 million in school costs, and up to $380 million in operating costs per year.[40] Fifteen more years of continued sprawl would cost Maryland $10 billion more than a compact pattern of growth, and, in Carroll County, Maryland, it has been determined that without new growth paying its fair share of infrastructure costs, $1.22 is paid out in services for every $1.00 collected from residential property taxes.[41] A 1989 Florida study demonstrated that planned concentrated growth would cost the taxpayer 50 to 75 percent less than continued sprawl.[42] Minneapolis-St. Paul would have to spend $3.1 billion more for sprawl by the year 2020 for new sewer and water services alone if it were to accommodate sprawl.[43] Even Las Vegas is studying smart growth to cope with its huge infrastructure deficit crisis.[44] Infrastructure costs have increased substantially more in comparison to the amount of revenue collected through local real estate and property taxes. For example, in Prince William County, Virginia, local authorities collected approximately $2,100 a year in real estate and other taxes per household.[45] However, public services per household cost the county $3,700. Generally, scattered development beyond the local service area accounts for much of this deficiency for many regions. Providing school facilities for a region has been costly as well. In Maine, the state lost 27,000 students between 1970 and 1995; however, it spent $434 million building new schools to accommodate the scattered development.[46] In New Jersey, school districts located in built-up areas or in corridors and contiguous development patterns will receive a $286-million, or 2 percent, annual financial advantage under the state plan because of the savings over sprawl.[47]

The fiscal impacts of sprawl versus planned growth are dependent upon two influences on development patterns.[48] First, the ability to influence development materializing from planned versus sprawl development can change the public service costs of development. (See Figure 2.1.) The second is the influence of sprawl in preventing greater densities, mixed use, pedestrian access to centers, and compactness of new neighborhoods. If planned development can provide more compact development patterns, public services costs will be less.[49] Development near transportation corridors or where public facilities already exist will help in the reduction of costs. In Florida, a study found public facility costs were between $16,000 and $17,000 per unit for corridor and nodal developments and almost $24,000 for scattered developments.[50] A New Jersey study found that infrastructure costs in dispersed growth areas were 9 percent more than those in planned development patterns.[51] Ongoing operating costs for infrastructure will be reduced if unneeded capital commitments are deferred.[52] One reality of our changing political climate is that it will no longer tolerate unacceptable fiscal, if not environmental, waste.

Nonetheless, many suburban communities that have grown with sprawl argue that the status quo should be maintained. These communities assert that real growth is occurring within the metropolitan area and that it is not just a game of corporate musical chairs. This growth creates jobs in construction, finance, banking, industry, and retail. It is asserted that commercial and residential decisions are based on the free market system—that people are drawn to the perceived quality-of-life benefits in the suburbs (such as better schools and lower crime rates); that retail/commercial entities pay a greater share of taxes compared to the services that they use, and that modern-day thinking encourages gated developments. The 1995 Bank of America report, *Beyond Sprawl*, counters most of these points and demonstrates that it makes good business sense to encourage development patterns that promote the economic health and diversity of the [metropolitan areawide] community.

Balanced growth means that both residential and commercial uses develop within a community. An early study by the Real Estate Research Corporation for the Council on Environmental Quality, Department of Housing and Urban Development, and the Environmental Protection Agency found that low-density, large-lot development required extremely high public investment for public facilities and services such as open space, schools, transportation, refuse collection, police and fire protection, utilities, postal services, administrative

Figure 2.1

Relative Infrastructure Costs of Sprawl versus Planned Development from Three Major Studies

Infrastructure Cost Category	Sprawl Development	Planned Development: Findings from Three Major Studies (in percent, relative to Sprawl)			Planned Development: Synthesis from Three Major Studies (in percent, relative to Sprawl)[2]
		Duncan Study	*Burchell Study*[4]	*Frank Study*[1]	
Roads	100%	40%	76%	73%	75%
Schools	100%	93	97	99	95
Utilities	100%	60	92	66	95
Other	100%	102	NA	100	NA

	Assumed Percentages[3]	
Density and Dwelling Types	*Sprawl Development*	*Planned Development*
1 dwelling unit/4 acres	6.8%	6.2%
1 dwelling unit/acre	20.4	6.2
3 dwelling units/acre	34.0	37.2
5 dwelling units/acre (clustered)	<u>6.8</u>	<u>12.4</u>
	68.0	**62.0**
10 dwelling units/acre (townhouse)	20.0	22.0
15 dwelling units/acre (multifamily)	<u>12.0</u>	<u>16.0</u>
	100.0%	**100.0%**

The above percentages are applied as weights to the Frank findings by dwelling type to derive a weighted unit distribution. It is further assumed that development will be leapfrog and at a 10-mile distance under sprawl, and contiguous and at a 5-mile distance under planned development.

Notes:

1. This is calculated from the base Frank findings as indicated in the text and applying the percentages shown above.

2. Represents a synthesis or consensus from the three studies noted in the text.

3. Derived from the Burchell, Robert W., et al., *1992 Impact Assessment of the New Jersey Interim State Development and Redevelopment Plan, Report II: Research Findings.* Report prepared for New Jersey Office of State Planning, Trenton. February 20.

4. Derived from the Burchell, Robert W., et al., *1992 Impact Assessment of the New Jersey Interim State Development and Redevelopment Plan, Report III: Supplemental AIPLAN Assessment.* Report prepared for New Jersey Office of State Planning, Trenton. April 30.

Source:

WILLIAM L. WHEATON & MORTON J. SCHUSSHEIM, THE COST OF MUNICIPAL SERVICES IN RESIDENTIAL AREAS (1955); WALTER ISARD & ROBERT E. COUGHLIN, MUNICIPAL COSTS AND REVENUES RESULTING FROM GROWTH (1957); REAL ESTATE RES. CORP., THE COSTS OF SPRAWL (1974); Alan Altshuler, *The Costs of Sprawl Volume 1: Executive Summary; Volume 2: Detailed Cost Analysis; Volume 3: Literature Reviews and Bibliography,* 43 J. AM. PLAN. ASS'N 279 (1979); ROBERT W. BURCHELL & DAVID LISTOKIN, THE BROOKINGS INST., LAND INFRASTRUCTURE, HOUSING COSTS, AND FISCAL IMPACTS ASSOCIATED WITH GROWTH; THE LITERATURE ON THE IMPACTS OF TRADITIONAL VERSUS MANAGED GROWTH (1995).

facilities, health care, and library services.[53] Another independent study, conducted by a team of planners and engineers, found that when land uses in an area are predominantly residential in character and distances are greater between residential and nonresidential uses, the revenue-to-cost ratio (in other words, the ratio of annual tax revenues generated by a use compared to the annual costs of providing facilities and services to that use) decreases. Contiguous, commercial uses pay, in tax revenues, as much as 136 percent of the cost of providing public facilities and services, whereas scattered, low-density residential developments pay as little as 41 percent in tax revenues for public facilities and services. Even the average revenue-to-cost ratio of 68 percent assumes that some degree of cross-subsidization is occurring, either that

1. some areas within a jurisdiction are contributing to making up the fiscal shortfall; or
2. intergovernmental transfers of funds contribute to subsidization of development.[54]

Political Impact

Sprawl causes fiscal strains on cities by drawing commercial development outward. The resultant lack of financial resources in central cities is inadequate as social needs of lower-income populations increase and community facilities age, deteriorate, and become deficient. Within the metropolitan area, first- and second-ring suburban communities inefficiently replicate facilities. This is not to say that some urban neglect has not been self-inflicted, for a lack of foresight to phase extraterritorial growth is evident. However, the resultant effect has left cities unable to maintain facilities and services or rebuild infrastructure. This has affected both central cities and landlocked first-ring suburbs.[55]

Cities that provide extrajurisdictional utility service without annexation effectively subsidize suburbs and finance sprawl. Annexation as a tool is defeated because of premature sprawl; development of land without adequate public infrastructure and services makes it a negative investment for the city, together with the concomitant factor that most annexation laws require separate votes to approve in the area to be annexed as well as the annexing city. Infrastructure for new fringe development has been financed by existing urban and suburban taxpayers, effectively subsidizing the process and luring new business and residents away from the central cities and first-ring and second-ring suburbs.[56] Moreover, cities have been prevented from tying growth management land use policies to their extraterritorial utility service.[57]

In the metropolitan area, sprawl contributes to the lack of regional coordination caused by the existence of numerous, autonomous local governments. This bureaucratic and jurisdictional layering, or governmental fragmentation, impedes the efficient provision of community facilities and services because many of these communities replicate existing services, some of which may alone have sufficient excess capacity to meet additional demand, while in other areas no effective facilities or services are provided. In many cases a community will allow development at its fringe that has fiscal and economic impact across its borders to adjacent communities without appropriate mitigation fees. Some tools have been developed to utilize regional general welfare as a state constitutional doctrine to address deficiencies across a metropolitan area; such programs have been applied to remedy housing and environmental inequities.[58] The result of the area's fragmentation is a duplication of services (rather than the intensification of services), decreasing effective service provision for the additional demand created.

Transportation Impact

Traffic congestion as a result of sprawl creates enormous societal costs in the form of environmental pollution, energy consumption, increased energy costs, decreases in economic productivity, and a general decline in citizens' quality of life. Automobile fuel combustion, due to greater distances traveled with fewer occupants, results in substantially greater air pollution. Personal time is lost as commuting times increase, as distances between population, employment, and recreational/cultural centers increase, putting more vehicles on the road for greater periods of time. Car time is one negative employment quality-of-life factor that results as sprawl increases. Emergency services suffer as congestion and accessibility from the lack of alternative transit cause slow response times, an issue especially prominent in growing suburban communities.[59]

Agricultural and Open Space Impact

Sprawl is the major factor for the loss of prime agricultural lands and open space, estimated to be as much as 1½ percent per year.[60] Translating that into real terms, every hour of every day, fifty acres of prime farmland are lost to

development.[61] If the trend continues unabated, by 2010 the United States could be a net importing agricultural nation.

Wetlands and open space also are being lost to development. "Sprawl eats up our open space. It creates traffic jams that boggle the mind and pollute the air. Sprawl can make one feel downright claustrophobic about our future."[62] Sprawl is an inefficient use of land, overutilizing energy sources, and creating a far poorer quality of life. When compared to compact planned development, sprawl growth patterns result in 600 percent higher police response times, 50 percent higher ambulance response times, and 33⅓ percent higher fire response times.[63]

In pursuing the goal of protecting sensitive environmental areas and preserving parks and open space, there are many tools available for a local government. There is no single correct approach to take, and many combinations of resources and tools exist for local governments to achieve this goal. For instance, Minneapolis, Minnesota, has a park and recreation board that operates independently of the city council. Thus, it possesses separate legislative authority to issue bonds, approve maintenance projects, and establish its own budget.[64] A recent $40 million spent "greening" a stretch of the Mississippi River near downtown has already generated close to $700 million in private redevelopment in formerly blighted areas.[65]

In Colorado, four western slope counties recently received a $500,000 grant from the National Telecommunications Infrastructure Administration Telecommunications and Information Applications Assistance Program to explore how geographic information systems technology can better serve growing rural communities.[66] Also out of Colorado, the Southwestern Colorado Data Center set up a web site that allows the public access to land inventory information previously only available to county planners.[67] Such access has helped ease the organizational burden of identifying possible conservation areas.

Finally, the federal Agricultural Improvement and Reform Act of 1996 authorized $35 million in matching funds to assist state and local agricultural conservation easement programs.[68] These few examples truly illustrate that if the will exists to preserve an area from development, a way to fund a conservation initiative can be found.

The Need for *Ramapo*'s System and Smart Growth

The costs of sprawl are rooted in broad socioeconomic issues. Unfortunately, unabated sprawl eventually will affect the very same suburban communities that are today promoting it. Fortunately, suburban communities have numerous opportunities to control this inefficient land use pattern. The key lies in utilizing two major concepts:

1. controlling patterns of development into transportation corridors, centers, contiguous development, and neotraditional mixed-use developments through the use of "an urbanizing tier" within a tier system based on the *Ramapo* system of requiring adequate public facilities to be available at the time of growth; and

2. requiring that new development pay for its one-time fair share of new capital costs, to incentivize growth in existing built-up areas and encouraging joint public/private investment to stimulate economic development.

Joint public/private ventures in which communities capture the benefit of public and private investment are tools and concepts that squeeze every drop of value from available tax and private investment dollars. It forces government and developers to seek out viable projects. It encourages reasonable and rational economic behavior. The bottom line is that we can no longer afford sprawl, either socially or fiscally. Wasted dollars make communities and the nation economically noncompetitive in a worldwide market and exacerbate energy and agricultural inputs that affect the trade balance adversely and contribute to disastrous environmental global warming effects. Containing sprawl is creating a sustainable environment.

The severe problems outlined above are the result of urban sprawl and leapfrog development. The following definition of sprawl is useful:

> A term of art employed to describe the uncontrolled development of land situated on the outskirts of America's major cities. It refers to an unfettered form of urban expansion which is characterized by the initial nonuniform improvement of isolated and scattered parcels of land located on the fringes of suburbia, followed by the gradual urbanization of the intervening undeveloped areas.

> Aside from its unpleasant aesthetic results, urban sprawl causes premature characterization of the nature of an area's future land use: the

unintentional planning decisions made by businessmen and developers who are rarely committed to the best interests of the entire community, and have a direct bearing upon the shape of subsequent development.

Further, this pattern of random development often results in the waste of valuable land resources, as the intermediate areas are not efficiently utilized. Moreover, there are high monetary costs accompanying urban sprawl since the price of providing municipal facilities and services such as sewers, waterlines, roads and public transportation is substantially increased when the population is scattered throughout a region.[69]

Controlling sprawl by redirecting growth would benefit central city dwellers through rehabilitation and revitalization of the central city,[70] would be environmentally beneficial by preserving agricultural land and open space, would aid in reducing energy consumption and would, by limiting the area over which services must be extended, reduce the cost of services to suburbanites and aid in the fiscal solvency of local governments.[71] Because so many various interest groups can benefit by effective growth management, it should now be possible to form coalitions to combat this hydra-headed problem.[72]

The climate for grappling with these crises was right during the late '60s and the '70s. But how were problems of this complexity and dimension approached? Earliest efforts were fragmented, isolated, and narrow, staying within the confines of two-dimensional traditional zoning concepts: type and location of land uses, often resulting in "exclusionary" effects.[73] Not until the case of *Golden v. Planning Board of Town of Ramapo* were timing and sequencing added as legitimate third and fourth dimensions of the regulatory zoning process.

Unplanned growth and the failure of the federal government to articulate an affirmative national growth policy can be seen as a result of congressional inability to broaden the scope of legislation beyond isolated solutions to individual problems. Typically, federal legislation reacts to problems only in a fragmented way—there is no attempt to confront problems within the context of society as a whole. Thus, we have legislation designed to improve air quality without considering the overall effect of such legislation upon sprawl, energy, housing, or other complex problems that are interrelated to the problem of air quality. It is clear that planning for the growth of a county, region, or state requires solutions that take into account the myriad complex and interrelated problems that must be addressed by comprehensive planning.[74]

These initial and ongoing deficiencies led to the development of the planning and legal principles implemented in the *Ramapo* program, and extended onward to utilization in a tier system for city/county, metropolitan, and regional approaches. The timing and sequencing of growth measured by the adequacy of public facilities over an eighteen-year comprehensive plan and capital improvement program, which was authorized by *Ramapo*, became embodied as the "Urbanizing Tier."

The 1990s has been a decade for renewed interest in land use reform. "Smart growth" is the new label given to the efforts in battling sprawl. Smart growth reduces the consumption of land for roads, houses, and commercial buildings by channeling development to areas with existing infrastructure. It centers growth around urban and older suburban areas and preserves green space, wetlands, and farmland. Smart Growth's goal is to reap the benefits of growth and development, such as jobs, tax revenues, and other amenitites, while limiting the disasters of growth, such as degradation of the environment, escalation of local taxes, and worsening traffic congestion. While there is no special formula for smart growth, there are common features in each of the communities that have adopted it. Wherever it occurs, smart growth

1. enhances a sense of community;
2. protects investment in existing neighborhoods;
3. provides a greater certainty in the development process;
4. protects environmental quality;
5. rewards developers with profitable products, financing and flexibility;
6. decreases congestion by providing alternative modes of transportation; and
7. makes efficient use of public money.[75]

Smart growth efforts have taken place on national, regional, and local levels.[76] In 1997, the Smart Growth Network was created to allow local government officials across the nation to share growth strategies and exchange information on the latest and best trends in sustainable development. The American Planning Association has produced a 1998 edition of its *Growing Smart Legislative Guidebook,* which offers models for comprehensive and neighborhood planning.[77]

Voters have responded positively to smart growth programs. In recent years,

voters have approved plans to preserve historical sites, parks, farmland, and open space and approved an estimated $7 billion for conservation, urban revitalization, and smart growth initiatives. Alabama, Arizona, Florida, Michigan, Minnesota, New Jersey, Oregon, and Rhode Island were some of the states that passed smart growth legislation in 1998.[78]

The remainder of this book will explore how *Ramapo* came into being and evolved into Smart Growth. Chapter III deals with the evolution of the *Ramapo* system; Chapters IV, V, and VI the extension of the *Ramapo* Smart Growth regional, local, and state systems (the Urbanizing Tier); Chapter VII with the revitalization of the urban core (the Urbanized Tier) and protection of agricultural, rural, and environmental land (the Nonurbanized Tier). Finally, Chapter IX will explore the new federal programs that are strenthening smart growth across the nation.

Endnotes

1. *See* Robert H. Freilich & Bruce G. Peshoff, *The Social Costs of Sprawl*, 29 URB. LAW. 183 (1997) [hereinafter Freilich & Peshoff].

2. *See generally* Robert W. Burchell, Ph.D., *Economic and Fiscal Costs (and Benefits) of Sprawl*, 29 URB. LAW. 159 (1997).

3. LINCOLN INSTITUTE OF PUBLIC POLICY, ALTERNATIVES TO SPRAWL, at 4 (1995).

4. *See* JOINT ECONOMIC COMMITTEE OF CONGRESS, HARD CHOICES: NATIONAL COUNCIL ON INFRASTRUCTURE FINANCE (1984).

5. In California, one-third of all new development in the last five years has been in gated communities with private governments. Neil Shouse, *The Bifurcation: Class Polarization and Housing Segregation in the Twenty-First Century Megalopolis*, 30 URB. LAW. 145 (1998).

6. Federal policy, but in particular the Federal Tax Code, is one of the major contributors to sprawl. The mortgage tax deduction permits homeowners, but not occupiers of rental housing, to deduct home mortgage interest and property taxes from taxable income, effectively and significantly lowering taxpayer liability. Staunchly supported by liberals and conservatives alike, even recent "flat tax" proponents acknowledge the deduction's widespread support and the likelihood of it continuing, in some form, indefinitely. To take full advantage of the deduction, higher incomes require higher home mortgages (and higher housing costs). This deduction encourages sprawl by providing the means to protect *more income* by buying *more home* on larger lots, which increases the amount of land consumed per capita. Freilich & Peshoff, *supra* note 1, at 187.

7. CHRISTOPHER TUNNARD, THE CITY OF MAN 362–85 (1953).

8. Kenneth L. Kraemer, *Developing Governmental Institutions in New Communities*, 1 URB. LAW. 268 (1969).

9. S. Mark White, AICP, and Dawn Jourdan, *Neotraditional Development: A Legal Analysis*, 49 LAND USE LAW & ZONING DIGEST 8 (Aug. 1997).

10. A-95; 1962 and 1991 Transportation Acts; 701 Planning.

11. For an excellent account of increasing federal involvement, *see* Hartke, *Toward a National Growth Policy*, 22 CATH. U. L. REV. 231 (1973); Ross Gelbspan, *A Good Climate for Investment*, ATLANTIC MONTHLY, June 1998, at 25.

12. S. 268, 92d Cong., 1st Sess., § 501(e) (1971).

13. *Id.*

14. *See* William Reilly, *New Directions in Federal Land Use Legislation*, in LAND USE CONTROLS: PRESENT PROBLEMS AND FUTURE REFORM 331, 340 (David Listokin ed., 1974).

15. Jayne E. Daly, *A Glimpse of the Past, a Vision for the Future, Senator Henry M. Jackson and National Land Use Legislation*, 28 URB. LAW. 1, 7 (1996).

16. Jeffrey Spivak, *KC Area Isn't Utilizing Growth Guru*, K.C. STAR, Mar. 7, 1996, at B1. For example, the Kansas City region, in which Freilich, Leitner & Carlisle is based, has only recently begun to see the need for growth controls, with none having been implemented.

17. National Housing Act of 1937, ch. 896, 50 Stat. 888, 42 U.S.C. § 1437 (1937).

18. Peter Dreier, *The Urban Crisis: The Kerner Commission Report Revisited: America's Urban Crisis: Symptoms, Causes and Solutions*, 71 N.C. L. REV. 1351 (1993).

19. *See generally* Charles M. Haar, SUBURBS UNDER SIEGE: RACE, SPACE, AND AUDACIOUS JUDGES (1996); Nico Calavita, et al., *Inclusionary Housing in California and New Jersey: A Comparative Analysis*, 8 HOUSING POL'Y DEBATE 109 (1997).

20. NATIONAL HOUSING TASK FORCE, A DECENT PLACE TO LIVE (New York, Ford Foundation, 1988); REPORT OF THE ADVISORY COMMISSION ON REGULATORY BARRIERS TO AFFORDABLE HOUSING, 102d Congress, 1st sess., No. 102-57, 1991; and the URBAN LAND INSTITUTE, FAIR HOUSING & EXCLUSIONARY LAND USE (1974). *See also* UNITED STATES COMMISSION ON CIVIL RIGHTS, EQUAL OPPORTUNITY IN SUBURBIA (1974).

21. John C. Boger, *Race and the American City: The Kerner Report in Retrospect—An Introduction*, 71 N.C. L. REV. 1289 (1993).

22. Florence W. Roisman, *Intentional Racial Discrimination and Segregation by the Federal Government as a Principal Cause of Concentrated Poverty: A Response to Schill & Wachter*, 143 U. PA. L. REV. 1351 (1995).

23. *See, e.g.,* United States v. City of Blackjack, 508 F.2d 1179 (8th Cir. 1974); Kennedy Park Homes Ass'n v. City of Lackawanna, 436 F.2d 108 (2d Cir. 1970); *cert. denied*, 401 U.S. 1010 (1971); Crow v. Brown, 332 F. Supp. 382 (N.D. Ga. 1971), *aff'd per curiam*, 457 F.2d 788 (5th Cir. 1972). *See also* U.S. COMMISSION ON CIVIL RIGHTS, HOME OWNERSHIP FOR LOWER INCOME FAMILIES (1971).

24. *Supra* note 20.

25. *See, e.g.,* Mahaley v. Cuyahoga Metropolitan Housing Authority, 500 F.2d 1087 (6th Cir. 1974); Cuyahoga Metropolitan Housing Authority v. City of Cleveland, 342 F. Supp. 250 (N.D. Ohio E.D. 1972), *aff'd sub nom.* C.M.H.A. v. Harmody, 474 F.2d 1102 (6th Cir. 1973).

26. United Farmworkers of Florida Housing Project, Inc. v. City of Delray Beach, 493 F.2d 799 (5th Cir. 1974).

27. *See, e.g.,* Gautreaux v. Chicago Housing Authority, 503 F.2d 930 (7th Cir. 1974); Shannon v. Department of Housing and Urban Development, 436 F.2d 809 (3d Cir. 1970); Hicks v. Weaver, 302 F. Supp. 619 (E.D. La. 1969); El Cortez Heights Residents and Property Owners Ass'n v. Tucson Housing Authority, 10 Ariz. App. 132, 457 P.2d 294 (1969).

28. The U.S. Supreme Court affirmed in *Village of Arlington Heights v. Metropolitan Hous-*

ing Development Corp., 429 U.S. 252 (1977), that *intent* to discriminate, not racial *effect*, was required in suits directly under the fourteenth Amendment. However, under Title VIII of the Fair Housing Act, discriminatory *effects* will be sufficient. Metropolitan Housing Development Corp. v. Village of Arlington Heights, 558 F.2d 1283 (7th Cir. 1973). Nevertheless, the decisions on effect have been rare. *See* Business Ass'n of University City v. Landview, 660 F.2d 867 (3d Cir. 1981) (refusal to find effects).

29. *See* James v. Valtierra, 402 U.S. 137 (1971); *see also* Note, *The Equal Protection Clause and Exclusionary Zoning After* Valtierra *and* Dandridge, 81 YALE L.J. 61 (1971).

30. Michael H. Schill & Susan M. Wachter, *The Spatial Bias of Federal Housing Laws and Policy: Concentrated Poverty in Urban America*, 143 U. PA. L. REV. 1285, 1312 (1995). *See, e.g.*, Hennelly, *Urban Housing Needs: Some Thoughts on Dispersal*, 17 ST. LOUIS U. L.J. 169 (1972); Silverman, *Homeownership for the Poor: Subsidies and Racial Segregation*, 48 N.Y.U. L. REV. 72 (1973); Stegman, *Low Income Ownership: Exploitation and Opportunity*, 50 J. URB. L. 371 (1973); Walker v. U.S. Dep't of Housing and Urban Dev., 734 F. Supp 1289 (N.D. Tex. 1989).

31. Robert E. Reiter, *The Impact of the Federal Highway Program on Urban Areas*, 1 URB. LAW. 76 (1969); Auerbach, *The Urban Freeway Manifesto*, 1 URB. LAW. (1969); Robert H. Freilich & S. Mark White, *Transportation Congestion and Growth Management: Comprehensive Approaches to Resolving America's Major Quality of Life Crisis*, 24 LOY. L.A. L. REV. 915 (1991).

32. Intermodal Surface Transportation Efficiency Act, 23 U.S.C. §§ 10, 1–40 (1991).

33. *Sprawl: Its Nature, Consequences, Causes, and Remedies*, LAND PATTERNS, Spring 1996 p. 1.

34. *E.g.*, Mike Anton, *School War Zone, Many Students Wounded in Shooting, Explosions, Fire at Jefferson County Columbine High*, DENVER ROCKY MOUNTAIN NEWS (Apr. 20, 1999), at 1A.

35. Robert D. Putnam, *Bowling Alone: America's Declining Social Capital*, DEMOCRACY, Jan. 1995 pp. 65-78.

36. BUREAU OF JUSTICE STATISTICS, SOURCEBOOK OF CRIMINAL JUSTICE STATISTICS, Kathleen Maguire and Ann L. Pastore, eds. (1997); FEDERAL BUREAU OF INVESTIGATION, CRIME IN THE UNITED STATES: UNIFORM CRIME REPORTS (1997).

37. ROBERT H. FREILICH, TO SPRAWL OR NOT TO SPRAWL: NATIONAL PERSPECTIVES FOR KANSAS CITY (CHARLES KIMBALL LECTURE) (Western Historical Manuscript Society 1998).

38. *See* FREILICH, THE SOCIAL COST OF SPRAWL, at 185; *see generally* JAMES DUNCAN ET AL., FLORIDA DEP'T OF COMMUNITY AFFAIRS, THE SEARCH FOR EFFICIENT URBAN GROWTH PATTERNS (1989); JAMES E. FRANK, THE COSTS OF ALTERNATIVE DEVELOPMENT PATTERNS: A REVIEW OF THE LITERATURE (1989); ROBERT W. BURCHELL ET AL., NEW JERSEY OFFICE OF STATE PLANNING, IMPACT ASSESSMENT OF THE NEW JERSEY STATE DEVELOPMENT AND REDEVELOPMENT PLAN, REPORT II: RESEARCH FINDINGS (1992); Maryann Froelich, *Smart Growth: Why Local Governments Are Taking a New Approach to Managing Growth in Their Communities*, PUB. MGMT. (May 1998), at 7 (traffic congestion levels have risen 22 percent between 1982 and 1994, according to a study by the Texas Transportation Institute, thus, traditional building of more roads only causes increased traffic conditions).

39. *See* Kevin Kasowski, *The Costs of Sprawl Revisited in Developments*, NAT'L GROWTH MGMT. LEADERSHIP PROJECT NEWSL. (Sept. 1992), at 1 (citing the study conducted for the Urban Land Institute in 1989 by James Frank).

40. NEW JERSEY OFFICE OF STATE PLANNING, REEXAMINATION REPORT OF THE STATE DEVELOPMENT AND REDEVELOPMENT PLAN (1997).

41. SIERRA CLUB FOUNDATION, SPRAWL COSTS US ALL (1997).

42. REPORT: GOVERNOR'S COMMISSION FOR A SUSTAINABLE SOUTH FLORIDA (1989).

43. WHAT'S SO BAD ABOUT SPRAWL? (Pioneer Press 1996).

44. Douglas R. Porter, *Keeping the Las Vegas Valley Livable Requires a Smart Growth Approach*, URB. LAND 58 Vol. 57, No. 6 (June 1998).

45. Maryann Froehlich, *supra* note 38, at 8.

46. *Id.* Bus service costs dramatically increased from $8 million to $54 million; *see* MAINE STATE OFFICE OF PLANNING, COSTS OF SPRAWL (1997).

47. *See* ROBERT W. BURCHELL ET AL., NEW JERSEY OFFICE OF STATE PLANNING, IMPACT ASSESSMENT OF THE NEW JERSEY INTERIM STATE DEVELOPMENT AND REDEVELOPMENT PLAN, REPORT II: RESEARCH FINDINGS (1992); ROBERT W. BURCHELL & DAVID LISTOKIN, BLUE-GRASS TOMORROW, THE ECONOMIC EFFECTS OF TREND VERSUS VISION GROWTH IN THE LEXINGTON METROPOLITAN AREA (1994), cited in Burchell, *Economic and Fiscal Costs (and Benefits) of Sprawl, supra* note 2, at 177.

48. A study of infrastructure costs "The Costs of Sprawl" was conducted in the early 1970s by the U.S. Department of Housing and Urban Development, the Council on Environmental Quality, and the Environmental Protection Agency. Additionally, a 1989 study by James E. Frank found that capital costs of infrastructure for a subdivision of three houses per acre can be reduced at least one-half by developing near basic public facilities and employment centers, at densities averaging twelve houses per acre. *See* James E. Frank, THE COST OF ALTERNATIVE DEVELOPMENT PATTERNS: A REVIEW OF THE LITERATURE (Washington, D.C.: U.S. Government Printing Office, 1989). *See also* Burchell, *supra* note 2, at 176.

49. Burchell, *supra* note 2, at 176.

50. A study by James Duncan and Associates, cited in PUB. MGMT. (May 1998), at 8.

51. FROEHLICH, *supra* note 38, at 8.

52. Burchell, *supra* note 2, at 180.

53. REAL ESTATE RESEARCH CORPORATION, THE COSTS OF SPRAWL: ENVIRONMENTAL AND ECONOMIC COSTS OF ALTERNATIVE RESIDENTIAL DEVELOPMENT PATTERNS AT THE URBAN FRINGE, DETAILED COST ANALYSIS, 105–31 AND EXECUTIVE SUMMARY, 3 (1974).

54. JAMES DUNCAN ET AL., *supra* note 34, at 18–19.

55. Kasowski, *supra* note 39, at 4.

56. MASSEY AND DENTON, AMERICAN APARTHEID, SEGREGATION AND THE MAKING OF THE UNDERCLASS (1993).

57. Robinson v. City of Boulder, 547 P.2d 228 (Colo. 1976). Legitimate utility-related reasons are required, such as insufficient facilities or shortage of capacity. Swanson v. Marin Mun. Water District, 128 Cal. Rptr. 485 (Cal. App. 1976).

58. *See* Southern Burlington County NAACP v. Township of Mount Laurel (Mount Laurel II), 92 N.J. 158, 456 A.2d 290 (1983) (municipalities have obligation to provide realistic opportunity for construction of that municipality's fair share of low- to moderate-income housing needs; Berenson v. Town of New Castle, 341 N.E.2d 236 (N.Y. 1975) (court must consider "not only the general welfare of the residents of the zoning township, but should also consider the effect of the ordinance on the neighboring communities); Township of Williston v. Chesterdale Farms, Inc., 341 A.2d 466 (Pa. 1975) ("it is not for any given township to say who may or may not live within its confines, while disregarding the interests of the entire area); Surrick v. Zoning Hearing Board, 382 A.2d 105 (Pa. 1977) ("suburban municipalities within the area of urban outpour must meet the problems of population expansion into its borders by increasing municipal services, and not by the practice of exclusionary zoning"); Associated

Homebuilders v. City of Livermore, 135 Cal. Rptr. 41 (Cal. 1976) (if an "ordinance may strongly influence the supply and distribution of housing for an entire metropolitan region, judicial inquiry must consider the welfare of that region"); Save a Valuable Environment (SAVE) v. City of Bothell, 576 P.2d 401 (Wash. 1978) (construction of major shopping center would have detrimental effects on areas outside city's jurisdiction; city may not act in disregard of the effect outside its boundaries).

59. *See* Freilich & White, *supra* note 35.

60. Shelby D. Green, *The Search for a National Land Use Policy: For the Cities' Sake, Loss of Agricultural Land*, 26 FORDHAM URB. L.J. 69, 79 (1998).

61. AMERICAN FARM LAND TRUST, FARMING ON THE EDGE (1997).

62. Christine Todd Whitman, Inaugural Address as New Jersey Governor, January 20, 1998.

63. JAMES H. KUNSTLER, HOME FROM NOWHERE 106 (Simon & Schuster 1996).

64. U.S. NEWS & WORLD REPORT, Jun. 8, 1998, at 31.

65. *Id.*

66. BUS. GEOGRAPHICS, Jan. 1998, at 34.

67. *Id.* at 35.

68. LAND TRUSTS & AGRIC. CONSERVATION EASEMENTS, 13 SUM. NAT. RESOURCES & ENV'T 336, 337 (1998).

69. Note, *A Zoning Program for Phased Growth: Ramapo Township's Time Controls on Residential Development*, 47 N.Y.U. L. REV. 723, 723–24 (1972).

70. Art Brisbane, *City Can Turn Eyes Inward*, K.C. STAR (Aug. 22, 1990) (saving the central city was one of the major focuses for my Minneapolis-St. Paul plan); George H. Gurley, Jr., *Where's the City's Vision?*, K.C. STAR (Feb. __, 1990) (I was quoted regarding my views on light rail and the need to revitalize downtown Kansas City).

71. Froehlich, *supra* note 38, at 5 (communities are "questioning the wisdom of abandoning brownfields in older communities, eating up the open space and prime agriculture lands at the suburban fringe, and polluting the air of an entire region by forcing more people to drive to get anywhere"). *See also* Robert H. Abrams, *Comment: Superfund and the Evolution of Brownfields*, 21 WM. & MARY ENVT'L L. & POL'Y REV. 265 (1997); and David L. Markell, *Legal Development: A Closer Look at Title 5 and Its Approach to the "Brownfields" Dilemma*, 60 ALB. L. REV. 1217 (1997) (describing New York's Environmental Bond Act of 1997 including provisions for remediation of brownfields).

72. Freilich & Davis, *Saving the Land: The Utilization of Modern Techniques of Growth Management to Preserve Rural and Agricultural America*, 13 URB. LAW. 27, 29 (1981).

73. *See* Cutler, *Legal and Illegal Methods for Controlling Community Growth on the Urban Fringe*, WIS. L. REV. 370 (1961).

74. Kendra H. Breichle, *A Better Way to Grow*, PUB. MGMT. (May 1998), at 4 (even prominent financial institutions, such as the Bank of America, encourage communities to move beyond sprawl to ensure that they remain vibrant places to live and work by requiring local governments to examine the basis of development decisions to ensure goals are met).

75. FROELICH, *supra* note 38.

76. Some smart-growth regulations have been criticized for the harmful possibilities resulting from converting smart growth into no growth, as where government places arbitrary caps on the number of building permits. If growth "gets too smart," can it cause the unconstitutional taking of private property? *See* Desiderio, *Growing Too Smart: Takings Implications of*

Smart Growth Policies, 13 NAT. RESOURCES & ENV'T 330 (Summer 1998); Ehrlich v. City of Culver City, 911 P.2d 429, 433 (Cal. 1996) (a reasonable relationship must exist between the monetary exaction imposed by the city and the public impact of the development).

77. For more information about the network, *see* <http://www.smartgrowth.org>; and for more information about the guidebook, *see* <www.planning.org/plnginfo/growsmar/gsindex. html.

78. Richard Moe, *Fed Up with Sprawl,* N.Y. TIMES (Nov. 12, 1998), at A24.

CHAPTER THREE

Ramapo

The *Ramapo* Experiment—
The Problem and the Solution

Coming to Ramapo

In 1960 I moved from a New York City law firm to become a partner in a small
real estate and land use firm in the northern suburbs of New York, in Rockland
County. My interest in pursuing a lifetime practice in land use law and plan-
ning had previously been piqued by my contacts as an undergraduate at the
University of Chicago, concentrating in the revitalization of cities as a public
affairs major and witnessing the first great renewal program of Hyde Park-
Kenwood under the leadership of Professor Julian Levi. I enrolled in Yale Law
School because of the pioneering efforts of Professor Myres McDougal in analyzing national policy for resource conservation and regional planning from the
New Deal on,[1] and watched with awe the extraordinary efforts of Mayor
Richard Lee during the early 1950s in making the small city of New Haven the
largest recipient of federal renewal funds of any city in America on a per capita
basis. Having graduated from Yale Law School in 1957 at the age of twenty-
one, I further pursued international planning at the Columbia School of International and Public Affairs, receiving a Master's in International Affairs in 1958.

Rockland County was at the zenith of a land boom craze that also
enveloped the southern suburbs of Connecticut, the northern suburbs of New
Jersey, and Westchester County, New York. This sleepy Dutch apple county
had been rudely awakened to suburban sprawl by the introduction of the toll-
free Palisades Interstate Parkway running thirty miles from the George Washington Bridge. It is another example of how the building of highways before the
advent of comprehensive planning is the cart leading the horse in opening up
untoward problems of suburban development without any corollary thought to
the need for adequate public facilities (schools, transportation, parks, open

space, stream preservation). All of that came unintentionally with the opening of the idyllic parkway leading to a vastly underused Harriman State Park.[2] No one thought of the consequences to the intermediate areas it paved through.

Historical-Economical Analysis of Town and Area

The Town of Ramapo is located in Rockland County, New York, approximately thirty miles northeast of New York City on the west side of the Hudson River.[3] The Town, consisting of eighty-nine square miles (larger than most cities, geographically, in New York State) and, at the time, seven different governmental units, experienced one of the fastest growth rates in the state after 1955 when the opening of the New York State Thruway, Tappen Zee Bridge, and Palisades Interstate Parkway made Rockland County a suburb of New York City. Since 1955, the County had experienced a growth rate of nearly 1,000 residential units per year in the unincorporated areas of the Town. In spite of the absence of adequate municipal facilities, almost all of it was reflected in large lot single-family residential subdivisions developed by commercial builders.

According to a population projection made in 1930, the Town of Ramapo, including its major villages of Spring Valley and Suffern, would have a population of 35,750 in 1980.[4] But by 1960, twenty years ahead of schedule, the Town's population had reached that level. In fact, growth was so rapid that between 1950 and 1963 population doubled and actually tripled between 1950 and 1968.

Due to the rapid growth in the area, the Town began to find it difficult to provide needed services and facilities at a pace that growth demanded. As a consequence, tax rates for schools and municipal services soared as the Town attempted to meet this added burden. For example, a family with a house whose market value was $25,000 might have paid $485 in taxes in 1960—but in 1968, by which time the population of the Town had increased by 90 percent, the family in the same house would be obliged to pay approximately $1,128 in taxes.[5]

The Basis for Growth Controls

In 1963, having become the founding president of the Young Democrats of Ramapo and on the Board of Directors of the New York State Young Democrats,[6] I began to formulate a concept that had been incubating in my mind for years: to plan and implement the control of suburban sprawl, accommodating the full fair share of population, but in a controlled, timed, and sequenced manner. I became fascinated with the earlier work of three planning and legal scholars. In 1955 Professor Charles Haar of Harvard Law School published his seminal articles[7] on comprehensive planning and the ways in which it could be used to guide and influence zoning, subdivision, and capital improvement decisions.

In the same journal, Professor Henry Fagin of North Carolina published an innovative article[8] on timing and sequencing growth in the suburbs to maintain quality of life. Fagin postulated five important goals to be achieved:

1. **The need to economize on the costs of municipal facilities and services** (through careful sequencing of facility provision).[9]
2. **The need to retain municipal control over the eventual character of development.** This prevents premature large lot zoning, which destroys the eventual ability to build at urban densities when utilities do arrive.[10]
3. **The need to develop a desirable degree of balance among various users of land.**[11] I was concerned that, by ensuring that a proper proportion of industrial and commercial development would coincide with residential development, a tax structure of reasonable proportions would be maintained, allowing a balance of low-income or affordable housing. This led to the creation of the Ramapo Housing Authority far in advance of the exclusionary zoning decisions of *Mount Laurel I et al.*[12] It was a thought that I tucked away and utilized in the Ramapo Plan, with great reward.
4. **The need to achieve greater detail and specificity in development regulations.** The ultimate linkage between the comprehensive plan, the capital improvement program, and the timing of development approval gave the Ramapo "points" system the specificity it needed.[13] One of the great stories of the *Ramapo* case was the comment by the New York Court of Appeals that the system was founded on a "four-volume master plan."[14]
5. **The need to maintain a high quality of community services and facilities.** This was translated by the Ramapo Plan I created into the now critical "concurrency of development with adequate level of public facilities" that is mandated by a growing number of states and is the keystone of all Smart Growth systems in the United States.[15]

The third major influence in the creation of my thinking toward timing and sequencing was a little-noticed article that appeared in the *Wisconsin Law Review.* Wisconsin had a distinguished land use planning law professor, Jacob Beuscher, who helped to introduce the official map to preserve highway and public utility rights of way.[16] One of Professor Beuscher's disciples, Richard Cutler, wrote an article entitled *Legal and Illegal Means for Controlling Community Growth on the Urban Fringe.*[17] Cutler's thesis was that communities were trying to limit growth but in ways that were completely counterproductive and even false in the intent. By designating huge areas for "holding zones" without reference to capital facilities or the timing and sequencing of development, these became excuses for approving rezoning for ad hoc development, creating suburban sprawl at will without planning. A second major method was to adopt larger and larger minimum lot sizes with the hope that developers would go away and come back some other day.[18] A third technique Cutler pointed out was to adopt noncumulative zoning, especially exclusive industrial, which prevented residential units from being built in large areas of a community despite the fact that only a small portion of land would ever be used for industrial purposes.[19] Finally, Cutler described minimum floor area restrictions that eliminated low- and moderate-income housing.[20]

In the development of the Ramapo Plan, all of these articles were taken into account to assure that multifamily and low-income housing were balanced between the unincorporated and village areas. Moreover, the Plan attempted to restore the vitality of the Town's villages by incentivizing commercial, industrial, and higher-density residential development to locate within the village centers. Later critics would complain that the unincorporated area lacked sufficient multiple-family housing and density as if each individual village and unincorporated area should be required to duplicate a full range of uses, that the political boundaries of fragmented cities and unincorporated areas were magically to be respected.[21] Ramapo thus was able to avoid the pitfalls of exclusionary zoning as enunciated by the courts just as the plan was completed and implemented in 1969. Without the benefit of regional planning, Ramapo met the regional general welfare.[22] It also demonstrated that the Ramapo Plan would become the precursor to County-City cooperation, as well as metropolitan or regional plans that would create tier systems focusing growth in established centers, limiting new growth to corridor centers and within urban growth boundaries, and protecting agricultural and rural areas.

The Campaign

In early 1965, I began my campaign for a seat on the Town Board by issuing a clarion call for controlled growth. Releasing a flyer entitled "A Formula for Victory," I called for replacement of the "nice guys" of the Republican Town Board with qualified leadership that would promote "ideas to forge a new constructive program of controlled growth." With the help of a key friend and chair-elect of the Young Democrats, Norman Rubinson, we campaigned the length and breadth of the Town. In those days there were no primaries—just smoke-filled rooms of "committeemen" from the precincts selecting the candidates to run for the Democratic slate. Although I lost in a close battle to Ned Siner, a veteran accountant from the Spring Valley coalition (the vote was 136 to 134), the Democrats knew that there was no way they could win without the Young Democrats and a vital campaign issue. In August of 1965, three months before the election, the Democratic chairman, Herb Reisman, a brilliant strategist, and the Town Democratic chairman, Morton Baron, together with the slate of candidates (John McAlevey for Supervisor, Ned Siner and Bernard Charles for Council), agreed to take me on as platform chairman and assured that if they won, I would be appointed Town Attorney to develop the controlled growth program.

The *Democratic News* of October 1965 promised that the number of new housing starts[23] allowed would depend on the ability of the Town to provide capital improvements such as schools, roads, sidewalks, recreation areas, and sewers.[24] Capital budgets would be developed at joint meetings with all school boards and service districts to afford a long-term planning basis for controlled growth. In an unbelievable upset, the three candidates won (Charles was last, winning by 100 votes), and, in January 1966, controlled growth began after my appointment as Town Attorney (one of the firm's clients—my job was not full time). The campaign was heartily contested by the builders[25] and we knew we were in for a long and historic battle.

The *Ramapo* Solution

Development of the Plan

Although the particular managed growth system that was later to come under attack in the courts officially began in 1966, it actually grew out of earlier attempts to deal with the problems of growth in the area.[26] The current history of planning in Ramapo began in 1964 when the Town applied for a planning assistance grant pursuant to section 701 of the Housing Act of 1954 to develop a master plan for the Town, the first since an unadopted proposal was prepared in 1930. The Town Planning Board, working with the County of Rockland Planning Board, the State of New York, and the federal government, prepared a master plan over a one-year period under the guidance of Planning Commission Chairman Norman Slovik. The plan was completed and presented to the public in May 1966, following numerous public hearings. The four-volume study covered every aspect of the history, existing land uses, public facilities, transportation, industry, commerce, housing needs, and population trends of the community. After final hearings, the newly completed master plan was adopted with amendments by the Town Planning Board pursuant to section 272(a) of the Town Law on July 26, 1966.

In August of 1967, the Town Board adopted an official map for the Town. The contents of the official map were derived initially from the master plan, particularly with respect to existing and proposed streets and highways, parks and drainage ways. As subsequent detailed facilities studies were accomplished, the official map was amended and refined to reflect the findings of those studies and helped to preserve the five major stream valleys of the Town.[27]

To supplement the master plan and official map, the Town conducted several detailed facility studies. The drainage plan, prepared under a grant from the federal government, provided a complete survey of all drainage ways. It was based on the capacity projected as necessary to carry off surface water when the Town would be developed at its maximum density to prevent extensive flooding from the five rivers that flow through the Town. The Town also prepared a similar map and plan for future sewer development, created sewer districts and a program of construction designed to provide sewers for all areas of the Town within the eighteen-year period of the capital improvement program. In addition, the Town completed an extensive recreation study and plan in 1969, analyzing all existing and potential public and private park and recreation sites, and making specific, detailed recommendations for their improvement and acquisition, if necessary.[28]

At the same time, a public housing authority was created and approval of several hundred units of low-income public housing and 500 units of moderate-income housing was granted by the Department of Housing and Urban Development in Washington. In a rare example of foresight and determination, the

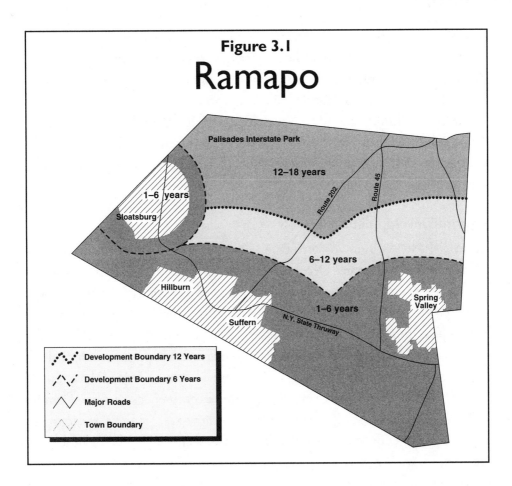

Figure 3.1

Ramapo

Palisades Interstate Park

12–18 years

1–6 years

Sloatsburg

6–12 years

Hillburn

1–6 years

Spring Valley

Suffern

N.Y. State Thruway

Route 202

Route 45

Development Boundary 12 Years

Development Boundary 6 Years

Major Roads

Town Boundary

Town and its housing authority proposed biracial, low-income family housing, and, in a series of legal battles with residents of the Town, won the right to construct the public housing it sought.[29]

After conducting the numerous studies discussed above, the Town adopted a capital improvements budget making a firm commitment for the development of necessary capital improvements specified in the master plan for a period of six years. To supplement the budget, the Town Board adopted a capital improvements program providing for the location and priority of capital improvement for the following twelve years. The two plans, covering a period of eighteen years, provided the capital improvements that would be required when the Town would be fully developed according to the specifications of the master plan.

The comprehensive zoning ordinance, adopted in 1966, along with the master plan, committed the Town to a policy of orderly growth and adequate provision of public facilities through a sequential development policy. This policy was developed through the long-range official map, sewer district, and drainage studies, and, finally, a capital budget and program that ensured a program of commitment to provide public improvements and facilities to all areas of the Town within a period of eighteen years. Final amendments, adopted in 1969, culminated the planning process and gave meaning to the goals of eliminating premature subdivision, urban sprawl, and development without adequate municipal and public improvements.[30] (See Figure 3.1.)

Interim Development Controls

To implement the new master plan, a comprehensive zoning ordinance was needed. Between May and December of 1966, an interim development law was enacted to prohibit, for six months, the issuance of building permits in those areas of the Town designated for change, and to protect the purposes of the master plan from an early demise at the hands of land speculators. In an important decision, *Matter of Rubin v. McAlevey,*[31] this interim measure was upheld as a valid protection of the planning process and orderly growth of the community. The Town Board was then able to adopt a comprehensive revised zoning ordinance on December 29, 1966, with a stated purpose "to limit development to an amount equal to the availability and capacity of public facilities and services."[32]

Although most cases have addressed the validity of interim development controls in the context of a town developing or amending a comprehensive plan, interim controls serve the same function when the municipality is amending and updating its zoning ordinance or subdivision regulations, undertaking an historic preservation project, evaluating the necessity of restricting development on a floodplain area, or establishing a redevelopment plan for a blighted area of the city.

An interim development control ordinance temporarily restricts the rezoning of land, approval of a new subdivision, and issuance of conditional or special use permits for a reasonable period of time in certain areas of a city or county that will be affected by the pending plan or amendment. A very practical function of interim controls is to provide a framework or structure for the planning process. Interim controls represent timetables and operate as an organizing system for an extremely complex process, ensuring that planning itself takes place. Third, and a corollary to the function of protecting the planning process, is the prevention of new nonconforming uses during the process. Thus, interim controls ensure that the effectiveness of the planning is not destroyed before it has a chance for zoning and subdivision regulations to be implemented by preventing the vesting of developers' rights. Generally, when the nature of plan revisions or proposed zoning changes become apparent, landowners and developers begin seeking building permits based on existing zoning, hoping to get approval before the changes are enacted. The municipality in response is pressed into making a hasty determination to adopt a permanent zoning ordinance. These competing behaviors have been termed "a race of diligence."[33] Interim controls eliminate this "race."

A fourth major function is the promotion of public debate on the strategies, goals, objectives, and policies of the plan and development techniques proposed to implement the plan. Public involvement is essential. It will often prevent the kind of planless implementation too often found in communities when action is precipitated without participation from the landowners and the public.[34]

Where does a municipality, county, or regional entity find the authority to enact interim development ordinances? Several sources have been identified and used by the courts to uphold interim controls. A number of states have enacted specific enabling legislation that permits a municipality to enact interim zoning ordinances with constraints of time and requiring diligent action by the municipality to enact new or revised regulations. Minnesota law provides:[35]

> If a county is conducting, or in good faith intends to conduct studies within a reasonable time, or has held or is holding a hearing for the purpose of considering a comprehensive plan or official controls or an amendment, extension, or addition to either, or in the event new territory for which no zoning may have been adopted, may be annexed to a municipality, the board in order to protect the public health, safety, and general welfare may adopt as an emergency measure a temporary interim zoning map or temporary interim zoning ordinance, the purpose of which shall be to classify and regulate uses and related matters as constitutes the emergency. Such interim resolution shall be limited to one year from the date it becomes effective and to one year for renewal thereafter.

In helping to enforce the Development Guide of the Metropolitan Council of Minneapolis-St. Paul, I successfully argued in the Minnesota Supreme Court that where specific statutory authority does not exist, the courts have relied on implied authority to exercise the police power to protect statutory planning processes or have looked to the general language in the state's zoning enabling act.[36]

Interim controls can also be achieved through informal techniques of administrative processing. The "administrative control theory" holds that a municipality can deny administratively the issuance of a building permit where the proposed use would conflict with a pending change in the zoning ordinance. A principle of administrative law prohibits an administrative officer from granting a permit in violation of a proposed law. Even though the Pennsylvania court found insufficient statutory authority for interim control ordinances in *Kline v. City of Harrisburg*, the court upheld a municipality's administrative procedures accomplishing the same objective in *A.J. Aberman, Inc. v. City of New Kensington*.[37]

Assuming legislative authorization, the validity of any given control depends on the reasonableness of the approach. The duration of the ordinance is of critical importance. Most statutes allow ordinances for a period of six months to one year with extensions. Without statutory limits, the courts have determined the reasonableness of the time period on a case-by-case basis. A primary determinant appears to be the complexity and scope of the plan being prepared.[38]

Even in the famous case of *First English Evangelical Lutheran Church v. Los Angeles County*,[39] which established that compensation, not invalidation, is the remedy for regulatory takings, on remand the California Court of Appeals found that an interim development ordinance to determine what uses or structures could be used in a flood-prone canyon was not a regulatory taking. The California Court of Appeal in *First English* stated:

> As an independent and sufficient grounds for our decision, we further hold the interim ordinance did not constitute a "temporary unconstitutional taking" even were we to assume its restrictions were too broad if permanently imposed on First English. This interim ordinance was by design a temporary measure—in effect a total moratorium on any construction on First English's property—while the County

conducted a study to determine what uses and what structure, if any, could be permitted on this property consistent with considerations of safety. We do not read the U.S. Supreme Court's decision in *First English* as converting moratoria and other interim land use restrictions into unconstitutional "temporary takings" requiring compensation unless, perhaps, if these interim measures are unreasonable in purpose, duration or scope. On its face, Ordinance 11,855 is reasonable in all these dimensions.

The ordinance had the legitimate avowed purpose of preserving the *status quo* while the County studied the problem and devised a permanent ordinance which would allow only safe uses and the construction of safe structures in and near the river bed. The restrictions in Ordinance 11,855 were reasonably related to the achievement of this objective. Given the seriousness of the safety concerns raised by the presence of any structures on this property, we find it was entirely reasonable to ban the construction or reconstruction of any structures for the period necessary to conduct an extensive study and fully develop persuasive evidence about what, if any, structures and uses would be compatible with the preservation of life and health of future occupants of this property and other properties in this geographic area.

We do not find the ordinance remained in effect for an unreasonable period of time beyond that which would be justified to conduct the necessary studies of this situation and devise a suitable permanent ordinance. The study was completed and a report containing recommended restrictions submitted in less than two years. County decision-makers took another six months to hold hearings, ponder and pass the somewhat less restrictive permanent ordinance. These periods are reasonable especially given the complexity of the issues to be studied and resolved. Nor were the restrictions imposed by the interim ordinance unreasonable in scope given the seriousness of the danger posed by the construction of new structures in Lutherglen and nearby properties. We cannot say that without a thoroughgoing study it would have been reasonably feasible to identify any structure which could be safely permitted on these properties. Thus we find the time taken by this study and the time this interim ordinance remained in effect to be well within the bounds of reason. The County owed this landowner no special duty to give priority to the study of Lutherglen over the study of other properties which might pose a danger to safety. Nor did it owe any of these landowners a duty to cut any corners in the study or take any risks that anything might be overlooked which could produce a permanent ordinance less restrictive than public safety concerns demanded.[40]

Interim controls also prevent the creation of vested rights that would have destroyed the plan and ordinance implementation before they could become effective, but in a limited way, not affecting all properties but only those inconsistent with the proposed plan. Vested rights in most states[41] require the developer to acquire a legal building permit plus substantial construction in order to use the preexisting law.[42] Most significantly, interim ordinances will not result in a "regulatory taking" because the economic use of the property is not *permanently* affected. Under the takings cases the property is looked at as a whole and if only a portion of the property[43] or only a small portion of time out of the entirety of time[44] is affected there will be no taking. The authority for interim controls can also be drawn from the Standard City Planning Enabling Act, which authorizes the implementation of planning.[45]

Implementing the Plan: The Timing and Sequencing Growth Management Ordinance

Having established the basic framework, the Town proceeded to develop a system of timing and sequential controls for subdivision residential development.[46] With a view toward managing growth in the area based upon objective standards and reasonable criteria, I drew up, and the Town adopted on October 23, 1969, a series of amendments to the zoning ordinance. The purposes of those amendments, based on the Fagin principles, were:

1. To economize on the costs of municipal facilities and services to carefully phase residential development with efficient provision of public improvements;
2. To establish and maintain municipal control over the eventual character of development;
3. To establish and maintain a desirable degree of balance among the various uses of the land;
4. To establish and maintain essential quality of community services and facilities.[47]

To implement the planning process, and to achieve the above goals realistically, the ordinance created a new class of special permit use known as "Residential Development Use."[48] That use classification requires that one who proposed to subdivide land obtain a special permit from the Town Board prior to the issuance of any building permit, special permit from the Board of Appeals, subdivision approval, or site plan approval by the Planning Board. When it considers the eligibility of each proposed residential project in deciding on the special permit, the Town Board is instructed to adhere to a specifically enumerated standard—as based upon the availability to the proposed development of five essential public improvements and services:

1. sewers or an approved substitute;
2. drainage facilities;
3. parks or recreational facilities, including public school sites;
4. state, county or town roads improved with curbs and sidewalks; and
5. firehouses.[49]

The degree of "availability" of each facility to the site is measured and scored on a scale specifically set out, and no permit may issue unless a minimum of 15 points are obtained.[50] The point system is as follows:

1. Sewers

   (a) Public sewers available   5 points

   (b) Package sewer plants   3 points

   (c) County-approved septic system   3 points

   (d) All others   0 points

2. Drainage

   Percentage of Required Drainage Capacity Available

   (a) 100% or more   5 points

   (b) 90% to 99.9%   4 points

   (c) 80% to 89.9%   3 points

   (d) 65% to 79.9%   2 points

   (e) 50% to 64.9%   1 point

   (f) Less than 50%   0 points

3. Improved Public Park or Recreation Facility
   Including Public School Site

(a) Within ¼ mile	5 points
(b) Within ½ mile	3 points
(c) Within 1 mile	1 point
(d) Further than 1 mile	0 points

4. State, County, or Town Major, Secondary, or Collector Roads,
   Improved with Curbs and Sidewalks

(a) Direct Access	5 points
(b) Within ½ mile	3 points
(c) Within 1 mile	1 point
(d) Further than 1 mile	0 points

5. Firehouse

(a) Within 1 mile	3 points
(b) Within 2 miles	1 point
(c) Further than 2 miles	0 points[51]

Pursuant to procedures set out in the ordinance, a developer who wished to develop a parcel of land had to file an application, with the requisite fee, to the administrative assistant for Boards and Commissions, along with a map showing the land proposed for development and a sketch of the proposed development.[52] The applicant had to indicate the basis for calculating his or her point score, demonstrating affirmatively a total of at least 15—the required number for issuance of a permit. The administrative assistant reviewed the application according to the standards established by the development point system and the capital improvement program and made a written report to the Town Board within forty-five days of the submission of the application.[53] The application was then posted for public hearing at the first regular meeting of the Board, not less than two weeks after submission of the written report. The Town Board had to render its decision within thirty days after the conclusion of the public hearing.

To relieve a residential subdivision owner of possible unreasonable restrictions on the use of his or her property that might obtain by an outright denial of future development, the ordinance contained several remedial provisions. First, the Board was required to issue an approval of an application giving the residential developer a present right to proceed with the proposed development in the year when such development would meet the point requirement.[54] The time that such permit is issued depends upon the scheduled completion date of the capital budget and capital program, but in no case could it be later than the final year of the capital program. Thus, under the provision, if a developer did not presently have the required 15 points, a special permit was, in effect, assigned for a future date when the requisite number of points would be available based upon the capital improvements program. As a result, no legitimate developer was deprived of the right to develop his or her property—development was merely phased until necessary municipal facilities were available, and such facilities had to be made available at some time within eighteen years. Second, a developer may advance the date of authorization by agreeing to provide such improvements as will bring the proposed development within the number of development points required for issuance of a special permit.[55] This may require the developer to make improvements to, or construct, off-site drainage or school, fire or recreation facilities, or make improvements to off-site roads. A developer who wished to make use of this option was required to post a cash deposit or surety bond sufficient to cover the cost of the proposed improvement.[56] Third, if a developer was denied authorization to proceed, he or she may apply for a variance to the Town Board.[57] If after a public hearing, the Board determined that such variance was consistent with the Town's comprehensive plan, the Board was empowered to grant the variance. A recent report on the ordinance as it has been implemented found that variances for one lot were almost always granted by the Board, those for two lots were usually granted, while those for three lots or more were usually denied.[58]

One of the most innovative remedial parts contained in the plan was a provision that within one year from the grant of the vested approval, the developer may request from the Town's Development Easement Acquisition Commission (DEACOM) a reduction in assessed valuation of the land if that valuation is affected by the temporary restriction or use of the land.[59] The Commission, consisting of seven members, was created in 1967 for the purpose of maintaining land as open space, to control the rate of development of the Town, and to enhance the conservation of natural and scenic resources. The law that created the Commission provides that, with the consent of the Town and property owners, the Town can acquire a developmental easement in the property for a period of not less than five years. When this occurs, the assessed valuation of the land subject to the easement is reduced in proportion to its decrease in value resulting from the limitation on future use of the land. By thus providing different remedial provisions to alleviate the burden of phased controls on individual developers, the plan ensured that reasonableness is the key to limitations on development. In addition, the grant of an easement to the Town was a charitable gift and entitled a grantor to a federal income tax deduction under section 170(h) of the Internal Revenue Code as well as property assessment reduction.[60]

The Effect of the Plan

As has been discussed above, the primary aims of the development points system established in the Town of Ramapo was: first, to control the rate of residential growth; and second, to establish priorities for the locations of residential development. Control over the rate of development can be viewed as an extension of traditional land use planning techniques, which have always had the effect of limiting the total residential buildout or capacity of a community. The second aim of the point system—that of determining the location of residential development—set location priorities by tying development to the adequacy of public facilities. Thus priority was given to residential areas the development of which will minimize future public investments. Because future growth is tied to the provision of facilities, it was certain that the plan would lead to a more desirable fiscal position on the part of the Town and a lower tax burden than would exist under conditions of uncontrolled growth.

In the past, it has been recognized that new residential development imposes more in the way of municipal costs than it contributes in the way of municipal revenues.[61] Thus, there is a net burden resting on the community at large. As a community grows, municipal expenditures increase because the school districts must provide educational facilities and services, and the town must provide municipal services and facilities to serve the increasing population.[62] At the same time, the increase in the number of new residential structures means more taxable properties to the community, both because of the structures themselves and because of increased commercial and industrial growth. A study of the Ramapo Plan conducted in 1971 found that under the controlled growth plan adopted by the Town, there would be a saving of about $5.4 mil-

lion over the entire eighteen-year period, or about $300,000 per year over a system of land use controls that had no provision for controlled growth.[63] The savings resulted because of fewer expenditures due to less residential construction, and the phasing of facility construction to coincide with needs. These savings were more than sufficient to offset the increases in tax revenue that would have occurred in an uncontrolled system and thus resulted in a projected net savings to the community.[64]

From the time the managed growth program began in October 1969 until 1974, there were 264 applications for special permits and variances.[65] All of the special permit applications—71 covering 991 lots on 1,084.12 acres—were granted and only three were set for a future date. The reason for the high success rate was that developers tended to meet informally with the administrative assistant prior to making formal application—if the required number of points were present, developers applied for permits; if not, they either applied for a variance, made their own improvements, or participated in the DEACOM program.[66] Of 158 variances applied for—covering 761 lots on 588.71 acres— 146 were granted and only 12 denied.[67] Of those denied, only one had more than two drainage points, the majority had no road access points, and only two had three firehouse points.[68] In 21 cases, a developer opted to make improvements to make up the point deficit.[69] In most cases, this meant constructing or committing drainage improvements, improved roads, or additional recreational facilities. In addition, since 1969, slightly more than 200 properties had taken advantage of the DEACOM program.[70] Over half of the properties that originally entered the program in 1969 for a five-year period renewed their participation for a similar time span or for a larger period, and as of July 1974, over 150 properties, constituting 1,700 acres of land, were still taking advantage of the DEACOM law. Normally these properties would have an assessed value of $7.5 million—under DEACOM, the combined assessment totaled $3.5 million.

After fourteen years elapsed of the eighteen-year Ramapo Plan (well into the third of the three six-year capital improvement programs), the Republicans, who had assumed control of the Town Board in March of 1983, decided to eliminate the program.[71]

The *Ramapo* Decision
Background of Litigation

The Ramapo Plan is based upon the concept of timing and sequential controls—that is, all residential development other than single lot development must proceed in accordance with the provision of adequate municipal facilities, because any development of two or more units has to be commercial in nature since the owner can only occupy one unit and must transfer or sell the others. The system was designed to avoid urban sprawl.[72] Earlier zoning did not handle the sprawl problem because early comprehensive plans did not consider these issues.[73] Restraints are only temporary in nature since none can exceed the eighteen-year period set by the capital program. The ordinance is implemented by the establishment of a system of special permits—before a permit can be granted for development, a total of fifteen developmental points must be accumulated from five different categories. The point accumulation is based upon the availability of five essential services or facilities, with differing numbers allocated depending upon proximity to those facilities.[74] Under the ordinance, the Town is committed to completion of public capital improvements to assure development of all areas of the Town within a maximum period of eighteen years. As a remedial provision, the ordinance provides for variance relief if the subdivision is consistent with the Town's comprehensive plan; reduction of assessed valuation in light of the temporary restrictions placed on the use of the land; and issuance of permits for development at such time as the capital plan indicates the facilities will be available. The developer is also given a right to speed up the development date by agreeing to provide the necessary facilities for accumulation of the required points.

As a result of the Ramapo Plan, a developer may be delayed from developing his property for up to eighteen years—unless he agrees to make required improvements, or obtains a variance from the Town Board. In October of 1969, shortly after enactment of the Plan, Ruth Golden, the owner of a parcel of undeveloped land within the Town and of the Ramapo Improvement Corporation, submitted a subdivision plan for approval by the Town Planning Board. The Planning Board denied approval on the ground that the applicant had failed to obtain the requisite special permit from the Town Board—under the provisions of the ordinance, subdivision approval by the Planning Board for residential development use could not be obtained unless the Town Board had

first issued a special permit for the use.[75] As a consequence of the denial, Golden and Ramapo Improvement Corp. (hereinafter referred to as Golden) brought an action against the Planning Board and the Town Board, seeking to annul the decision of the former and invalidate the Zoning Ordinance.[76]

The allegations brought by Golden were based both on the United States Constitution and the Constitution of the State of New York.[77] She alleged first that the power exercised by the Town to regulate the timing of development had not been delegated to it by the state, and that the ordinance was therefore invalid under both statutory law and substantive due process.[78] Second, Golden alleged that even if the ordinance was not *ultra vires*, it had not been adopted in accordance with a comprehensive plan, as required by the state law.[79] Third, the ordinance was alleged to be violative of Golden's Fifth Amendment right not to have her property taken "for public use without just compensation."[80] Fourth, and last, the ordinance was alleged to be exclusionary in nature.[81]

In response to the allegations, the Rockland County, New York, Supreme Court found, in an opinion written by Judge Galloway, that the ordinance was a valid exercise of the Town Board's zoning powers.[82] On appeal, a sharply divided bench in the appellate division reversed specifically on the *ultra vires* issue.[83] Justice Martuscello, writing for the majority, held that the Town had "usurped power by regulating its population growth in a manner which has not been delegated to it."[84] Although it recognized minimum lot size zoning as an authorized means of controlling population density, the court felt that such means were clearly distinguishable from regulating population growth.[85] The court also felt that the discrimination among developers inherent in allowing some "to build earlier than others"[86] could not be relieved by the tax abatement feature of the Ramapo Plan. The Town subsequently appealed the case to the New York Court of Appeals, and in a decision already referred to as a zoning classic,[87] the court reversed the appellate decision and held that the Plan was indeed constitutional.[88]

The *Ramapo* Opinion

The Authority Issue

The first allegation raised by petitioner Golden in the *Ramapo* case was that the particular zoning scheme enacted by the Town of Ramapo exceeded the scope of authority vested in the municipality by the state, and that the ordinance was therefore *ultra vires*. The basis of this argument is that since the primary purpose of the amending ordinance is to control or regulate population growth within the Town, the enactment is invalid because that purpose is not among those authorized by the zoning enabling legislation. The legislation applicable to the case were sections 261 and 263 of the New York Town Law. Section 261 states:

> For the purpose of promoting the health, safety, morals, or the general welfare of the community, the town board is hereby empowered by ordinance to regulate and restrict the height, number of stories and size of building and other structures, the percentage of lot that may be occupied, the size of yards, courts and other open spaces, the density of population, and the location and use of buildings, structures and land for trade, industry, residence or other purposes. . . . [89]

Section 263 reads:

> Such regulations shall be made in accordance with a comprehensive plan and designed to lessen congestion in the streets, to secure safety from fire, flood, panic and other dangers; to promote health and general welfare; to provide adequate light and air; to prevent the overcrowding of land; to avoid undue concentration of population; **to facilitate the adequate provision of transportation, water, sewerage, schools, parks and other public requirements.** . . . [90] (Emphasis supplied.)

The specific issue involved was whether those two provisions of New York Town Law delegated to the Town Board the power to promulgate ordinances restricting population density and land use based upon a system of timing and sequential control. Even though section 263 includes within its provisions an express sanction for ordinances that have the purpose of facilitating the introduction of adequate municipal services and facilities, it was argued that the Town did not have the power under section 261 to employ timing controls to attain those ends.

The authority issue is raised in zoning cases because historically, local governments have been viewed as mere creatures of the state. As creatures of the state, municipalities have no inherent power to legislate[91]—only where there is a specific delegation of legislative authority can a municipal government exercise the police power.[92] Even when there is a specific grant of authority to a local body, most courts have traditionally limited local discretion by restricting exer-

cises of authority to situations in which the power to act is expressly granted by the enabling act, or where the particular function is clearly implied in state laws.[93]

In facing the authority issues in *Ramapo,* the court of appeals was able to imply the power to utilize timing and sequential controls from the language of sections 261 and 263 of the Town Law.[94] In so doing, the court said:

> The power to restrict and regulate conferred under Section 261 includes within its grant, by way of necessary implication, the authority to direct the growth of population for the purposes indicated, within the confines of the township. It is the matrix of land use restrictions, common to each of the enumerated powers and sanctioned goals, a necessary concomitant to the municipality's recognized authority to determine the lines along which local government shall proceed, though it may divert it from its natural course.[95]

Further finding that the Ramapo ordinance was enacted to further "legitimate zoning purposes"[96] as enumerated in section 263, the court held that the power to further those purposes through timing and sequential controls was indeed authorized under the standard zoning enabling act incorporated in New York Town Law.

The Comprehensive Plan Issue

The second argument raised in *Ramapo* was that the ordinance, as enacted, was not in accordance with the comprehensive plan. This argument was based on a central assumption underlying the law of zoning—that restrictive land use techniques are employed as means to an end, and not as ends in themselves.[97] This assumption, which derives from the Due Process Clause, mandates that there be a rational relationship between the regulation as applied and the objective posited,[98] and is essentially a prohibition against arbitrariness in the enactment of zoning ordinances.[99] In addition, the zoning enabling acts expressly define and limit the permissible ends that a zoning ordinance may serve, and New York's enabling acts further require that zoning regulations be adopted in accordance with a comprehensive plan.[100]

The most viable defense against a claim of arbitrariness is conformity to a comprehensive plan.[101] The requirement is met if it can be demonstrated that there exists a systematic rational land use scheme, and zoning laws enacted by the town that conform to that scheme. An important factor to consider is whether there is some evidence of a planning process at work.[102]

In the *Ramapo* decision, the comprehensive plan requirement was easily met because a detailed master plan had been devised over a two-year period providing an overall basis for the Town's immediate and long-range plans for land use and development. In equating the master plan with the concept of a comprehensive plan,[103] the court felt that because the plan was aimed at insuring systematic and orderly growth throughout the township, and because it was based upon exhaustive facility studies designed to identify public needs, the means of implementation—timing and sequential controls—and the plan were not inconsistent. Thus, the court concluded that phased zoning is not an arbitrary device because it is rationally related to difficult planning problems. If the phased zoning ordinance is adopted in the context of overall planning, the evidence is much stronger that the local government's efforts are reasonable, and that they are rationally related to their conceived purposes.

The Taking Issue

This argument is based upon the Fifth Amendment prohibition against taking "private property . . . for public use without just compensation," which has been held applicable to the states through the Fourteenth Amendment.[104] An ordinance that seeks to restrict permanently the use of property so that it may not be used for any reasonable purpose has been held to effect a taking. If a taking results, the power of eminent domain must be used to accomplish the objective of the ordinance—the government cannot simply impose total restrictions upon the use of one's land without paying for it.

In the *Ramapo* case, Golden argued that by delaying development of her property for a period of eighteen years, the ordinance had the effect of taking her property without just compensation. The court of appeals, however, rejected her argument, holding that the restrictions upon subdivision and development imposed by the ordinance did not result in a taking without just compensation, even though some land might be burdened for a full generation.[105] Recognizing that every restriction upon the use of property has an adverse effect upon some individual owners, the court found that unless those restrictions are "unreasonable in terms of necessity," or the resulting "diminution in value [is] such as to be tantamount to a confiscation," the regulation would pass muster.[106] Golden's property was not taken, because although the limitations imposed were "substantial in nature and duration," they were not "absolute."[107] For one thing, all residential property within the township could be subdivided within a maximum period of eighteen years.[108] In addition, Golden could accelerate the date of development of her land by providing, at her expense, the facilities and services required to obtain a special permit.[109] Finally, the restrictions imposed by the ordinance, although they may have the effect of diminishing the value of Golden's property, that diminution would be offset by future financial benefit from the orderly development of the township [110] and reduced local property taxes during the period of restriction.[111] Thus, the court felt that the restrictions imposed were only temporary in nature—the property could be put to a profitable use within a reasonable time—and not sufficient to result in an invalid taking.[112]

By accepting full population and employment growth through timed and sequenced development, property is afforded an urban use when public facilities become available and thus is not deprived of "all" use under the *First English* and *Lucas* decisions.[113] Beginning with *Golden v. Planning Board,*[114] and continuing through current decisions, both state and federal courts have uniformly upheld growth-timing planning techniques against taking challenges. The standard for these cases, and the standard required of a regulation to avoid a taking claim, is "reasonable use over a reasonable period of time" as measured by the comprehensive plan.[115]

The *Lucas* decision emphasized over eighteen times that there is no categorical take unless *all value and use* has been permanently deprived. In *Golden,* the court considered a growth management plan that phased growth over eighteen years to be reasonable,[116] and therefore land that will not be serviced within the life of the plan is appropriately regulated for nonurban, rural, or agricultural uses and is constitutional for providing a reasonable use—which is nonurban.[117] When a community seeks to time and phase growth on the basis of adequacy of public facilities, courts will enforce an obligation on the part of the government to build the facilities within a reasonable period of time (that is, that the governing body make a good faith effort to comply with a comprehensive plan).[118]

The Exclusionary Issue

The fourth argument put forth by Golden in the *Ramapo* case was that the concept of timing and sequential controls as embodied within the Ramapo scheme was exclusionary in nature.[119] This argument rests upon an analogy of the Ramapo Plan to techniques utilized in recent years by many communities attempting to isolate themselves from the increasing pressures of population growth, sprawl, and increasing tax burdens. The most popular of such techniques is large minimum lot size requirements that so inflate the cost of housing that the influx of low- and moderate-income families is effectively barred.[120] In recent years, there has been an increasing trend toward invalidating such ordinances on the ground that they are exclusionary in nature and thus promote no valid zoning purpose.[121]

In its decision in *Ramapo,* the court of appeals recognized the invalidity of exclusionary zoning techniques when it stated that:

> There is, then, something inherently suspect in a scheme which, apart from its professed purposes, effects a restriction upon the free mobility of a people until sometime in the future when projected facilities are available to meet increased demands.[122]

And, when it said:

> What we will not countenance, then, under any guise is community efforts at immunization or exclusion.[123]

But the court also realized the essential difference between the Ramapo Plan and other techniques:

> But far from being exclusionary, the present amendment merely seeks, by the implementation of sequential development and timed growth to provide a balanced cohesive community dedicated to the efficient utilization of land.[124]

The restrictions on development imposed by the Ramapo Plan thus are recognized as an affirmative attempt to provide a balanced cohesive community dedicated to the efficient utilization of land. They are not imposed to freeze population at present levels, or to exclude low- or moderate-income groups from the community, but to ensure continuous development commensurate with the Town's obligation to provide essential municipal facilities.[125] Evidence of such purposes can be found both in the fact that the restrictions imposed conform to the community's considered land use policies as expressed in its comprehensive plan, and in the Town's affirmative attempts to provide for low-

and moderate-income housing in the community.[126] Because the plan was based upon exhaustive facility studies and was implemented through affirmative controls designed to promote ordered community growth, the court felt that the Town had made a reasonable attempt to deal with the problems it sought to correct.

The Dissent

The dissenting opinion in *Ramapo,* written by Judge Breitel, expresses the view that timing and sequential controls are not authorized by enabling legislation that delegates the power to regulate subdivision development to the Town.[127] His main criticism of the majority opinion is its implication of that power from the language of section 261 of the Town Law.[128] The fear expressed by Judge Breitel is that without specific legislative language authorizing such restrictions, communities may utilize controlled growth techniques as a means of excluding low- and moderate-income families from these communities and thus have a negative impact upon regional growth patterns.[129] To the extent that Judge Breitel attempts to make an analogy between traditional exclusionary techniques, and the system of timing and sequential controls utilized in the Ramapo Plan, his opinion differs fundamentally from that of the majority, which distinguishes between the essentially negative approach exemplified by the traditional techniques and the positive attempt to encourage planned, efficient development evidenced by the Ramapo Plan.

Ramapo in the Courts

Ramapo was ranked the most significant land use regulation case in America, other than *Euclid,* by Dozier & Hagman in 4 *Environmental Comment* 4 (1978) after a survey of over 100 academics and leading land use practitioners.

A noted treatise on zoning and land use controls makes the following observation regarding the significance of *Ramapo*:[130]

> The *Ramapo* decision shifted the balance of power from the developer to public land use agencies. The developer no longer has an absolute right to proceed with development, irrespective of whether public facilities can reasonably accommodate the development. Instead, the developer can be made to wait a reasonable period to allow public facilities to catch up or be forced to expend funds to ripen the land for

development. . . . The *Ramapo* decision and rationale also permanently altered the court's perception of the land use regulatory process and paved the way for subsequent decisions that have favored public regulation over the developer or landowner's immediate right to develop property (irrespective of the harm such development might inflict upon the public good). . . .

Ramapo has achieved tremendous success in the courts. During the twenty-five-year period from 1972 to 1997 the case has been cited approvingly in eighty New York cases, seven federal courts of appeal cases, eighteen state appellate courts including Arizona, California, Connecticut, Florida, Idaho, Illinois, Maine, Maryland, Massachussetts, Michigan, Montana, New Hampshire, New Jersey, North Dakota, Ohio, Pennsylvania, and South Carolina, and thirty-four law review articles.

Thus, in *Maryland National Capital Park & Planning Commission v. Rosenberg*,[131] the court of appeals, citing *Ramapo*, related that timing and sequential controls "are said by professional planners to be the most important advance in planning and zoning law since *Village of Euclid*. . . ." The federal court decisions uniformly uphold the constitutionality and public purpose of linking the adequacy of public facilities to infrastructure planning. *Steel Hill Development, Inc. v. Town of Sanbornton*.[132] *Schenk v. City of Hudson*[133] approved a growth control system that slowed the rate of growth to allow the city to improve its infrastructure to meet existing and future needs without straining resources. The district court had enjoined the system for failing to meet *Ramapo* standards.[134]

Perspectives

The decision in *Ramapo* marked the first time that any court in the United States had upheld the concept of restricting development in metropolitan areas through comprehensive planning or zoning without compensation. Now, for the first time, states,[135] regions, and even the federal government, as well as municipal governments, had the tool to develop a rational urban growth policy that can balance suburban development with inner-city revitalization and new community development. By recognizing that timing and sequential controls, over a period of eighteen years, is a necessary concomitant of the police power to regulate urban growth, the court in *Ramapo* vitalizes a tool for controlling the direction of growth and the public capital investment in metropolitan areas.[136]

As contrasted with traditional techniques, time controls emphasize controlling both population and community expansion until the municipality is able to provide adequate facilities and services. The aim is coordination between the pace of development and its sequence.[137] Growth is not only phased, but rather it is encouraged in those areas where municipal facilities are readily available to service new development. Only in areas where insufficient service is available is development discouraged, and then only for a reasonable time. Thus the concept means that municipal growth can be channeled into areas where development can be adequately provided for, and out of areas where services cannot be efficiently provided until a later time. The result is economic provision of quality services, municipal control over characterization of the area, and affirmative planning that can provide the potential for orderly, efficient growth.

As has been discussed previously, timing and sequential control also enable a community to plan affirmatively for the accommodation of low- and moderate-income housing, maintain a desirable balance between commercial and residential use within the community, and, by limiting uncontrolled sprawl on the urban-rural fringe, such controls can provide impetus for rehabilitation of built-up suburban and urban areas, long neglected because of overemphasis on suburbia.[138] In addition, time coordination offers the potential of viable planning over city-county, regional, state or even national settings. By basing future development on the efficient provision of services to meet the needs of that development, many of the problems that have plagued local, regional, state, and national planning could now be effectively solved. The remaining chapters will discuss the application of timing and sequential control to these broader settings, ensuring the Smart Growth key to solving the problem of suburban sprawl in America.

Extending *Ramapo's* Eighteen-Year Timing and Phasing into an Urbanizing Tier for Metropolitan, City/County, and State Systems for the Control of Sprawl: The Constitutional Requirements

The majority of national growth in America since World War II has taken place on the urban-rural fringe.[139] As overall metropolitan area population has increased, so have myths and perceived conditions of:

1. abandonment and blight of central cities and older suburban built-up areas;
2. higher crime rates,[140] deterioration and deficiencies of existing infrastructure have pushed large numbers of mobile citizens to the quiet, spacious existence of a suburban ideal.[141]

Given impetus by federal housing and tax policies, as well as by the creation of a vast federal highway system that allowed commuters to relocate their residences in suburbia and even propelled an industrial migration away from the central city, this great movement of people and industry to the suburbs has led to wasteful and inefficient urban sprawl and leapfrog development.[142]

As a concomitant of uncoordinated development on the urban-rural fringe, the burden of bearing the cost of capital investment to provide services for developments outside of areas with adequate municipal facilities has shifted to the public sector.[143] Soaring general property tax rates reflected in many communities attest to the increased need for public facilities,[144] and the general subsidization by most communities of new growth leading to massive deficiencies.[145] This transfer of the true cost of development from the developer, landowner, and consumer to the public sector has led to:

- land speculation;
- destruction of environmental and agricultural resources;
- inefficient use of energy resources because of sprawling roads and utility lines;
- poor quality in those services provided due to the extensive demands on the limited resources of the communities;
- an unwillingness to provide adequate housing for diverse racial, economic, and ethnic groups;
- defensive incorporations and annexations; and
- an increase in the cost of public services.[146]

Most local governments in high-growth areas find themselves unable to cope with the imbalance of sprawl growth. A major reason for the failure to deal adequately with these problems is that most municipalities are not capable of solving what are essentially regional problems. Because of governmental fragmentation, which is characteristic of governmental structure on the urban-rural fringe, most municipal governments lack the jurisdictional power base to govern over more than limited territorial areas.[147] Even though the problems of sprawl do not stop at municipal boundary lines, the power of local govern-

ments to cope with those problems does. As a result, a multiplicity of fragmented local governmental units attempt to deal with problems that by their very nature demand county-city intergovernmental, regional, or national solutions.[148]

There are few quick fixes to sprawl or the social effects and costs of sprawl. The only proven method of controlling the negative effects of sprawl is through state, regional, and city-county coordination that guides local governments to determine which areas are appropriate for development or should be protected from development, analyzes corridor location and capacity, and identifies appropriate development patterns. This accepts the premise that accommodating growth is not bad, but that unchecked sprawl will damage the metropolitan area. Growth coordination makes development responsive to a community's ability to provide facilities and services efficiently, phasing growth by timing its development to the availability of public facilities and making planning decisions with an understanding of the consequences of development.[149]

It is in this sense that the Ramapo Plan can become an "urbanizing" tier which organizes growth in nonsprawl patterns (corridors, centers, contiguous development). Tier I will be existing downtowns, Tier II existing residential areas, Tier III will be the "urbanizing" tier, and Tier IV the nonurban rural, agricultural, and environmental tier. Managing sprawl creates joint partnerships between developers and communities, and among communities— relationships that foster interdependence and encourage cooperation and coordination, not confrontation.

Urban communities can learn from suburban communities, by becoming more responsive to "internal" issues. Though central cities may find it difficult to compete with the "sizzle" of suburban development patterns, they can compete by promoting diverse, cosmopolitan alternatives and providing desired and basic services to its citizens, and by creating new joint public-private development adjacent to marinas, universities, hospitals, transit stations, arterial interchanges, and public facilities.[150] Alternatives exist to provide for, and eliminate barriers to, affordable housing. Education can be improved through the use of magnet and neighborhood-based schools. Cities can respond to the crime issue by refocusing police department programs and staffing based on community and neighborhood need. Infrastructure can be improved for streets, parks, and cultural facilities, and services enhanced. They can learn to reverse the decline of their residential and economic base.

Incentives have been used successfully to entice businesses to relocate, and their applicability to lure homeowners is equally justified. San Diego required that outlying new growth in the Urbanizing Tier pay its fair share of the cost it generates in off-site facilities while making available equity financing in existing urban areas (the Urbanized Tier), which balanced infill and suburban growth. Portland, Oregon; Boulder, Colorado; and Dayton, Ohio, have marketed the advantages of their cities' neighborhoods, transit, open space, and cultural/ethnic diversity.[151] The Puget Sound region has proposed spending $12 billion to construct and expand the mass transit system to channel growth within corridors and centers (the Urbanizing Tier) and to encourage economic development.[152] Cities also can encourage development to reestablish urban neighborhoods in the Urbanized Tier. Champaign, Illinois, in a plan I devloped, encouraged infill development and emphasized performance zoning by using realistic goals that were attainable and not frightening to current residents, for the in-town neighborhood.

Suburban communities can respond by limiting growth in areas not yet ready for development and requiring that development pay fully for facilities and services generated by new growth in the Urbanizing Tier. Urban and suburban communities can reduce the costs of sprawl by addressing connectivity, and encouraging the use of urban villages and neotraditional neighborhoods, both of which emphasize a neighborhood's role and reduced trips by locating commercial activities within walking distance (within the Urbanizing Tier). Once a tier system is adopted you can have different goals, objectives, policies, and strategies within each tier and meet equal protection. It is a marvelous system.

The metropolitan area needs to develop regional plans, which are translated into county and city implementation for infrastructure and other social services. The transportation network is a tool to accomplish regional cooperation by rebuilding more roads within developed areas rather than exclusively building urban bypasses, and finding ways to incorporate mass transit (even on a limited basis). Government, though politically unlikely to consolidate, can enter into intergovernmental agreements to share responsibilities and revenues, undertake unified development and growth planning, and provide coordinated and nonconfrontational tax and development incentives at local, state, and federal levels.[145] A regional plan offers equity among both the wealthy and poor areas within a metropolitan area and matches environmental, fiscal, and social needs with resources.

One can be an advocate for the suburbs and for the metropolitan area—they are not mutually exclusive. It is more, and not less, coordination that will lead to greater wealth in our metropolitan area. When governments come together and work with each other instead of against each other, infrastructure costs will decline and sprawl will slow.[153] If communities refrain from adopting efficient, coordinated growth management strategies, development will continue to sprawl across the countryside, because sprawl is a *process* that pits new development areas against old. As the decay spreads outward, third-ring suburbs will be affected, and the "doughnut hole" will expand. Suburban cities already are finding evidence of "urban decay" in their neighborhoods, such as deferred maintenance of structures, absentee property owners, and neighborhoods with declining income levels and infrastructure deficiencies. In addition, sprawl breeds increased governmental fragmentation and inefficiencies, as more independent levels of government, each with its own agenda, impact more people and businesses.

Solutions require broad-based regional, city/county, and state support to help manage growth within the urbanizing tier. History has taught that lasting fiscal growth occurs within a strong economy—one based as much on the quality of life and successful business practices as on collaborative, rather than adversarial, government participation. Planning for growth, though primarily a local function, is largely dependent on government's perception of its role in the marketplace. Government participation, whether at the regional level, through coordinated efforts between the cities and counties, or through statewide legislation and mandates, utilizing the *Ramapo* planning and legal principles of concurrency have accomplished controlled growth and prevented urban sprawl. Due to innovative outreaches of *Ramapo*, these legal and planning principles have been challenged. Courts will examine constitutional issues including taking claims and good faith criteria, as well as the overall effect upon the region under the Regional General Welfare Doctrine. It is necessary for local officials to examine these issues when enacting timed and sequenced growth management controls, but if it is done correctly, the tier system is the most defensible Smart Growth system.

The Takings Issue

Many regions and states should be aware of the "takings" issues that can arise when implementing techniques for controlling growth.[154] The "taking" issue permits opponents of growth-control measures to challenge the constitutionality of the plans and ordinances as applied to a particular piece of property.[155] Under the United States Constitution, private property is afforded protection under both the Due Process Clause[156] and the Fifth Amendment Taking Clause,[157] as incorporated into the Fourteenth Amendment.[158] In addition, most state constitutions contain "taking" clauses—some requiring compensation for "taking or damaging."[159]

Primarily as a result of Justice Holmes's opinion in *Pennsylvania Coal v. Mahon*,[160] the Fifth Amendment Taking Clause has come to be seen as a limitation upon the state's proper exercise of the police power. Prior to that decision, regulation under the guise of the police power had been held not to be circumscribed by the Fifth Amendment but merely by the Fourteenth Amendment mandate of "reasonableness." *Pennsylvania Coal*, however, seemed to say that the police power and eminent domain are at opposite ends of a continuum and that, somewhere in between, a line can be drawn to divide the one from the other, and that the difference between regulation and taking is a matter of degree, not kind.[161] The problem, however, is that the Supreme Court has never drawn that line—it has been left to the states, resulting in a confused and nonuniform disposition of the problem.

The theory that has received the most judicial acceptance seems to be the balancing theory, wherein the court attempts to balance the impact of the regulation against the importance of the state's interest supporting the regulation. Pursuant to this test, an ordinance that totally deprives a landowner of all reasonable use of his property invariably results in an unconstitutional taking without due process of law. However, application of the test turns upon what the court believes to be a reasonable economic use. For example, the Wisconsin court in *Just v. Marinette County*[162] has stated that:

> An owner of land has no absolute and unlimited right to change the essential natural character of his land so as to use it for a purpose which it was unsuited in its natural state and which injures the rights of others. The exercise of the police power in zoning must be reasonable and we think it is not an unreasonable exercise of that power to prevent harm to public rights by limiting the use of private property to its natural use. . . . The changing of wetlands and swamps to the damage of the general public by upsetting the natural environment and the nat-

ural relationship is not a reasonable use of that land which is protected from police power regulation.[163]

Similarly, the First Circuit Court of Appeals in *Steel Hill Development, Inc. v. Town of Sanbornton*,[164] dismissed the taking issue, finding that "though the value of the tract has been decreased considerably, it is not worthless or useless so as to constitute a taking."[165] The New York Court of Appeals in *Ramapo*[166] held that an ordinance that merely restricts the use of property for a reasonable time does not amount to an unconstitutional taking. Once the issue of the impact of the ordinance upon the individual is settled, the court must determine the importance of the state interest sought to be protected by the ordinance. A state interest is more likely to be substantial when regulating a use that presents an immediate threat to the public. Thus, regulation that seeks to protect the public health and safety will be afforded the highest priority and will therefore sustain the greatest degree of impact. On the other hand, aesthetics, historical considerations, and preservation of a community's character are objectives universally given the lowest priority. This does not mean that regulations seeking to accomplish these objectives will not be sustainable; it merely means that they will not usually be sustainable if the resulting impact upon the individual is overly burdensome. Preservation of the economy, planned growth, and the efficient provision of adequate services and facilities will sustain a heavier impact on the individual than purely aesthetically-related goals.

The case law has evolved that concurrency programs and adequate public facilities ordinances that involve timing and sequencing must comport with constitutional principles of due process, equal protection, substantive due process, and the Takings Clause. These restrictions on development may lead to takings claims in several distinct situations. First, as with any restriction on development, the value of the project in monetary terms may be reduced, especially for projects within the Urbanizing Tier, which may not be serviced for a long period of time. This may result in a reduction in the monetary value of the land or an interference with the landowner's plans to build on the property. Second, classical versions of adequate public facilities ordinance have included an "escape clause" allowing developers to avoid this waiting period by constructing the necessary facilities themselves.[167] "Escape clauses" must be part of a program whereby development is phased or denied on the basis of the adequacy of public facilities, rather than an unlawful exaction designed to require developers to pay for existing facility deficiencies.

A regulation, as opposed to a physical occupation[168] or an exaction on development permission, constitutes a taking where "it imposes too heavy a burden on property rights to be sustained as a police power regulation."[169] To avoid characterization as a taking, an adequate public facilities ordinance must leave the property owner with a reasonable use of his or her property for a reasonable period of time.[170] The question of reasonableness will turn on whether

1. the regulation substantially advances a legitimate public purpose; or

2. whether it denies a landowner economically viable use of its property.[171] The "substantial advancement" test balances the interests asserted by the government against the economic impact of the regulation.[172] This test is used to determine whether the government has violated the policy of the Takings Clause to avoid the transfer of public burdens to a relatively small group of property owners.[173] The second test focuses on whether the landowner has been deprived of all reasonable use of its property.

The validity of a timed and sequenced concurrency program under the substantial advancement inquiry will turn on the diligence of the studies and planning underlying the ordinance, since these studies may be examined for the purpose of characterizing the nature of the local government's action. The relative weight assigned to the government's interest will be tested against two factors:

1. the nature of the government's action; and

2. the "reciprocity of advantage" conferred by the ordinance.[174]

Uses deemed "injurious to the health, morals, or safety of the community,"[175] such as nuisance regulation, may be prohibited notwithstanding an almost complete deprivation of property value or use since no one has the right to create a nuisance in the first place.[176] Where it can be demonstrated that an adequate public facilities ordinance is needed to prohibit the creation of a public danger, such as the failure of a sewer treatment plant or the avoidance of flood-prone conditions through the requirement of adequate drainage facilities, the extent of deprivation allowed under this inquiry is great. However, the lesser the relationship of the required facilities to public health or safety, the lesser the deprivation allowed before the regulation is invalidated.

The determination of whether a landowner has been deprived of all reasonable use of its property focuses on two factors:

1. the economic impact of the regulation; and
2. the extent to which the landowner's "distinct investment-backed expectations" have been defeated.[177]

This inquiry focuses only on the reasonableness of the remaining use, and not the amount of deprivation.[178]

Most adequate public facilities ordinances (APFOs) and concurrency programs allow developers to "buy time" by providing facilities before their scheduled date in the capital improvements program. Normally, APFOs are subject to attack only as a regulatory taking, since their only effect is to use the police power of the local government to preclude (temporarily) the development of land. However, if a court can be convinced that the ordinance is simply a form of "extortion" designed to shift a disproportionate amount of public facilities costs onto a developer, or to continously deny all development in a circuitous approval process, the developers may be excused from compliance with the ordinance.[179] The legitimacy review for regulatory takings challenges to adequate public facilities ordinances would implicate the looser "rational basis" standards applied in Fourteenth Amendment due process or equal protection cases.[180] However, including the requirement that a developer provide all scheduled public improvements needed to rectify existing level of service deficiencies could raise takings challenges on the basis that the requirement is not "proportionate" to the impact of the development. The question is whether the ordinance is truly designed to relieve the harshness of a valid regulation, which would survive judicial scrutiny, or whether the local government is using its police powers to extort payments for existing deficiencies or the provision of excess facility capacity that will not be caused by or used by the development onto the developer. Where the APFO is coupled with a realistic, financially feasible capital improvements program, including funding sources other than developer contributions, there is little question that the ordinance is designed to achieve legitimate growth management and public facilities goals. However, where a capital improvements program is lacking, or where mandatory dedications or impact fees are listed as the sole source of new capital improvements funding despite the presence of existing service deficiencies, the ordinance may become subject to judicial scrutiny.[181]

Pundits predicted that a series of land use takings decisions decided in 1987 would send the planning profession into a tailspin. While those cases decided for the first time that "regulatory" takings are subject to the Fifth

Amendment's compensation requirement[182] and announced a heightened standard of scrutiny for development exactions,[183] they did nothing to stultify the range of public purposes (absent bad faith) recognized as sufficiently important to justify substantial diminutions in property values without compensation. In the recent case *City of Monterey v. Del Monte Dunes at Monterey, Ltd.*, decided in May of 1999, the U.S. Supreme Court held that continuous denial (five times) of development applications that met previous conditions constituted a taking on two grounds: failure to advance legitimate state interests, and denial of all reasonable use.[184] In particular, the *First English* decision raised the question whether temporary bans on construction, such as moratoria and interim development controls, are subject to invalidation as "temporary takings."[185]

If the restriction upon the property is not permanent, time is used as an element of the taking equation to determine what use is left for the land after the timing restriction terminates.[186] It is critical to distinguish between the time that a taking occurs (that is, from the date of enactment of the ordinance once a taking has been found[187]) and time as a factor in determining whether a taking has occurred in the first place. Thus, on the remand of the *First English* case, the California Court of Appeals found that the interim ordinance prohibiting construction within the flood plain did not rise to the level of a taking (despite six years' passing from the time of original adoption of the interim ordinance until the case reached the United States Supreme Court). The Court held that time is but one factor in the takings equation:

> We do not read the U.S. Supreme Court's decision in First English as converting moratoriums and other interim land use restrictions into unconstitutional "temporary takings" requiring compensation unless perhaps, **if these interim measures are unreasonable in purpose, duration or scope.** (Emphasis supplied.)[188]

This result is compelled because the duration of the controls is a significant factor in determining the remaining reasonable use of the land. If the regulation is temporary, all reasonable use has not been denied because there is future use remaining. Thus for adequate public facilities ordinances, the test is whether the regulation has left a reasonable use over a reasonable period of time.[189] The U.S. Supreme Court identifies this principle as the nonsegmentation theory—that, in determining whether a taking has occurred, the property interest, both

present and future, horizontal and vertical, must be viewed in its entirety.[190] As one commentator suggests:

> *Keystone* and *Penn Central* require that present use and future use be recognized solely as separate strands in the bundle of rights that comprise property. Thus the loss of the present use strand, standing alone, does not constitute a facial taking. Even if all present use is denied, there is no taking because future use remains. When the time dimension in property is taken as a whole, property rights are accorded their constitutional protection due if the land owner is given a reasonable use of property measured over a reasonable period of time.[191]

The *First English* decision expressly recognizes the validity of "normal delays" in the development approval process,[192] and several decisions subsequent to *First English* have upheld moratoria despite taking claims.[193] In *First English*, the United States Supreme Court held, on a motion for summary judgment, that a landowner could receive compensation for restrictions imposed by a floodplain development moratorium adopted by the City of Los Angeles, provided the landowner could demonstrate that the restrictions amounted to a confiscatory taking. On remand, the California courts in the *First English* litigation found that the plaintiff failed to state a cause of action despite the outright prohibition of construction on its property, finding that the regulatory taking issues presented did not even present a "close issue."[194] Its discussion of the balance between public necessity and private deprivation is particularly relevant to the issues raised by adequate public facilities ordinances. The *First English* decision distinguished the goal of "preventing premature urbanization"—which has been recognized as advancing a legitimate state interest[195]—from the goal under consideration in that case, which was the preservation of lives and health. The court stated that the latter goal would support the deprivation of all use of a landowner's property, while the former would not:[196]

> If there is a hierarchy of interests the police power serves—and both logic and prior cases suggest there is—then the preservation of life must rank at the top. Zoning restrictions seldom serve public interests so far up on the scale. More often these laws guard against things like "premature urbanization" [citations omitted] to orderly development and

the mitigation of environmental impacts [citations omitted]. When land use regulations seek to advance what are deemed lesser interests such as aesthetic values of the community they frequently are outweighed by constitutional property rights. [citations omitted] Nonetheless, it should be noted [that] even these lesser public interests have been deemed sufficient to justify zoning which diminishes—without compensation—the value of individual properties.[197]

Adequate public facilities ordinances serve a number of purposes related to public health and safety as well as "minor" concerns related to urban design. Tying the level of growth to the adequacy of water and sewer, transportation, fire, and school facilities promotes both physical and psychological well-being and inhibits the deleterious effects of sewer system failures, traffic congestion and accidents, and insufficient educational capacity. "Premature urbanization," which in *Agins* was an aesthetic goal, is not the major minor justification for adequate public facilities concerns. Instead, the concern is over the ability of communities to provide public facilities and services essential to individual health, safety, and welfare and to maintain a balance between development and infrastructure that ensures the overall economic, environmental, and psychological well-being of a community. This multiplicity of purposes should rank higher than the zoning restrictions mentioned in *First English*.

As has been discussed in detail in Chapter II, the New York Court of Appeals in *Golden v. Planning Board of the Town of Ramapo*[198] upheld the timing and sequential control system (TASC) as embodied in the Ramapo Plan. In so doing, the court held that the Ramapo Ordinance was not outside permissible statutory authorization, it was not unconstitutionally exclusionary, and it came within the bounds of the Taking and Due Process Clauses. As to the exclusionary issue, the court said:

What we will not countenance, then, under any guise, is community efforts at immunization or exclusion. But, far from being exclusionary, the present amendments merely seek, by the implementation of sequential development and timed growth, to provide a balanced cohesive community dedicated to the efficient utilization of land.[199]

[T]he obvious purpose is to prevent premature subdivision absent essential municipal facilities and to insure continuous development commensurate with the Town's obligation to provide such facilities.

They seek, not to freeze population at present levels but to maximize growth by the efficient use of land, and in so doing testify to this community's continuing role in population assimilation.[200]

In discussing the taking and due process issues, the court emphasized the temporary nature of the restrictions and the effort the town had made to mitigate the hardship to affected landowners:

> An ordinance which seeks to permanently restrict the use of property so that it may not be used for any reasonable purpose must be recognized as a taking. . . . An appreciably different situation obtains where the restriction constitutes a temporary restriction, promising that the property may be put to a profitable use within a reasonable time. . . . The proposed restraints, mitigated by the prospect of appreciated value and interim reductions in assessed value, and measured in terms of the nature and magnitude of the project undertaken, are within the limits of necessity.
>
> In sum, where it is clear that the existing physical and financial resources of the community are inadequate to furnish the essential services and facilities which a substantial increase in population requires, there is a rational basis for "phased growth" and hence, the challenged ordinance is not violative of the Federal and State Constitutions.[201]

It is clear from the discussion above that timing and sequential controls do not violate constitutional standards as long as such controls are based intelligently and logically upon the economic, social, and environmental necessities of the area. By accepting full population and employment growth through timed and sequenced development, property is afforded an urban use when public facilities become available and thus are not deprived of "all" use under the *First English* and *Lucas* decisions.[202] Beginning with *Ramapo* and continuing through current decisions, both state and federal courts have uniformly upheld growth-timing planning techniques against taking challenges. The standard for these cases, and the standard required of a regulation to avoid a taking claim, is "reasonable use over a reasonable period of time" as measured by the comprehensive plan.[203] The *Lucas* decision emphasized over eighteen times that there is no categorical taking unless all value and use has been *permanently* deprived. In *Ramapo,* the court considered a growth management plan that phased growth over eighteen years to be reasonable,[204] and therefore land that will not be serviced within the life of the plan is appropriately regulated for nonurban, rural, or agricultural uses and provide for a reasonable use—which is nonurban.[205] When a community seeks to time and phase growth on the basis of adequacy of public facilities, courts will enforce an obligation on the part of the government to build the facilities within a reasonable period of time (that is, that the governing body makes a good faith effort to comply with a comprehensive plan). As long as such controls are based on a comprehensive plan that entails restrictions upon private property on a temporary basis, and provide for affirmative goals of providing a fair share of low- and moderate-income housing, efficient provision of services, and environmental and energy conservation, they should be upheld in the courts. The key again is "reasonableness"; the TASC concept presents an imminently reasonable means of dealing with complex urban problems.

The Good Faith Requirement of Concurrency and Adequate Public Facility Regulation

Concurrency regulations tie the issuance of development permits, such as rezoning, planned unit development approvals, subdivision plats, site plans, and building permits, to level of service (LOS) standards identified in a comprehensive plan.[206] Most concurrency ordinances are tied to roadway LOS standards. Few concurrency ordinances tie the issuance of development permits to public transit capacity. However, many concurrency or adequate public facilities regulations—such as those used in Montgomery County, Maryland— apply a lower roadway LOS where public transit is available. This technique maintains the integrity of the concurrency management system while encouraging development to occur in areas where alternative transportation capacity is available.

A municipality's concurrency program, as well as any adequate public facilities plan, must be accompanied by "good faith" efforts to resolve existing deficiencies in addition to efforts to mitigate the externalities of new growth-related impacts.[207] There are two essential rationales for this requirement. First, the constitutional Takings Clause requires that new development can only be compelled to mitigate its proportionate impacts;[208] and, second, without an even-handed approach, courts will look for an improper ulterior motive.[209]

The courts will recognize the broad powers of local governments to com-

bat deficiencies through comprehensive planning. A wide range of fiscal and police power devices are available to resolve infrastructure deficiencies. However, to avoid placing an undue burden on new development for ills it has not created, the courts have developed a set of "good faith" doctrinal requirements. Courts have consistently upheld growth controls imposed pursuant to a balanced and even-handed comprehensive plan designed to resolve infrastructure deficiencies.[210] When a comprehensive plan is not in place, the courts have presumed good faith efforts by a municipality as long as plan studies to develop a comprehensive plan are under way,[211] and such studies will also defeat allegations of hidden illegal motives to deter growth.[212] These principles have been illustrated by a series of New York cases where the court has held that notwithstanding constitutional restrictions on the use of development controls to require new construction to pay for existing deficiencies, new development can be denied pending the resolution of those deficiencies as long as good faith efforts are being used to resolve those deficiencies,[213] but would be an unconstitutional taking where the city had not taken good faith steps to provide an adequate system[214] or where the ban was not adopted pursuant to a comprehensive plan.[215]

Regional General Welfare Doctrine

Coordination between the local governments and service providers within the same tier or between tiers is essential to ensure that adequate growth controls will promote timed and sequenced development within the entire region. The Regional General Welfare Doctrine can be a tool for each tier to make further assurances that the other tiers are working in the best interest of the state or region. Regional General Welfare is conceptually based on a fundamental limitation on the sovereign government's exercise of the police power—that furthers the health, safety, and general welfare of the citizens. [216] Because the state's police powers must promote the welfare of all citizens of the state, it is impossible for the state to delegate police powers to local governments that would be exercised contrary to the general welfare of the citizens of the state. Where a locality acts in its own parochial "best interest" to the detriment of significant state or regional interests, the regional general welfare doctrine would be used to challenge the action as a violation of substantive due process.

The basis of the Regional General Welfare Doctrine, as it pertains to land use controls, can be found in the landmark decision of the United States

Supreme Court upholding the constitutionality of zoning regulations in *Village of Euclid v. Ambler Realty Company*.[217] The Court noted that the village of Euclid was located in the Cleveland metropolitan area and suggested the future "possibility of cases where the general public interest would so far outweigh the interest of the municipality that the municipality would not be allowed to stand in the way."[218] The substantive due process test used to judge the constitutionality of the zoning ordinance in *Euclid* for purposes of the federal Constitution has been uniformly applied in the states for state constitutional purposes as well (that is, that a zoning ordinance must have a substantial relation to the public health, safety, and general welfare to be constitutional).[219]

Most successful regional general welfare cases have addressed municipal ordinances that have effectively excluded, through various regulations and restrictions, development of affordable housing. The courts have generally found the exclusionary effect unreasonable due to the burdens of housing shortages placed on surrounding communities and those seeking housing.[220] While a cooperative effort is needed between all the tiers of a region, each tier can examine its own urban forms and specific techniques to contribute to the regional goal of controlled, timed, and sequenced growth.

Acceptance of the concept of "regional" general welfare is also implicit, if not explicit, in cases finding that nonresidents have standing to challenge a governmental entity's zoning decisions. The general rule is that as long as the applicable statutory or case law requirements for standing are satisfied, the nonresident has standing to challenge the decision based upon the effects of the decision on property outside the jurisdiction of the zoning authority. The classic case in this regard is *Borough of Cresskill v. Borough of Dumont*.[221] In *Dumont*, several municipalities challenged the rezoning of a tract from residential to commercial in a neighboring jurisdiction. The court held:

> The public health, morals and welfare are not limited by the boundaries of any particular zoning district, nor even by the boundaries of the municipality adopting the ordinance. . . . Hence, it becomes a legal requirement that the restrictions and regulations in a zoning ordinance must be made with reasonable consideration to the character of the land and also to the character of the neighborhood lying along the border of the municipality adopting the ordinance.

In the case of *Duffcon Concrete Products v. Borough of Cresskill*,[222] the court said: "What may be the most appropriate use of any particular property depends not only on all the conditions, physical, economic and social, prevailing within the municipality and its needs, present and reasonably prospective, but also to the nature of the entire region in which the municipality is located and the use to which the land in that region has been or may be put most advantageously." In the case of *De Benedetti v. River Vale TP., Bergen County*,[223] the court said: "[I]t is, accordingly, necessary to obtain a broad perspective of the municipality and the region in which it is located."[224] In *City of Hickory Hills v. Village of Bridgeview*,[225] the Illinois Supreme Court held that a local government had standing to challenge the rezoning of land in a neighboring municipality to a higher intensity. The plaintiff was under a court order to supply services to the rezoned area, and alleged that public services were inadequate to accommodate the proposed development. While the court cited numerous Illinois cases finding a lack of statutory authority to challenge neighboring zoning ordinances, the court recited the general rule in other jurisdictions that an "aggrieved person" with a real interest in the subject matter of the controversy may challenge a neighboring city's zoning ordinance.[226] While the prior obligation to provide services to the property seemed to provide a special circumstance of unique impact, the Illinois Supreme Court in *Village of Barrington Hills v. Village of Hoffman Estates*,[227] held that the reasoning of the case could be extended to include more generalized impacts on fiscal health and infrastructure.[228]

The *Dumont* and *Duffcon* decisions have had profound implications for the practice of local zoning, many of which apply equally to boundary adjustments and other exercises of the police power. The doctrine simultaneously expanded the concept of general welfare while limiting the constitutional authority of local governments to act for purely local interests. The most common application of the doctrine has been the invalidation of ordinances for failing to consider regional needs adequately,[229] or upholding zoning actions in light of regional considerations such as the availability or unavailability of proscribed uses elsewhere.[230] *Dumont* was also mentioned in a decision striking flat fees on taxis as an unreasonable restraint on the ability of taxicab companies not headquartered in the enacting community to operate there.[231] Decisions following the *Creskill* cases prior to *Mt. Laurel*, below, exhibited a reluctance to apply *Dumont* in an affirmative manner by requiring localities to zone for high-intensity uses forming outside of municipal boundaries.[232] However, this situation changed with the advent of *Mt. Laurel* and the exclusionary zoning cases, which imposed an affirmative obligation under the constitutional regional general welfare doctrine to consider the need for housing in adjoining areas when developing zoning ordinances.

The most extensive use of the regional general welfare doctrine has been in exclusionary zoning cases. Although the Pennsylvania courts were actually the first to apply the doctrine to such cases, the blockbuster case was the 1975 decision of the New Jersey Supreme Court in *Southern Burlington NAACP v. Township of Mt. Laurel*,[233] (hereinafter *Mount Laurel I*). In holding that exclusionary zoning violates substantive due process guarantees of the state Constitution, the New Jersey Supreme Court stated:

> [I]t is fundamental and not to be forgotten that the zoning power is a police power of the state and the local authority is acting only as a delegate of that power and is restricted in the same manner as is the state. So, when regulation does have a substantial external impact, the welfare of the state's citizens beyond the borders of the particular municipality cannot be disregarded and must be recognized and served.[234]

Although the regional general welfare doctrine is generally discussed by the courts in constitutional terms, this quote from *Mount Laurel I* reveals that the issue might also be viewed in terms of an abuse of the delegated power to regulate land use (that is, *ultra vires* exercise of the police power) as well as an unconstitutional act. *Mount Laurel I* was later expanded upon in *Southern Burlington County NAACP v. Township of Mount Laurel*,[235] (*Mount Laurel II*). A year after the *Mount Laurel I* decision, the California Supreme Court addressed the regional general welfare doctrine and its relationship to housing opportunities in the *Livermore* decision. The *Livermore* case involved an initiative growth management adequate public facilities ordinance enacted by the voters of the City of Livermore that prohibits issuance of further residential building permits until local educational, sewage disposal, and water supply facilities complied with specified standards. The court stated:

> When we inquire whether an ordinance reasonably relates to the public welfare, inquiry should begin by asking *whose* welfare must the ordinance serve. In past cases, when discussing ordinances without sig-

nificant effect beyond the municipal boundaries, we have been content to assume that the ordinance need only reasonably relate to the welfare of the enacting municipality and its residents. But municipalities are not isolated islands remote from the needs and problems of the area in which they are located; thus, an ordinance, superficially reasonable from the limited viewpoint of the municipality, may be disclosed as unreasonable when viewed from a larger perspective.

These considerations impel us to the conclusion that the proper constitutional test is one which inquires whether the ordinance reasonably relates to the welfare of those whom it significantly affects. If its impact is limited to the city boundaries, the inquiry may be limited accordingly; if, as alleged here, the ordinance may strongly influence the supply and distribution of housing for an entire metropolitan region, judicial inquiry must consider the welfare of that region.[236]

The court went on to describe a balancing test to determine whether or not a challenged land use regulation reasonably relates to the regional general welfare. The regional general welfare doctrine as applied to low- and moderate-income housing has since been codified by the New Jersey and California legislatures. The doctrine has been adopted, to one degree or another, in cases involving housing or exclusionary zoning in Pennsylvania, New York, and New Hampshire.[237]

The most significant extension of the regional general welfare doctrine outside of the area of housing and exclusionary zoning is found in the 1978 decision of the Supreme Court of Washington in *Save a Valuable Environment (SAVE) v. City of Bothell.*[238] That case involved a challenge by an environmental group to a rezoning for a regional shopping center that was alleged to have substantial external impacts relating to the loss of desirable agricultural land and the need for substantial investments in highways, sewers, and other services and utilities. The Washington court concluded:

Under these circumstances, Bothell may not act in disregard of the effects outside its boundaries. Where the potential exists that a zoning action will cause a serious environmental effect outside jurisdictional borders, the zoning body must serve the welfare of the entire affected community. If it does not do so it acts in an arbitrary and capricious manner.[239]

All localities should be aware of takings issues, concurrency and good faith requirements, and the regional welfare policies when implementing proper timed and sequenced growth programs to withstand constitutional and legal challenges.

Endnotes

1. Professor McDougal, along with a talented Associate Professor David Haber, had written the classic work in the field, PROPERTY, WEALTH & LAND (Michie Press, 1946), which called for national policy and regional planning initiatives to conserve resources. It was the first major casebook written for law schools in the still unborn field of land use planning law. Previously, almost all work in the field was confined to treatises on zoning law or completely separate planning works focusing more on architecture, landscape planning, open space, and the city-beautiful movement.

2. For a similar story of unplanned growth, see the two marvelous studies of the great city builders, Miller, CITY OF THE CENTURY: THE EPIC OF CHICAGO AND THE MAKING OF AMERICA (Simon & Schuster, 1996) (describing the chaotic growth of the City of Chicago and its suburbs in the nineteenth century, despite Burnham's magnificent lakefront plan), and Robert A. Caro, THE POWER BROKER: ROBERT MOSES AND THE FALL OF NEW YORK, (Knopf 1974) (the incredible story of how Robert Moses, the Utopian engineer, broke open sprawl in the New York region by building "parkways" to the suburbs in lieu of mass transit). *See also* Rexford G. Tugwell, *The Moses Effect,* in URB. GOV'T at 463 (Edward C. Banfield ed., New York Free Press, 1961). *See* Fausold, *A Summary of Land Use in America,* 24 ENVTL. & URB. ISSUES 1, 6 (1997) (describing how Chicago and Atlanta have reached a fifth generation of suburban sprawl forty-five and seventy miles outside of the cities, respectively).

3. For a summary of the economic and planning history of the Town, see Chung, CONTROLLING THE RATE OF RESIDENTIAL GROWTH: A COST-REVENUE ANALYSIS FOR THE TOWN OF RAMAPO (1971); Freilich & Greis, TIMING AND SEQUENCING DEVELOPMENT: CONTROLLING GROWTH IN FUTURE LAND USE, ENERGY, ENVIRONMENT AND LEGAL CONSTRAINTS, 59–106 (D. Burchell & D. Listokin, eds. 1975).

4. *Id.* Chung at 2.

5. *Id.* Chung at 4.

6. Until the 1965 elections when growth control swept the Democrats into control of the Town Board, not one single majority slate of Democrats had ever won election in the Town since the Civil War.

7. Haar, *The Master Plan: An Impermanent Constitution,* 20 LAW & CONTEMP. PROBS. 353 (1955); Haar, *In Accordance with a Comprehensive Plan,* 68 HARV. L. REV. 115 (1955).

8. Henry Fagin, *Regulating the Timing of Urban Development,* 20 LAW & CONTEMP. PROBS. 298, 300-01 (1955).

9. A study that came out two years after the historic *Ramapo* decisions in the New York Court of Appeals and U.S. Supreme Court had demonstrated that more efficient forms of planned unit development for 10,000 dwelling units would save just under $11 million (approximately 15 percent) in road and utility costs over typical leapfrog development with the

same number of residents. REAL ESTATE RESEARCH CORPORATION, THE COSTS OF SPRAWL, DETAILED COST ANALYSIS at 8 (1974). For similar results *see* the Statewide New Jersey Plan in which I was a principal consultant; *see generally* Robert Burchell, *Economic and Fiscal Costs of Sprawl*, 29 URB. LAW. 199 (1997). A recent study by James Duncan shows that infrastructure costs for housing units in transportation corridors or neotraditional centers are only $16,000 per dwelling unit compared to $24,000 for sprawl, single-family units, *cited in* Maryann Froehlich, *Smart Growth: Why Local Governments Are Taking a New Approach to Managing Growth in Their Communities*, PUB. MGMT. 5, 8 (May 1998). *See also* FREILICH, TO SPRAWL OR NOT TO SPRAWL: NATIONAL PERSPECTIVES FOR KANSAS CITY (CHARLES KIMBALL LECTURE) 14 (Western Historical Manuscript Society 1998), showing that residential development pays only about 60 percent of its total cost of capital and operational needs over the lifetime of the development in comparison with commercial and industrial development, which pays 130 percent over its useful life. A balanced, mixed community is essential to capital and operating costs and efficiencies. BANK OF AMERICA REPORT, BEYOND SPRAWL: NEW PATTERNS OF GROWTH TO FIT THE NEW CALIFORNIA (1995). Moreover, because new developments in the suburbs do not pay their full cost of capital improvements, the need for which generates, existing built-up areas are required to subsidize the new growth from the general tax base. *See* Helen F. Ladd, *Population Growth, Density and the Cost of Providing Public Services*, 29 URB. STUDIES 273, 292 (1992): "In addition the results suggest that rapid population growth imposes fiscal burdens on established residents in the form of lower service levels." *See also* Paul Oyaski, Mayor, *Economic Erosion: The Case Against Urban Sprawl*, 22 STATE AND LOCAL LAW NEWS 5, Spring 1999; Franklin James, *Evaluation of Local Impact Fees as a Source of Infrastructure Funding*, 11 MUN. FIN. J. 1407 (1990).

10. *Compare* (1) "Growth has helped fuel California's unparalleled economic and population boom and has enabled millions of Californians to realize the enduring dream of home ownership . . . but sprawl has created enormous costs that California can no longer afford. Ironically, unchecked sprawl has shifted from an engine of California's growth to a force that now threatens to inhibit growth and degrade the quality of our life." [BANK OF AMERICA REPORT, BEYOND SPRAWL: NEW PATTERNS OF GROWTH TO FIT THE NEW CALIFORNIA (1995), *cited in* Briechle, *A Better Way to Grow*, PUB. MGMT., May 1998, at 4]; *with* (2) "Controlling sprawl by redirecting growth would benefit central city dwellers through rehabilitation and revitalization of the central city, would be environmentally beneficial by preserving agricultural land and open space, would aid in reducing energy consumption and would be limiting the area of which services must be extended, reduce the cost of services to suburbanites and aid in the fiscal solvency of local governments. Because so many interest groups can be benefitted from effective growth management, it should now be possible to form coalitions to combat this hydra-headed problem." Freilich & Davis, *Saving The Land: The Utilization of Modern Techniques of Growth Management to Preserve Rural and Agricultural America*, 13 URB. LAW. 27, 29 (1981).

11. In 1965 an influential article was published on the utility of using planned unit development in lieu of conventional sprawl subdivision. *See* Jan Krasnowiecki, Richard F. Babcock & David N. McBride, *Legal Aspects of Planned Unit Development*, URB. LAND INST. TECHNICAL BULL. NO. 52 (1965). This article was a precursor to much of today's "neotraditional development" theory. *See* S. Mark White & Dawn Jourdan, *Neotraditional Development: A Legal Analysis*, LAND USE LAW & ZONING DIG. 17 (August 1997). *See also Editorial*, ROCHESTER (MINN.) POST BULL., October 9, 1998, calling for "neotraditional" development to break the pattern of single-family detached sprawl; Jeffrey Spivak, *Suburbs as Urban Centers, Planners*

Seek Neo-Traditional Communities as Alternatives to Sprawl, K. C. STAR, April 2, 1999 at A-2. Other works that influenced my thinking in the early 1960s toward maintaining mixed-use communities go back to my readings of the early days of the New Town movement. *See* EBENEZER HOWARD, GARDEN CITIES OF TOMORROW (1946 ed.), and CLARENCE STEIN, TOWARDS NEW TOWNS IN AMERICA (1928). For recent efforts toward mixed-use transit-oriented development along transportation corridors, *see* Robert H. Freilich, *The Land Use Implications of Transit-Oriented Development: Controlling the Demand Side of Transportation Congestion and Urban Sprawl,* 30 URB. LAW. 3 (Summer 1998) (lecture delivered in Berlin to the U.S. German Marshall Fund Conference on Transportation Sustainability), and Amy E. Freilich and Michael Bernick, *Transit Villages and Transit-Based Development,* 30 URB. LAW. 1 (Winter 1998).

12. In 1965 the Pennsylvania Supreme Court decided *National Land and Investment Co. v. Easttown Township Bd. of Adjustment,* 215 A.2d 597 (Pa. 1965), which required communities in the path of urbanization to assimilate its fair share of regional growth. It was the forerunner to *Mount Laurel I, Southern Burlington County NAACP v. Township of Mt. Laurel* (Mount Laurel I), 67 N.J. 151, 336 A.2d 726 (1975) and the regional general welfare doctrine. Associated Home Builders of the Greater East Bay Inc. v. Livermore, 557 P.2d 473 (Cal. 1976) (requiring that if a zoning ordinance influences the supply and distribution of housing for an entire metropolitan region, judicial inquiry must consider the "welfare of that region"). Similar "regional general welfare" holdings have been made by the courts in New York (Berenson v. Town of New Castle, 341 N.E.2d 236 (N.Y. 1975)); Washington (S.A.V.E. v. City of Bothell, 576 P.2d 401 (Wash. 1978)); Virginia (Board of Supervisors of Fairfax County v. DeGroff Enterprises, Inc., 198 S.E.2d 600 (Va. 1973)); New Hampshire (Britton v. Town of Chester, 595 A.2d 492 (N.H. 1991)); Pennsylvania (Township of Williston v. Chesterdale Farms, Inc., 341 A.2d 466 (Pa. 1975)).

In its ultimate decision in the *Ramapo* case, the New York Court of Appeals relied heavily on the provision of public housing in the Town. The court noted that Ramapo "utilized its comprehensive plan to implement its timing controls and has coupled with these restrictions provisions for low and moderate income housing on a large scale." (285 N.E.2d at 303). Ramapo was the first suburban town in New York State to develop voluntarily, as part of its planning, integrated public housing for low-income families, often over vociferous objections of its own residents. For Ramapo to develop two federal public housing areas with over two hundred duplex units, the Town had to win multiple lawsuits with its own citizens. *See Greenwald v. Town of Ramapo,* 35 A.D.2d 958, 317 N.Y.S.2d 839 (A.D. 2d 1970); Farrelly v. Town of Ramapo, 317 N.Y.S.2d 837 (A.D. 2d 1970); and Fletcher v. Romney, Secretary of U.S. Dep't of Housing and Urban Development, 323 F. Supp. 189 (S.D.N.Y. 1971).

In addition, the Town prevented urban sprawl by incentivizing thousands of multifamily housing units within the villages of the Town (Suffern and Spring Valley) and thus encouraged regional general welfare and urban infill.

13. As recently as *Schenck v. City of Hudson,* 114 F.3d 590 (6th Cir. 1997) which overruled 937 F. Supp. 679 (1996), the court of appeals held that a points allocation system tied to adequate public facilities standards was essential to meeting federal substantive due process. *See* Stoney-Brook Development Corporation v. Town of Fremont, 479 A.2d 561 (N.H. 1984), where the court invalidated a growth management system based on inadequate study and assessment of the community's needs.

14. *See* F. BOSSELMAN, D. CALLIES & J. BANTA, THE TAKING ISSUE 290 (1973):

The importance of a sound presentation is apparent in the urban context as well. The Town of Ramapo successfully defended a growth management ordinance before New York's highest court with success due in no small part to a thorough presentation of their case . . . .

The Town was able to present a vast array of planning data in their defense. In its statement of facts in *Golden v. Planning Board of the Town of Ramapo* . . . the Court of Appeals pointed to the Town Master Plan whose "preparation included a *four volume* study of the existing land uses, public facilities, transportation, industry and commerce, housing needs and projected population trends. . . .

15. At the time I was formulating the concepts for the Ramapo Plan and Ordinance, a neighboring Town of Clarkstown was also experimenting with requiring off-site improvements as a condition of rezoning. This effort was led by the excellent planning firm of Raymond & May. It was a useful introductory tool but it was limited to *discretionary* changes, requesting rezoning and conditional use permits and didn't reach to the whole level of development activity in a sprawling community, permitted as of right: *Josephs v. Town Board of Clarkstown*, 198 N.Y.S.2d 695 (N.Y. Sup. Ct. 1960). (In *Josephs* the court reviewed the town board's denials of a *special permit* seeking *increased density and lower lot sizes* based on inadequacy of the town's school facilities.).

16. I later used the official map concept to protect the five major streams that flowed through Ramapo into the Passaic River and ultimately New York Bay. The preservation of these stream corridors was one of the signal achievements of the Plan. In 1995 I argued and won the case of *Palm Beach County v. Wright*, 641 So. 2d 50 (Fla. 1994), which reversed four years of adverse decisions and held that a county major street right-of-way protection plan (or official map) was not an unconstitutional facial taking. *See* Robert H. Freilich and David W. Bushek, *Integrating Land-Use and Transportation Planning: The Case of* Palm Beach County v. Wright, ABA STATE & LOCAL LAW NEWSLETTER, Vol. 18, No. 2 (Winter 1995) at p. 1.

17. 1961 WIS. L. REV. 370.

18. The "large lot" minimum lot size has been the bane of rational planning and the godfather of suburban sprawl. In 1968, the REP. OF THE NAT'L COMM'N ON URB. PROBS. (DOUGLAS COMM'N REP.), BUILDING THE AMERICAN CITY, 91st Cong., H.R. Doc. 91-34 (1968) reported that two-thirds of all vacant zoned land in the United States was zoned for minimum lot sizes in excess of two acres, creating vast areas of urban sprawl. For a history of urban sprawl and its fiscal and social impacts, *see* Freilich, *supra* note 9. Many decisions at the time the Ramapo Plan was being formulated were decrying "minimum lot sizes"; *see* National Land & Investment Co. v. Easttown Township, 215 A.2d 597 (Pa. 1965); Appeal of Kit-Mar Builders, 268 A.2d 765 (Pa. 1970).

19. *See* Pierro v. Baxendale, 118 A.2d 401 (N.J. 1955) *and* Katobimar Realty Company v. Webster, 118 A.2d 824 (N.J. 1955) with a strong dissent by Justice William J. Brennan, Jr. before he was elevated to the U.S. Supreme Court; *State ex rel.* Howard v. Village of Roseville, 70 N.W.2d 404 (Minn. 1955) (excluding manufactured housing and trailer parks).

20. Lionshead Lake, Inc. v. Wayne Township, 89 A.2d 693 (N.J. 1952).

21. Herbert Franklin, *Controlling Growth but for Whom? The Social Implications of Development Timing*, 2 MGM'T & CONTROL OF GROWTH 78 (S. Scott ed., Scoffeld 1975) (suggesting that the unincorporated town should have been looked at without regard to the villages).

22. Thus in *In re* Kit-Mar Builders, 268 A.2d 765, 769 (Pa. 1970), the court held:

Neither Concord Township, nor Easttown Township nor any other local governing unit may retreat behind a cover of exclusive zoning. We fully realize that the overall solution to these problems lies with greater regional planning, but until that time comes that we have such a system, we must confront the situation as it is. The power currently resides in the hands of each local governing unit, and we will not tolerate their abusing that power in attempting to zone out growth at the expense of neighboring communities.

23. Simpson, *Democrats Demand New Building Quota,* SPRING VALLEY RECORD, September 9, 1965; DeSalvo, 3 *Ramapo Candidates Urge Building Edict,* ROCKLAND COUNTY J. NEWS, Sept. 9, 1965.

24. Gruber, *Ramapo Democrats Emphasize Long Term Construction Plans,* ROCKLAND COUNTY J. NEWS, Sept. 10, 1965.

25. *Builders Lambast Democrats for Party's Plank on Housing,* SPRING VALLEY RECORD, Sept. 15, 1965.

26. For a summary of the plan and its development, *see* Manuel Emanuel, Ramapo's *Managed Growth Program: A Close Look at* Ramapo *After Five Years Experience,* 4 PLANNER'S NOTEBOOK 1 (Oct. 1974). *See also,* Chung, *supra* note 3.

27. Years later I argued the critical case in the Supreme Court of Florida, *Palm Beach County v. Wright,* 641 So. 2d 50 (Fla. 1994), which upheld the constitutionality of the official map for entire county transportation thoroughfare maps. *See infra,* Chapter V, "Palm Beach County: Preserving Transportation Corridors." But such a period cannot be unlimited in time. The New York General City Law § 35 provides that a city can utilize an official map for ten years without providing for compensation. Where a period of fifty years was used, the courts must at least consider whether a de facto regulatory taking has occurred. *Ward v. Bennett,* 214 A.D.2d 741, 625 N.Y.S.2d 609 (A.D.2d., 1995).

28. Emanuel, *supra* note 26, reprinted in 3 MGM'T & CONTROL OF GROWTH 302 (S. Scott ed., Scoffeld 1975).

29. Fletcher v. Romney, 323 F. Supp. 189 (S.D.N.Y. 1970); Greenwald v. Town of Ramapo, 35 A.D.2d 958 (A.D.2d 1970); Farrelly v. Town of Ramapo, 317 N.Y.S.2d 837, 35 A.D.2d 958 (A.D.2d 1970).

30. Elliott & Marcus, *From Euclid to Ramapo, New Directions in Land Development Controls,* 1 HOFSTRA L. REV. 56 (1973).

31. 54 Misc. 2d 338, 282 N.Y.S.2d 564 (1967), *aff'd,* 29 A.D.2d 874, 288 N.Y.S.2d 519 (A.D.2d 1968). The continuing validity of *Rubin v. McAlevey* was enunciated recently by the New York Appellate Division in *Ward v. Bennett,* 214 A.D.2d 741, 625 N.Y.S.2d (A.D.2d 1995). "While the City has the power to temporarily restrict the use of land without compensation for the purpose of conducting studies toward a comprehensive regulatory scheme, the duration of such period cannot be unreasonable." (*See* Matter of Russo v. New York State Department of Environmental Conservation, 55 A.D.2d 935, 391 N.Y.S.2d 11 (1977) [citing Matter of Rubin v. McAlevey, 54 Misc. 2d 338, 282 N.Y.S.2d 564, *aff'd* 29 A.D.2d 874, 288 N.Y.S.2d 519]; de St. Aubin v. Bigane, 51 A.D.2d 1054, 1055, 381 N.Y.S.2d 533 (1976), citing Matter of Rubin v. McAlevey, *supra*).

32. Freilich, *Interim Development Controls: Essential Tools for Implementing Flexible Planning and Zoning,* 49 URB. LAW. 65 (1971) (describes the entire system utilized in Ramapo and nationally).

33. This phrase was made famous in the leading case of *Downham v. City Council of Alexandria,* 58 F.2d 784, 788 (E.D. Va. 1932), where the court also noted that to disallow interim zoning power would be "like locking the stable after the horse is stolen." *Id.*

34. Freilich, *Interim Development Controls: Essential Tools for Implementing Flexible Planning and Zoning,* 49 Urb. Law. 65 (1971).

35. Minn. Stat. Ann. § 394.34.

36. *See* Collura v. Town of Arlington, 329 N.E.2d 733 (Mass. 1975) (court found authority to adopt zoning in the enabling act that represented a broad delegation of police power to cities and towns), and Almquist v. Township of Marshan, 245 N.W. 819 (Minn. 1976), a case I argued to the Minnesota Supreme Court (general language of the planning enabling act "to implement a plan"); the court found a second source of local zoning authority in a home rule amendment to the state constitution). *See also* Matter of Rubin v. McAlevey, 54 Misc. 2d 338, 282 N.Y.S.2d 564 (1967), aff'd, 29 A.D.2d 874, 288 N.Y.S.2d 519 (A.D.2d 1968) (interim ordinances enacted by the Town of Ramapo while developing its landmark timing and sequencing regulations were upheld).

37. 105 A.2d 586 (Pa. 1954) (a municipality may properly refuse a building permit for a land use repugnant to a pending and later enacted zoning ordinance even though applied for when the intended use conforms to existing regulations). *See also* Hunter v. Adams, 4 Cal. Rptr. 776 (Cal. Dist. Ct. App. 1960); and Russian Hill Improvement Association v. Board of Permit Appeals, 56 Cal. Rptr. 672, 423 P.2d 824 (Cal. 1967).

38. *Compare* Conway v. Town of Stratham, 414 A.2d 539 (N.H. 1980) (upholding interim controls on condition that the town implement master plan within one year) *with* Campana v. Clark, 197 A.2d 711 (N.J. Law Div. 1964) (sustaining an interim control ordinance for thirty-one months) and Peacock v. County of Sacramento, 77 Cal. Rptr. 391 (Cal. Ct. App. 1969) (finding that an interim ordinance that prevented development for three years gave the county reasonable time to complete its study, but was a taking without compensation when it extended beyond that time).

39. 482 U.S. 304 (1987).

40. 258 Cal. Rptr. 893, 906 (Cal. App. 1989).

41. Elizabeth Garvin and Martin Leitner, *Drafting Interim Development Ordinances: Creating Time to Plan,* Land Use Law, 3, 6 (American Planning Association, June 1996).

42. Arden Rathkopf, The Law of Zoning and Planning, § 50.04[3][a] (4th ed. 1994); Richard Carlisle & S. Mark White, *Administrative and Legislative Techniques for Resolving Vested Rights and Condemnation Issues in* Nichols, Law of Eminent Domain, ch. 25 (1993).

43. *See* Concrete Pipe & Products of California, Inc. v. Construction Laborers Pension Trust, 508 U.S. 602, 113 S. Ct. 2264, 2290 (1993) (diminution of economic value of 78 percent (*Euclid*) and 91.5 percent (*Hadacheck*) are mere diminutions; in determining whether a taking has occurred, the entirety of the property must be utilized as the measure of diminution of loss of all substantial use or value); *see* Ward v. Bennett, 214 A.D.2d 741, 625 N.Y.S.2d 609, 612 (A.D.2d 1995) (upholding temporary restrictions) but rejecting a fifty-year reservation as a taking.

44. In 1993 I argued a critical interim development takings case, utilizing the principle of *Concrete Pipe, supra, Woodbury Place Partners v. City of Woodbury,* 492 N.W.2d 258 (Minn. App. 1993), which held that a moratorium of two years to complete an interchange study was not a taking even though the City admitted *all* use of the property had been prevented for the two-year period.

45. When the Metropolitan Council of Minneapolis-St. Paul adopted its tiered development guide plan, an interim development ordinance prevented a subdivision of hundreds of homes from destroying the effectiveness of Tier IV, the rural and agricultural tier. Having

developed the plan, Freilich & Ragsdale, *Timing and Sequential Controls: The Essential Basis for Effective Regional Planning: An Analysis of the New Directions for Land Use Control in the Minneapolis-St. Paul Region*, 58 MINN. L. REV. 1009 (1974), I argued the case in the Minnesota Supreme Court and had a lower court decision, awarding the developer damages, reversed and dismissed. *Almquist v. Town of Marshan*, 245 N.W.2d 819 (Minn. 1976), based upon authority found in the Standard Planning Enabling Act.

46. In 1968 I left my firm and the position of Town Attorney to become the Rubey M. Hulen Professor of Law at the University of Missouri-Kansas City School of Law. I had just completed my residency for my Doctor of Juridical Science at Columbia University School of Law; the J.S.D. was awarded in 1975. The thesis was entitled "Timing and Sequencing of Growth."

47. AMENDMENTS TO TOWN OF RAMAPO BUILDING ZONE AMENDED ORDINANCE , § 46-13.1(A)(1969).

48. *Id.* at § 46-13.1(B).

49. *Id.* at § 46-13.1(D).

50. *Id.*

51. *Id.*

52. *Id.* at § 46-13.1(C).

53. *Id.*

54. *Id.* at § 46-13.1(E)(1)(a).

55. *Id.* at § 46-13.1(E)(1)(b).

56. *Id.*

57. *Id.* at § 46.13.1(F).

58. Emanuel, *supra* note 26.

59. DEVELOPMENT EASEMENT ACQUISITION LAW OF TOWN OF RAMAPO (1967).

60. *See* Thomas A. Gihring, *Incentive Property Taxation: A Potential Tool for Urban Growth Management*, 65 J. AMERICAN PLANNING ASS'N 62 (1999), citing Robert H. Freilich, Developing an Effective Concurrency Management System for Jurisdictions in Washington State, Symposium on Levels of Service, Puget Sound Council of Governments, March 13, 1992, at 4-5. *See also Symposium, Urban Sprawl*, 29 URB. LAW. 157 (1997).

61. For a brilliant review of this problem, see THE SIERRA CLUB, THE DARK SIDE OF THE AMERICAN DREAM: THE COSTS AND CONSEQUENCES OF SUBURBAN SPRAWL (1998); ROBERT W. BURCHELL AND DAVID LISTOKIN, LAND INFRASTRUCTURE, HOUSING COSTS AND FISCAL IMPACTS ASSOCIATED WITH GROWTH: THE LITERATURE ON THE IMPACTS OF SPRAWL VERSUS MANAGED GROWTH (Lincoln Inst. of Land Policy, 1995); Jerry Weitz and Terry Moore, *Oregon's Empirical Evidence of Contiguous Urban Form*, 64 J. A.P.A. 424, 430–34 (1998); THE COSTS OF SPRAWL, REAL ESTATE RESEARCH CORP. (1974). *See* note 9 *supra*.

62. *See* ERIC D. KELLY, COMMUNITY GROWTH: POLICIES, TECHNIQUES AND IMPACTS 20 (1993).

63. Chung, *supra* note 3, at 34.

64. *See* Report of the National Council on Public Works Improvements (1987). The Council's analysis is set out in Nancy S. Rutledge, *Public Infrastructure as a National Concern*, 11 STATE AND LOCAL L. NEWSL. 1, No. 1 (Fall 1987). Rutledge states that from the nine volumes of reports, four themes emerged. One theme which is directly confirming of the Ramapo approach is to utilize financing options with the basic goal "to make more efficient use of existing facilities as a partial substitute for major expansions in capital funds." The others are:

1. Full cost pricing in rate setting for water supply, wastewater treatment and solid waste.

2. Capital solutions that encourage better use of existing facilities.

3. Public-private partnerships.

4. Changes in the federal financial role.

5. Increased reliance on the "beneficiary pays principle" to finance public works at all levels of government.

6. Promote developer financing of new infrastructure investments.

Id. at 17. Ramapo was the precursor to requiring developers to advance public facilities to meet infrastructure needs.

65. Emanuel, *supra* note 26, at 7.

66. *Id.* at 6.

67. *Id.* at 7.

68. *Id.* at 8.

69. *Id.*

70. *Id.* at 7.

71. Geneslaw & Raymond, PLANNING (June 1983), at 8.

72. Urban sprawl is characterized by two dimensions: (1) scattered, noncontiguous development, measured by the number of vacant parcels lying with predominantly developed urban areas; and (2) low density development. The antithesis of these sprawl conditions can be found in most state Smart Growth legislation: (1) centralization; (2) contiguous development patterns; (3) more intensive land utilization; (4) infill development; (5) preservation of rural open space and resource lands; (6) directing new growth to existing centers, neotraditional communities and transit-oriented development; and (7) reduce automobile dependency. Thomas A. Gihring, *Incentive Property Taxation: A Potential Tool for Growth Management,* 65 J. A.P.A. 62 (1999). *Compare* Reid Ewing, *Is Los Angeles Style Sprawl Desirable?* 63 J. AM. PLAN. ASS'N 107 (1997) (criticizing sprawl) *with* Peter Gordon and Harry W. Richardson, *Are Compact Cities a Desirable Goal?* 63 J. AM. PLAN. ASS'N 95 (1997) (asserting benefits of urban sprawl).

73. *See* Edward J. Kaiser and David R. Godschalk, *Twentieth Century Land Use Planning,* 61 J. AM. PLAN. ASS'N 365 (1995).

74. For a complete discussion of the Plan, *see* Chapter IV, *infra.*

75. AMENDMENTS TO TOWN OF RAMAPO BUILDING ZONE AMENDED ORDINANCE, § 46-13.1(B)(1)(1969).

76. Petition of Ruth Golden & Ramapo Improvement Corp., filed in Supreme Court, Rockland County, at 9 (Feb. 1970).

77. *Id.* at 11.

78. Brief for Petitioners-Respondents at 13-14, Golden v. Planning Board of the Town of Ramapo, 30 N.Y.2d 359, 285 N.E.2d 291, 334 N.Y.S.2d 138 (1972) [hereinafter called Brief].

79. *Id.* at 23–25.

80. Citing Arverne Bay Constr. Co. v. Thatcher, 278 N.Y. 222, 15 N.E.2d 587 (N.Y. 1938) (delay of eight years in bringing sewer to a development held to be a taking and denial of substantive due process).

81. *Id.* at 15–19, 26-30.

82. Golden v. Planning Board of the Town of Ramapo, No. 525-1970 (Sup. Ct. Rockland County, Nov. 19, 1970).

83. Golden v. Planning Board of the Town of Ramapo, 37 A.D.2d 236, 324, N.Y.S.2d 178 (1971).

84. 37 A.D.2d at 243, N.Y.S.2d at 186.

85. *Id.*, 324 N.Y.S.2d, at 183.

86. *Id.*, 324 N.Y.S.2d, at 185.

87. HAGMAN, PUBLIC PLANNING AND CONTROL OF URBAN LAND DEVELOPMENT 386 (1973).

88. 30 N.Y.2d 359, 334 N.Y.S.2d 138, 285 N.E.2d 291 (1972), *appeal dismissed.*, 409 U.S. 1003 (1972). The decision in *Ramapo* has been the subject of many articles. *See, e.g.*, Bosselman, *Growth Management and Constitutional Rights—Part I: The Blessings of Quiet Seclusion*, 8 URB. L. ANN. 3 (1974); Bosselman, *Can the Town of Ramapo Pass a Law to Bind the Rights of the Whole World?*, 1 FLA. ST. L. REV. 234 (1973); Clark & Grable, *Growth Control in California: Prospects for Local Governmental Implementation of Timing and Sequential Control of Residential Development*, 5 PAC. L.J. 570 (1974); Elliott & Marcus, *From Euclid to Ramapo: New Directions in Land Development Controls*, 1 HOFSTRA L. REV. 56 (1973); Freilich, Golden v. Town of Ramapo: *Establishing a New Dimension in American Planning Law*, 4 URB. LAW. ix (1972); Landman, *No, Mr. Bosselman, the Town of Ramapo Did Not Pass a Law to Bind the Rights of the Whole World: A Reply (Part I)*, 10 TULSA L.J. 169 (1974); Note, *Phased Zoned: Regulation of the Tempo and Sequence of Land Development*, 26 STAN. L. REV. 585 (1974); Note, *Zoning for Timed Development*, 1 REAL EST. L.J. 279 (1973); Note, *Time Control, Sequential Zoning: The Ramapo Case*, 25 BAYLOR L. REV. 318 (1973); Note, Golden v. Planning Board: *Time Phased Development Control through Zoning Standards*, 38 ALB. L. REV. 142 (1973); Note, *A Zoning Program for Phased Growth: Ramapo Township's Time Controls on Residential Development*, 47 N.Y.U. L. REV. 723 (1972); Note, *Time Controls in Land Use: Prophylactic Law for Planners*, 57 CORNELL L. REV. 827 (1972).

89. N.Y. TOWN LAW § 261 (McKinney 1965).

90. N.Y. TOWN LAW § 261 (McKinney 1965).

91. *See, e.g.*, 1AC. ANTIEAU, MUNICIPAL CORPORATION LAW, ch. 7 (1955); 1C. RATHKOPF, THE LAW OF ZONING AND PLANNING, ch. 2 (3d ed. 1974).

92. *See, e.g.*, Roberson v. Montgomery, 285 Ala. 421, 233 So. 2d 69 (1970); First Nat'l Bank of Lake Forest v. Village of Northbrook, 2 Ill. App. 1082, 178 N.E.2d 533 (1971).

93. J. DILLON, COMMENTARIES ON THE LAW OF MUNICIPAL CORPORATIONS, at 448 (5th ed. 1911). *See also* Ottawa v. Carey, 108 U.S. 110 (1883).

94. *Supra* note 16.

95. 30 N.Y.2d, at 370, 334 N.Y. Supp. 2d, at 146.

96. *Id.*

97. ROBERT M. ANDERSON, AMERICAN LAW OF ZONING, §§ 1.11 to 1.12, at 20-22 (1968).

98. *See, e.g.,* Village of Euclid v. Ambler Realty Co., 272 U.S. 365 (1926).

99. *See* Heyman & Gilhool, *The Constitutionality of Imposing Increased Community Costs on New Suburban Residents through Subdivision Exactions*, 73 YALE L.J. 1119, at 1124 (1964).

100. N.Y. TOWN LAW § 263 (McKinney 1965).

101. *See generally* Charles Haar, *In Accordance with a Comprehensive Plan*, 68 HARV. L. REV. 1154 (1955).

102. *See, e.g.,* Udell v. Haas, 21 N.Y.2d 463, 235 N.E.2d 897, 288 N.Y.S.2d 888 (1968). *See also* Note, *Comprehensive Plan Requirement in Zoning*, 12 SYRACUSE L. REV. 342 (1961).

103. 30 N.Y.2d, at 367-68, 334 N.Y.S.2d, at 143.

104. Chicago, B. & O. R.R. v. Chicago, 166 U.S. 226 (1897). *See also* Michelman, *Property, Utility, and Fairness: Comments on the Ethical Foundations of "Just Compensation" Law*, 80 HARV. L. REV. 1165 (1967); Sax, *Takings and the Police Power*, 74 YALE L.J. 36 (1964).

105. 30 N.Y.2d, at 383, 334 N.Y.S.2d, at 156.

106. *Id.* at 381, 334 N.Y.S.2d, at 155.

107. *Id.* at 382, 334 N.Y.S.2d, at 155.

108. *Id.*

109. *Id.*

110. *Id.*

111. *Id.*

112. *See* Freilich & Garvin, *Takings After* Lucas: *Growth Management, Planning and Regulatory Implementation Will Work Better Than Before*, 22 STETSON L. REV. 409 (1993).

113. First English Evangelical Lutheran Church v. County of Los Angeles, 482 U.S. 304 (1987); Lucas v. South Carolina Coastal Council, 112 S. Ct. 2886 (1992).

114. 285 N.E.2d 291 (N.Y.), *appeal dismissed sub nom.* Rockland County Builders Ass'n v. McAlevey, 409 U.S. 1003 (1972).

115. The concept of "reasonable use" was enunciated in *Village of Euclid v. Ambler Realty Co.*, 272 U.S. 365, 395 (1926), and *Nectow v. City of Cambridge*, 277 U.S. 183, 187 (1928). The reasonable period of time standard was added by *Golden*, 285 N.E.2d 291 (N.Y.), *appeal dismissed sub nom. Rockland County Builders Ass'n v. McAlevey*, 409 U.S. 1003 (1972). It is important to distinguish these previously mentioned cases, where time was a factor in the taking, from those cases trying to determine the time of the taking, once a taking has been determined to have occurred. The *First English, supra* note 113, case held that once a taking has been determined, compensation is due from the effective date of the take regardless of how short the period of time the take has been in effect. In determining whether a take has occurred in the first place, reasonable timing and sequencing regulations will not effect the take because the property has not been permanently deprived of value or use. It will have an urban use within a reasonable period of time as measured by the comprehensive plan.

116. *Golden*, 285 N.E.2d, at 304–05.

117. Taking challenges are almost always ineffective against timed and sequenced growth if based upon an integrated and comprehensive plan. *See, e.g., Wincamp Partnership v. Anne Arundel County*, 458 F. Supp. 1009 (D. Md. 1978). The authority to deny development approval based on facility or service availability is provided by state statutes, which expressly authorize such growth management timing controls. N.H. REV. STAT. ANN. § 674:21 (1986 & Supp. 1992) (setting forth "innovative" land use controls and expressly authorizing regulation and control of the timing of development); MD. CODE ANN. ENVTL. § 9-512(b)(1) (1987 & Supp. 1992) (building permits may not be issued unless adequate public facilities are available to serve proposed construction); WASH. REV. CODE § 36.70A.010 (1991). The authority to adopt timed and sequenced controls based on adequacy of public facilities measured by capital improvement programs and comprehensive plans has been upheld against taking challenges under the zoning enabling statute, *Golden*, 285 N.E.2d at 291 (N.Y. 1972); the authority to plan, *Norbeck Village Joint Venture v. Montgomery County Council*, 254 A.2d 700 (Md. 1969); *Smoke Rise, Inc. v. Washington Suburban Sanitary Comm'n*, 400 F. Supp. 1369 (D. Md. 1975); the authority to regulate subdivision, *Guiliano v. Town of Edgartown*, 531 F. Supp. 1076 (D. Mass. 1982); the power to enter into intergovernmental contracts, *Unity Ventures v. County of Lake*, 631 F. Supp. 181 (N.D. Ill. 1986), *aff'd*, 841 F.2d 770 (7th Cir.), *cert. denied sub nom. Alter v. Schroeder*, 488 U.S. 891 (1988); the power to rezone, *Larsen v. County of Washington*, 387 N.W.2d 902 (Minn. Ct. App. 1986); site plan approval, *Chase Manhattan Mortgage & Realty Trust v. Wacha*, 402 So. 2d 61 (Fla. 4th DCA 1981); *Long Beach Equities v. County of*

Ventura, 282 Cal. Rptr. 877 (Ct. App. 1991) (no taking if developer denied annexation to city and county zoned property rural unless annexed to city).

118. *See* Q.C. Constr. Co. v. Gallo, 649 F. Supp. 1331 (D.R.I. 1986), *aff'd*, 836 F.2d 1340 (1st Cir. 1987); Wincamp Partnership v. Anne Arundel County, 458 F. Supp. 1009 (D. Md. 1978); Rancourt v. Town of Barnstead, 523 A.2d 55 (N.H. 1986); Charles v. Diamond, 360 N.E.2d 1295, 1301 (N.Y. 1977); Belle Harbor Realty Corp. v. Kerr, 323 N.E.2d 697, 699 (N.Y. 1974); Lake Illyria Corp. v. Town of Gardiner, 352 N.Y.S.2d 54 (A.D. 1974); *cf.* Associated Home Builders v. City of Livermore, 557 P.2d 473 (Cal. 1976) (development restrictions scrutinized and upheld under state regional general welfare constitutional doctrine); Beck v. Town of Raymond, 394 A.2d 847 (N.H. 1978) (absence of comprehensive plan); 303 W. 42nd Street Corp. v. Klein, 396 N.Y.S.2d 385 (App. Div. 1977) (development restrictions without concurrent comprehensive planning effort prompted the court to search for illegal ulterior motives); Estate of Scott v. Victoria County, 778 S.W.2d 585 (Tex. Ct. App. 1989) (seven-and-a-half-year sewer hookup moratorium was validated).

119. 334 N.Y.S.2d at 1515.

120. *See, e.g.*, Southern Burlington County N.A.A.C.P. v. Township of Mt. Laurel, 336 A.2d 713 (N.J. 1975); Oakwood at Madison, Inc. v. Township of Madison, 117 N.J. Super. 11, 283 A.2d 353 (1971). *See also* Freilich & Bass, *Exclusionary Zoning: Suggested Litigation Approaches*, 3 URB. LAW. 344 (1971); Sager, *Tight Little Islands: Exclusionary Zoning, Equal Protection, and the Indigent*, 21 STAN. L. REV. 767 (1969).

121. *Id. See also* Chapter II, *supra.*

122. 30 N.Y.2d, at 375; 334 N.Y.S.2d, at 149.

123. 30 N.Y.2d, at 378, 334 N.Y.S.2d, at 152.

124. *Id.*

125. *Id.*

126. *See* Chapter IV, *infra.*

127. 30 N.Y.2d, at 382, 334 N.Y.S.2d, at 156.

128. *Id.*, at 389, 334 N.Y.S.2d, at 159.

129. *Id.*, at 389, 334 N.Y.S.2d, at 162.

130. ROHAN, 1 ZONING AND LAND USE CONTROLS § 4.05 (Matthew Bender & Co. 1984, 1998).

131. 307 A.2d 504 (Md. 1973).

131. 469 F.2d 956, 962 (1st Cir. 1972).

133. 114 F.3d 590 (6th Cir. 1997) (reversing injunction issued by district court (937 F. Supp. 679, N.D. Ohio, 1996)).

134. 937 F. Supp. 679, 691.

135. *See* Chapter IV, *infra. Ramapo's* requirement that links development approval with the availability of public facilities, known as "concurrency" spread to Florida in 1985, Washington in 1990, Maryland in 1992, Georgia in 1997, Tennessee in 1998, and a host of other states. *See* John DeGrove, *The New Frontier for Land Policy: Planning and Growth Management in the States* (with Mines, 1992); Boggs & Apgar, *Concurrency and Growth Management: A Lawyer's Primer*, 7 J. LAND USE & ENVTL. L. 1 (1991); Patricia Salkin, MODERNIZING STATE LAND USE LAWS INTO THE 21ST CENTURY: AN INSIDE VIEW OF CURRENT INITIATIVES (Government Law Center, Albany Law School 1998).

136. *See* Eric D. Kelly, *Planning Growth and Public Facilities: A Primer for Local Officials* 16 (Am. Plan. Ass'n, Planning Advisory Serv. Report No. 447, 1993).

137. *See* Fagin, *Regulating the Timing of Urban Development*, 20 LAW & CONTEMP. PROBS. 298 (1955).

138. *See* Chapter I, *supra.*

139. *See* UNITED STATES PRESIDENT (NIXON), REP. ON NAT'L GROWTH (1972). *See also* detailed discussion in Chap. 1.

140. In reality, inner-city crime rates have decreased: "A few positive recent trends in cities such as falling crime rates, [reduced welfare loads] and balanced municipal budgets belie a dismal and fundamental trend." Brendan L. Koerner, *Cities That Work*, U.S. NEWS & WORLD REPORT, June 8, 1998 at 26, 28. *See* Nick Anderson, *Crime Is Down*, L.A. TIMES, Feb. 26, 1998, at B10 (report shows that California, mirroring the nation, is reporting statewide that crime in urban areas is declining sharply); *see also* CUOMO, THE STATE OF THE CITIES SECRETARY OF HOUSING AND URBAN DEVELOPMENT REPORT. (1998), which reflects dropping crime rates and significant improvement in employment of welfare and low-skilled employees in cities, citing a recent study of seventy-four urban aras by the Conference of Mayors. Janofsky, *An Urban Improvement, But Not Quite Fat City*, N.Y. TIMES, June 18, 1998, at A16. ("But the gains continue to pale beside job growth in the suburbs, the report says, or disparity that reflects a domino effect of adverse urban circumstances. As urban problems like crime and poor schools steadily persuade many middle class residents to leave for the suburbs, commercial investment follows, draining cities of their tax base.").

141. Middle-class families—"the bedrock of a stable community," according to the Department of Housing and Urban Development's most recent "State of the Cities" report—continue to leave; suburbs contain 75 percent more families than cities, compared with 25 percent more in 1970. For every American who moved to a city in that period, four relocated to a suburb. Koerner, *supra* note 401, at 28.

142. Jennifer Preston, *Battling Sprawl, States Buy Land For Open Space*, N.Y. TIMES, June 6, 1998, at A1.

143. Bill Collier, *City Council Will Get Growth Plan*, AUSTIN AMERICAN-STATESMAN Jan. 18, 1980 ("urban sprawl is inefficient and costly and the city should use developer incentives to encourage development downtown instead of on the city's fringes," per Robert Freilich).

144. *See* Stevens, *Tax Revolt*, N.Y. TIMES, Sept. 14, 1970, at 32.

145. *Hard Choices*, SUMMARY REP. OF THE NATIONAL INFRASTRUCTURE STUDY PREPARED FOR THE JOINT ECON. COMM. OF THE U.S. CONGRESS (February 1984); Nancy Rutledge, *Public Infrastructure as a National Concern, Report of the National Council on Public Works Improvement*, 11 STATE AND LOCAL L. NEWSL. No. 1 (1987).

146. Freilich & Ragsdale, *supra* note 45, at 1013 (1974).

147. *See* Becker, *Municipal Boundaries and Zoning: Controlling Regional Land Development*, 1966 WASH. U. L.Q. 1.

148. *See* DOUGLAS R. PORTER, MANAGING GROWTH IN AMERICA'S COMMUNITIES 247 (1997).

149. Austin, Texas's comprehensive plan identifies the concern about destructive effects of continued urbanization on the natural environment of the city as a major motivating force behind development of the plan. Growth areas were delineated for urbanization and ranked by reference to concepts of environmental development suitability and revitalization of the inner city. The City desires to encourage growth along an environmentally suitable corridor. Two areas were identified as being less desirable for continued growth because of the existence of limiting environmental factors: steep slopes, clay solid and bedrock, floodplain, prime

agricultural lands and a contribution zone for aquifer recharge, and the Lake Austin watershed. Performance principles were developed for each environmentally limiting factor. The City of Austin intended to investigate the feasibility of applying TDRs, taxing modifications, and public purchase of development rights to mitigate the effects of restrictions on development and encourage landowners to leave the land in an undeveloped state. *See* DEPARTMENT OF PLANNING, AUSTIN TOMORROW 148-56 (1980) *cited in* CALLIES & FREILICH (1st ed. 1986) at 873. *See also Land-use Controls: A Case of More Being Better*, AUSTIN AMERICAN-STATESMAN, Jan. 18, 1980, at A6 ("more attention should be paid to the fiscal policies on development" per panelist Robert Freilich).

150. Robert H. Freilich & Brenda L. Nichols, *Public-Private Partnerships in Joint Development: The Anatomy of Large Scale Urban Development Projects,* 7 MUN. FIN. J. 5 (1986).

151. A perfect example is the redevelopment of the old airport site in Denver, Colorado. *See* James Brooke, *Denver Calls Old Airport Ground Zero for Growth,* N.Y. TIMES, Sept. 16, 1998, A13 at col. 1. *See also ULI 1999 Real Estate Forecast,* URB. LAND, May 1999 at 34, showing that Austin, Seattle, San Diego, Oakland, and Minneapolis-St. Paul are experiencing dramatic increases in demand and higher rents for downtown office space.

152. Robert H. Freilich, Elizabeth A. Garvin & S. Mark White, *Economic Development and Public Transit: Washington Growth Management,* 16 U. PUGET SOUND L. REV. 949 (Spring 1993).

153. Professor Freilich's implementation of growth management in Minneapolis, Minnesota, for example, has resulted in savings of about $2 billion every ten years. Freilich has compared Kansas City to Minneapolis, suggesting that this city is at the same crossroads Minneapolis faced in the mid-'70s. "The Mid-America Regional Council has projected the same scenario Minneapolis was facing 20 years ago—more growth and more highway construction in the outer rings of the metropolis." *City Can Turn Eyes Inward,* K.C. STAR, Aug. 22, 1990.

154. For an excellent analysis of growth management and takings issues, *see generally* Robert H. Freilich & Elizabeth A. Garvin, *Takings After* Lucas: *Growth Management, Planning, and Regulatory Implementation Will Work Better than Before,* 2 STETSON L. REV. 409 (1993); Robert H. Freilich, *Solving the "Taking" Equation: Making the Whole Equal the Sum of Its Parts,* 15 URB. LAW. 447 (1983); Daniel R. Hyatt, *Murky Law Governs Regulatory Takings,* AGRIC. J., Mar. 28, 1997; Fred Strasser, *Just Whose Land Is It, Anyway?,* NAT'L L.J. (Dec. 22, 1986) at 1.

155. *See generally* Nectow v. City of Cambridge, 277 U.S. 183 (1928). For other significant takings cases, *see* Dolan v. City of Tigard, 512 U.S. 374 (1994) (holding that a municipality must conduct sufficient planning to document the connection between a land dedication requirement imposed pursuant to the issuance of a building permit and the impacts that are created upon the municipality as a result of the development for which a building permit is sought); *see also* Robert H. Freilich & David W. Bushek, *Thou Shalt Not Take Title without Adequate Planning: The Takings Equation after* Dolan v. City of Tigard, 2 URB. LAW. 187 (1995); Lucas v. South Carolina Coastal Council, 112 S. Ct. 2886 (1992); First English Evangelical Lutheran Church v. County of Los Angeles, 482 U.S. 304 (1987); Nollan v. California Coastal Comm'n, 483 U.S. 825 (1987); Keystone Bituminous Coal Ass'n v. DeBenedictis, 480 U.S. 470 (1987); Kaiser Aetna v. United States, 444 U.S. 164 (1979) (holding that owners of a private lagoon are subject to a taking when the United States makes the lagoon accessible to navigable water and public use); Andrus v. Allard, 444 U.S. 51 (1979) ("the denial of one traditional property right does not always amount to a taking. At least where an owner possesses

a full 'bundle' of property rights, the destruction of one 'strand' of the bundle is not a taking, because the aggregate must be viewed in its entirety"). For a full discussion of the major Supreme Court cases that comprise the modern takings doctrine, *see* REGULATORY TAKING: THE LIMITS OF LAND USE CONTROLS (G. Richard Hill ed., 1990) and AFTER *LUCAS*: LAND USE REGULATION AND THE TAKING OF PROPERTY WITHOUT COMPENSATION (David L. Callies ed., 1993), both published by the Section of Urban, State and Local Government Law of the American Bar Association; Robert Freilich, *Solving the "Takings Equation": Making the Whole the Sum of Its Parts*, 15 URB. LAW. 447 (1983).

156. U.S. CONST. amend. XIV, § 1.

157. U.S. CONST. amend. V.

158. Chicago, B. & O. R.R. v. City of Chicago, 166 U.S. 226 (1897).

159. The Fifth Amendment of the United States Constitution merely forbids private property from being "taken for public use, without just compensation"; however, about half of the states require compensation when private property is either "taken" or "damaged." *See generally* CAL. CONST. art. I, § 14; NEB. CONST. art. I, § 21.

160. 260 U.S. 393 (1922).

161. *See* F. BOSSELMAN, D. CALLIES & J. BANTA, THE TAKING ISSUE, at 118-38 (1973).

162. 56 Wis. 2d 7, 201 N.W.2d 761 (1972).

163. *Id.* at 201 N.W.2d 768.

164. 469 F.2d 956 (1st Cir. 1972).

165. *Id.* at 963.

166. Golden v. Ramapo Planning Board, 30 N.Y.2d 359, 285 N.E.2d 291, *app. dismissed*, 409 U.S. 1003 (1972).

167. *See, e.g.*, Golden v. Ramapo Planning Board, 30 N.Y.2d 359, 285 N.E.2d 291, *app. dismissed*, 409 U.S. 1003 (1972).

168. Regulatory takings must be distinguished from physical occupations, which are takings regardless of the legitimacy of the public purpose served or extent of diminution of property. *See* Loretto v. Teleprompter Manhattan Corp., 458 U.S. 419 (1982).

169. D. HAGMAN & J. JUERGENSMEYER, URBAN PLANNING & LAND DEVELOPMENT CONTROL LAW § 10.7 (2d ed. 1986). The classic statement of this facet of the takings analysis is that "while property may be regulated to a certain extent, if regulation goes too far it will be recognized as a taking." Pennsylvania Coal v. Mahon, 260 U.S. 393 (1922).

170. Freilich & Chinn, *Finetuning the Takings Equation: Applying It to Development Exaction: Part 1*, 40 LAND USE L. & ZONING DIG., no. 2, at 3 (1988), citing Golden v. Ramapo Planning Board, 30 N.Y.2d 359, 285 N.E.2d 291, *app. dismissed*, 409 U.S. 1003 (1972) (deprivation of some property owners' right to develop their properties under an adequate public facilities ordinance for an eighteen-year time period).

171. Keystone Bituminous Coal Ass'n v. De Benedictus, 480 U.S. 470, 486 (1987); Estate of Friedman v. Pierce County, 112 Wash. 2d 68, 768 P.2d 462 (1989).

172. Penn Central Transportation Co. v. City of New York, 438 U.S. 104 (1978); Freilich & Chinn, *Finetuning the Takings Equation: Applying It to Development Exaction: Part 1*, 40 LAND USE L. & ZONING DIG., no. 2, at 3, 9 (1988).

173. Keystone Bituminous Coal Ass'n v. De Benedictus, 480 U.S. 470, 492 (1987) (quoting Agins v. Tiburon, 447 U.S. 255, 260-61 (1980)).

174. Keystone Bituminous Coal Ass'n v. De Benedictus, 480 U.S. 470, 488-92 (1987).

175. *Id.* at 489 (citing Mugler v. Kansas, 123 U.S. 623, 668–69 (1887)); *see also* First Eng-

lish Evangelical Lutheran Church v. County of Los Angeles, 258 Cal. Rptr. 893, 210 Cal. App. 3d 1353 (Cal. App. 2d Dist. 1989), *cert. denied,* 493 U.S. 1056 (1990).

176. *Supra* note 167 at 491.

177. Penn Central Transportation Co. v. City of New York, 438 U.S. 104, 124 (1978), *rehearing denied,* 439 U.S. 883 (1978).

178. Estate of Friedman v. Pierce County, 112 Wash.2d 68, 768 P.2d 462 (1989); Penn Central Transportation Co. v. City of New York, 438 U.S. 104, 124 (1978), *rehearing denied,* 439 U.S. 883 (1978). Of course, the amount of deprivation is relevant to the remedy issue. It is, however, not relevant to a determination of liability where a reasonable use remains. The following factors are probably, among others, relevant to this inquiry:

1. The reasonableness of the landowner's asserted expectations. Is it reasonable for landowners on the urban fringe to expect to develop their properties in the near future, given the market for urbanized development in that area and the amount of time needed to extend facilities necessary for development?

2. The character of the government interest asserted. Is the government trying to protect the public from a real danger or merely trying to provide a public benefit at the expense of a small, discrete class of property owners? Is the ordinance reasonably necessary to effectuate the interest?

3. Are existing uses made commercially impractical by the adequate public facilities ordinance? A farm placed in an agricultural holding zone or rendered usable as a farm only through the operation of an adequate public facilities ordinance should not give rise to a successful takings claim, since the use of the property is not changed.

4. Does the balance between public benefit and private burden favor the government or the property owner?

5. Does the ordinance implement a comprehensive plan, or does it appear to discriminate against a single piece of property?

179. *See* Nollan v. California Coastal Commission, 483 U.S. 825 (1987).

180. *See* Batch v. Town of Chapel Hill, 376 S.E.2d 22, 29 (N.C. App. 1989) (citing Freilich & Chinn, *Finetuning the Takings Equation: Applying It to Development Exaction: Part 2,* 40 LAND USE L. & ZONING DIG., no. 3, at 3 (1988)), *rev'd on other grounds,* 387 S.E.2d 655 (1990), *cert. denied,* 496 U.S. 931 (1990).

181. Based on the foregoing analysis, the following factors are relevant to a takings challenge asserted against an adequate public facilities ordinance:

1. The remaining economic worth of the property;

2. The amount of time that the landowners will have to wait before facilities are extended to the property or areawide facilities are brought up to standard. (In Ramapo, some landowners were forced to wait as long as eighteen years before their property was allowed to be developed);

3. The urgency of the regulation. Where a nuisance regulation is involved, the deprivation may be severe. To the extent that the studies and plans establish a compelling need for the regulation, the municipality is on solid footing against deprivation challenges;

4. The extent to which the landowner benefits from the regulation to determine whether there is an "average reciprocity of advantage."

182. First English Evangelical Lutheran Church v. County of Los Angeles, 482 U.S. 304 (1987).

183. Nollan v. California Coastal Commission, 483 U.S. 825 (1987).

184. City of Monterey v. Del Monte Dunes at Monterey, Ltd., 119 S. Ct. 1624 (1999), S.W. 320798 (1999), aff'g 95 F.3d 1422 (1997). In an amicus brief which I submitted on behalf of the American Planning Association, I argued that the Court should not follow the "rough proportionality" *Dolan* rule applied to dedications and exactions where the case involves a regulatory zoning ordinance which requires a permanent deprivation of all or substantially all use and value. The Court agreed: ". . . we have not extended the rough proportionality test of Dolan beyond the special context of exactions—land-use decision conditioning approval of development on the dedication of property to public use." at p. 8.

185. Pre-1987 sewer moratoria and interim development control cases upholding restraints on development for significant but nonpermanent periods of time have been held by the courts not to constitute a taking of property.

(A) SEWER MORATORIA

Wincamp Partnership, OTC v. Anne Arundel, County, Maryland, 458 F. Supp. 1009 (D. Md. 1978); Smoke Rise, Inc. v. Washington Suburban Sanitary District, 400 F. Supp. 1369 (D. Md. 1975); Candlestick Properties, Inc. v. San Francisco Bay Conservation and Development Commission, 11 Cal. App. 3d 557, 89 Cal. Rptr. 897 (1970); Cappture Realty Corp. v. Board of Adjustment of Borough of Elmwood Park, 313 A.2d 624 (N.J. Super., 1973) *aff'd,* 336 A.2d 30 (App. Div. 1975); Donohoe Construction Co. v. Montgomery County Council, 567 F.2d 603 (4th Cir., 1977); City of Dallas v. Crownrich, 506 S.W.2d 654 (Tex. Civ. App. 1974).

(B) INTERIM DEVELOPMENT CONTROLS

Almquist v. Town of Marshan, 245 N.W.2d 819 (Minn. 1976); Collura v. Town of Arlington, 329 N.E.2d 733 (Mass. 1975); Matter of Rubin v. McAlevey, 54 Misc. 2d 338, 282 N.Y.S.2d 564 (1967), *aff'd,* 29 A.D. 2d 874, 288 N.Y.S.2d 519 (A.D.2d 1968); Russian Hill Improvement Association v. Board of Permit Appeals, 56 Cal. Rptr. 672, 423 P.2d 824 (Cal. 1967); Valley View Industrial Park v. City of Redmond, 733 P.2d 182, 195-96 (Wash. 1987).

For a general discussion of this area, *see* Freilich, *Interim Development Controls: Essential Tools for Implementing Flexible Planning and Zoning,* 49 J. Urb. L. 65 (1971); Heeter, *Interim Zoning Controls: Some Thoughts on Their Uses and Abuses,* 2 Mgmt. & Control of Growth 409, 411 (S. Scott ed., 1975).

(C) POST-1987 CASES

Zilber v. Town of Moraga, 692 F. Supp. 1195 (N.D. Cal. 1988); First English Evangelical Lutheran Church v. Los Angeles County, 482 U.S. 304, 107 S. Ct. 2378, 96 L. Ed. 2d 250 (1987), *on remand* 210 Cal. App. 3d 1353, 258 Cal. Rptr. 893 (Cal. App. 1989), *cert. denied,* 493 U.S. 1056 (1990); Estate of Scott v. Victoria County, 778 S.W. 2d 585 (Tex. App. 1989); Friel v. Triangle Oil Co., 543 A.2d 863 (Md. App. 1988).

186. *See* Freilich, *Solving the Taking Equation: Making the Whole Equal the Sum of Its Parts,* 15 Urb. Law. 447, 460-62 (1983); Bozung & Alessi, *Recent Developments in Environmental Preservation and the Rights of Property Owners, "Moratoria as Regulatory Takings after First English,"* 20 Urb. Law. 969, 1014–30 (1988).

187. *First English, supra* note 182.

188. *Supra* note 178, Bozung & Alessi at 1–14: "Even before *First English* a group of distinguished land-use lawyers and scholars had warned that if the temporary regulatory theory espoused by Justice Brennan in *San Diego Gas & Electric* were adopted, then 'a way must be found to avoid tossing development moratoria on the judicial ash heap . . .,' " citing Williams,

Smith, Siemon, Mandelker & Babcock, *The White River Junction Manifesto*, 9 Sup. Ct. Rev. 193, 218 (1984); *but see contra*, Berger, *The Supreme Court Lays Down the Law (Land Use Style)*, 1989 Zoning & Planning L. Handbook 197, 208–12, (failing to distinguish between temporary restraints on development and ordinances that amount to temporary takings).

189. Golden v. Planning Board of the Town of Ramapo, 30 N.Y.2d 359, 285 N.E.2d 291, *appeal dismissed*, 409 U.S. 1003 (1973); First English Evangelical Lutheran Church v. County of Los Angeles, 482 U.S. 304 (1987); Freilich & Greis, *Timing and Sequencing Development: Controlling Growth, in* R. Burchell & D. Listokin, Future Land Use (Rutgers 1975), at 59–106.

190. Keystone Bituminous Coal Ass'n v. DeBenedictus, 480 U.S. 470, 107 S. Ct. 1232, 94 L. Ed. 2d 472 (1987) (total prohibition of mining of coal in support estate not a taking when entire mineral estate considered); Penn Central Transportation Co. v. New York City, 438 U.S. 104, 98 S. Ct. 2646, 57 L. Ed. 2d 631 (1978), *rehearing denied*, 439 U.S. 883, 99 S. Ct. 226, 58 L. Ed. 2d 198 (1978) (regulation that prohibited construction of building in air rights but allowed the property owner to transfer the development rights—not a taking); Andrus v. Allar, 444 U.S. 51, 100 S. Ct. 318, 62 L. Ed. 2d 210 (1979) (restrictions on sale or disposition of eagle feathers not a taking where the property can still descend through inheritance); Deltona Corp. v. United States, 228 Ct. Cl. 476, 657 F.2d 1184 (1981), *cert. denied*, 455 U.S. 1017, 102 S. Ct. 1712, 72 L. Ed. 2d 135 (1982) (no taking of three fingers of land where total restriction on development is required pursuant to federal wetlands regulations and development of two fingers out of five is allowed); Gorieb v. Fox, 274 U.S. 603, 47 S. Ct. 675, 71 L. Ed. 1228 (1927) (upholding zoning setback laws—despite total loss of setback area—based on total area of entire lot); Presbytery of Seattle v. King County, 787 P.2d 907 (Wash. 1990) *overruling* Allingham v. City of Seattle, 749 P.2d 160 (Wash. 1988) (which had held that a regulation requiring buffer area of one-third of lot for open space reservation was a partial taking).

191. Bozung & Alessi, *supra* note 188, citing Freilich, *Solving the Taking Equation: Making the Whole Equal the Sum of Its Parts*, 15 Urb. Law. 447, 478 (1983).

192. *First English, supra* note 182.

193. Sun Ridge Development v. City of Cheyenne, 787 P.2d 583 (Wyo. 1990); Estate of Scott v. Victoria County, 778 S.W.2d 585 (Tex. App. 1989).

194. First English Evangelical Lutheran Church v. County of Los Angeles, 258 Cal. Rptr. 893, 210 Cal. App. 3d 1353 (Cal. App. 2d Dist. 1989), *cert. denied*, 493 U.S. 1056 (1990).

195. Agins v. Tiburon, 447 U.S. 255 (1980).

196. First English, 258 Cal. Rptr. at 903. The court did not rest on this issue, since it went on to decide, based on the type of use involved, that the plaintiff had not been deprived of all reasonable use of its property.

197. *Id.* at 903–04.

198. 334 N.Y.S.2d 138 (1972).

199. *Id.* at 152.

200. *Id.*

201. *Id.* at 156.

202. First English Evangelical Lutheran Church v. County of Los Angeles, 482 U.S. 304 (1987); Lucas v. South Carolina Coastal Council, 112 S. Ct. 2886 (1992).

203. The concept of "reasonable use" was enunciated in *Village of Euclid v. Ambler Realty Co.*, 272 U.S. 365, 395 (1926) and *Nectow v. City of Cambridge*, 277 U.S. 183, 187 (1928). The reasonable period of time standard was added by *Golden v. Planning Board*, 285 N.E.2d

291 (N.Y. 1972) *appeal dismissed sub nom. Rockland County Builders Ass'n v. McAlevey*, 409 U.S. 1003 (1972). It is important to distinguish these previously mentioned cases, where time was a factor in the taking, from those cases trying to determine the time of the taking, once taking has been determined to have occurred. *First English*, 482 U.S. at 304, 319 (1987). The *First English* case held that once a taking has been determined, compensation is due from the effective date of the take regardless of how short the period of time the take has been in effect. In determining whether a take has occurred in the first place, reasonable timing and sequencing regulations will not affect the take because the property has not been permanently deprived of value or use. It will have an urban use within a reasonable period of time as measured by the comprehensive plan.

204. *Ramapo*, 285 N.E.2d at 304-05.

205. Taking challenges are almost always ineffective against timed and sequenced growth if based upon an integrated and comprehensive plan. *See, e.g.,* Wincamp Partnership v. Anne Arundel County, 458 F. Supp. 1009 (D. Md. 1978). The authority to deny development approval based on facility or service availability is proved by state statutes, which expressly authorize such growth management timing controls. N.H. REV. STAT. ANN. § 674:21 (1986 & SUPP. 1992) (setting forth "innovative" land use controls and expressly authorizing regulation and control of the timing of development); MD. CODE ANN. ENV'T § 9-512(b)(1) (1987 & SUPP. 1992) (building permits may not be issued unless adequate public facilities are available to serve proposed construction); WASH. REV. CODE § 36.70A.010 (1991). The authority to adopt timed and sequenced controls based on adequacy of public facilities measure by capital improvement programs and comprehensive plans has been upheld against taking challenges under the zoning enabling statute, *Golden v. Planning Board of the Town of Ramapo*, 285 N.E.2d 291 (N.Y. 1972); the authority to plan, *Norbeck Village Joint Venture v. Montgomery County Council*, 254 A.2d 700 (Md. 1969); *Smoke Rise, Inc. v. Washington Suburban Sanitary Comm'n*, 400 F. Supp. 1369 (D. Md. 1975); *Long Beach Equities v. County of Ventura*, 282 Cal. Rptr. 877 (Ct. App. 1991) (no taking if developer denied annexation to city and county zoned property rural unless annexed to city). *See also* FREILICH & GARVIN, TAKINGS AFTER *LUCAS*, at 426.

206. S. Mark White, *Using Adequate Public Facilities Ordinances for Traffic Management*, in PLANNING ADVISORY SERVICE REPORT NO. 465, (American Planning Association, August 1996).

207. Robert H. Freilich & S. Mark White, *Transportation Congestion and Growth Management: Comprehensive Approaches to Resolving America's Major Quality of Life Crisis*, 4 LOY. L. REV. 915, 955 (1991).

208. Paradyne Corp. v. State Dept. of Transportation, 528 So. 2d 921 (Fla. App. 1 Dist. 1988); Unlimited v. Kitsap County, 750 P.2d 651 (Wash. App. 1988); *and see* Justice Scalia's dissent in *Pennell v. City of San Jose*, 483 U.S. 1, 19-20, 108 S. Ct. 849 (1988), elaborating on the now famous "nexus" requirement in his majority opinion in *Nollan v. California Coastal Commission*, 483 U.S. 825 (1987). Justice Scalia observes that the Fifth Amendment's Takings Clause bars government from forcing some people alone to bear public burdens that, in all fairness and justice, should be borne by the public at large:

> Traditional land-use regulation (short of that which totally destroys the economic value of property) does not violate this principle because there is a cause-and-effect relationship between the property use restricted by the regulation and the social evil that the regulation seeks to remedy. Since the owner's use of the property is (or, but for the regulation, would

be) the source of the social problem, it cannot be said that he has been singled out unfairly. Thus, the common zoning regulations requiring subdividers to observe lot-size and set-back restrictions, and to deduct certain areas to public streets, are in accord with our constitutional traditions because the proposed property use would otherwise be the cause of excessive congestion.

See also Dolan v. City of Tigard, 512 U.S. 374, 395 (1994) (noting that traditional land use planning tools such as dedications for streets will generally be considered as reasonable).

209. *See* 303 W. 42nd Street Corp. v. Klein, 58 A.D.2d 778, 396 N.Y.S.2d 385 (1977), where the Mayor of the City of New York "declared war" on business exploiting sexually-oriented material. In furtherance of these efforts, the Buildings Department required that plaintiff's building be fully sprinklered. In a bitter dissent, several judges questioned whether the City was using the public safety rationale to eliminate a legitimate—although politically unpopular—use. In California, development restrictions are often scrutinized for illegal exclusionary purposes; *see* Associated Homes Builders v. City of Livermore, 18 Cal. 3d 582, 135 Cal. Rptr. 41, 557 P.2d 473 (1976).

210. *See* Golden v. Planning Board of the Town of Ramapo, 30 N.Y.2d 359, 334 N.Y.2d 138, 285 N.E.2d 291, *app. dismissed,* 409 U.S. 1003 (1972) (Town had adopted eighteen-year capital improvement program demonstrating where capital facilities to deal both with new growth and deficiencies would be located); Freilich & Greis, *Timing and Sequencing Development, Controlling Growth, in* FUTURE LAND USE, ENERGY, ENVIRONMENT AND LEGAL CONSTRAINTS, 59-106 (R. Burchell and D. Listokin eds., Rutgers 1975).

211. Conway v. Town of Stratham, 414 A.2d 539 (N.H. 1980); Beck v. Town of Raymond, 394 A.2d 847, 852 (N.H. 1978) (good faith efforts to increase the capacity of municipal services accompanying growth controls).

212. In *Wincamp Partnership, OTC v. Anne Arundel County, Maryland,* 458 F. Supp. 1009 (D. Md. 1978), the court rejected a substantive due process challenge, noting the county's comprehensive planning efforts, including the appropriation of substantial sums of money toward other wastewater treatment plants in the current budget and the presence of a $100 million "capital facilities program" for wastewater treatment. Citing *Smoke Rise, Inc. v. Washington Suburban Sanitary Commission,* 400 F. Supp. 1369 (D. Md. 1975), the court reasoned that "the comprehensive plans to improve wastewater facilities belied any hidden purpose to hinder growth." *Id.* at 1027.

213. Belle Harbor Realty Corp. v. Kerr, 35 N.Y.2d 507, 364 N.Y.S.2d 160, 323 N.E.2d 697 (1974). *See also* Beaver Meadows v. Board of County Commissioners, 709 P.2d 928 (Colo. 1985) (county could deny PUD approval on basis of lack of adequate off-site road capacity but could approve the project and then apportion the cost of building the facilities disproportionately to the developer).

214. Charles v. Diamond, 41 N.Y.2d 318, 392 N.Y.S.2d 594, 360 N.E.2d 1295 (1977) (denying a landowner permission to tie into the city sewer system on the basis of system inadequacies would be an unconstitutional taking where the city required connection to the sewer system as a condition precedent to development and had not taken good faith steps to provide an adequate system).

215. Westwood Forest Estates, Inc. v. Village of South Nyack, 23 N.Y.2d 424, 244 N.E.2d 700 (1969) (invalidating outright ban on multifamily construction that had been imposed to alleviate the burden on the city's sewage disposal plant, where the plant had capacity; and the real problem—inadequate sewage treatment—predated the advent of new construction). For

a similar case, *see Q.C. Construction Co. Inc. v. Gallo,* 649 F. Supp. 1331 (D.R.I. 1986) invalidating a moratorium pending the resolution of sewer system inadequacies. Noting that the expansion of the sewer system had occurred in a "piecemeal" fashion rather than pursuant to a comprehensive plan, the court, citing *Goldblatt v. Town of Hempstead,* 369 U.S. 590 (1962), required "measurable" efforts to improve the system (including developer contributions) rather than stop-gap, burdensome measures that only perpetuated existing deficiencies. The Court cited a number of other cases that had approved development restrictions or moratoria imposed pursuant to a comprehensive plan *to remedy deficiencies* and that would not impose *a permanent* ban on development; *id.* at 1337-38 citing *Schaffer v. City of New Orleans,* 743 F.2d 1086 (5th Cir. 1984), *Golden, Smoke Rise,* and *Wincamp Partnership.*

216. ROBERT H. FREILICH & S. MARK WHITE, REGIONAL GENERAL WELFARE AND INTERGOVERNMENTAL PLANNING, at 1 (1998); Dwight Merriam.

217. 272 U.S. 365 (1926).

218. 272 U.S. at 390.

219. *See* Associated Home Builders v. City of Livermore, 557 P.2d 473, 485-86 (Cal. 1976) [hereinafter *Livermore*].

220. *See, e.g.,* Southern Burlington County NAACP v. Township of Mount Laurel (Mount Laurel II), 92 N.J. 158, 456 A.2d 290 (1983) (municipalities have obligation to provide realistic opportunity for construction of that municipality's fair share of low- to moderate-income housing needs); Berenson v. Town of New Castle, 341 N.E.2d 236 (N.Y. 1975) (court must consider "not only the general welfare of the residents of the zoning township, but should also consider the effect of the ordinance on the neighboring communities"); Township of Williston v. Chesterdale Farms, Inc., 341 A.2d 466 (Pa. 1975) ("it is not for any given township to say who may or may not live within its confines, while disregarding the interests of the entire area"); Surrick v. Zoning Hearing Board, 382 A.2d 105 (Pa. 1977) ("suburban municipalities within the area of urban outpour must meet the problems of population expansion into its borders by increasing municipal services, and not by the practice of exclusionary zoning"); Associated Homebuilders v. City of Livermore, 135 Cal. Rptr. 41 (Cal. 1976) (if an "ordinance may strongly influence the supply and distribution of housing for an entire metropolitan region, judicial inquiry must consider the welfare of that region"). The theory of regional general welfare was also applied in an environmental context by the Washington Supreme Court in *Save a Valuable Environment (SAVE) v. City of Bothell,* 576 P.2d 401 (Wash. 1978) (construction of a major shopping center would have detrimental effects on areas outside of city's jurisdiction; city may not act in disregard of the effect outside of its boundaries). *See also* Britton v. Town of Chester, 595 A.2d 492 (N.H. 1991).

221. 15 N.J. 238, 100 A.2d 182 (1953), *aff'd,* 15 N.J. 238, 104 A.2d 441 (1954).

222. 1 N.J. 509, 64 A.2d 347 (N.J. 1949).

223. 21 N.J. Super. 430, 91 A.2d 353 (N.J. Super. Ct. App. Div. 1952).

224. While the New Jersey Supreme Court did not decide the standing issue, later decisions affirmed the position of the lower court in *Creskill* on standing. Borough of Roselle Park v. Township of Union, 113 N.J. Super. 87, 272 A.2d 762 (1970); Borough of Allendale v. Township Committee, 169 N.J. Super. 34, 404 A.2d 50, 51 (1979) (standing to challenge upzoning on neighboring jurisdiction).

225. 67 Ill. 2d 399, 367 N.E.2d 1305 (1977).

226. 367 N.E.2d at 1307 (citing 49 A.L.R.2d 1126).

227. 81 Ill. 2d 392, 410 N.E.2d 37 (1980).

228. Few cases have applied the regional general welfare concept to annexation. In asserting a regional general welfare challenge to an annexation action or statute, the principles set forth in *Hunter v. City of Pittsburgh*, 207 U.S. 161, 28 S. Ct. 40, 52 L. Ed. 151 (1907) will have to be distinguished. In *Hunter*, the City of Pittsburgh consolidated a smaller city into its boundaries. Residents of the smaller city challenged the action, claiming that the consolidation would violate due process by drastically increasing their tax burdens. In rejecting this argument, the court noted that municipal governments are merely creatures of the state, which may modify the boundaries of a local government or change its obligations without running afoul of the Constitution—even without the consent of the affected citizens.

A well-established line of New Jersey cases establishes that zoning must take into consideration the character of neighboring communities to be considered a legitimate exercise of the police power. 104 A.2d at 445–47; *see Duffcon Concrete Products, Inc. v. Borough of Creskill*, 1 N.J. 509, 64 A.2d 347, 349 (1949) (upholding zoning ordinance excluding heavy industry from a community due to regional considerations). Citing several provisions of the state constitution and statutes authorizing zoning, the court rejected the plaintiff's argument that the "responsibility of a municipality for zoning halts at the municipal boundary lines without regard to the effect of its zoning ordinance on adjoining and nearby land outside the municipality." *Id.*, 104 A.2d, at 445. In a widely cited passage, the court reasoned that "[t]o do less would be to make fetish out of the invisible municipal boundary lines and a mockery of the principles of zoning." *Id.* at 446. Consequently, the court invalidated the rezoning as invalid spot zoning.

229. Southern Burlington County NAACP v. Township of Mt. Laurel, 67 N.J. 151, 336 A.2d 726 (1974) (invalidating exclusionary zoning ordinance—see discussion below); Vickers v. Gloucester Township, 37 N.J. 232, 181 A.2d 129, 140-50 (1962) (Hall, J., dissenting from majority opinion upholding ban on manufactured homes from a suburban community).

230. Fobe Associates v. Mayor & Council of Demarest, 74 N.J. 519, 379 A.2d 519, 46-48 (1977) (upholding ban on multifamily residences and denial of variance to construct an apartment building, strong dissent stressing need to consider regional factors when making zoning decisions); Pascack Association, Ltd. v. Washington Township, 74 N.J. 470, 379 A.2d 6, 24-27 (1977) (upholding ban on multifamily housing in fully developed community; strong dissent stressing need to consider regional need for housing); Shephard v. Woodland Township Committee, 71 N.J. 230, 364 A.2d 1005, 1010 (1976) (upholding special district for senior citizens, taking into consideration regional need for suitable senior citizen housing); Quinton v. Edison Park Development Corp., 59 N.J. 571, 285 A.2d 5 (1971) (buffer requirement for shopping center development held applicable to protection of adjacent residential areas outside boundaries of municipality); Kunzler v. Hoffman, 48 N.J. 277, 225 A.2d 321 (1966) (upholding grant of variance for mental hospital based on statewide and regional need therefor); Gartland v. Borough of Maywood, 45 N.J. Super. 1, 131 A.2d 529 (1957) (upholding rezoning from residential to business uses); Hochberg v. Borough of Freehold, 40 N.J. Super. 276, 123 A.2d 46, 53 (1956) (zoning amendment permitting business use adequately considered regional needs, but vitiated due to personal interest of planning board member). *See also* Beshore v. Town of Bel Aire, 237 Md. 398, 206 A.2d 678, 686 (1965) (town not required to follow county use restrictions when annexing property, although agreeing generally with proposition that municipality should take character of surrounding areas into consideration).

231. Taxis Inc. v. Borough of East Rutherford, 149 N.J. Super. 294, 373 A.2d 726 (1977).

232. Gross v. Allan, 117 A.2d 275, 279 (N.J. Super. 1955) (concentration of excluded uses

in neighboring jurisdiction held not determinative); Barone v. Bridgewater Tp., 45 N.J. 224, 212 A.2d 129 (1965) (upholding residential-agricultural use classification barring commercial uses concentration of commercial uses in neighboring areas).

233. 67 N.J. 151, 336 A.2d 726 (1975).

234. 336 A.2d at 726.

235. 456 A.2d 390 (1983).

236. 557 P.2d at 487.

237. *See* CHARLES M. HAAR, SUBURBS UNDER SIEGE: RACE, SPACE AND AUDACIOUS JUDGES (Princeton, 1996); CHARLES M. HAAR AND JEROME KAYDEN, ZONING AND THE AMERICAN DREAM: PROMISES STILL TO KEEP (Chicago, 1989); CHARLES M. HAAR AND DANIEL FESSLER, THE WRONG SIDE OF THE TRACKS (New York, 1986).

238. 576 P.2d at 401.

239. 576 P.2d at 405.

CHAPTER FOUR

Regional America: *Ramapo* in Action

Regional America: *Ramapo* in Action

The techniques upheld in *Ramapo* were quickly[1] utilized in other jurisdictions (cities, counties, metropolitan areas, and states) over the next twenty-seven years to expand the role of planning, managing, and channeling growth not in suburban cities and counties on the developmental fringe and metropolitan areas.[2] Many governments have elevated planning for public services and facilities to the metropolitan level,[3] because planning and growth management activities of all areas are continuously affected by the actions of other jurisdictions in the area. The coordination of multigovernmental planning and management activities is essential if growth management efforts are to succeed. A number of states and metropolitan areas, through statutory enactments, have implemented *Ramapo* urbanizing tiered growth and adequate public facility (concurrency) growth management planning.[4] In these jurisdictions, growth management measures are employed for two principal reasons: "(1) to prevent sprawl development and associated demands on public services from outstripping available resources, and (2) to slow down, if not stop, adverse changes in community character and 'quality of life' which are perceived to result from suburban sprawl development."[5] Growth coordination techniques, however, have greater potential than simply slowing the pace of development.[6] Used correctly, tools such as transportation congestion management,[7] timing and sequencing controls that require development approval to be concurrent with adequate public facilities,[8] development exactions that place the cost of newly required infrastructure development on new development,[9] environmentally sensitive land regulations, tiers, corridors, centers,[10] and urban growth boundaries can be used to focus permanent nonsprawl growth locations on an areawide basis.[11]

Growth management techniques can be used to provide incentives for growth in central cities, maintain and strengthen first-ring suburbs, and organize development and prevent sprawl in the Urbanizing Tier through a *Ramapo* timing and phasing program linked to adequate public facilities. The principles and techniques upheld in *Ramapo* stimulated an expanded view of the planning, management, and channeling of residential and commercial growth not only in suburban areas on the developing fringe but as a major element in structuring, incentivizing, and enhancing economic development in an entire metropolitan area.[12] The metropolitan areawide plans then are translated into areawide implementation for infrastructure concurrency and delivery of services. Government, though politically unlikely to consolidate, can enter into intergovernmental agreements to share responsibilities and revenues, undertake unified development codes and comprehensive planning, and provide coordinated and nonconfrontational tax and development incentives for economic development. An areawide plan may offer the opportunity to provide equity among both wealthy and poor areas within a metropolitan area which would match environmental, fiscal, and social needs appropriate with resources. Beginning in the 1970s with Minneapolis-St. Paul, many metropolitan areas have centered their growth policies around *Ramapo* concepts and the need to time and sequence growth in the Urbanizing Tier. The Central Puget Sound area in Washington; Portland, Oregon; San Diego, California; Montgomery, Baltimore, Howard, and Prince George Counties, Maryland; Reno-Washoe County, Nevada; Lexington-Fayette County; and Palm Beach and Sarasota Counties, Florida, are among the principal areas in the nation incorporating the *Ramapo* legal principles of concurrency on a regionwide basis.[13]

Minneapolis-St. Paul, Minnesota: Urban Growth Boundaries and the Tier Concept

The idea of broadening specific growth management techniques based upon *Ramapo* to geographic and functional areas within a metropolitan area was first incorporated when I went to work as the lead consultant for preparing the Metropolitan Development Framework for the Minneapolis-St. Paul Metropolitan area exactly one year after the *Ramapo* decision came down from the New York Court of Appeals (May 1973).[14] In the 1960s, the Minneapolis-St. Paul Region had experienced the same sprawl pattern of growth and development endured by other areas of the nation—scattered, leapfrog development, urban sprawl, and urban core deterioration.[15] A side effect of this scattered development was competition between communities, which produced further fragmentation, imbalance in the provision of housing and public services, and serious energy problems. The solution began in 1967 when the Minnesota legislature passed the Metropolitan Council Act (hereinafter the Council).[16] Since its creation, the Council's main function has been to develop a comprehensive metropolitan planning strategy for the Minneapolis-St. Paul[17] area. Minnesota was one of the first states to recognize the importance of areawide solutions to the problems facing its largest metropolitan area. Two reports found the following trends occurring in the 1970s Twin Cities metropolitan area:[18]

1. Agricultural activities were moving further away from the urban core, opening up large amounts of vacant land for housing developments in a twelve-county area within a fifty-mile radius of Minneapolis-St. Paul;

2. The population of the region was rapidly growing in a wide band of middle-outer suburbs, tapering off in the inner suburbs and declining in the two central cities;

3. Development was dispersing into pockets of housing at sites scattered along lakes and roads far out into the previously rural countryside, resulting in the creation of twenty-five new municipalities within a ten-year period;

4. More than 85 percent of the predicted 830,000–880,000 population increase in the Region by 1990 and 1,005,000 by 1993 would fall within the middle-outer suburban rings, and beyond;

5. Rapidly expanding urban sprawl and increasingly scattered development would result in more costly public and private facilities, inefficient use of capital investment in built-up areas, loss of valuable open space, high costs in abating substantial surface and groundwater pollution, and vastly increased rates of taxation.[19]

To deal with the problems caused by rapid and uncontrolled growth, the Council was charged with coordinating the planning and development of the metropolitan area surrounding Minneapolis and St. Paul.[20] The Council has jurisdiction over a 3,000-square-mile, seven-county area that at the time of its organization included roughly 1.8 million people, in 320 separate but overlapping governmental units, of which 189 were incorporated cities or villages. Composed of fifteen members—fourteen appointed by the governor from legislative districts, and one, the chairman, appointed by the governor, at large,[21] the legislation created a mechanism for achieving coordination in the metropolitan area through a system of mandatory referrals to the Council from various entities within the jurisdictional areas including independent boards, commissions, agencies, municipalities, and counties applying for federal funds.[22]

Every comprehensive plan of those local entities, which the Council determined to have an areawide, multicommunity, or substantial metropolitan development effect, would be submitted to the Council for review before it could be implemented. The Council had sixty days to review the plan. If it found that the plan was inconsistent with the Council's own comprehensive guide for the metropolitan area, or detrimental to the orderly and economic development of the area, it had the power to suspend the plan indefinitely.[23] The Council also was empowered to review implementing land use regulations and policies of municipalities and counties in the seven-county area if they had a substantial effect on metropolitan area development. However, it could not suspend regulations indefinitely since the review process was only for "comment and recommendation." In addition, the Council was empowered to review applications for federal funds commenting on each application's conformity to metropolitan comprehensive planning.[24] To initiate its overall review function effectively, the Council prepared a Metropolitan Comprehensive Development Guide, which was "a compilation of policy statements, goals, standards, programs, and maps prescribing guides for an orderly and economic development, public and private, of the metropolitan area."[25] In the preparation of the Guide, the Council was required to consider the development and impact of such matters as land use, parks, open space, airports, highways, transit facilities, public hospitals, libraries, schools, and other public buildings.[26]

In an effort to cope with the many problems confronting the Twin Cities area, I was retained by the Council to prepare a physical development framework proposing a regional policy for managed growth based on timing and sequential controls and incorporating maximum local government involvement and decision making.[27] The Physical Development Framework Policy divided the metropolitan Region into five separate tiers or planning areas: Planning

Area I consisted of the metro centers, the downtown areas of Minneapolis and St. Paul; Planning Area II, the central city and older suburban existing built-up areas; Planning Area III, the areas of active urbanization (the Ramapo "urbanizing tier"); Planning Area IV, the agricultural, open space, environmental, and rural areas; and Planning Area V, freestanding new towns and cities within Planning Area IV. Specific goals and different policies, strategies, and objectives were set for each planning area, and the framework suggested how development and redevelopment would be uniquely impelmented in each area consistent with these objectives.

At the time of the development of the physical development framework, the population of the metropolitan area was slightly under two million but scheduled to reach two million over the twenty-year life of the plan. Planning Area III would contain 530 square miles of land for the absorption of the third million of population in lieu of the estimated 1,600 square miles of sprawl, which would have occurred if no urbanizing tier had been in place. The outside boundary of Tier III was denoted as the MUSA line—the Metropolitan Urban Service Area boundary. The first million population consumed only 180 square miles of land; the second million, 530 square miles. Thus by adopting the "Urbanizing Tier," 1,000 square miles of the best agricultural land in the state was saved. Sprawl would have consumed for the third million almost ten times as much land area per capita as for the first million, despite Minneapolis and St. Paul being very low-density cities.[27]

The plan can be illustrated as on next page. (See Figure 4.1.)

At the inner and outer areas of the region, the policies were clear. In Planning Area I, the Council's objectives included attracting financial institutions, specialized professional and retail functions, office space users, and metropolitan cultural and entertainment complexes, and encouraging a broader socioeconomic mix. The primary tools were incentives, tax increment financing, infrastructure grants, CDBG funds, redevelopment assistance through clearance, and eminent domain.

Planning Area II objectives emphasized the maintenance of structures and neighborhoods in generally sound condition, the redevelopment or rehabilitation of deteriorating neighborhoods, the construction of new houses in types and densities consistent with the market preferences of the population at large, the removing of uncertainties about the future of older neighborhoods and the reduction of concentrations of minorities and low-income families.

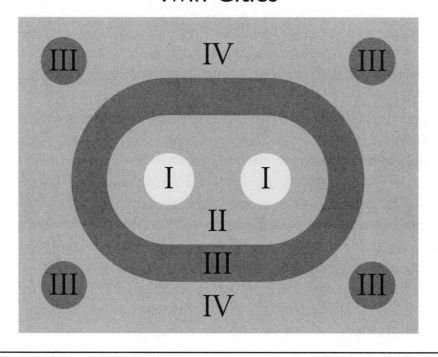

Figure 4.1

Twin Cities Lessons

- Clearly define metropolitan issue
- Secure funding
- Obtain sufficient authority for carrots and sticks
- Evaluate and refine the plan

Twin Cities

Planning Area IV would remain primarily rural, with provisions for the optional development of freestanding new towns and expansion of existing farm town communities. The restriction of growth and prevention of sprawl in Planning Area IV was expected to result in greater reinvestment in Planning Areas I and II and a revitalization of the core of the area. One of the critical tools adopted was the Minnesota Fiscal Disparities Act, which redistributes 40 percent property tax revenue from industrial and commercial development to a general tax metropolitan to be distributed to cities and counties based on pop-

ulation.[28] This unique redistribution tool particularly deprives the motivation for suburban raids on existing tax base. The policies for Planning Area IV centered around the preservation of the agricultural economic base and lifestyle, primarily through the enforcement of standards for development that would prevent public health and pollution problems and prohibit the extension of urban scale facilities or services into the area. Finally, the Council suggested that Planning Area III also be reserved for limited growth around existing free-standing rural towns in which development of a purely local economic base for growth would be emphasized. Each rural center would thus be surrounded by a Planning Area III development of staged, contiguous growth to prevent scattered development and sprawl.[29] Throughout all the areas designated in the regional plan, low- and moderate-income housing would be encouraged. Where necessary to preserve environmental and agricultural land development easements with federal tax credits, preferential tax assessment and rural cluster techniques were available.

Planning Area III covered the area of active urbanization and sprawl (the Urbanizing Tier). Most municipalities, counties, and metropolitan areas are forced to react to development in the Urbanizing Tier with little control over where and when development takes place. The result is sprawl, leapfrog development, and a waste of land, resources, and energy.[30] Several commentators, recognizing the extent of these problems and the inability of most municipalities to address them effectively, have suggested that the impetus of sprawl might be reversed if development were made responsive to timed and sequential provision of public facilities.[31]

In an attempt to deal with the problems discussed above, working with the Council, I proposed the implementation of timing and sequential controls by designating Planning Area III as the Ramapo "urbanizing tier"—the area experiencing the sprawl and rapid urbanization . The goals set for Planning Area III included supporting growth and additional public investment as needed to complete development of leapfrogged land in municipalities that had already invested in capital facilities, opening up new land for urbanization in a staged, contiguous manner through capital budgeting of public service extensions, and providing balanced housing types for a variety of income levels. In Planning Area III, development would be timed in accordance with the availability of adequate public facilities. The timing and sequencing techniques in *Ramapo* played a major role in Planning Area III.[32] Development in that area was tied to fifteen- to twenty-year capital improvements programs of area service providers, which separated the existing urban areas from the rural areas. Timing and sequencing of facilities mitigated the confiscatory impact of the regulations on the rural landowners, who had no basis for investment-backed expectations of urban use for their property.[33] The Council had found that tremendous economic savings would result from the use of such controls.[34] The studies also showed that if timing controls are imposed, housing costs should not increase, while substantial savings should result from adequate provision of transportation, sewage, and drainage facilities. In most communities undergoing rapid growth, this should also produce savings in housing, gasoline, and tax costs for middle-income families.[35]

In addition to economic savings, the implementation of *Ramapo's* timing and sequential controls also promoted social and environmental goals. Not only were such controls utilized to gain more efficient density with offsetting public open space, but a mix of housing and population was promoted. The Metropolitan Council was committed to the concept of balanced housing uses throughout the area, and particularly to dispersed and scattered-site housing for low- and moderate-income families.[36] The Council adopted as one of its major goals the provisions of housing opportunities for lower-income persons in new development areas.[37] At the same time, the Council desired to upgrade inner-city areas and stabilize older transitional areas in the central cities and first-ring suburbs. By limiting sprawl development on the urban fringe through the implementation of timing and sequential controls, a redistribution of construction to inner-city, transitional neighborhoods, and neotraditional or new towns in-town could be achieved. Such controls were utilized in conjunction with other affirmative policies in the inner-city areas, and a positive program was initiated designed to fulfill these objectives.[38]

Because of more efficient development resulting from the implementation of timing and sequential controls in Planning Area III, increased energy savings of almost two billion dollars every ten years were anticipated.[39] For one thing, better planning, clustering, and higher density significantly reduced reliance on auto travel and thus reduced the amount of energy expended. Additionally, by clustering employment centers in corridors and centers, and by creating neotraditional communities with balanced uses,[40] incentives were provided for effective and efficient public transportation systems and for greater economic development opportunities.[41]

The Metropolitan Council adopted the Metropolitan Development Framework (MDF) in 1975, a Metropolitan Investment Framework (MIF) in 1977, a Metropolitan Development Framework in 1986, Policies for the Rural Service Area in 1991, and Regional Blueprints in September of 1994 and December of 1996 (the latter including a Year 2040 areawide growth strategy).[42] The development framework concentrated on using the Ramapo system for guiding growth into a more compact pattern of development within an urban growth boundary (designated as the MUSA line—Metropolitan Urban Service Area line—Tier III) and a tier system[43] so that the extension of areawide facilities would be more economical.[44] The investment framework concentrated on monitoring the capital improvement programs and operations of metropolitan agencies to implement the timed and sequenced development framework policies.[45]

In 1986, the MDF and MIF were combined into the comprehensive Metropolitan Development and Investment Framework (MDIF). The 1986 plan focused on a broader strategy, managing areawide resources with priority to existing facilities and the public dollars used to maintain or expand them. The MDIF continued the division of the area into a metropolitan urban service area and a rural service area. The growth management strategy encouraged the development to occur within the urban service area. Public improvements would be limited to meet the needs of the people living in the urban service area. The delineation between the urban service area and the rural service area came to be known as the MUSA line, an Urban Growth Boundary. The MUSA line was determined by using forecasts of population, households, and employment to indicate where growth would be occurring in the region.[46] Such forecasts were also to be helpful in determining plans for growth and subsequent prioritized timed and sequenced investment decisions within the urban service area. The MDIF also included development policies for geographic areas or tiers within both the urban service area and the rural service area. In total, there were eight tiered geographic policy areas: five in the urban service area and three in the rural service area, as opposed to five in the original development framework.

The five policy areas in the urban service area were: metro centers, areawide business concentrations, and fully developed, developing, and freestanding growth centers. The categorization of these areas served a primary purpose: It helped determine the priorities for expenditure of public funds. The metro centers are the downtown areas of Minneapolis and St. Paul. The goal of this policy was to maintain the areawide facilities serving the metro center, thus preserving the metro centers as vital centers of economic activity and housing. Metropolitan business concentrations are entity areas that have large employment bases and where clusters of economic development are found, usually in large office complexes or major shopping centers. The MDIF supported continued growth of these areas and encouraged increased development densities. Thus Tier I was to be the fully developed, built-up, centrally located hub of the metropolitan area, typically referred to as the core cities and the first-ring suburbs.

Additionally, the Twin Cities have taken measures to ensure limited growth in the rural area.[47] The Council's framework and policies on the rural service areas consisted of a ranking of land into "primary protection areas" and "secondary protection areas."[44] Primary protection areas receive the most protection and are lands covenanted into permanent agriculture and rural preserves, which will have dwelling unit thresholds of no more than one unit per forty acres for permanent agricultural areas and one unit for ten acres with cluster for permanent rural areas.[48] Urban facilities are generally prohibited in this area unless strong documentation exists that no other locations in the metropolitan area will adequately meet the siting and selection criteria.

While the MDIF secured growth for a time, the metropolitan area has grown to its urban growth boundary. In its December 1996 Regional Blueprint, the Council adopted an areawide growth strategy with the intended result of accommodating an additional 330,000 households and 650,000 more people by the year 2020.[49] In adopting its strategy, the Council used the "alternatives" mechanism, described later in this chapter, which I used for the Reno-Washoe County Plan to engage all of the special interest groups and emerge with a preferred alternative, or a "hybrid option."[50]

The major policies continue from the 1976 Metropolitan Development Framework. Two-thirds of all growth to the year 2020 will be contained within the current urban boundary area (the year 2000 Metropolitan Urban Service Area boundary).[51] At most, only one-third of new development to the year 2020 would occur on no more than 80,000 acres at the urbanizing edge of the area. A further "urban reserve" of 120,000 acres is earmarked for urban development after the year 2020. Its outer boundary will permanently divide the urban and rural parts of the region. Without the plan, development at the edge would likely consume 170,000 acres.[52] The policies continue to encourage the infill of vacant land, utilization of higher minimum densities, and, for the first time, concentrating job growth along transportation and transit corridors and centers; it will define a geographic pattern of growth within the urban boundary area.[53]

What is notable is that the Council is continuing to discuss the nature and pattern of growth including *timing and phasing* within the Metropolitan Urban Service Area (MUSA) boundary, retaining the full dimension of the Ramapo system, instead of allowing growth to reach out immediately to the outer edge of the MUSA line.[54]

Final problems remain due to the lack of a state land use growth management statute for areas in Minnesota and adjacent Wisconsin outside the seven-county council region. Some growth is leapfrogging over the seven-county boundary needlessly, consuming large areas of prime farmland, forests, and rural open space.[55]

In recent years, the State of Minnesota has become a leader in the enaction of legislation encouraging areawide approaches to modern growth problems. Minnesota legislators and judges have formulated a state policy of annexation whereby municipal boundary changes depend upon the objective condition of the territory involved rather than upon the often parochial and subjective desires and interests of inhabitants of either the territory sought to be annexed or of the annexing body.[56] The creation of the Minnesota Municipal Commission (MMC)[57] to serve as an administrative overseer of most municipal boundary changes, including annexation and defensive incorporations within Minnesota, is further evidence of a state policy favoring orderly and controlled growth. In establishing the Commission, the legislature announced that "sound urban development is essential to the continued economic growth of this state" and empowered the Commission "to promote and regulate development of municipalities so that the public interest in efficient local government will be properly recognized and served."[58] To effectuate this policy, the state legislators recently enacted a statute allowing for a process of "orderly annexation," which permits the MMC to set aside designated territory for future annexation to a municipality until such time as the annexing entity is found to be willing and prepared to furnish urban services and the territory to be annexed is or is about to become urban or suburban in nature.[59] When these conditions are met, the Commission may allow annexation. After annexation, the taxes in the annexed territory increase over a period of three to five years to the same rate as that of the annexing unit. As the MMC has said, "[t]his procedure allows the village to plan today to service the growth that everyone concedes will take place while not annexing any land until that growth actually does occur."[60]

San Diego, California:
Urban Infill and Transportation Corridors
Using *Ramapo* Tiers and Impact Fees

San Diego was the second major metropolitan area that selected the *Ramapo* techniques to manage growth in an Urbanizing Tier. The use of the technique has been hugely successful, both in creating economic growth in Tier II corridors and in stimulating growth in the central city and vacant areas in the urban service area.[61] In November of 1972, after the U.S. Supreme Court dismissed the appeal in *Ramapo*, I spoke on growth management and the *Ramapo* case at a land use conference sponsored by the American Law Institute and American Bar Association (ALI-ABA) in San Diego. Mayor Pete Wilson attended the conference as a keynote speaker, and we talked about using the *Ramapo* case to deal with severe problems of infrastructure deficiencies that the city was facing with its new suburban growth, particularly on the I-15 suburban corridor (Mira Mesa and beyond). I continued to consult with the city during 1973 to 1974. Some three years later, in 1975, when I returned from a visiting professorship at the London School of Economics, the mayor invited me to become a permanent consultant to the city and develop a complete growth management system—with the aim of making it one of the most effective in the nation.

The City of San Diego was determined to adopt land development policies discouraging leapfrog, suburban sprawl development and to encourage residential and economic development in established infill areas and transportation corridors and transit centers.[62] Encouraging development to occur first within the transportation corridors ensures that transit facilities will be financially feasible and that the community will not evolve as a single-use sprawl development. San Diego recognized that, whether mandatory or incentive-based, developers will avoid building in corridor or center areas unless adequate incentives are created or unless land use controls are in place that channel development.

In San Diego, rather than utilizing a simple urban growth boundary line that separates urban from rural areas, the city decided that a tiered system should be utilized. The tier concepts include an urbanized area, urbanizing area, and future urbanizing areas.[63] An urban growth boundary (UGB) is a

mapped line that separates urbanizing land from rural land and within which urban growth is contained for a specified time period, usually the life of the plan. Edges and UGBs are advocated by many neotraditionalists as a way to channel growth into higher-density, mixed-use nodes and centers. Because UGBs require large areas to contain growth effectively, they are often designated on an areawide basis or by intergovernmental agreement. In fact, Oregon and Washington require UGBs.[64] The problem with using a UGB system as the sole basis of control is that there is no distinction within the growth boundary, so the sprawl can reach out to the edges of the boundary immediately without timing and phasing of intermediate areas. Therefore, areas beyond the boundary are recognized as simply rural or agricultural, leaving no reserve for future urbanization. This creates enormous conflict and pressure to enlarge the boundary immediately.

A more sophisticated application of the UGB approach is the use of a "tier system," which was applied in San Diego. A principal tenet of the "tier system" involves the division of the planning area into subareas ("tiers"), so that different areas of the community that present different problems relating to growth and development can be treated with different policies. Nevertheless, while individual areas may need to be separated for specialized treatment, they must still be viewed in terms of their interrelationships with other areas and with the community as a whole. The tier system divided the community into "growth" and "limited growth" categories and added the tiers as subdivisions of those general categories. Tiers within the growth category are commonly designated "Urbanized" and "Planned Urbanizing." The tiers within the limited growth category would be "Future Urbanizing," "Rural," "Agricultural," and "Conservation/Open Space."

Each of the tiers has specific geographical boundaries and is capable of being mapped. The Urbanized Tier consists of those areas that are at or near build-out and served by public facilities including central city, city neighborhoods, first- and second-ring suburban communities. The Planned Urbanizing area represents the "new" growth area, which may take the form of corridors, centers, neotraditional mixed communities, contiguous areas, or areas ending up to UGBs. The Rural area should be a permanent rural density development area. If a temporary "holding" zone is needed until growth areas are built out, a Future Urbanizing tier should be designated that contains lands presently unsewered but needed for future growth as the Planned Urbanizing (Ramapo) tier moves outward in an orderly way. The Rural-Agricultural tier is intended to identify those lands that should be preserved permanently for rural densities and agricultural production. Last, the Environmental, Conservation/Open Space tier consists of lands containing natural resources or environmentally sensitive areas; it may overlay the other tiers.[65]

Transportation corridors, as areas that would be targeted for future growth, can be integrated into the framework by inclusion in the area mapped and designed as Planned Urbanizing. Transportation corridors may also pass through more than one tier and therefore may require the use of differing techniques. For instance, techniques utilized in transportation corridors in the Urbanized Tier will likely have a redevelopment/infill focus while techniques utilized in transportation corridors in the Future Urbanizing Area would likely consist of advance acquisition, excess condemnation, and use of an official map or thoroughfare right-of-way plan to prevent development in the bed of proposed thoroughfares to be built or widened.[66] Joint development through public-private enterprise[67] and transit villages[68] is a technique that is commonly used in all areas mapped as transportation corridors.

These alternatives were designed to redirect where a greater percentage of new development would occur.[69] San Diego's plan incorporated three major areas (exclusive of environmentally sensitive zones that overlaid all tiers but was never adopted until a later date. ". . . thus becoming the first step towards resurrecting Freilich's proposal for a citywide environmental tier"[70]) for which separate objectives and techniques were proposed: Urbanized Areas, Planned Urbanizing Areas (the "Urbanizing Tier"), and Future Urbanizing Areas. This tier system was designed to create urban infill by transferring a greater proportion of new growth to the Urbanized Area. (See Figure 4.2.)

The extent of the shift in development patterns to the Urbanized Area in a period of just over four years from plan adoption was remarkable. Much of it was due to the incentive to build in the downtown, waterfront, and built-up neighborhoods because they already had sewer, water, parks, roads, schools, and community fire, police, park, and recreational facilities; conversely, in the new growth Planned Urbanizing Area, development was required to bear the prime responsibility for financing the infrastructure through facility benefit assessments (FBAs) (impact fees).[71]

Prior to 1979, the year the FBAs were introduced along with adoption of the plan, the estimated proportion of new growth was 90 percent in the

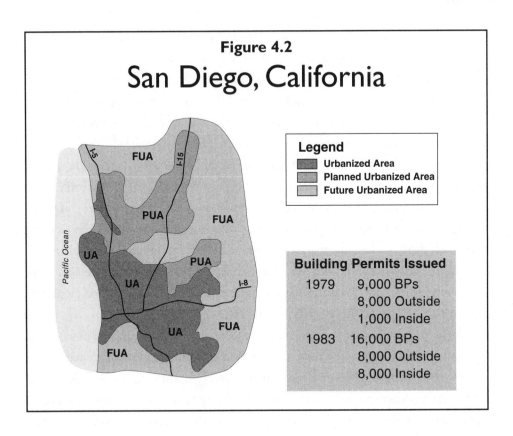

Figure 4.2

San Diego, California

Legend
- Urbanized Area
- Planned Urbanized Area
- Future Urbanized Area

Building Permits Issued

1979	9,000 BPs	
	8,000 Outside	
	1,000 Inside	
1983	16,000 BPs	
	8,000 Outside	
	8,000 Inside	

Planned Urbanizing (PUA) and Future Urbanizing (FUA) Areas, and 10 percent in the 167-square-mile built-up Urbanized Area (UA). A goal was established to change the percentages to 60 percent in the PUA and 40 percent in the UA to utilize more efficiently over 25,000 vacant serviced areas of land in the UA that had been "leapfrogged." These goals were substantially achieved as noted in a June 24, 1983, Planning Department Information Report (No. 83-289):

1979–1983 Population Growth	1979–1983 Housing Units
46,233 UA (60%)	15,921 UA (Added 62%)
28,216 PUA (36%)	9,958 PUA (Added 38%)
2,951 FUA (4%)	

Total 77,400

A major factor contributing to the dramatic reversal in the location of growth was the fiscal incentive favoring the UA. Building in older areas where public services were available reduced housing costs in comparison to new growth areas where development was required to finance capital infrastructure, the need for which was generated by new development.[72]

The San Diego Progress Guide and General Plan defined the Urbanized Area as the central portion of San Diego and the city's remaining older sections. This area was divided into the central area, which included downtown, the area designed to be the focus of metropolitan San Diego, with land use and transportation patterns expected to emphasize its function as the areawide center, and the remaining older communities, which were expected to become more diverse in land use, emphasizing activity nodes in older communities. The central area objectives focused on attracting the most intensive and varied land uses, including office, administrative, financial, residential, and entertainment. The objectives for the remaining older communities stressed conservation of social-environmental characteristics and deteriorating neighborhoods' rehabilitation through compatible infill policies.[73]

San Diego's Planned Urbanizing Area consisted of the newly developing communities with the objective of supporting additional public investment necessary to complete development and to allow communities already served by capital facilities to grow. Land was to be opened for urbanization in a staged, contiguous manner through orderly public facilities extension and infrastructure improvements, which was the prime responsibility for new growth to bear through a facility benefit assessment system; it also included housing provision for a variety of income levels. Facility provision was designed to coincide with development. Criteria for evaluating development in this area included a determination of transportation, schools, emergency services, libraries, parks, open space, drainage, water supply, water distribution systems, and sewer system capacity. The Future Urbanizing Area included land that was vacant and generally zoned agricultural.[74] This land was to be held as an urban reserve, released for development only through tightly constrained transition policies as the planned communities were built out or as opportunities to implement the city's balanced housing or land use goals arose.[75] It was recommended that land within this area that was zoned agricultural or low-density residential/recreational use for extended time periods should be given tax relief through preferential tax assessments.[76]

Special assessments and impact fees were incorporated into the three-tier system, eliminating a Tier II that would consist of existing built-up areas outside of downtown (Tier I); and Tier V, an overlay evirnomental tier that would

cover the entire downtown.[77] New developments within the Planned Urbanizing Area were required to participate in public infrastructure financing through the application of a facilities benefit assessment (FBA).[78] The FBA apportioned the costs of traffic, park, library, school, fire, and other facilities to each new unit of residential, commercial, and industrial development. Payment of the FBA occurred at the building permit stage.[79] Overall, use of these combined growth management techniques (tiered growth and facility financing) resulted in a major shift of development into the designated Urbanized Area, effectively creating infill development.

The San Diego plan was a fundamental combination of three major elements:

1. to utilize the Ramapo Plan to time and sequence growth through the three-tier system—especially in the "Planned Urbanizing Tier";
2. to organize growth in the Planned Urbanizing Tier through a transportation corridor approach; and
3. to require that new growth not be subsidized by existing built-up areas through the general fund but would pay for the one-time capital costs generated by that growth through facility benefit assessments.[80]

Accomplishing the last element of the plan required extraordinary integration of economics, finance, planning, and law on our part, working with a former student of mine, Tom Clark, who had become one of California's leading bond attorneys. California had not yet recognized through statutory authority the creation of impact fees[81] and therefore we utilized new wine in old wineskins—a special assessment on newly developing areas so that the general fund would not subsidize the new growth-related facilities, yet avoid the labelling of a special tax that would be void under Proposition XIII.[82] The FBAs covered the new planned community and corridor areas in the urbanizing tier. Moreover, built-up property in the area of assessment was excluded from the assessment since the existing properties did not contribute to the need for new capital facilities generated by the new growth.[83] Particularly significant were the policies in the General Plan that a piecemeal approach to dealing with large development in planned urbanizing areas would inevitably lead to haphazard sprawl growth and fiscal imbalance, putting heavy burdens on those seeking early development and lighter loads upon those coming into development at a later time.[84] Thus the plan and FBA ordinance recognized that the aggregation of all improvements (some twenty-five separate urban-type improvements: school, roads, drainage, library, parks, fire, police, recreation, open space, and so on) into one FBA and the spread of that cost to all undeveloped parcels was held by the court of appeal to be appropriate.[85]

Last, the vision of the city that controlling urban sprawl required the three major policies was recognized by the court. "San Diego's general plan is the instrument through which the City seeks to manage an explosive growth with land use controls, development of new and urbanizing communities over a period of years and the financing of public facilities . . . by imposing a present lien on undeveloped properties to pay in the future an apportioned share of the costs of public facilities required to accommodate the needs of future residents of the properties upon their development."[86] The result was revitalization of depressed neighborhoods in both the downtown and waterfront areas.[87]

Additionally, I developed for San Diego a Transportation Congestion Management and Development Phasing Ordinance with an annualized "phasing limit," which limited new development to the capacity of existing transportation facilities and new facilities included in a twenty-year capital improvements plan. Similar to *Ramapo,* if developers wish to build earlier than anticipated, they could advance the facilities needed to avoid a deterioration in the planned level of service or make a voluntary advance payment to cover the cost of the facilities. To support the development phasing requirements and to correct existing infrastructure deficiencies,[88] a separate ordinance established a Capital Facilities Plan that shows the capacity-adding roadway and transit facilities to be added over the next twenty years.[89]

Following the guidelines of the transportation ordinance and the tier concept, growth is continuing in the Urbanized and Planned Urbanizing Areas.[90] Recently, through a political decision to promote preservation and development, San Diego adopted a nature conservation plan where specific undeveloped sections of land will be purchased and permanently set aside for protected natural habitat, and other open space will be set aside for unrestricted development.[91] While this program appears to involve some compromises, the Future Urbanizing Area will not face transition into swift development. Proper soil analysis and habitat studies must take place to ensure that appropriate open space will not be utilized for development. With San Diego's growth, the city will now continue to concentrate higher densities within the Urbanized Area and the Planned Urbanizing Area.[92]

In addition to the transit villages, San Diego incorporated major mixed-residential-use villages into the Planned Urbanizing Area with the aim of capturing its full fair share of regional population and to meet the regional general welfare requirements of *Associated Homebuilders of City of Livermore,* 557 P.2d at 473 (Cal. 1976). The city adopted a nine-phase, mixed-use North City West community plan along the I-5 corridor in the PUA. The Carmel Valley Precise Plan (the first phase of nine phases) was situated on 358 acres and was approved in 1979 along with the growth management plan to contain 2,065 units of single-family, duplex, cluster, and garden apartments, with population projected at approximately 5,000 persons.

In 1982 the court of appeal, in one of the first approvals of neo-traditional development in the United States, found that the plan fully met the city's regional general welfare needs:

1. it provided needed housing in the region to meet regional demand;
2. it aided in distribution of new development along major transportation corridors with residences and employment near corridor centers;
3. it relieved sprawl growth pressures in the north, thus decreasing transportation congestion and air quality degradation.[93]

Lexington-Fayette County, Kentucky: Urban County Government and Urban Growth Areas

Lexington-Fayette County is located in the heart of the famous Bluegrass region of Kentucky. Growing from a small community to the region's economic, educational, health, and cultural activities center, the Lexington area has had a successful history of growth management. In 1976, I was retained by the county to deal with sprawl growth resulting from municipal services being extended to areas increasingly distant from the urban center.[94]

A relatively simple technique for channeling urban growth and managing the soaring costs of utilities associated with leapfrog development was pioneered by Wolfgang Roesseler of Ladislas, Segoe & Associates in Lexington, Kentucky, in 1958 as well as in several Wisconsin cities. Basically, the technique involved designating an Urban Service Area (USA), which planning studies showed to be most adaptable to the extension of municipal services such as streets, sewers, and water, and a rural service area where development is restricted. Lexington, Kentucky, established a USA line to achieve the following goals:

1. make the most efficient use of public tax money providing necessary service to developing areas;

2. maintenance of agricultural uses, especially protection of the famous Kentucky horse farms;

3. efficient municipal or county services; and

4. promotion of public health through sewer services.[95]

The 1958 system consisted of two documents: a 1953 "Segoe" Report, which had previously been adopted by the Planning and Zoning Board; and a 1958 Master Plan Supplement compiled by Wolfgang Roesseler. The two documents comprised the Master Plan for the Development of the then-separate City of Lexington and Fayette County. The Future Land Use Plan was a part of the 1958 Master Plan Supplement. An imaginary line roughly in the form of a circle was drawn completely around the City of Lexington varying from three to five miles from the center of the city. The line was irregular because it followed the outline of eleven public sewerage basins that had been ascertained by the J. Steven Watkins Engineering firm. The area within this line was designated as the "Urban Service Area," which contemplated the accommodation of a population of 200,000 people.[96]

A major element of the 1958 Urban Service Area, the first "Urban Growth Boundary" in the United States was upheld by a court as constitutional against taking[97] and substantive due process challenges because there still was value (the diminution was from $1,650/acre for residential to $600 to $1,200/acre without the rezoning) and that boundary lines of demarcation must be drawn somewhere.[98] (See Figure 4.3.)

One of the major problems I faced in working with the Lexington "Urban Service Area" concept was to incorporate the planners' contemplation of reaching 200,000 inhabitants when the present population was 125,000. A liberal allowance in acreage had to be made over and above the acreage that would accommodate exactly 200,000 in population in recognition of the fact that if only the bare amount of acreage was included in the area to accommodate the future population, a land monopoly would be created. If some of the land would not be developed because owners would not sell or the land could not meet health or environmental tests, inflation in land and housing prices would ensue.[99] This concept of including more acreage than needed, but not more than about 1¼ to 1½ times, was incorporated in the Metropolitan Council and San Diego growth management systems—and most smart growth systems since.[100]

In 1973, pursuant to authorizing state legislation[101] voters of the City of

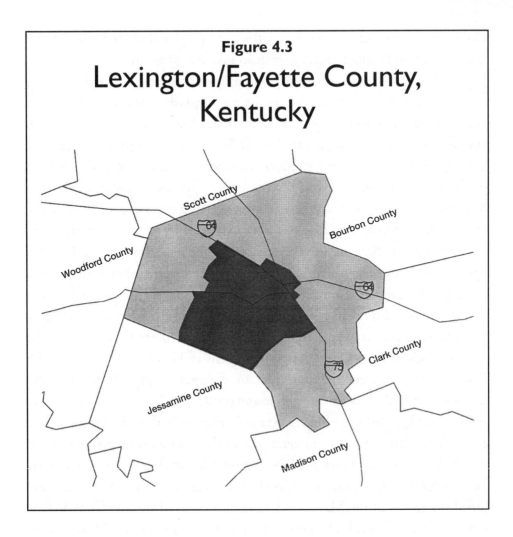

Figure 4.3
Lexington/Fayette County, Kentucky

Lexington and Fayette County elected to merge into an urban county government. In the same year, the state passed enabling legislation for urban county governments to provide for the establishment of urban/rural service areas:

> The territory of an urban county government may be divided into service districts. Each service district shall constitute a separate tax district within which the urban county government shall levy and collect taxes in accordance with the kind, type, level and character of the services provided by the urban county government in each of these districts. The legislative body of the urban county government may abolish or alter existing districts or create new districts.[102]

The stage was now set for introducing the Ramapo plan into the Urban Service Area concept to facilitate smart growth and control of sprawl.

In 1976, I was invited to Lexington-Fayette County because defects in the 1973 plan began to emerge. The use of a single Urban Service Area (Urban Growth) boundary had allowed for urbanization right up to the line without any timing or phasing of growth. The ability to plan and prioritize a capital improvements program and to phase development in accord with adequate public facilities led to sprawl within the Urban Services Area and serious conflict with land in the rural service area immediately adjacent to the USA. Thus, in 1973 the Urban Service Area had to be expanded by over 7.5 square miles[103] to accommodate these pressures. Nevertheless, the plan was successful in containing growth outside the USA, in that even with the expansion to 74.4 square miles, it still represented only 26 percent of the county's 283 square miles within the USA—and only 50 percent of the land within the USA was developed. All of those problems were outlined in the report I delivered in early 1977.[104]

The Freilich & Leitner 1980 Comprehensive Plan (Plan), working with Dale Thoma, the new planning director, focused on growth management strategies as a tool to coordinate public and private development to effect urban infill, as well as distinguishing functional subareas within the urban service area.[105] The Plan became an integral part of the community's overall Growth Planning System and represented the combination of county and city cooperation. Adoption of the Plan completed a four-year planning process that combined the efforts of the Mayor's Advisory Task Force, Planning Commission, Urban County Council, Division of Planning, citizens, and the Urban County Government as a whole.

The 1980 Plan was created to deal with the explosive population growth then occurring in an attempt to prevent sprawl from encroaching upon horse farms, agricultural lands, and environmental lands. The Plan proposed six new functional areas located within the USA consisting of a downtown, employment centers, urban activity centers, urban growth areas, existing neighborhoods, and horse farms. This delineation better suited the implementation strategy and techniques. The Plan utilized *Ramapo's* sequential timing of growth in accordance with adequate public facilities as the next step to providing the necessary linkages for the urbanizing tier within the USA.[106]

The division of the USA into the six functional "tier" areas created a two-part Urbanizing Tier consisting of Urban Activity Centers (UAC) and Urban

Growth Areas (UGA). The UACs were distinct areas of concentrated high- and medium-density residential uses with supporting retail trade, personal services, and community facility concentrations. Each activity center functioned as a focal point for the surrounding geographic area and accommodated the needs of its population. The remainder of the Urbanizing Tier was encompassed in the UGA where the largest share of growth and development in the county would be accommodated. The development in the UGAs were to be timed and sequenced where the new development was contiguous to existing built-up areas. Many factors were reflected in the delineation of the UGA including the location, timing, sequencing, quantity, type, and quality of growth based on the capital improvement program. The implementation strategy related to two major actions: first, zoning was adopted to reflect densities and uses suitable for urban development; and second, ensuring that when urban development occurs, the necessary public facilities and services are available and adequate to serve the development. These two actions were closely related and supported by the appropriate planning and Capital Improvements Programming. The Kentucky enabling legislation provided for the planning and implementation approaches necessary in the UGA.[107]

In the years following the 1980 comprehensive planning revision, little change was made in the Urbanizing Tier policies. Emphasis shifted toward protecting the remaining rural and green space areas and avoiding major USA expansions, despite over fifty petitions with 10,000 additional acres requesting inclusion in the 1993 to 1995 plan revision.[108] In 1995 the Planning Commission hired a well-known planning attorney, Charles Siemon, to update the Land Use Element. In May of 1996, an Expansion Area Master Plan was adopted, adding only 1,600 additional acres to the USA. Major emphases shifted to impact fees for development-generated facilities, transfers of development rights, and establishing rural land-carrying capacity (basing rural subdivision approval on rural levels of service standards).[109] A similar rural capacity approach was utilized in the New Jersey State Plan when I worked as Principal Legal Consultant with Charles Siemon. Lexington-Fayette County continues to represent a successful example of utilizing the *Ramapo* approach through an Urbanizing Tier growth boundary system.

Upon adopting the 1996 Comprehensive Plan, the Lexington-Fayette County Region has shaped its land use controls for the next twenty to fifty years. The key *Ramapo* techniques continue to be utilized through expansion

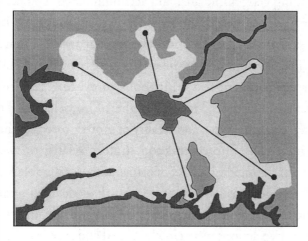

Figure 4.4

Washington, DC

- Radial Corridors
- Corridor Centers
- Joint Development
- Enhanced Air Quality
- Transportation Congestion Management

area criteria for housing, public facilities, infrastructure, boulevards, greenways, and open space.[110] Most recently, the nonprofit, community-based organization Bluegrass Tomorrow, which works within a seven-county area promoting sustainable, efficient, livable communities, has sponsored a conference focusing on smart growth choices for the region.[111] Bluegrass Tomorrow aims to keep intact the legacy of Lexington as a large urban center with surrounding smaller, yet self-contained, communities. The conference discussed many smart growth options, including incentive-based development, preserving environmentally sensitive agricultural and open space areas, infill of older urban areas, and creating communities with a sense of place.[112] No doubt these options will help keep this strong metropolitan area thriving.

Washington and Baltimore Regions:
Corridors, Centers, and Joint Public-Private Development
in Baltimore, Montgomery, and Howard Counties, Maryland

Subsequent to World War II, as with many regions, the Washington-Baltimore area experienced a surge of outward growth. In 1969 the region adopted a Year 2000 Radial Corridor Plan to channel growth. Note that in lieu of an urban growth boundary, the "Urbanizing Tier" would become transportation corri-

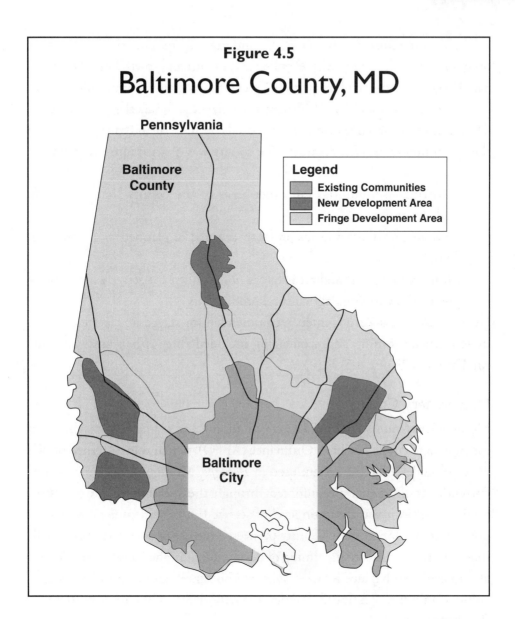

Figure 4.5

Baltimore County, MD

Pennsylvania

Baltimore County

Legend
- Existing Communities
- New Development Area
- Fringe Development Area

Baltimore City

dors.[113] (See Figure 4.4.) Nevertheless, the outer communities were deluged by new jobs and population. These counties were, for the most part, not prepared for the growth.

Baltimore County

Upon being designated legal consultant to develop Baltimore County's growth management plan, I helped to institute an interim development ordinance until the plan could be adopted and implemented.[114]

Baltimore County, Maryland, in undertaking its growth management program, stressed, unlike Minneapolis-St. Paul's urban growth boundaries and San Diego's tiered-corridors plan, a series of Town and Community Urban Activity Centers as its Tier III (urbanizing tier) areas for accelerated growth.[115] These centers included existing or designated commercial and town centers and their surrounding residential areas. The county was divided into the following tiers:

1. Existing communities (all other areas of the county that are largely urbanized);
2. Fringe growth areas (areas presently sewered or planned to be sewered); and
3. Rural and agricultural areas (areas not planned for sewer extensions or with soils with high agricultural productivity).

New Development Area Centers recommended for staged accelerated growth under Ramapo timing and sequencing included three urban areas and one rural area (see Figure 4.5).[116]

Montgomery County

Montgomery County adopted a successful timing and sequencing system called the Adequate Public Facilities Ordinance (APFO), which was patterned on the *Ramapo* model. Like the system used in *Ramapo*, Montgomery County's concurrency requirements are enforced through the subdivision process; but, unlike *Ramapo*, it was based on level of service (LOS) standards rather than a point system. Montgomery County pioneered the use of adequate public facilities not only to regulate the timing of development in the Urbanizing Tier but also to achieve a balance between jobs and housing[117] and to preserve its agricultural lands through transfers of development rights to its corridor systems.[118] (See Figure 4.6.)

The Montgomery County system divides the jurisdiction into policy areas in which growth ceilings are established for jobs and housing. Flexible growth ceilings and level of service standards are established for areas served by public transit and for affordable housing. Montgomery County enforces its APFO through the subdivision process, imposing adequate public facilities requirements at the preliminary plat stage.[119] The APFO applies a lower roadway level of service where public transit is available. This technique maintains the integrity of the concurrency management system while encouraging development

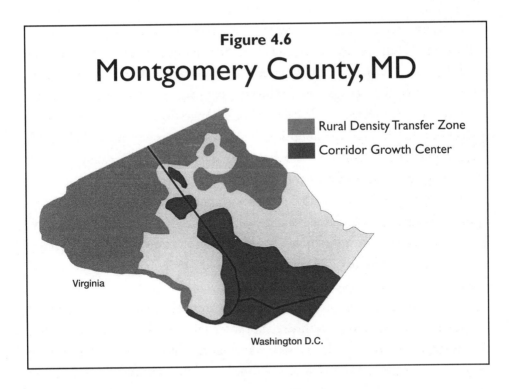

Figure 4.6

Montgomery County, MD

Rural Density Transfer Zone

Corridor Growth Center

Virginia

Washington D.C.

to occur in the Urbanizing Tier where alternative transportation capacity is available. I worked with the county to establish excise taxes for development-generated transportation needs along the corridors.[120]

Specifically, the LOS standards are assigned within "policy areas," which are aggregations of traffic zones. A "staging ceiling" is established for the policy area. The staging ceiling is the maximum amount of residential and employment growth that may occur within the policy area without exceeding the adopted LOS. LOS standards apply to the *entire* policy area and are used to calculate the maximum level of congestion and development that can occur without exceeding the assigned LOS. Separate staging ceilings are calculated for residential and employment-generating growth to effectuate an appropriate jobs-housing balance. Where subceiling limits are exceeded by approved and approved-but-unbuilt ("pipeline") traffic, a moratorium is declared for subdivision applications for that type of use. LOS standards are assigned to reflect the availability of public transportation. A lower LOS applies where transit facilities are available, to reflect the fact that heavy congestion increases the likelihood that transit facilities will be utilized (this is the principle of "substitution"). A special ceiling allocation is established for affordable housing.

Local area review is applied where (1) the project is above a certain threshold size and (2) the project is near a congested intersection (level of service D), or if the policy area is within 5 percent of the staging ceiling. This level of review is required in recognition of the fact that some projects could otherwise satisfy policy area review while causing local congestion. The APFO is monitored annually through the adoption of an "annual growth policy" in which various political subdivisions of the county interested in its enforcement review the staging ceiling and administrative reform.[121]

Montgomery County combines transportation management with its development staging approach in certain areas. No successful legal challenges have been raised against the ordinance. The state's highest court rejected a challenge to the county's differential LOS standards based on takings, due process, and equal protection theories in the *Schneider* decision.[122]

An important feature of Montgomery County is the use of joint public-private development along its three major interstate corridor interchanges. The transportation corridor includes both vehicular transportation (I-270) and the major rail line coming out of Washington, D.C. The county has been able to assemble land around the interchanges; install sewer, water, and other essential public facilities; and lease the land out to private development, retaining a percentage of revenue earned.[123] This power is essential to governments that wish to participate in the equity side of the global economy.[124]

A recent article described how joint development is proceeding in San Diego, Los Angeles, Washington, D.C. ("Arlington and Montgomery counties have assembled land and utilized other incentives to build transit based, mixed use developments at the following stations: Bethesda . . ."), San Francisco Bay Area, St. Louis, Atlanta, Santa Clara, Chicago, and New Jersey.[125] In working with the Florida Department of Transportation, I helped develop the Florida legislation that permits each city and county in Florida to utilize joint public-private development at every major arterial interchange in the state.[126] Even federal agencies are utilizing innovative new concepts such as enhanced leasing to promote equity positions in government-held property.[127]

Howard County

Howard County is located in the path of growth from both Washington and Baltimore. While the growth control efforts in Montgomery County and Baltimore County in the late 1970s effected some progress in halting sprawl, many

felt it was ineffective in its implementation. The growth slowdown was temporary and the high cost and short supply of land served by water and sewer service and the continuing pressure for jobs and housing in the Washington and Baltimore areas forced development into rural areas. With the construction of I-95 and replacement of US 1, the beltway centers began to expand along the new highway. With this, outlying Howard County began to grow even as the surrounding counties remained steady. In the 1980s, Howard County became the "development frontier."[128] The stringent growth management techniques of neighboring counties and increased funding for additional transportation arterials (that is, US 29, I-95, US 1, and I-70) only seemed to reinforce the attractiveness of Howard County for urban development. It was estimated that by the year 2010, 50 to 60 percent of all travel in Howard County will be through-traffic. These future traffic problems caused Howard County to retain Freilich, Leitner, and Carlisle to help prepare a new comprehensive plan with a strong implementation element. I proposed a series of alternative development scenarios, similar to my solutions for Reno-Washoe County, so that a "preferred scenario" could be selected.

After a two-year effort, between my firm and the county's brilliant planning director Uri Avin, in which we acted as principal legal and planning consultant, the 1990 Howard County General Plan was adopted and subsequently received the prestigious 1991 American Planning Association Award for Outstanding Comprehensive Planning. The plan is oriented toward environmental protection and growth management providing for a beneficial level of economic development. The plan took previous general plans further, which traditionally relied on zoning and subdivision regulations, by providing timed and sequenced growth in its growth management strategy.[129] Previously, comprehensive zoning plans regulated the type and intensity of development; however, only a few of the zoning districts provided standards for evaluation of the impacts of development. The system was very weak in preventing premature development, and the ability to install needed roads, facilities, and public services was overlooked. Insufficient state funding for schools and roads, the increased need to upgrade the local road network, the need for additional public transit, and the elimination of federal funding for water and sewerage facilities helped diminish the effectiveness of the existing limited powers to match growth effectively with the needed infrastructure. The Phased Growth program in the 1990 General Plan provided the timing and phasing of land use designations, development actions, and prioritized provision of public facilities over the next two decades.

Limited state and federal funding also caused transportation concerns in the region. Even if no growth occurred in the county over the next twenty years, traffic conditions would significantly worsen if current regional trends continued and no alternatives were put into place.[130] Local government intervention became essential to prevent the breakdown of the traffic network. After an analysis of existing locations with deficient levels of service (LOS), the county developed polices to guide in the selection of future roads:

1. use of existing rights-of-way, where possible, to minimize intrusion into existing subdivisions, neighborhoods, and communities; and

2. developing new alignments and reservation of future rights-of-way only where existing rights-of-way could not be used and where the new alignments would provide sufficient capacity to serve the required function in the road network.

The road improvements proposed in the General Plan over the next twenty years would greatly improve traffic conditions above those that would occur under the previous plan.

Planning for transit has become an essential part of Howard County's balanced growth. The utilization of each transit mode to its maximum efficiency and cost effectiveness within the context of a broad spectrum of transportation needs and dependency is important.[131] Techniques such as identifying, acquiring, and building park-and-ride lots for carpooling, as well as the encouragement of shifting to other higher-occupancy vehicles, has been part of that plan. To ensure a system that will facilitate employment and stimulate economic development and increase the opportunities of transportation-dependent persons, Howard County's comprehensive transportation plan will be based on analysis and assessment, evaluation of present quasi-public transportation services, and study of current and potential system users. Through the year 2010, the county will pursue the construction of road improvements, provide incentives to the State Highway Administration to accelerate and enhance its road-building program in the county, and support the eastern alignment of the I-95 Virginia-Delaware bypass.[132]

Howard County also used a broad-based development easement program, coupled with federal tax deductions, preferential assessment, cluster development, and TDRs, to preserve over 80 percent of its agricultural lands by

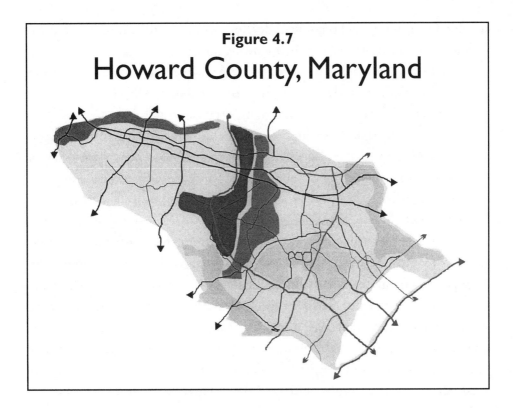

Figure 4.7

Howard County, Maryland

demonstrating to farmers that with the appropriate incentives it was more economical to retain the land than to sell to sprawl developers; *see* chapter 8, *infra.* This assured that new development would be encouraged to build in corridors, centers, and existing communities (in other words, the "new town" of Columbia).[133] (See Figure 4.7.)

Central Puget Sound Metropolitan Area, Washington: Transportation and Concurrency

Rapid growth in the Central Puget Sound Metropolitan Area threatened to destroy the area's quality of life and, with it, the jobs and industrial base needed to sustain future growth.[134] In the early 1990s, the region faced traffic congestion, population increases that caused pressures on the environment, and a resulting concern for the need to protect natural resources and environmentally sensitive areas.[135] In response to these issues, the Washington State legislature adopted a planning framework for harnessing this growth and simultaneously encouraging the potential for economic development. Statewide growth management and planning legislation was passed to incorporate the *Ramapo* techniques of timing and phasing of development in accordance with adequate public facilities by establishing the following goals:

1. reduce urban sprawl by encouraging growth to occur where "adequate public facilities and services can be provided in an efficient manner";
2. provide "efficient multimodal transportation systems"; and
3. to "[e]nsure that those public facilities and services necessary to support development shall be adequate to serve the development at the time the development is available for occupancy and use without decreasing current service levels below locally established minimum standards."[136]

The 1990 Growth Management Act (GMA)[137] involved all levels of government requiring local governments to adopt comprehensive plans and implementing regulations, while the 1991 Growth Strategies legislation[138] established a cooperative framework for planning between cities and counties.[139] The counties that were required to plan were required to adopt integrated city and county planning policies that served as the framework for both the county and city comprehensive plans. The state mandated specific elements in the city and county comprehensive plans.[140] All counties were required to adopt development regulations that protect critical areas.[141] The GMA outlined consistency requirements for planning, including the following:

1. city and county plans must be consistent with state goals;
2. city and county plans must be internally consistent; and
3. city and county plans must be consistent with neighboring city and county plans.[142]

Counties that were required to plan were also required to delineate twenty-year urban growth areas (UGA).[143] The legislation also required transportation concurrency, a policy that requires the cities or counties to identify funding for transportation facilities, transportation facility deficits, and the future needs on a ten-year time frame.[144] Thus, the Washington legislation recognized the *Ramapo* concurrency concept and its implementation at the local level of government.[145] Cities and counties with specified population and growth rate characteristics are required to adopt a comprehensive plan including a mandatory transportation element that contains comprehensive structural, financial, and police power strategies founded on concurrency principles.[146]

The most beneficial approach to solving metropolitan problems relied primarily on a set of targeted incentives designed to encourage and foster development in selected locations, rather than on a heavy-handed set of regulatory

tools. With this, I recommended to the Central Puget Sound region that the incentives should target development in two key geographic locations: corridors and centers of economic development and infill development areas, to control sprawl beyond the Urbanizing Tier.[147] Either separately established or designated within tiers, transportation corridors can serve as unifying frameworks for the construction and utilization of transportation facilities, financing mechanisms, and regulatory techniques.[148] A transportation corridor is defined as a specific geographic area including:

1. the maximum right-of-way required to meet population and employment growth; and
2. adjacent areas reasonably necessary to be included in order to accomplish the corridor plan.

The transportation corridor reflects a far broader concept than a mere highway system. The corridor is a legislatively defined or mapped area whose central focus is a proposed or existing transportation facility.[149]

The Washington system provides for a unique combination of urban growth boundaries and concurrency management of transportation facilities. The growth management system requires local governments to adopt and enforce ordinances that allow development only if the affected transportation facility will not decline below the predetermined level of services (LOS), unless those improvements or strategies for providing the facilities are made concurrent with the development. Concurrent with development means that "[the transportation facility] improvements or strategies are in place at the time of development, or that a financial commitment is in place to complete the improvements or strategies within six years."[150] The LOS standards are established locally to judge the transportation system's performance.[151] The transportation system is coordinated by the metropolitan transportation planning organization.

The combination of these two techniques allows the use of transportation corridors designed to encourage infill development and permit the creation of urban centers within the Urbanizing Tier. The infill areas/centers will accommodate mixed land uses and pedestrian amenities while providing new opportunities for development and investment.[152] The impetus for location in infill areas/centers is provided through a concurrency management program. In close-in areas, LOS standards may be difficult to meet because of existing congestion.[153] This tends to push development out of the urban core to fringe areas where LOS standards are easier to meet. Two techniques of concurrency management, however, can be applied to encourage development infill:

1. the averaging of transportation LOS; and

2. the waiving of concurrency requirements in existing urbanized areas.

Averaging can be done at a metropolitan level to establish a regional carrying capacity. This capacity can be allocated to infill areas/centers to allow increased development in those areas while diminishing the allocation to rural, fringe areas. Development in the Urbanizing Tier can be further encouraged through selective concurrency waivers for development at corridor centers that allow development to be exempt from concurrency review. Infill development can rely on alternative transportation and transit modes, bicycle and pedestrian systems, and mixed-use development, all of which will reduce roadway impact and length of trips.

In the early 1990s, the Central Puget Sound Metropolitan Area began the growth containment process that Portland, Oregon, started in the 1970s.[154] The Puget Sound area has enjoyed a strong economy that brought changes to the region.[155] During the late 1980s, the region had the fastest-growing economy in the nation, with population increases of more than 100,000 a year. Rapid economic growth ushered in a building boom that consumed land at a fast rate. The preference for the private automobile and decentralized workplaces combined with the fast pace of growth and resulted in traffic congestion and air pollution. In addition, the strong demand for housing increased the price of housing so that many low- to moderate-income families could not afford it.

Due to the regional impact of land loss, the Puget Sound Regional Council (PSRC) was established to address the regional issues of the natural environment, the economic region, the transportation system, and the housing market.[156] The PSRC, consisting of King, Kitsap, Pierce, and Snohomish Counties, is the regional planning entity that replaced the Puget Sound Council of Governments. PSRC makes the key decisions on regional growth and transportation issues consistent with the state goals identified in the GMA.[157] It has established a full integration of transportation and land use policies in the region due to the collaborative efforts at the federal, state, and regional levels.[158]

Beginning in July of 1991, the GMA required the Central Puget Sound region to adopt multicounty planning policies.[159] In response, PSRC took interim action in 1992 and identified *Vision 2020* as the multicounty planning polices for the four-county region.[160] *Vision 2020* was the regional plan in place at the time, having been adopted in October of 1990.[161] The Council decided to conduct the required multicounty planning policy work in two phases: first, the framework policies; and second, the strategic policies. In 1993, the first phase was accomplished when the Council amended *Vision 2020* and established framework policies addressing the topics identified in the GMA.[162] The second planning phase began in the summer of 1993, focusing on developing strategic policies and updating the framework policies to incorporate the actions of other planning processes.[163]

Vision 2020 establishes a hierarchy of "central places" to guide growth to fifteen mixed-use centers that are served by a more efficient transportation system (see Figures 4.8 and 4.9). The central places concept is a growth management technique used to achieve compact development with a reordering of transportation investment priorities.[164] This growth strategy involved classifying development in the region into six central places.[165] All land areas not classified as central places are designated as open space or as an existing noncenter employment area.[166] The classification process was a collaborative effort between the cities, counties, tribal governments, countywide agencies, the metropolitan agencies, the state, and the public.[167] Classification was based on the type of existing development, the capacity of existing infrastructure, the role the area will play in accommodating future development, and the type of planned transportation services.[168]

Transportation planning plays a key role in the Puget Sound area; it emphasizes more travel options for people wishing to avoid congested roadways.[169] The PSRC (Puget Sound Regional Council) serves as the designated Metropolitan Planning Organization (MPO) for the four counties, which fulfills the metropolitan urban transportation planning required by the Federal Highway and Urban Mass Transit statutes.[170] The PSRC also performs transportation planning responsibilities required by the state by serving as the Regional Transportation Planning Organization (RTPO) authorized under the State Growth Management Act.[171] The RTPOs are required to:

1. prepare and update a transportation strategy;
2. prepare a regional transportation plan;
3. certify transportation elements of local comprehensive plans;
4. certify countywide planning policies;
5. develop a six-year regional transportation improvement program; and

6. establish guidelines and principles that provide direction for preparation and implementation of the transportation elements of comprehensive plans.[172]

PSRC developed and adopted *Vision 2020* to serve as the planning document that fulfills both the state and federal transportation requirements.[173]

A few of the key implementation efforts of PSRC include the monitoring of planning, the review of multilevel plans and policies, the designation of central places, and the development of a program that ensures citizen participation in regional planning efforts. PSRC systematically monitors the progress in achieving the policies outlined in *Vision 2020* and submits an annual status report to the regional assembly.[174] PSRC has responsibility for developing criteria for the designation of central places;[175] however, the designation of central places will be based on a collaborative effort between all levels of government in that region and the public. The Council is also responsible for developing and implementing a process whereby citizen participation will occur in regional planning.[176]

The Regional Council plays an important role as a reviewing agency for multilevel plans and policies to determine if they meet various legislative requirements for conformance and consistency.[177] The Council has studied the various review requirements and proposed review procedures. The proposal identifies three types of review:

1. Coordination and consultation regarding local comprehensive plans, transportation agency plans, and *Vision 2020*;
2. Consistency review of countywide planning policies and *Vision 2020*;
3. Certification of transportation elements for conformance with the Growth Management Act requirements.[178]

The method of remedy for inconsistencies found during the review of plans and policies depends upon the type of review. For reviews in Type I, "coordination and consultation," there is not a mandate for resolution of differences; therefore, PSRC will work with the agencies to resolve the differences if possible.

When inconsistencies are found in Type II review, "consistency review of countywide polices and *Vision 2020*," PSRC will work with the county and/or planning groups to discuss potential problems. If the problems are not successfully addressed, PSRC and the county's policy group discuss possible remedies. If inconsistencies remain, PSRC can petition the Growth Planning Hearings Board to determine remedies or changes in policy.[179] If, during Type

III review, inconsistencies are identified during the certification of transportation elements in local plans, discussion would take place between the Regional Council staff and the jurisdictions's staff. If discussions do not successfully resolve differences, the issue is referred to the Council's Executive Board. The Board may take action. Local governments are able to appeal the Board's action to a board of hearing examiners who are charged to resolve the conflict, "in a manner that would establish consistency between the local transportation element and *Vision 2020.*"[180]

Of the entire Central Puget Sound Region, Pierce-Tocava County holds about 21 percent of the regional population.[181] The county extends from the lowlands of Puget Sound to Mount Rainier, 1,793 square miles of mountains and valleys, rivers and streams, lakes and islands, forests and meadows, and with a population of over 640,000 people.[182] The county experienced 84 percent growth in its unincorporated areas in the 1980s.[183] Pierce County provides services to all of the unincorporated areas and to some areas within incorporated areas.[184] In 1984, the county initiated comprehensive planning.[185] A comprehensive plan was developed and adopted, but voters instituted a referendum on the comprehensive plan and it was voted out in 1986. After 1986, several of the county council members lost the next election. A few of the decisive components in the 1986 plan included the designation of an urban growth boundary and the downzoning of rural and resource lands. From 1986 until the passage of the State Growth Management Act (GMA), the county had not attempted comprehensive planning; instead, planning was done by the individual unincorporated communities.[186]

In 1991, Pierce County retained Freilich, Leitner, and Carlisle to develop the countywide policies with the cities and the county's comprehensive plan. The current Pierce County Comprehensive Plan, which we developed, covers all unincorporated parts of the county, but the countywide policies cover both the unincorporated and incorporated county.[187] The incorporated cities and towns have responsibility for growth management plans for their corporate limits and for adjacent areas where spillover growth is expected. The municipalities are encouraged to reach interlocal agreements with neighboring entities and the county where growth areas overlap to ensure coordination of planning, the provision of public facilities and services, and to provide consistent application of growth management controls. The areas covered by interlocal agreements are designated as joint planning areas with the Pierce County

Comprehensive Plan.[188] The comprehensive plan for the county includes ten elements, of which six are required by the GMA. The six required elements include land use,[189] rural, housing, transportation, utilities,[190] and capital facilities elements. The additional elements address economic development, the environment, community plans, and essential public facilities.[191] The organization of each planning element includes a hierarchy of policies. These include the state goals, state mandates and county mandates that are derived from other documents, and the objectives, principles, and standards established in the countywide planning policies and the county comprehensive plan.[192]

The county identifies a master goal to guide planning in the county: "[to] ensure that the location of land use optimizes the combined potential for economic benefit and the enjoyment and conservation of natural resources while minimizing the threat to health, safety and welfare posed by hazards, nuisances, incompatible land uses, and environmental degradation. . . ."[193] The plan utilizes a growth management concept whereby the county identifies "where new housing, shopping and economic development should be encouraged and where open space, rural areas, farmlands and forested lands should be protected."[194] This concept is furthered by designating seven major *Ramapo-*type tiers:

1. urban growth areas;
2. urban reserve;
3. rural areas;
4. urban/special areas;
5. resource lands;
6. open space areas; and
7. government lands.[195]

Additionally, Pierce County and its municipalities were required, under an interlocal agreement with the Central Puget Sound Region, to develop and adopt countywide planning policies. The county commissioned me to develop the polices where expected growth areas overlap to ensure coordination of plans, public facilities and services, and consistent application of growth management controls.[196] The GMA identifies the development of urban areas where adequate public facilities and services exist or can be provided in an efficient manner, the reduction of sprawl is needed, and a provision of adequate public facilities and services necessary to support urban development at the time the development is available for occupancy and use as planning goals to guide the

development and adoption of comprehensive plans and development regulations.[197] I helped develop policies through the examination of these GMA mandates, including:

- the delineation of urban growth areas;
- the determination and delineation of tiers including an Urbanizing Tier;
- the linkage of tier delineations to capital improvements programming;
- timing and phasing of growth;
- public facility and service adequacy;
- public facility and service availability at the time of development—concurrency;
- facility service provision and extension policies, with a particular focus on sanitary sewer service;
- financing of facility and service provision and extension and imposition of full but fair share of costs on new development; and
- joint county/municipal planning in the Urbanizing Tier.

The result of this process was a series of written policy statements used for establishing a countywide framework from which county and municipal comprehensive plans are to be developed and adopted.[198] Specifically, the Urban Growth Area was designed to time and sequence development supported with historical and typical urban governmental services and facilities such as sewer systems, domestic water systems, street cleaning services, fire protection services, and public transit services. These areas were intended to control the fiscal and environmental implication of unplanned, sprawled growth. The Plan gave the Pierce County Council the responsibility to designate unincorporated Pierce County's UGA as well as individual city and town UGAs.

Economic Development Incentives

I was also deeply involved with the establishment of the Metropolitan Transit System, particularly in integrating the use of the $11.5 billion transit plan with the metropolitan land use economic development policies. Several of the major implementation devices that I recommended were:

1. waiving impact fees to encourage commercial office and industrial facilities locating at transit centers;
2. lowering LOS requirements for development around transit centers;
3. providing for "programmatic" (public-provided) environmental, facility,

and fiscal impact analyses at transit centers so that individual developments would have accelerated processing; and

4. utilizing joint public-private partnerships for economic development at
   transit centers.

These provisions that have been enacted have helped accelerate economic
growth in the region and discourage sprawl.[199]

The growth management legislation also establishes a regional transportation planning process recognizing the multijurisdictional control and inter-
connectedness of the state transportation system. The statute establishes that
regional transportation planning organizations and local transportation plans
must be consistent with the regional transportation plan. Comprehensive road
programs consistent with the comprehensive plan must be established at the
county and municipal level. From this transportation planning process, the
Central Puget Sound Region recently developed a proposed Rapid Transit Plan,
which compared different transit-based development alternatives and sought to
develop a scenario best suited to attract economic development while meeting
the transportation needs of the region. The group preparing the plan, Metro,
recommended the development of a regional rail system and enhancements to
existing bus service at an estimated cost of $11.5 billion.[200] Whether through
public-private partnerships or transportation planning, the State of Washington
has led the way in tailoring the basic growth management techniques to fit
areawide issues and solve community-based problems. (See Figure 4.8.)

Even before the 1990 GMA mandates, King County's concern for preserving its agricultural environment called for action. In 1979, I examined King
County's agricultural land resources in an attempt to preserve and maintain
agriculture as a productive economic activity, particularly on prime agricultural lands that were in proximity to existing urban areas.

Agricultural Preservation

I was retained in 1980 by King County (Seattle) to develop a system for preserving the county's agricultural lands along its major river valleys. As part of
the process I recommended that basic concepts be applied in developing an
agricultural preservation strategy, classifying and delineating the appropriate
categories of agricultural land through the county, describing the purpose
and intent of each category in the overall system, relating these categories to
other functional planning areas in the growth management program for King

Figure 4.8
Puget Sound Regional Rail and HOV System

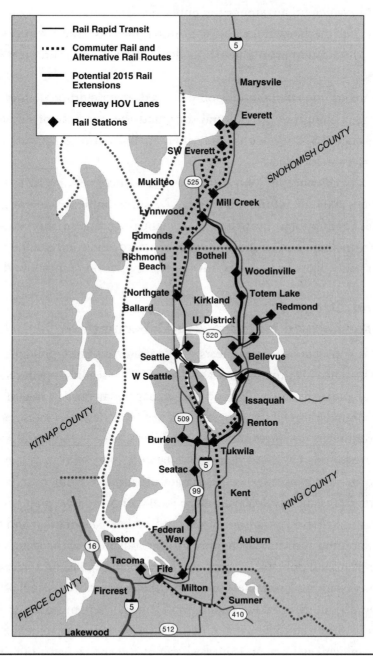

County, and applying compensatory, regulatory, tax, long-term bonds, or incentive techniques to each category to achieve the specified objectives.[201] The county distinguished those areas that were currently or projected in the long-range comprehensive plan to be urbanized within the build-out of the county, similar to *Ramapo*, from those areas that were permanently rural and agricultural and in which urban-supporting public facilities and services would not be provided. The mechanism for distinguishing these two basic categories of land would be the creation of an urban/rural demarcation line within the urban services area.

The major implementation tools consisted of agricultural density zoning, clustering on nonprime agricultural soils, and the purchase of development rights through a $100 million bond program. The entire agricultural strategy has been very successful.

These basic concepts went a long way toward preserving King County's river valleys and agricultural land. Today, Washington boasts one of the most successful metropolitan growth management programs in the nation.[202] Its state, metropolitan, and local distribution of control and strategies has been followed in many plans and Smart Growth state legislation that followed.

Portland, Oregon:
State-Authorized Metropolitan Coordination

Oregon is truly one of the pioneers of state-directed metropolitan planning through its statewide program initiated in 1969.[203] Oregon's system relies upon a series of nineteen statewide land use management goals. Oregon's Urban Growth Boundaries (UGB) program is the first statewide requirement that local governments designate and enforce UGBs. Goal 14 requires local governments to establish UGBs so that public facilities and services (Goal 12) are extended in such a manner as to separate urbanizable from rural land. The transportation element (Goal 12) of the local comprehensive plan emphasizes the relationship between transportation and land use. The number and location of transportation facilities are required to be consistent with "state and local land use plans and policies designed to direct urban expansion to areas identified as necessary and suitable for urban development" (Goal 12(B)(1)). To show how serious this goal is, Washington County, Oregon, recently paid Intel to *reduce* its plan to locate its major national headquarters by reducing the size of the employment force and physical size of the site so as to not create an

urban sprawl effect, to better compatibility with the surrounding area, ensure adequate public facilities to service the site, and promote greater infill in existing county centers.[204]

Plans for new facilities or the expansion of existing facilities are required to identify, *inter alia,* the impact on local land use patterns and existing transportation systems. The goal encourages the utilization of existing transportation facilities. Capital investment policies are designed to buttress the separation of urbanized from nonurbanized areas enforced through the urban growth boundary. Local governments are required to design, phase, and locate transportation facilities (including air, marine, rail, mass transit, highways, bicycle, and pedestrian facilities) in such a manner as to encourage growth in urbanized areas while discouraging growth in rural areas.[205] The Land Conservation and Development Commission (LCDC) is charged with the administration and enforcement of the land use planning program where it oversees counties, cities, and special districts that are responsible for most planning and plan implementation in the state.[206] The Oregon system requires counties and cities to adopt a comprehensive plan that conforms with the statewide planning goals established by LCDC.[207] Counties and cities may form a regional planning authority to exercise the coordination responsibilities.

Between 1963 and 1971 the Portland Metropolitan Study Commission identified several areawide issues caused by the growth of urban and suburban populations. These problems were considered metropolitanwide because they extend beyond and were unable to be solved by the individual local governments.[208] Problems were found in the areas of water supply, sewage disposal, transportation, parks, police and fire protection, air pollution, planning, and zoning.[209] The Portland area has been particularly innovative in growth management strategies. Representatives from many governments and agencies play critical roles in growth management. In 1978, voters in Multnomah, Washington, and Clackamas Counties created an elected areawide government called the "metropolitan service district" to oversee issues that overstepped the traditional city and county boundaries.[210] It became known popularly as Metro.[211] Metro was established in an effort to eliminate duplication of services and overlapping jurisdictions by consolidating the regional governments into an elected governing body to allow accountability and responsiveness to the citizenry.[212] Its responsibilities included amending the regional Urban Growth Boundary (UGB) and adopting planning goals and objectives for the region called the

Regional Urban Growth Goals and Objectives (RUGGOs) that are consistent with state goals.

While these plans indicated the direction the area would follow, they were deemed unspecific; and in 1990, the Oregon Constitution was amended to allow Metro jurisdiction over all matters of "metropolitan concern" as set forth in a charter that was adopted in November 1992.[213] The state legislature authorized Metro to define and apply planning procedures in the areas of air quality, water quality, and transportation.[214] In addition, Metro may adopt functional plans to control the impact on air and water quality, transportation, and other aspects of metropolitan development the Council may identify.[215] The new charter required adoption of the Regional Framework Plan (Plan) in which the 2040 Growth Concept was included. Local officials brought together several past plans into the Plan, which is a comprehensive set of policy guidelines for managing the region's future growth.[216] It will help create an integrated land use, transportation, parks, and open space planning program for the region. The Region 2040 Growth Concept program is a fifty-year planning process designed to look at the problems and potential of actively shaping growth. Officials are examining Urban Reserves, which are areas just outside the current UGB that may be brought into the UGB at some point in the future to accommodate future growth. The new Metro's responsibilities include areawide coordination, comprehensive metropolitan planning, and the delivery of regional services in the Portland metropolitan area.[217] It governs a geographic area that encompasses twenty-four cities and portions of three counties. While these efforts will still only control growth up to the UGB, it does address and increase density levels. However, if Portland had utilized timing and sequencing within the Urbanizing Tier including concentrating growth near developed public facilities, transportal growth would not already be sprawling the urban area fringes.

Oregon's state requirement of UGBs[218] has established a clear limit to long-range urban sprawl. However, because of the abundance of open space within the boundaries early on, orderly development of infrastructure did not become an important strategy. Twenty years ago, the lack of timing and sequencing, when the UGBs were first utilized in Oregon, did not appear detrimental. Populations were steady and growth remained around developed infrastructure. However, in the Portland metropolitan area, where the population is expected to increase by 500,000 by 2017, local officials are currently facing significant growth issues. While Portland has many supporters of its UGBs, a problem exists about whether enough capacity exists within the UGB to accommodate the substantial and newly expanded increase in population.[219] One of the critical questions for metropolitan land use control systems is to ensure that there is no interference with economic growth and expansion The Portland system has mixed results on that score.[220] The region is also currently debating whether to expand the UGB up to 10,000 acres to accommodate growth. Without a tier system it has been too easy to change the UGB boundaries and convert agricultural land; *1000 Friends of Oregon v. LCDC, Lane County,* 752 P.2d 271 (Or. Sup. en banc 1988).[221] Pressures are developing from commercial developments on prime farmland that results from the ever-tightening urban boundary.[222] A tier system would more effectively control sprawl by establishing more definitive standards. Oregon's statewide system has been subject to the most litigation of any Smart Growth state. The application of the statewide goals to particular land use decisions has been a constant source of litigation.[223] Despite these critical issues, Metro has successfully addressed and established regional strategies under the Oregon state growth management law ahead of most other regions in the United States.[224]

Endnotes

1. *See* Broward County and Pinellas County, Florida, which asked me to develop strategies for their growth management plans several years after the *Ramapo* decision. Ron LaBrecque, *Planners Buck the "Puzzle" Picture,* MIAMI HERALD, Aug. 4, 1975, at 1B. "The Planning Council has based many of its legal conclusions on the advice of Robert H. Freilich, a law professor at the University of Missouri in Kansas City. More than a year ago the city of Hollywood contracted with Freilich for legal advice on land-use planning. Freilich is generally considered one of the foremost authorities in the field and is best known for the so-called Ramapo plan"; *see also* Ron Sympson, *Still Time to Control Growth in County, Planner Maintains,* MIAMI HERALD, May 23, 1975, at 1; addressing the fifth urban affairs seminar on Oklahoma City's comprehensive plan ("Robert Freilich, recognized as an authoritative expert on urban growth management"), *see* Marilyn Duck, *Urban Sprawl Curtailment Needed,* OKLA. CITY TIMES, Dec. 12, 1977, at 6S; *Decision Needed on Growth,* Norman Oklahoma Transcript (Dec. 1, 1977); one of the earliest expansions of *Ramapo* occurred in Pinellas County, Florida, when I addressed the Pinellas County Commission of Florida in 1973 on utilizing the curtailed availability of water supplies as adequate public facility timing and phasing regulation; Ralph Golden, *Pinellas Seminar Set on Controlled Growth* (1973); Patti Bridges, *New Methods Said a Must to Control Growth,* Tampa (1973).

2. *See* DAVID L. CALLIES, ROBERT H. FREILICH & THOMAS E. ROBERTS, CASES AND MATE-RIALS ON LAND USE 630 (West 3d ed. 1999) [hereinafter CALLIES, FREILICH & ROBERTS]. For an excellent summary of metropolitan growth management, *see* Porter, 223–42; *see also* Douglas R. Porter, *Tough Choices: Regional Governance for San Francisco*, URB. LAND (Mar. 1992).

3. Some Areawide Planning Councils include: Portland, Oregon Metro Organization; San Diego Association of Governments (eighteen city governments and the county government in San Diego County); Metropolitan Council in Minneapolis/St. Paul; and Triangle J Council of Governments (Chatham, Durham, Johnston, Lee, Orange, and Wake Counties); Dane County City-County Planning Commission in Madison, Wisconsin, *see* Ruth Eckdish Knack, *Go Badgers, Fight Sprawl*, PLANNING 14 (May 1997); and the Windham Area, Vermont (includes twenty-seven towns within three counties and covers 928 square miles in the southeast corner of Vermont).

4. *See, e.g.,* FLA. STAT. ANN. §§ 163.001 *et seq.* (1999) (county and city planning subject to mandatory State Department of Community Affairs review), 187.101–.201 (state plan) (1999); HAW. REV. STAT. §§ 205-1 to 205-37 (1999); ME. REV. STAT. ANN. tit. 12 §§ 683-685D (planning), tit. 38 §§ 481-490 (site development) (1999); N.J. STAT. ANN. §§ 52:18A-196 to -199 (1999); OR. REV. STAT. §§ 197.005–.860 (1999) (comprehensive land use planning coordination); VT. STAT. ANN. tit. §§ 6001–6108 (1999); WASH. REV. CODE, ch. 36.07A (1999). *See also* JOHN M. DEGROVE AND D. A. MINESS, THE NEW FRONTIER FOR LAND POLICY: PLANNING AND GROWTH IN THE STATES (Lincoln Institute of Land Policy, 1994); Daniel J. Curtin & Ann R. Danforth, *Looking Beyond the City Lights, Regional Approaches to the Growth Crisis*, 22 URB. LAW. 701 (1990). *See* Sturges v. Town of Chilmark, 402 N.E.2d 1346, 1352 (Mass. 1980) (when the small town of Chilmark on Martha's Vineyard wanted to preserve its unique character, it passed an ordinance pursuant to a state regional planning statute limiting and phasing building permits over a ten-year period. The court in upholding it stated: "regional needs, which are often important considerations. . . . ").

5. Robert H. Freilich, Elizabeth A. Garvin & S. Mark White, *Economic Development and Public Transit: Washington Growth Management*, 16 U. PUGET SOUND L. REV. 949, [hereinafter Freilich & Garvin] at 954 (1993); *see also* Katherine E. Stone & Phillip A. Seymour, *Regulating the Timing of Development: Takings Clause and Substantive Due Process Challenges to Growth Control Regulations*, 24 LOY. L.A. L. REV. 1205, 1207 (1991).

6. For a survey of techniques available and their potential use, *see* Gary A. Pivo, *Taking Stock of Growth Management in the U.S.*, LANDLINES 1 (Newsletter of the Lincoln Inst. of Land Policy, Sept. 1992); Ch. 4: *Zoning and Land Use Controls in* GROWTH MANAGEMENT PROGRAMS (Eric D. Kelly ed., Matthew Bender, 1996).

7. *See* Freilich & White, *The Interaction of Land Use Planning and Transportation Management: Lessons from the American Experience*, TRANSP. POL'Y 101 (U.K. 1994). An earlier version of this article was presented by me as the keynote speaker on November 9, 1993, at the Royal Town Planning Institute Conference, "Planning for Sustainable Transport, London," and was utilized in the draft note on PLANNING POLICY GUIDANCE ON TRANSPORT, U.K. DEP'T OF ENVIRONMENT. A later version, "The Land Use Implications of Transit-Oriented Development: Controlling the Demand Side of Transportation Congestion and Urban Sprawl," was delivered at a workshop on Sustainable Transportation in Urban Areas sponsored by the German Marshall Fund of the United States in Berlin, October 28, 1997, and was published in 30 URB. LAW. No. 3 (1998).

8. S. Mark White, *Using Adequate Public Facility Ordinances for Traffic Management*, PLAN.

ADVISORY SERVICE REP. No. 465, (American Planning Association, Aug. 1996); *see* Kelly, *supra* note 6. "Of the four techniques (adequate public facilities, phased growth, rate of growth, urban growth boundaries) adequate public facilities requirements are the most basic, the most useful, and the most easily defensible." *Id.* at § 401 (2), pp. 4–5.

9. *See, e.g.,* ROGER FELDMAN ET AL., FINANCING INFRASTRUCTURE: TOOLS FOR THE FUTURE (1988).

10. Freilich & Garvin, *supra* note 5, at 955; *see* Linda Bozung & Deborah J. Alessi, *Recent Developments in Environmental Preservation and the Rights of Property Owners,* 20 URB. LAW. 969 (1988).

11. For an in-depth discussion of these techniques and their effect on communities, *see* Eric Damian Kelly, *Zoning and Land Use Controls, Growth Management Programs* § 4.05 URB. GROWTH BOUNDARIES (Matthew Bender & Co., 1996); and MICHAEL MANTELL ET AL., CREATING SUCCESSFUL COMMUNITIES: A GUIDEBOOK TO GROWTH MANAGEMENT STRATEGIES (1990).

12. D. Callies, R. Freilich and T. Roberts, Ch. 7: *From* Ramapo *to the Metropolitan Council: Crystallization of the Tie-Concept in* GROWTH MANAGEMENT PROGRAMS 630 (Eric D. Kelly ed., Matthew Bender, 1996).

13. *See id.*

14. *Enforcing Metropolitan Policies,* MPLS TRIB., Dec. 5, 1973, at 6A.

15. CITIZENS LEAGUE PLANNED UNIT DEVELOPMENT COMMITTEE, MINNEAPOLIS, GROWTH WITHOUT SPRAWL (Sept. 19, 1973); TWIN CITIES METROPOLITAN COUNCIL, DISCUSSION STATEMENT ON METROPOLITAN DEVELOPMENT POLICY (Oct. 17, 1973).

16. MINN. STAT. ANN. ch. 473 (1967).

17. Arthur Naftalin, *Making One Community Out of Many: Perspectives on the Metropolitan Council of the Twin Cities Area,* 1, St. Paul, Minn., Metropolitan Council of the Twin Cities Area, 1986).

18. *See supra* note 15.

19. Freilich & Ragsdale, *Timing and Sequential Controls—The Essential Basis for Effective Regional Planning: An Analysis of the New Directions for Land Use Control in the Minneapolis–St. Paul Metropolitan Region,* 58 MINN. L. REV. 1009, at 1015–16 (1974).

20. Metropolitan Council Act, Minnesota Session Laws 1967, ch. 896, § 1. For an excellent presentation of the early history of the Council, *see* F. BOSSELMAN & D. CALLIES, THE QUIET REVOLUTION IN LAND USE CONTROL, at 136-63 (1971) [hereinafter BOSSELMAN & CALLIES].

21. Metropolitan Council Act, MINNESOTA SESSION LAWS 1967, ch. 896, § 2, subd. 3.

22. Bosselman & Callies, *supra* note 20, at 139.

23. MINNESOTA SESSION LAWS 1971, ch. 541.

24. Metropolitan Council Act, MINNESOTA SESSION LAWS 1967, ch. 896, § 6, subd. 5.

25. Bosselman & Callies, *supra* note 20 at 1016.

26. Metropolitan Council Act, MINNESOTA SESSION LAWS 1967, ch. 890, § 6, subd. 5.

27. *See* MYRON ORFIELD, METROPOLITICS, A REGIONAL AGENDA COMMUNITY AND STABILITY (Washington, D.C.: Brookings Inst. 1997): "As long as different towns in a metro region have widely disparate tax rates—and thus disparate levels of public services—municipalities will continue to compete among themselves for businesses and residents."; Chris Lester, *Tax Breaks Are Misused,* K.C. STAR, November 24, 1998, at D-8, 9: "For example, Dallas-based Ameriserve recently announced plans to build a $14 million distribution center in Shawnee at the far west of the metropolitan area, removing facilities from Kansas City and Omaha, and sought

property tax abatement and below-market interest rate bonds. The rationale for such public largesse was that drivers will have to book more mileage to the new facility on the edge of civilization. Such standards defy logic."; *see also* Michael J. Smith, *First the Commuter Tax, Now the Water,* N.Y. TIMES, June 5, 1999, at A-25, col. 2: "The suburbs are preparing to give New York City another kick in the teeth to follow up repeal of the commuter tax."

28. *Supra,* note 19, at 1046.

29. Robert Freilich & David Greis, TIMING AND SEQUENCING DEVELOPMENT, CONTROLLING GROWTH, IN FUTURE LAND USE, ENERGY, ENVIRONMENT AND LEGAL CONSTRAINTS 59-106 (Burchell & Listokin, eds., Rutgers Center for Environmental Policy 1975); Robert Freilich, *Development Timing, Moratoria and Controlling Growth,* 1974 Institute on Planning, Zoning and Eminent Domain (Southwestern Legal Foundation) 147 (Matthew Bender, 1974). For a detailed account of this process, *see* ch. I, *supra,* and works cited therein.

30. Schmandt, *Municipal Control of Urban Expansion,* 29 FORDHAM L. REV. 637 (1961).

31. *See* Kelly, *supra* note 6 at § 403: "Probably the most famous phased growth program is that of Ramapo, New York."

32. For a detailed analysis of the Metropolitan Plan, *see* Freilich & Ragsdale, *supra* note 19. *See also* Freilich & Garvin, *supra* note 5, and the takings discussion, *supra* in ch. 3.

33. Twin Cities Metropolitan Council, Discussion Statement on Metropolitan Development Policy, at 10 (Oct. 17, 1973).

34. *Id.* at 10; *see also* discussion of "costs of sprawl" *in* ROBERT W. BURCHELL AND DAVID LUTOKIN, LAND, INFRASTRUCTURES, HOUSING COSTS, AND FISCAL COSTS ASSOCIATED WITH GROWTH ch. 3 (Lincoln Institute, 1995).

35. *See* Hills v. Gautreaux 425 U.S. 284 (1976); Shannon v. U.S. Dep't of HUD, 436 F.2d 809 (3d Cir. 1970); Walker v. Dallas Housing Authority and U.S. Dep't of HUD, 734 F. Supp. 1289 (N.D. Tex. 1989); Metropolitan Housing Dev. Corp. v. Village of Arlington Heights, 616 F.2d (7th Cir. 1980) (all of which required that concentration of minority housing in desegregated areas was a violation of Title VIII of the Fair Housing Act and ordered integrated site selection dispersal in the suburbs).

36. *Supra* note 33 at 4, 8

37. For discussions of the programs, *see* Freilich & Ragsdale, *supra* note 19, at 1085-89.

38. *See* JAMES J. MACKENZIE, ROGER C. DOWER AND DONALD D. T. CHEN, THE GOING RATE: WHAT IT REALLY COSTS TO DRIVE, at VII (World Resources Institute, June 1992); and same authors, ROAD KILL: HOW SOLO DRIVING RUNS DOWN THE ECONOMY (Boston: Conservator Law Foundation, 1994).

39. *See* DAVID BOLLIER, HOW SMART GROWTH CAN STOP SPRAWL (Essential Books, 1998) (discussing the "New Urbanism," including neotraditional planning, traditional neighborhood development (TND), transit-oriented development (TOD)); J. Spivak, *Suburbs As Urban Centers,* K.C. STAR, April 2, 1999, at A-13.

40. Michael S. Bernick & Amy E. Freilich, *Transit Villages and Transit-Based Development: The Rules Are Becoming More Flexible; How Government Can Work with the Private Sector to Make It Happen,* 30 URB. LAW. 1 (1998) [hereinafter Bernick & Freilich]; Freilich, Garvin & White, *supra* note 5.

41. METROPOLITAN COUNCIL, REGIONAL BLUEPRINT, METRO 2040: A GROWTH STRATEGY FOR THE REGION (1996).

42. *See* CALLIES, FREILICH & ROBERTS, *supra* note 2.

43. METROPOLITAN COUNCIL, METROPOLITAN DEVELOPMENT AND INVESTMENT FRAME-

WORK 1 (1988); *see also* Amendments to the Metropolitan Development and Investment Framework: Policies for the Rural Service Area (1991) [hereinafter Rural Service Policies]; Options for Change: Metropolitan Development and Investment Framework, Public Discussion Paper (1993); *see supra* note 41 at 8.

44. *See supra* notes 41, 43.

45. *See* V. GAIL EASLEY, STAYING INSIDE THE LINES: URBAN GROWTH BOUNDARIES, at 16, (American Planning Association Planning Advisory Service Report No. 440, 1992).

46. Rural Service Policies, *supra* note 43 at 7.

47. Rural Service Policies, *supra* note 40, at 7, 8; *see* ch. 3 on LESA programs, which finish the basis for the distinction.

48. *See supra* note 43, at 8.

49. *See id.*

50. *See id.*

51. METROPOLITAN COUNCIL, METRO 2040 UPDATE, A GROWTH STRATEGY FOR THE TWIN CITIES METROPOLITAN AREA 1 (Apr. 1998).

52. *Id.* In 1976 in adopting the first Metropolitan Development Framework, Tier III (the "Urbanizing Tier") contained 530 square miles of land in lieu of 1,600 square miles of sprawl, which would have occurred at existing zoning without the MUSA boundary.

53. *Id., More Compact Development, Activity Centers and Transit Routes* p. 1. (*See also* San Diego and Washington, D.C., transportation corridors.).

54. "Communities at the growing edge of the region will define and *stage* their 2020 MUSA development. . . ." *supra* note 49, at 8.

55. John M. DeGrove, *Regional Successes in the Making and Old Success Falling Apart,* A.L.I.–A.B.A. INST. ON PLAN., REG. & EMINENT DOMAIN II (1997).

56. Freilich & Ragsdale, *supra* note 20, at 1030.

57. MINN. STAT. § 414.01 (1971).

58. *Id.*

59. *Id.,* at § 414.032.

60. Minn. Mun. Comm'n, Forrst Lake Memorandum, at 3 (Dec. 21, 1972).

61. CALLIES , FREILICH & ROBERTS, *supra* note 2, at 631.

62. PROGRESS GUIDE AND GENERAL PLAN, CITY OF SAN DIEGO, CALIFORNIA [hereinafter PROGRESS GUIDE]. *See also* Robert H. Freilich & Martin L. Leitner, *Keep Growth Plan Updated,* S.D. TRIB., Feb. 1984; Jeff Ristine, *City OKs Landmark Growth Measure,* S.D. TRIB., June 23, 1987, at 1; Michael Abrams, *City Growth Cap Draws Heated Debate,* S.D. UNION, June 23, 1987, at 1; Charles W. Ross, *Freilich Is Man in the Middle,* S.D. UNION, Apr. 17, 1977; David M. Kinchen, *Realtors Scan Property Tax-Reform Initiative Hailed at Convention,* L.A. TIMES, Oct. 16, 1977, at 2; Charles W. Ross, *Planner Predicts "White Flight,"* S.D. UNION, Aug. 19, 1977; Gary Shaw, *Freilich Doctors His Growth Plan,* S.D. DAILY TRANSCRIPT, Aug. 27, 1980, at 1A; Bob Dorn, *Builders Hear Debate on Managed Growth,* S.D. EVENING TRIB., Aug. 18, 1977; Frank Stone, *Drop Seen in Growth Rate Here,* S.D. EVENING TRIB., Apr. 14, 1977, at 1; Roger Hedgecock, *Continuing Economic Health Depends on Limiting Sprawl, Saving Environment,* S.D. UNION, Apr. 15, 1977 at B11; *San Diego Urban Plan Explained, question and answer by Robert Freilich,* S.D. UNION, Mar. 21, 1977, at 1; Robert H. Freilich, *Return to Center Can Stop Sprawl,* S.D. UNION, June 9, 1976, at B11.

63. *See* Nico Colavita, *Vale of Tiers,* 63 PLANNING 18 (American Planning Association 1997).

64. Easley, *supra* note 45.

65. Robert H. Freilich & Stephen P. Chinn, *Transportation Corridors, Shaping and Financing Urbanization Through Integration of Eminent Domain, Zoning and Growth Management Techniques,* 55 UMKC L. REV. 153 (1987) [hereinafter Freilich & Chinn]. *See* Colavita, *supra* note 63, at 20. Ironically Colavita reports that I wanted to adopt a five-tier system (including a downtown tier and an environmental overlay tier), but the city opted for a simpler structure. Ultimately half of the future urbanizing area was converted into an open space, environmental tier, incorporating my recommendations fifteen years later. Colavita at 21.

66. Robert H. Freilich & David W. Bushek, *Integrating Land Use and Transportation Planning, The Case of* Palm Beach v. Wright, 18 STATE & LOCAL LAW NEWS, Winter 1995, at 1; Palm Beach County v. Wright, 641 So. 2d 50 (Fla. 1994); Robert H. Freilich & Stephen P. Chinn, *supra* note 65.

67. Robert H. Freilich & Brenda Nichols, *Public Private Partnerships in Joint Development: The Legal and Financial Anatomy of Large Scale Urban Development Projects,* 7 MUN. FIN. J. 5 (1986) [hereinafter Freilich & Nichols]; Richard Babcock, *The City As Entrepreneur: Fiscal Wisdom or Folly?* 29 SANTA CLARA L. REV. 931 (1989); Judith Wegner, *Utopian Visions: Cooperation Without Conflicts in Public-Private Ventures,* 31 SANTA CLARA L. REV. 313 (1991).

68. Bernick & Freilich, *supra* note 40.

69. Note that the State of Florida has adopted such a statewide policy; *see* GOVERNOR'S COMM'N FOR A SUSTAINABLE SOUTH FLORIDA, EASTWARD HO! REVITALIZING SOUTH FLORIDA'S URBAN CORE (DCA 1996).

70. *Supra* note 63.

71. Some commentators criticized the program because instead of seeing the extraordinary growth back into the downtown and existing built-up areas (raising land and housing values) as a reversal of sprawl, they narrowly could see only that "overbuilding became particularly frantic in the urbanized tier," and single-family neighborhoods were being invaded by multifamily buildings (a typical NIMBY response). Colavita, *supra* note 63 at 20, 21. That was exactly what made the city so strong—that a financial incentive was created to return to the built-up areas with office buildings, a marina, residential condominiums, shopping centers (Horton Plaza), convention centers, hotels, restaurants. From 1979 to 1999 when the tier system became effective, growth in the city's built-up areas was five times as great as the period from 1959 to 1979. In fact, Colavita admits in his report:

> By the mid-1980s, the growth management plan seemed to be working fairly well. Infill development was taking place at a brisk pace in the urbanized tier. . . . In the words of a planning department report, by 1984, "San Diego was considered a model for effective growth management."

Supra note 63 at 20.

72. Franklin James, *Evaluation on Local Impact Fees as a Source of Infrastructure,* 11 MUN. FIN. J. 407, 413 (1990): "Impact fees have normative merit as sources of local government revenue, because they allocate the costs of new infrastructure to the beneficiaries of the infrastructure: landowners, developers, and consumers of the new development. The use of impact fees is expanding throughout the nation by state legislation." *See* Martin Leitner and Susan Schoettle, *A Summary of State Impact Fee Enabling Legislation,* 25 URB. LAW. 49 (1993).

73. Impact fees or special benefits assessments were not changed in the urbanized area in order to provide growth incentive. When deficiencies reached levels that required attention, the Council adopted impact fees to the urbanized area. *See supra* note 63, at 21.

74. *Id.* at 27. Specific "transition policies" were adopted that tightly regulated the reclassifi-

cation of land from future urbanizing to a Planned Urbanizing classification. *See* ROBERT H. FREILICH, A TIERED GROWTH MANAGEMENT PROGRAM FOR SAN DIEGO, 2-4 to 2-11 (1976). *See* Oregon policies for transition, Goal 14. Goal 14 sets out seven factors that are to be considered in connection with the establ;ishment or change of a UGB. The first two factors are connected with "need," that is, the amount of land required for urban uses and growth, taking into account vacant bypassed land. The remaining five factors are "locational," that is, what land to use to accommodate urban uses and growth. *See* City of Salem v. Families for Responsible Government, 668 P.2d 395 (Or. App. 1983); Baker v. Marion County, 852 F.2d 254, 255 (Or. App. 1993). The statute now authorizes density increases with the UGB to meet housing needs as an alternative to boundary expansion. OR. REV. STAT. § 197.296(4)(b).

75. *Id.* Subsequently, this area was permanently preserved as rural and open space in the Charter and Comprehensive Plan through Proposition "A" adopted by initiative, which legally protected the future urbanizing area from premature conversion, *supra* note 63 at 20, 21, where the author states that "the plan that came out of the process . . . [had] redeeming features [in] that almost half of the future urbanizing area was to remain open space, thus becoming the first step toward resurrecting Freilich's proposal for a citywide environmental tier."

76. PROGRESS GUIDE, *supra* note 62, at 34.

77. Robert H. Freilich, *supra* note 73. The five-tiered system was ultimately reduced by political decision to the three tiers: urbanized, urbanizing, and future urbanizing; *see also* DOUGLAS R. PORTER, PROFILES IN GROWTH MANAGEMENT 81–87 (Urban Land Institute 1996).

78. Robert H. Freilich & S. Mark White, *Transportation Congestion and Growth Management: Comprehensive Approaches to Resolving America's Major Quality of Life Crisis*, 24 LOY. L.A. L. REV. 931 (1991).

79. The entire San Diego facility benefit assessment system was upheld by the California Court of Appeals, in J.W. Jones Companies v. City of San Diego, 157 Cal. App. 3d 745, 203 Cal. Rptr. 580 (Ct. App. 1984).

80. J.W. Jones Companies v. City of San Diego, 157 Cal. App. 3d 745, 747, 203 Cal. Rptr. 580, 582 (1984), in which the Court reversed the lower court finding that the FBAs were special taxes and not appropriate benefit assessemnts. Nevertheless, both the lower court and the appeal court agreed that the FBA was a new financing device developed by San Diego to pay for public improvements which in the past had been financed out of the general fund. 157 Cal. App. 3d at 582.

81. The court of appeal determined that the FBA is a valid exercise of the city's [assessment] power to impose changes upon property within a designated area to pay for public facilities serving the needs of those who will reside in that area. 157 Cal. App. 3d at 748.

82. CAL. CONST., art. XIII A, § 4 (Prop. 13). The court of appeal found that there was specific statutory and home rule authority for the FBAs under the Improvement Acts of 1911 and 1913 and home rule power conferred by CAL. CONST., art. XI, § 5, *City Council v. South*, 146 Cal. App. 3d, 320 (1983).

83. This the court found had a reasonable basis. "The aggregation of all the improvements in the FBA and the spread of their costs to the undeveloped parcels in the area of benefit was proper." 157 Cal. App. 3d at 757. The court found that the public facilities were needed to accommodate the population increase and "while improved property may derive incidental benefit from the new facilities we perceive no discriminatory classification," citing *Associated Home Builders, Inc. v. City of Walnut Creek*, 4 Cal. 3d 633, 639–40, 484 P.2d 606 (1971).

84. *See* Easley, *supra* note 45 at 5 (tier and UGB systems promote efficient and economical

provision of services); Gerritt Knapp, *The Price Effects of Urban Growth Boundaries,* 61 LAND ECON. 26 (1985); Arthur C. Nelson, *Using Land Markets to Evaluate Urban Containment Progress,* 52 J. AM. PLAN. ASS'N 156 (1986).

85. 157 Cal. App. 3d at 589. "The North University City FBA encompasses some 25 separate improvements to be erected between 1981 and 1989. Each of these elements of the public facilities are integral to the *planned* development of the area of benefit . . . and [the lower court wrongly] declined to permit the City to aggregate all of the projected public facilities in the whole area of benefit in the belief [that] each of the 25 projects were to be viewed in isolation one from the other." 157 Cal. App. 3d at 587.

86. 157 Cal. App. 3d at 587.

87. Freilich & Chinn, *supra* note 65, at 162 n.52.

88. Dedications, exactions, and impact fees are confined to changes related to facilities the need for which is generated by the new growth. They may not be used to correct existing deficiencies. Marblehead v. City of San Clemente, 277 Cal. Rptr. 550 (Cal. App. 1991); thus the proper use of impact fee financing is to avoid the creation of new deficiencies.

89. *See* City of San Diego, Emergency Congestion Management and Development Phasing Ordinance of 1990 § 5(A) (draft of July 5, 1990) (unpublished proposal on file at Loyola of Los Angeles Law Review); *see* note 62 *supra.* The ordinance also promoted the use of transportation corridors and transit-oriented development. *See* Marla G. Boarnet & Nicholas S. Cowpin, *Transit-Oriented Development in San Diego County: The Incremental Implementation of a Planning Ideal,* 65 J. A.P.A. 80 (1999).

90. Transit-based residential developments have been built at two of the La Mesa stations as well as at 47th Street and Barrio Logan station. The transit agency has been active in planning a transit village at Rio Vista West on the Mission Valley Line and conversion of a parking lot at the Moreno Boulevard station into transit-based housing. Bernick & Freilich, *supra* note 40 at 5.

91. B. Drummond Ayres, Jr., *San Diego Backs "Model" Nature-Habitat Plan,* N.Y. TIMES, Mar. 20, 1997, at A10.

92. Peter Jensen, *San Diego's Vision Quest,* PLANNING, March 1997, at 5.

93. City of Del Mar v. City of San Diego, 133 Cal. App. 3d 401, 183 Cal. Rptr. 898 (1982).

94. ROBERT H. FREILICH & MARTIN L. LEITNER, 1980 COMPREHENSIVE PLAN, GROWTH PLANNING SYSTEM (adopted Oct. 30, 1980) by the Lexington-Fayette Urban County Planning Commission [hereinafter Freilich & Leitner].

95. ROBERT H. FREILICH, STATUTORY AUTHORITY FOR A GROWTH PLANNING SYSTEM IN LEXINGTON-FAYETTE COUNTY, KENTUCKY, (Feb. 1977).

96. The above description is taken from the findings of fact of *Provincial Development Co. v. Webb,* No. 7973 (Fayette Cir. Ct. Ky. 1960), which upheld the system and denied a request for a rezoning to urban intensity (Residence-1 or Suburban-1 from Agriculture-1). The court found that even though the line ran through the farm, more than half of the farm was outside the line.

97. Provincial Development Co. v. Webb, citing Shemwell v. Speck, 265 S.W.2d 468, 470 (Ky. 1954): "It must be remembered that the purpose of zoning is not to protect the value of the property of particular individuals, but rather to promote the welfare of the community as a whole."

98. Provincial Development Co. v. Webb, citing Sunolow v. City of Philadelphia Zoning Board of Adjustment, 137 A.2d 251 (Pa. 1958).

99. Provincial Development Co. v. Webb, No. 7973 (Fayette Cir. Ct. Ky. 1960).

100. *See* ch. 6, *infra.*

101. *See* KY. REV. STAT. 67A.010 (1973) ("in order to facilitate the operation of local government, to prevent duplication of services, and to promote efficient and economical management of the affairs of local government").

102. KY. REV. STAT. 67A.150 (1973). Lexington-Fayette County, in carrying out this statutory authority, actually created full urban service districts and partial urban service districts depending on the kind, type, level, and character of the services provided. The delineation of the districts was consistent with the urban and rural service areas shown in the Comprehensive Plan. *See* FREILICH & LEITNER, *supra* note 94. The entire statutory scheme for urban and rural taxing districts was upheld against a charge of violation of the uniformity of taxation clause of the state constitution. *Holsclow v. Stephens,* 507 S.W.2d 462 (Ky. 1973). For a discussion of how excise taxes for improvements generated by new development and how they can differentiate between built-up and newly developing areas, see my facility benefit assessment system for San Diego, approved in *J. W. Jones Company v. City of San Diego,* 203 Cal. Rptr. 580, 587 (1984); David Bushek, *Infrastructure Financing and the Excise Tax Alternative,* J. PROBATE & PROP. L. (ABA, Jan./Feb. 1999); Terry Morgan & Martin Leitner, *Financing Public Facilities with Development Excise Taxes,* 11 ZONING AND PLANNING L. REP. 17–22 (Mar. 1988). A similar urban/rural service area differential taxation scheme was upheld for the Nashville-Davidson County consolidation. *Frazer v. Carr,* 360 S.W.2d 449 (Tenn. 1962). For a detailed discussion of using a single land tax without tax on structures in order to encourage development on closer infill lots (the Henry George concept), *see* Thomas A. Gihring, *Incentive Property Taxation: A Potential Tool for Urban Growth Management,* 65 J. A.P.A. 62, 63 (1999). "A two-rate tax system's expected outcomes can be summarized as follows: (1) discourage urban sprawl; (2) encourage infill development. . . ." *Id.* at 64.

103. The Urban Services Area expanded from its base of 67 square miles to 74.4 square miles in a 1973 update. *See supra* note 95.

104. Al Marsh, *Lexington to Receive Proposed Growth Goals,* LEXINGTON HERALD, Jan. 26, 1978 (reporting that Robert H. Freilich pointed out shortcomings in the 1973 growth management methods including the weaknesses of the urban service areas where the concept failed to address the question of what happens inside the urban service area boundary, and did not address the costs of development and whether that development would be timed in sequence with the availability of public facilities, such as streets, sewers, and schools and parks); *see also* Rich Dozier, Jr., *Council Hires Expert to Guide Growth Plan,* LEXINGTON HERALD, May 20, 1977 ("Dr. Freilich is one of a handful of experts in this country who has an intimate familiarity with the frontiers of the law in this area"); Tom Carter, *Lexington Is "Dazzling" to New Growth Manager Freilich,* LEXINGTON HERALD, May 22, 1977; Pam Sprague, *Urban Council Hires Controversial Planner,* LEXINGTON LEADER, May 20, 1977, at 1.

105. Robert S. Joice, Planning at the Edge of Lexington: Urban Service Area Boundary at 40 Years of Age, Planning and Zoning for Community Land-Use Management paper, University of Wisconsin, (May 4-6, 1998).

106. Freilich & Leitner, *supra* note 94, at 28–29.

107. *Id.* n.128.

108. *Id.* at 35.

109. *Id.* at 38.

110. *Supra* note 95.

111. Land Lines, January 1999.

112. Land Lines, January 1999.

113. METRO WASHINGTON COUNCIL OF GOVERNMENTS, YEAR 2000 PLAN: THE RADIAL CORRIDOR, THE CHANGING REGION: A COMPARISON OF PLANS AND POLICIES WITH DEVELOPMENT TRENDS (1969).

114. *See* Pietila Antero, *Council Resolves to Act on County Growth Curbs*, THE BALTIMORE SUN (Feb. 2, 1977) (a controversial interim development control bill I advocated was a channel to Baltimore County's future residential building activities to areas where sufficient water, sewer, police, and fire services were available. "This interim bill [would] slow the county's development until sufficient studies [could] be prepared for drafting a permanent adequate-facilities law for the county"); *see also* Elizabeth A. Garvin & Martin L. Leitner, *Drafting Interior Development Ordinances,* __ LAND USE LAW AND ZONING DIGEST (June 1996).

115. BALTIMORE COUNTY GROWTH MANAGEMENT PROGRAM 1979–1990, Freilich & Leitner, coprincipal consultant (with Wallace Roberts & Todd and Hamer, Siler & George).

116. CALLIES, FREILICH & ROBERTS, *supra* note 2, at 604.

117. Freilich & White, *supra* note 7; *see also* Freilich & White, *supra* note 77.

118. Agricultural land preservation as accomplished through TDRs in Montgomery County was approved by the courts. Dufour v. Montgomery County Council (Cir. Ct. No. 56964, 1983); *see also* Gardner v. New Jersey Pinelands Comm'n, 593 A.2d 251 (N.J. 1991) (approving agricultural TDRs in New Jersey).

119. Montgomery County, Maryland, Code ch. 50, § 50-35(k) (1973).

120. An earlier system of impact fees was rejected by the courts as lacking statutory authority, but the excise tax was upheld. *Eastern Diversified Properties v. Montgomery County*, 570 A.2d 850 (Md. App. 1990). Excise taxes are far superior to impact fees since no nexus is required. Morgan & Leitner, *Financing Public Facilities with Development Excise Taxes: An Alternative to Exaction and Impact Fees*, 11 ZONING & PLANNING L. REP. 17-22 (March 1988); *Bloom v. City of Fort Collins*, 784 P.2d 304 (Colo. 1989) (identifies five methods of raising funds for infrastructure finance: utility fees, excise tax, special assessment, impact fees, and ad valorem taxation).

121. *See* S. MARK WHITE, ADEQUATE PUBLIC FACILITIES ORDINANCES AND TRANSPORTATION MANAGEMENT (American Planning Association Planning Advisory Service Report No. 465).

122. Schneider v. Montgomery County, 328 Md. 239, 614 A.2d 84 (1991).

123. For a complete description, *see* Freilich & Nichols, *supra* note 67: "Cities and counties are joining with private developers in a variety of endeavors such as the construction of hotels, sports stadium complexes, convention centers, private hospitals, regional business headquarters, regional retail shopping centers, power plants and mixed use complexes around mass transit stations."

124. California's Public Utilities Code § 30600 provides for the Metropolitan Transit Authority: "That property includes . . . property necessary . . . for joint development. . . . The board may *lease, jointly develop* . . . if it is for the best interests of the district to do so." (Emphasis added.)

125. Bernick & Freilich, *supra* note 41.

126. Freilich & Chinn, *supra* note 59 (describing how joint development meets public purpose, condemnation, authority, value capture, excess land acquisition, tax increment financing bonding, constitutional public credit clauses, underwriting of land and infrastructure costs and the use of fee-simple with easements or leasehold arrangements and describing the Florida legislation).

127. *See* Anatolji Kushnir & Michael Simmons, *The Department of Veterans Affairs's Public-Private Venture Asset Programs,* 30 URB. LAW. 361 (1998). Section 3(a)(1)(D) of the Federal Transit Act, 49 U.S.C. § 5309(a)(5) (authorizes the Secretary of Transportation to make grants and loans for transportation projects including through economic development by sale or lease).

128. 1990 General Plan, Howard County, Maryland, at 15.

129. *Id.* at 229.

130. *Id.* at 87.

131. *Id.* at 98.

132. *Id.* at 101.

133. *See* Chapter VII, III B and D for a description of this very successful strategy.

134. Freilich & Garvin, *supra* note 5.

135. Larry G. Smith, *Planning for Growth, Washington Style, in* STATE & REGIONAL COMPREHENSIVE PLANNING: IMPLEMENTING NEW METHODS FOR GROWTH MANAGEMENT 138 (Buchsbaum & Smith eds., 1993); John M. DeGrove & Deborah A. Miness, THE NEW FRONTIER FOR LAND POLICY: PLANNING & GROWTH MANAGEMENT IN THE STATES 121 (1992).

136. *See* Act approved Apr. 24, 1990, ch. 17, 1990 Wash. Legis. Serv. 1375 (West). The Washington "Urban Growth Areas" legislation, WASH. REV. CODE § 36.70A, requires each county adopting a comprehensive plan shall designate an urban growth area or areas within which urban growth shall be encouraged and outside of which growth can occur only if it is not urban in nature. Each city in the County must be included in an urban growth area. An urban growth area may also include territory outside of existing city boundaries only if such territory is already characterized by urban growth or is adjacent to territory already characterized by urban growth. Urban growth should be located first in areas already characterized by urban growth that have existing public facility and service capacities to serve such development, and second in areas already characterized by urban growth that will be served by a combination of both existing public facilities and services and any additional needed public facilities and services that are provided by either public or private sources. PETER BUCHSBAUM & LARRY SMITH, STATE AND REGIONAL COMPREHENSIVE PLANNING: IMPLEMENTING NEW MODELS FOR GROWTH MANAGEMENT (A.B.A. 1993).

137. 1990 Wash. Laws 1972, 1st Ex. Sess., ch. 17 (amended by 1991 Wash. Laws 2903, 1st Sp. Sess., ch. 32, and 1992 Wash. Laws 1050, ch. 227) (codified at WASH. REV. CODE ch. 36.70A (1992), WASH. REV. CODE ch. 47.80 (1992), and WASH. REV. CODE ch. 82.02 (1992)) *cited in* Freilich & Garvin, *supra* note 5, at 955.

138. 1991 Wash. Laws 2903, 1st Sp. Sess., ch. 32.

139. *Id* at § 36.70A.040 (1991 & Supp. 1996) (describing two categories of counties that are mandated to adopt comprehensive land use plans and development regulations and are also required to adopt countywide planning policies. Category 1 includes counties with a population of 50,000 or more and characterized by population increase of more than 10 percent in the prior ten years. All cities located within these counties must adopt comprehensive plans. Category 2 includes counties that experienced population increases of more than 20 percent in the prior ten years. All cities located within these counties must adopt comprehensive plans).

140. *Id.* at § 36.70A.070 (mandating elements including land use, housing, capital facilities, and transportation. County plans must also contain a rural element).

141. *Id.* at § 36.70A.060(2); Smith, *supra* note 135, at 145.

142. WASH. REV. STAT. §§ 36.70A.070, 36.70A.100, 36.77.010, 36.81.121, 35.58.279 (other consistency requirements are, state agency actions that relate to public facilities must be

consistent with city and county plans and the transportation element in plans must be consistent with the land use element and consistent with the six-year transportation plans of neighboring cities, counties, and multicounty areas).

143. Freilich & Garvin, *supra* note 5, at 955.

144. *Id.* at § 36.70A.110; Smith, *supra* note 135, at 124.

145. *See* Richard L. Settle & Charles G. Gavigan, *The Growth Management Revolution in Washington: Past, Present and Future,* 15 U. Puget Sound L. Rev. 869 (Spring 1993); and Freilich & Garvin, *supra* note 5.

146. *See* A Legacy of Excellence for the Washington Region, Task Force Report on Growth and Transportation (June 1991).

147. *See* James A. Kushner, *Urban Transportation Planning,* 4 Urb. L. & Pol'y 161, 173 (1981); *see generally* Freilich & Garvin, *supra* note 5.

148. *See* Freilich & Chinn, *supra* note 65, at 170–71 (1987); *see also* Montgomery County v. Woodward & Lothrop, Inc., 376 A.2d 483, 488 (Md. 1977), *cert. denied sub nom. F*unger v. Montgomery County, 434 U.S. 1067 (1978).

149. Freilich & Garvin, *supra* note 5, at 962.

150. See *supra* note 142, at § 36.70A.070(6).

151. *Id.* at § 36.70A.(6)(b)(ii).

152. Freilich & Garvin, *supra* note 5, at 963.

153. Transportation facilities must be available within six years of development. Wash. Rev. Code § 36.70A.070(6)(e)(1991).

154. Michael J. Major, *Containing Growth in the Pacific Northwest,* Urb. Land 17 (Mar. 1994).

155. Robert H. Freilich & S. Mark White, Regional General Welfare and Intergovernmental Planning 27 (Jan. 15, 1998).

156. The Puget Sound Regional Council, Vision 2020, Growth and Transportation Strategy for the Central Puget Sound Region, i, 2, 3, (1990 & 1993 amendment); [hereinafter Vision 2020] & Freilich & White, *supra* note 155.

157. Vision 2020, *supra* note 156.

158. Remarks by John M. DeGrove, *Regional Successes in the Making and Old Success Falling Apart,* ALI-ABA Course of Study Materials, Land Institute: Planning, Regulation, Litigation, Eminent Domain and Compensation, Aug. 14–16, 1997 (Vol. II).

159. "Multi-county planning policies shall be adopted by two or more counties, each with a population of four hundred fifty thousand or more, with contiguous urban areas and may be adopted by other counties, according to the process established under this section or other processes agreed to among the counties and cities within the affected counties through the multi-county region." Wash. Rev. Code Ann. § 36.70A.210(7) (West 1991 & Supp. 1993) *cited in* Freilich & White, *supra* note 155, at 28.

160. The four counties in the region include King, Kitsap, Pierce, and Snohomish counties; Freilich & White, *supra* note 155, at 27.

161. Vision 2020 was adopted in 1990. It combined the role of two previous plans, the 1982 Regional Transportation Plan and the 1979 Regional Development Plan, and extended the planning time frame to a thirty-year period. *See supra* note 156.

162. The GMA requires policies for:

1. designation of urban growth areas;
2. contiguous and orderly development and urban services;

3. transportation facilities & strategies;

4. siting regional capital facilities;

5. interjurisdictional planning;

6. economic development; and

7. affordable housing.

WASH. REV. CODE ANN. § 36.70A.210 (3) (West 1991 & Supp. 1993) (the fiscal impact analysis is addressed by countywide planning efforts within the region; another topic identified as an important issue, and thus planned for regionally, is open space linkages, resource protection, and critical areas).

163. VISION 2020, *supra* note 156, at i.

164. *Id.* at 10.

165. *Id.* at 20 (the six central places classifications are: a regional center, metropolitan centers, subregional centers, activity clusters, pedestrian pockets, and small towns).

166. *Id.*

167. *Id.* at 38.

168. *Id.* at 20. Development was divided into the following land use categories: major urban centers, activity centers, employment areas, and residential neighborhoods. Major Urban Centers are areas that contain high concentrations of housing and employment, with direct service by high-capacity transit, and a wide range of other land uses such as retail, recreational, public facilities, parks, and open space. Major Urban Centers are a focus of regional activity and provide services to the general region. Activity Centers are locations that contain many of the same land uses as Urban Centers but tend to be more automobile-oriented because of their physical layout. Low Density/Intensity Employment Areas include office parks, industrial areas, and manufacturing locations that are developed at relatively low densities. These areas are typically automobile-oriented, single-use areas and do not generate a high degree of transit use. Residential Neighborhoods generally include single family residences with varying degrees of multifamily, depending on location. Commercial services can range from numerous and convenient to nonexistent.

169. Several of the planned transportation improvements include: a regional rapid transit system, high-occupancy vehicle lanes for ride-sharing and buses, passenger ferry service improvements, local transit improvements, freeway and arterial improvements, highway efficiency improvements, auto ferry capacity improvements, and employer-based demand management. VISION 2020, *supra* note 156, at 32–34.

170. 23 U.S.C. 134 and 49 U.S.C. 1607 (among other responsibilities, the MPO must prepare and adopt a multimodal regional transportation plan and a six-year transportation improvement program).

171. The GMA allows cities and counties to form RTPOs, which may perform the mandatory transportation planning functions.

172. WASH. REV. CODE ANN. § 47.80.

173. VISION 2020, *supra* note 156, at 25.

174. VISION 2020, *supra* note 156, at 38.

175. *Id.* The criteria will address "employment targets and densities for centers and non-centers, housing densities, ratio of jobs to housing, type and level of transportation service, timing of transportation investments, transit compatible urban design, regional form, incentives for implementing the centers concept, regional parking pricing and maximum and minimum parking requirements."

176. *Id.* at 36.

177. The Puget Sound Regional Council conducts review responsibilities that are mandated by federal and state legislation, regional plans, and interlocal agreements. Federal statutes requiring regional review for conformance or consistency requirements include: the Federal Clean Air Act, the Americans with Disabilities Act, the High Capacity Transportation Systems Act, and the Surface Transportation Efficiency Act. State requirements for regional review are found in the Growth Management Act and the Washington Administrative Code. Regional review is also required by the Interlocal Agreement for Regional Planning of the Central Puget Sound Area—VII.A.4 and VII.A.5. For a thorough analysis of the Puget Sound Regional Council's responsibilities for coordination of plans, consistency review and certification, see the Issue Paper developed by the Council in 1994, *infra* note 178.

178. THE PUGET SOUND REGIONAL COUNCIL, ISSUE PAPER: COORDINATION OF PLANS, CONSISTENCY REVIEW, AND CERTIFICATION (March 3, 1994) (this paper will be updated to include 1994 amendments to the Growth Management Act).

179. THE PUGET SOUND REGIONAL COUNCIL, ISSUE PAPER: COORDINATION OF PLANS, CONSISTENCY REVIEW, AND CERTIFICATION 4–11 (March 10, 1994) (the petition may be filed by the PSRC Executive Board, the countywide policy body, a local jurisdiction, a state agency, or any other individual or organization with standing according to the Growth Management Act).

180. *Id.* at 4–13.

181. PIERCE COUNTY COUNCIL, PIERCE COUNTY COMPREHENSIVE PLAN: EXECUTIVE'S PROPOSAL, I-12 (Draft Dec. 1993).

182. *Id.* at II-35.

183. *Id.* at II-34.

184. *Id.* at I-13.

185. The county's last planning efforts were in 1962. That plan had become outdated, and county officials wanted a comprehensive plan that was up to date and that could guide growth.

186. Telephone interview with the long-range planner for the Department of Planning and Land Services, Pierce County, Washington, July 1, 1994.

187. FREILICH, LEITNER & CARLISLE, COUNTY-WIDE PLANNING POLICIES FOR PIERCE COUNTY, WASHINGTON (June 30, 1992).

188. *Supra* note 181, at I-3.

189. The land use element is divided into 15 subsections, which include: 1) urban growth area, 2) urban reserve area, 3) centers and corridors, 4) agriculture, 5) forest lands, 6) mining, 7) residential, 8) master planned communities, 9) commercial, 10) industrial, 11) recreation, 12) open space, 13) public facilities, 14) utilities, 15) nonconforming use, and 15) storm water. *See supra* note 181, at I-18.

190. The utilities elements is divided into seven subsections, which include: 1) general policies, 2) electricity, 3) natural gas, 4) telecommunications & cable TV, 5) sewer and wastewater, 6) solid waste, and 7) domestic water systems. *Id.*

191. *Id.* at I-15.

192. The state goals are taken from RCW 36.70A.020, the state mandates are from RCW 36.70A.020 and WAC 365- 195, the county mandates are directives from the County-Wide Planning Policies, the Multi-County Policies of VISION 2020, the Nisqually River Management Plan, and the Joint Land Use Study. *Id.* at I-16.

193. *Id.* at II-1.

194. *Id.* at II-3.

195. Urban growth areas include incorporated areas, unincorporated areas with moderate to intensive development, and lands appropriate for urban growth. "Urban special areas are areas in an UGA which currently have low levels of development. . . . The urban reserve is an area of land that is in transition from rural to urban. . . . Rural areas include lands for agriculture, forest, rural living and employment." *Id.* at II-3, -4.

196. Pursuant to the agreement, a steering committee, consisting of one elected official from the County and one elected official from each of the municipalities was created. The Steering Committee was responsible for drafting the policies. A Growth Management Coordinating Committee was also created to give technical/staff support to the Steering Committee. The Steering Committee then hired the national and regional consulting firms of Freilich, Leitner & Carlisle and Northwest Strategies.

197. FREILICH, LEITNER & CARLISLE, COUNTY-WIDE PLANNING POLICIES FOR PIERCE COUNTY, WASHINGTON at 47 (June 30, 1992)

198. *Id.*, FREILICH, LEITNER & CARLISLE, COUNTY-WIDE PLANNING POLICIES (June 30, 1992).

199. For a complete analysis of these economic development incentives, *see* R. Freilich, E. Garvin, and S.W. White, *Economic Development and Public Transit: Making the Most of the Washington Growth Management Act,* 16 UNIV. OF PUGET SOUND LAW REV. 949, 957 1993).

200. *See* Freilich, Garvin & White, *supra* note 199 at 1091; in November of 1997, the voters passed Proposition 1, which mandates that creation of a public development authority charged with building a forty-mile monorail and light rail system utilizing public-private funds from developers at station stop opportunities. GRANT COGSWELL, ATLANTIC COAST, at 16 (June 1998) (voters passed Proposition 1, building a forty-mile monorail with public-private funds).

201. FREILICH & LEITNER, P.C., A PROPOSED AGRICULTURAL LANDS PRESERVATION STRATEGY FOR KING COUNTY, WASHINGTON, KING COUNTY, WASHINGTON PLANNING DIVISION (1980). The County ultimately used $100 million in bonds to purchase development rights in the agriculturally rich river valleys.

202. Larry G. Smith, *Planning for Growth, Washington Style, in* STATE & REGIONAL COMPREHENSIVE PLANNING: IMPLEMENTING NEW METHODS FOR GROWTH MANAGEMENT 153 (Buchsbaum & Smith eds., 1993).

203. *See generally* Robert E. Lang & Steven P. Hornburg, *Planning Portland Style: Pitfalls and Possibilities,* 8 HOUSING POL'Y DEBATE 1 (1997); Buchsbaum & Smith, *Oregon Blazes a Trail,* EDWARD J. SULLIVAN 51 (1993). Oregon's statutory program was initiated in the same year that the Ramapo Plan was adopted. Oregon Laws ch. 324, 1969.

204. *See* Sam H. Verhovels, *Fighting Sprawl, Oregon County Makes Deal with Intel to Limit Job Growth,* N.Y. TIMES, June 9, 1999, at A-1.

205. As a general rule, a local government is not permitted to establish an urban growth boundary containing more land than the locality "needs" for future growth. *City of Salem v. Families for Responsible Government,* 668 P.2d 395, 398–99 (Or. Ct. App. 1983).

206. Buchsbaum & Smith, *supra* note 203, at 79. Original jurisdiction over contested land use matters rests with a separate Land Use Board of Appeals (LUBA) with appeals taken directly to the state appellate courts. *See Younger v. City of Portland,* 752 A.2d 262 (Or. 1988) for scope of LUBA's review powers.

207. *See generally* Carl Abbott, *The Portland Region: Where City and Suburbs Talk to Each*

Other—and Often Agree, 8 HOUSING POL'Y DEBATE 11 (1997); *see also* Buchsbaum & Smith, *supra* note 203, at 79.

208. FREILICH & WHITE, *supra* note 155, at 8.

209. METRO HOME RULE CHARTER COMMITTEE, HISTORICAL DEVELOPMENT OF THE MET-ROPOLITAN SERVICE DISTRICT, 8 (Portland, May 1991) *cited in* FREILICH & WHITE, *supra* note 155, at 8.

210. REGIONAL FRAMEWORK PLAN—PORTLAND, OREGON, at 2 (Dec. 11, 1997).

211. *Id.* at 5 (Dec. 11, 1997) (Metro's partners in the region are twenty-four cities, three counties, and more than 130 special service districts, the State of Oregon, Tri-Met, the Port of Portland, and the Portland Area Boundary Commission). For an excellent summary of Metro, *see* DOUGLAS R. PORTER, MANAGING GROWTH IN AMERICA'S COMMUNITIES, 222–29 (1997).

212. OR. REV. STAT. § 268.015; *see also* FREILICH & WHITE, *supra* note 155.

213. *Supra* note 210; for an interesting analysis that the traditional "Dillon's Rule," which limits local government authority to expressed state legislation and which has been overturned as unconstitutional by the U.S. Supreme Court, in *Romer v. Evans,* 517 U.S. 620 (1996), *see* Lawrence Rosenthal, Romer v. Evans *as the Transformation of Local Government Law,* 31 URB. LAW. 257, 263 (1999).

214. FREILICH & WHITE, *supra* note 155, at 8.

215. FREILICH & WHITE, *supra* note 155; OR. REV. STAT. § 268.390.

216. The Regional Framework Plan includes contents from the Future Vision, Regional Urban Growth Goals and Objectives, the 2040 Growth Concept, and the Urban Growth Management Functional Plan.

217. FREILICH & WHITE, *supra* note 155.

218. Local governments are required to establish and implement local plans including twenty-year growth boundaries.

219. Remarks by John M. DeGrove, *Visions and Visioning: What's It All About? And Is It Important? Can You Get Where You Want To Go Without It?,* ALI-ABA COURSE OF STUDY MATE-RIALS, LAND INSTITUTE: PLANNING, REGULATION, LITIGATION, EMINENT DOMAIN AND COM-PENSATION, Aug. 14–16, 1997 (Vol. II) (the current UGB area is approximately 233,000 acres). *See generally* Arthur C. Nelson, *Blazing New Planning Trails in Oregon,* URB. LAND (Aug. 1990).

220. For contrary views, *see* Niemi, *Oregon's Land Use Program and Individual Development: How Does the Program Affect Oregon's Economy?* 14 ENVT'L L.. 707 (1984); Wendi Kellington, *Oregon's Land Use Program Comes of Age: The Next 25 Years,* 50 LAND USE L. AND ZONING DIG. 3 (No. 10, Oct. 1998).

221. *See* Duncan, *Agriculture as a Resource: Statewide Land Use Programs for the Preservation of Farmlands,* 14 ECOL. L.Q. 401, 402 (1987); Baker v. Marion County 852 P.2d 255 (Or. App. 1993).

222. Gordon Oliver and R. Gregory Nokes, *Land Use Law Showing Its Age,* THE SUNDAY OREGONIAN, May 31, 1998, at B-1.

223. *See* Jurgenson v. County Court, Union County, 600 P.2d 1241 (Or. 1979) (subdivision approval); Still v. Board of Commissioners, Marion County, 600 P.2d 733 (Or. App. 1979) (subdivision approval); and Columbia Hills Development Co. v. LCDO, 624 P.2d 157 (Or. App. 1984) (building permit).

224. *See* PORTER, *supra* note 211, at 227–28; *see generally* Phillip Langdon, *How Portland Does It,* URB. DESIGN (Nov. 1992); R. Gregory Nokes & Gordon Oliver, *Urban Growth Boundary Unites Future of 24 Cities,* THE SUNDAY OREGONIAN, May 31, 1998, at B-4.

Smart Growth in Use in City and County Areas

Smart Growth in Use in City and County Areas

County and city governments must cooperate and coordinate their efforts in controlling urban sprawl.[1] Interlocal agreements between cities and counties have become important in securing direction over development within the Urbanizing Tier. The necessity for the city and county to cooperate lies in the city's inability to control growth outside its boundaries, without the county's efforts to time and sequence growth in the region outside the city. While counties can easily implement standards without the intervention of the city, enforcing such standards aids the central city in attracting needed development through incentives. Some states are promoting joint city-county planning through intergovernmental agreements in setting transportation, land use, and air quality controls.[2]

Arizona has passed legislation that promotes cooperative planning between cities and counties for the purpose of adopting and implementing joint development plans.[3] I developed the legislation and was able to assist Mohave County, Arizona, to update its comprehensive plan by entering into intergovernmental agreements with the cities located in the county.[4] This process involves city/county identification and agreements on areas to be included in the joint planning process, a study of the development and facility needs in the joint planning areas outside of the cities, and further agreements regarding orderly annexation for cities, common development standards in each area, and provisions for financing of public facilities to support development in each area.[5]

Similarly, the Puget Sound Region is requiring mandatory local government, county, and regional "planning policies" to be developed as part of a comprehensive growth management planning act.[6] The cities of Reno and Sparks and Washoe County, Nevada; Park City and Summit County, Utah; Palm Beach County and Monroe County, Florida; the Boulder regional area and Grand Junction and Mesa County, Colorado; Simi Valley and Ventura County as well as Riverside, California; and Howard County, Maryland, are other examples of areas that have implemented cooperative growth management strategies.

Washoe-Reno County, Nevada: Use of the "Alternatives" Process to Develop Ramapo "Tiered" Systems

The process for developing the Truckee Meadows-Washoe County Regional Plan began in early 1989, with the passage of legislation by the Nevada State legislature requiring mandated compliance with Master and Area Plans by Cities and the County.[7] The Regional Planning Commission hired me to develop its plan to escape the imminent threat of the state developing its own plan for the area under the mandatory legislation. The Regional Plan is a first for the area in which a unifying cooperative framework was implemented for the development policies of the cities of Reno and Sparks and Washoe County.

These mandatory state compliances proved necessary for a region where substantial growth was expected. The Regional Plan was designed to accommodate anticipated population and employment needs up to the year 2007 in which it would minimize the effects of growth on the Region's environment and quality of life. The Commission found that, for the continuing growth of the area to be coordinated, there must be agreement among various public and private entities about future development. A shared vision would allow each agency the ability to make decisions that could support and further the creation of the regional form. Without a shared vision, each agency could take on a different approach, resulting in overdevelopment and inefficient public infrastructure. The key component to the regional planning process was the agreement on a regional urban form that would direct action by all state, local, and other affected entities.

Figure 5.1
Washoe County Alternatives

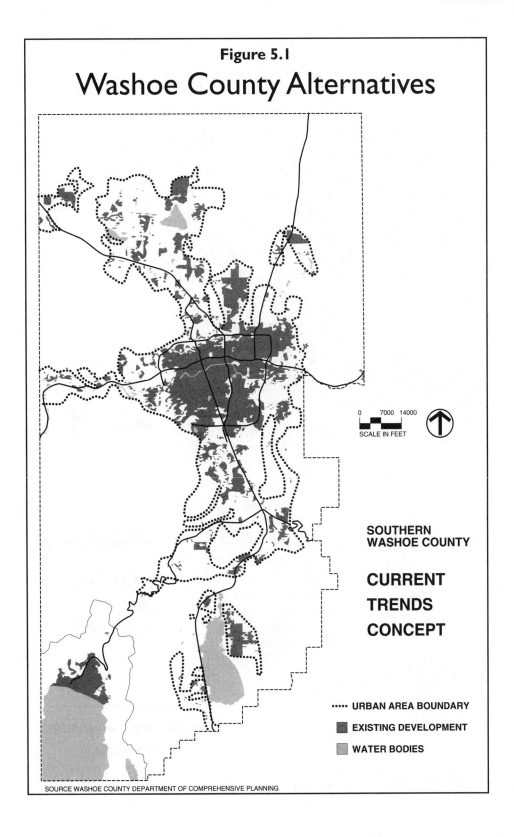

SOUTHERN
WASHOE COUNTY

CURRENT

TRENDS

CONCEPT

0   7000   14000
SCALE IN FEET

•••••• URBAN AREA BOUNDARY

■ EXISTING DEVELOPMENT

▨ WATER BODIES

SOURCE WASHOE COUNTY DEPARTMENT OF COMPREHENSIVE PLANNING

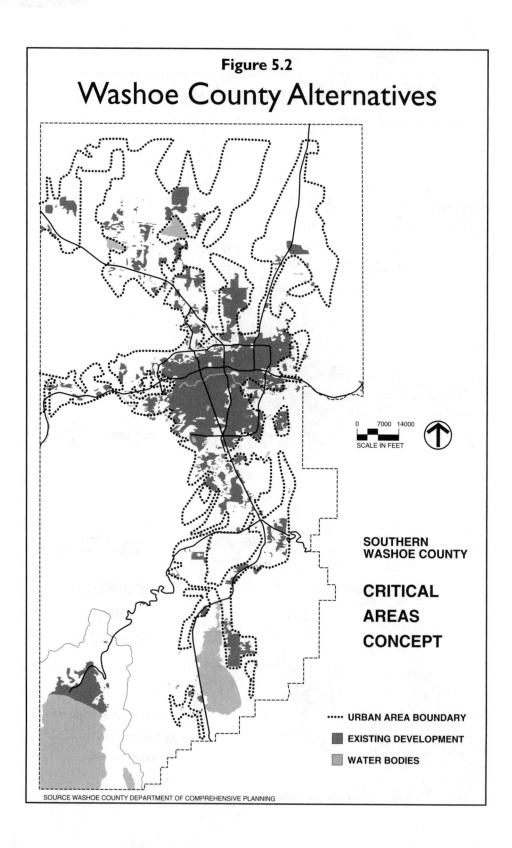

Figure 5.2

Washoe County Alternatives

SOUTHERN
WASHOE COUNTY

CRITICAL

AREAS

CONCEPT

0   7000 14000
SCALE IN FEET

······ URBAN AREA BOUNDARY

EXISTING DEVELOPMENT

WATER BODIES

SOURCE WASHOE COUNTY DEPARTMENT OF COMPREHENSIVE PLANNING

To reach a shared vision, the various public and private groups with competing interests must reach an agreement on a regional urban form. If only one alternative is presented to five different, competing groups, all would surely reject and oppose it because the alternative would only represent, at most, 20 percent of each group's total interest. Therefore, multiple alternatives are necessary to achieve a proactive stance from each competing interest group. Each group supports the alternative that serves its interests the most. From the alternatives and the input of the interest groups, a final preferred alternative arrives, resulting in a shared vision.

After the growth trends in the region were analyzed, four alternative growth management concepts (urban forms) were proposed.[8] The first was the "Current Trends" of the region and how continuing exactly what has been done in the past would negatively affect the area (see Figure 5.1). The first alternative pointed out the dangers of continuing down the path of the current trend. It depicted the five major crises necessitating a growth management plan:

1. decline in existing built-up areas;
2. degradation of the environment;
3. overutilization of energy sources and transportation congestion;
4. fiscal strain linked with deficiencies in adequate public facilities and overburdened transportation facilities; and
5. loss of agricultural lands and open space.

The second alternative placed priority on preserving critical environmental areas (including hillsides, floodplains, stream valleys, aquifer recharge areas, and wetlands), accommodating future growth, but in areas that could be developed without impairing the environmental systems and features of the region (see Figure 5.2). This alternative served environmental protection groups.

The third alternative presented was capital-driven expansion, emphasizing fiscal efficiency. The main purpose of this form was the ability to use existing infrastructure cost-effectively. Instead of studying existing natural systems, easily identifiable in the environmental alternative, this urban form relied on service area designations to determine timing for improvements and expansion of capital facilities—primarily water, sewer, and roads. This alternative was attractive to suburban taxpayers, who would like to see greater provision of adequate public facilities and payment from the new development as opposed to subsidy from the general fund. (See Figure 5.3.)

Additionally, a Sphere of Influence boundary for each city would be

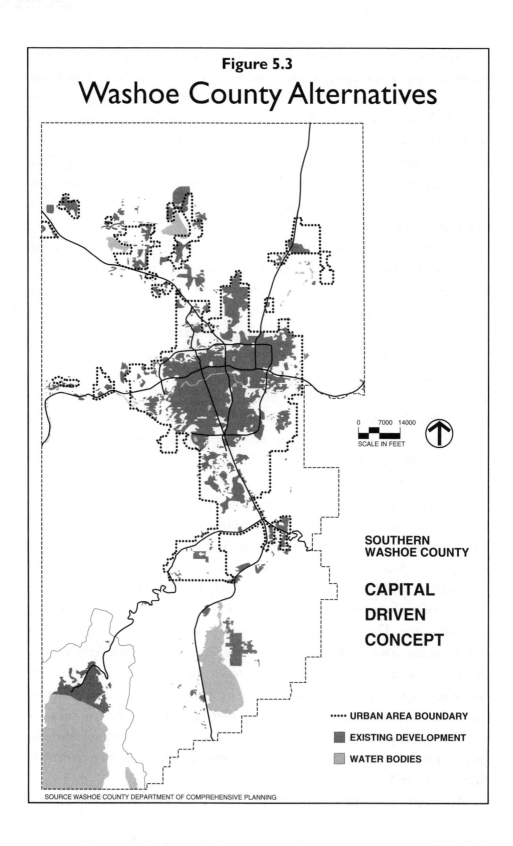

Figure 5.3

Washoe County Alternatives

0 7000 14000
SCALE IN FEET

SOUTHERN
WASHOE COUNTY

CAPITAL

DRIVEN

CONCEPT

····· URBAN AREA BOUNDARY

▉ EXISTING DEVELOPMENT

▉ WATER BODIES

SOURCE WASHOE COUNTY DEPARTMENT OF COMPREHENSIVE PLANNING

identified to provide a definition of areas that would, at some point in the future, be annexed and become part of the city. A second major concept in this alternative was community identity, with the two existing urban cores of Reno and Sparks forming the focal points for the Region's most intensive urban development. This alternative would revitalize urbanized areas and would be supported by those living in the older areas of the Region.

The fourth alternative presented was the "quality of life" emphasis. This urban form was based less on geographic subareas and more on policy consid-erations—a performance-based approach of lessening air pollution and traffic congestion. The purpose of this alternative was to establish several statements or standards that defined a desired quality of life for the Region. The report also outlined potential implementation strategies for the chosen growth manage-ment system. These included:

1. land and/or benefit acquisition;
2. capital improvements;
3. environmental controls;
4. zoning;
5. subdivision review;
6. population controls;
7. tax and fee systems;
8. geographic limits; and
9. numerical restraints.

The four alternatives were compared and evaluated based on their consis-tency with regional goals and objectives and their relative impacts on environ-mental and infrastructure systems.[9] Eventually, the Regional Planning Commission and Regional Governing Board adopted a "preferred alternative" that depicted the tier development concepts emphasizing the development of a compact urban area through the use of "tiers" of focused growth, including urban area and future urban areas, suburban communities, and rural areas. Additionally, the form emphasized maintenance of the vitality and identity of existing cities and suburban communities, the preservation of areas of rural development, the creation of new centers with a mix of employment and hous-ing, and the definition of economic activity centers.[10] The Regional Plan also included *Ramapo*'s phasing of urban and suburban development over time con-sistent with growth demands and the availability of adequate public services and facilities. Finally, the Plan focused on the protection of flood plains,

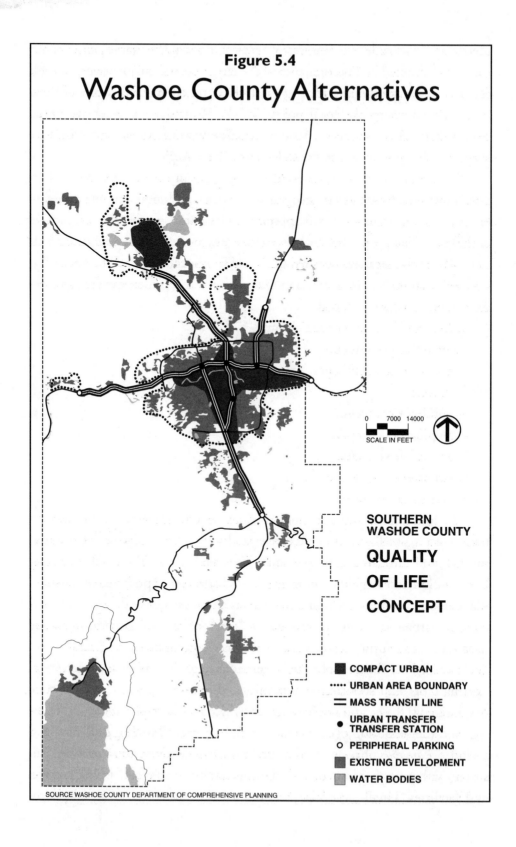

Figure 5.4

Washoe County Alternatives

SOUTHERN
WASHOE COUNTY

QUALITY

OF LIFE

CONCEPT

0   7000   14000
SCALE IN FEET

■ COMPACT URBAN
••••• URBAN AREA BOUNDARY
═ MASS TRANSIT LINE
● URBAN TRANSFER
  TRANSFER STATION
○ PERIPHERAL PARKING
■ EXISTING DEVELOPMENT
▨ WATER BODIES

SOURCE WASHOE COUNTY DEPARTMENT OF COMPREHENSIVE PLANNING

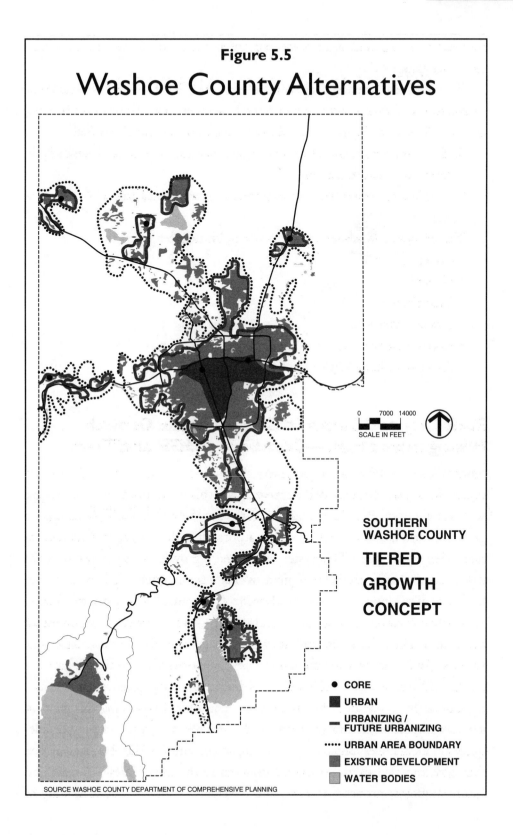

Figure 5.5

Washoe County Alternatives

SOUTHERN
WASHOE COUNTY

TIERED

GROWTH

CONCEPT

- ● CORE
- ■ URBAN
- — URBANIZING / FUTURE URBANIZING
- ⋯ URBAN AREA BOUNDARY
- ■ EXISTING DEVELOPMENT
- ▨ WATER BODIES

SOURCE WASHOE COUNTY DEPARTMENT OF COMPREHENSIVE PLANNING

0 7000 14000
SCALE IN FEET

the creation of regional open space, and the retention of hillsides in nonurban uses. (See Figure 5.5.)

The adopted "preferred alternative" was the "Tiered Growth Concept," similar to the *Ramapo* systems mentioned previously in Minneapolis-St. Paul and New Jersey (see Figure 5.3). The key policies of the tiers included:

1. designation of areas within the region that are to be treated similarly in terms of urbanization; and
2. creation or preservation of community identities as part of that urbanization.

The proposed Washoe County tiers would include:

- Core;
- Urban;
- Urbanizing;
- Future Urbanizing;
- Urban Reserve; and
- Permanent Rural/Open Space.

Park City and Summit County, Utah: Growth Management Plan—Combining UGB and Tiers

Summit County, Utah, has experienced rapid growth largely due to the success of area ski resorts. Because of this growth, the county retained me to strategize with the County, Park City and the Park City School District to develop a growth coordination strategy to be incorporated with a newly drafted general plan. (See Figure 5.6.) This system proposed a growth management element to be included with the general plan, which was designed to promote sound land use decisions within the Snyderville Basin area.[11] The pattern of land uses—their location, timing, mix, and density—was a critical component of any community's character. The Growth Management Element was organized to work conjunctively with the Land Use Element to plan sufficient land for residential, commercial, industrial, and public uses and to locate these uses appropriately to enhance the community character. It was also designed to preserve important natural resources and to enable the county to provide adequate public services efficiently to the future community. The Basin's General Plan was intended to give everyone involved in the use of land—current and future residents, property owners, and developers—a clear understanding of

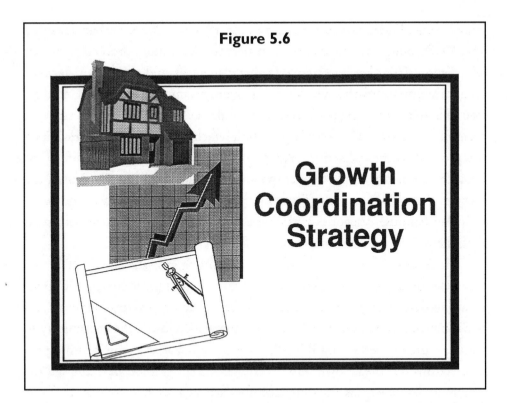

Figure 5.6

Growth
Coordination
Strategy

the development patterns the community has found to be most appropriate.

The Land Use Element was divided into Land Use Categories and Growth Management. Land use preferences and densities were designated on the Land Use Map. Conversely, the Growth Management Element designated *Ramapo's* timing and sequencing of the use of the land. While these elements were distinguishable, they were ultimately applied in combination to determine how development would occur in the Snyderville Basin.

The growth management system consisted of four interrelated techniques that operated at varying levels of detail. This system included the designation of an urban growth boundary, delineation of tiers, transportation corridors and joint planning areas, adoption of adequate public facility requirements, and the implementation of impact fees. The urban growth boundary was designed to separate urban, urbanizing, and potential future urbanizing areas of the Basin from permanent rural, natural resource, and environmentally sensitive lands. It separated areas suitable for urban growth from those areas unsuitable for urban growth but suitable for other uses. By discouraging growth in outlying areas while encouraging or facilitating growth in existing, developed areas, the UGB would channel development into those areas most suitable for urban densities. The UGB could then be divided into tiers to create more detailed standards and criteria. This plan was unique in that it incorporated either short-term or long-term urban growth strategies based on geographic delineations. The adoption of a long-term geographic restraint would be done through the establishment of a perimeter or a boundary beyond which no urban scale development was presently contemplated. Intended to be a fixed boundary for the life of the Plan, the boundary would be incorporated into the Land Use Element of the General Plan. The Land Use Element and Map would ensure that the delineation of land use categories within and outside of the UGB were consistent with the purposes and intent of the UGB.

The Basin's UGB was more refined by defining growth "tiers," which further delineated subareas within the UGB and allowed for more specific application of density regulations, impacting fees, concurrency requirements, and environmental considerations. The tier framework allowed the community to address major issues aiding both the county and Park City in planning for future growth. A breakdown into functional and geographic areas allowed the county to describe goals and objectives for each area, to evaluate market forces and growth trends selectively for each area, and to consider implementation techniques that were specific for, and responsive to, the needs of each area.[12]

The fundamental premise of the tier delineations was that the Basin could be divided into geographical subunits based upon functional distinctions. (See Figure 5.7.) The tiers were divided into growth area tiers—Urbanizing, Planned Urbanizing, and Future Urbanizing—and limited growth area tiers—Rural and Joint Planning Area/Rural Protection. The Urbanizing Tier included those areas that were undergoing active urbanization and that were presently serviced by public facilities. The Urbanizing Tier was designated based on factors such as the proximity to existing highway collector systems, traffic flows to Salt Lake City, largely developed areas, existing or approved subdivision plats, recognition of planned public capital improvement projects currently served by sewer and local capital improvements phasing, the development of commercial centers and major recreational centers, the availability for high-density infill development, and adjacency to joint planning area-urban expansion. Together, the urban growth boundary and the Tiers were designed to create an urban form with the attributes varying from compact and efficient development patterns with phased urbanizing areas to the protection of floodplain.[13]

Figure 5.7

Summit County, Utah
Snyderville Basin Development Tiers

RURAL

TIER I

TIER III

TIER I

TIER II

Snyderville

RURAL

Park City

RURAL

Figure 5.8

Alternatives Analysis

- Define possible policy options
- Examine effects on the community's future
- Invite community discussion and comment
- Develop a preferred alternative
- Build consensus for Comprehensive Plan proposals

The Planned Urbanizing Area (Tier II) was characterized by "new" growth areas where some existing development was not served by a full range of necessary public facilities and services. Some urban growth might be served by a combination of both existing public facilities and services, and any additional needed public facilities and services that would be provided by either public or private sources where logical capital improvements phasing would occur over a ten- to twenty-year-time period. This could include areas where no public sewer expansions were approved, road designs did not meet ultimate capacity standards, water quality and supply were poor, large tracts of undeveloped areas remained, and transfer of development rights were a possibility. The Future Urbanizing Area (Tier III) was restricted from development until the Urbanizing and Planned Urbanizing Areas were significantly built out. Any growth was related to long-range planning and capital improvements. To allow landowners reasonable use of their land, the area could utilize various techniques in Tier III including conservation easements, preferential tax assessments, cluster housing, planned unit development, transfer of development rights, and open space corridor and greenbelt designation. The Rural Area was the permanent rural density development area. These areas tended to be predominately rural and agricultural in use, or were sensitive lands that lacked public facilities because of their distance from existing urban centers.

Another key factor in Summit County's plan was the existence of designated transportation corridors. These transportation corridors might be separately mapped to overlay the tier delineations. Some transportation corridors might pass through more than one tier requiring the use of differing techniques. For

instance, the Urbanizing Tier techniques would likely have a joint development, corridor center, or infill focus. However, the Future Urbanizing Tier would consist of advanced land acquisition and corridor preservation.

To summarize, an alternatives analysis is critical in reaching consensus for controlling urban sprawl. (See Figure 5.8.)

Palm Beach County: Preserving Transportation Corridors and Neotraditional Developments, Florida

Florida has mandated consistency among plans at the city/county level through intergovernmental coordination.[14] The state plan mandates local comprehensive planning,[15] local plan consistency with the regional and state plans,[16] county membership in a Regional Planning Council,[17] and an adequate public facilities provision requiring development concurrency.[18] Early on I developed Sarasota's Public Facilities Financing Ordinance, which evolved from a municipal services taxing unit for roads and parks into a full-fledged impact fee system for roads, parks, and beach facilities countywide.[19] While land use is generally local, Florida's legislature found that certain types of activities affect the state as a whole.[20] Growth management has been necessary especially to Southern Florida. The current statutes address critical problems such as the restoration of the Everglades, Florida's future water supply, the loss of agricultural lands, and the need to preserve and restore Florida's environmental systems.[21]

Florida's southeast coast is now implementing growth management techniques designed to provide a meaningful channel for growth in Southeast Florida to lands other than those adjacent to the Everglades, thereby protecting the environment, encouraging more compact energy-efficient development patterns, and redirecting growth to the older coastal cities requiring revitalization and infill.[22]

In 1982 I was appointed as the principal consultant to restore the distressed South Beach area of Miami Beach. The district was dilapidated, had terribly deficient sewer, water, and road infrastructure, and an eroded beach. Its buildings were rundown and mostly abandoned. In a series of coordinated moves that I recommended, the city adopted a $100 million infrastructure bond, an arrangement with the federal government to restore the beach, the adoption of an Historic District to prevent the destruction of the glorious but rundown art deco hotel, and an incentive zoning plan to assemble lots for new restaurants, hotels, housing, and commercial through incentives.[23] The Plan has become the most successful urban redevelopment program in the U.S. and one of the most successful tourist designation spots in the word. It won both the national and Florida APA awards for best project.

In 1977 I was hired by the City of Hollywood, Florida, to protect North Beach, where a land firm had proposed building a 4,872-unit development on the east side of Route A1A, affecting the sand dunes of 2.75 miles of ocean beach. Through the use of transfers of development rights, the entire east side of the highway was protected and all development rights transferred to the inland side of the highway. The program was upheld in an historic decision involving the first use of TDRs for environmental purposes.[24]

I also developed for Monroe County, Florida (the Florida Keys), an innovative approach to identifying and quantifying the carrying capacity of the Keys.[25] Under the comprehensive plan update required by Florida's Growth Management Act (and considering a variety of factors), the county integrated the rate-of-growth program with *Ramapo*'s permit allocation system by granting points to various applicants.[26] After examining major issues such as Florida's traffic standards for U.S. Highway 1, the need to provide open space, potable water, drainage facilities, and solid waste disposal, and the need to meet Florida's standards on hurricane evacuation times, the county justified its rate of growth program system on public safety and the lack of carrying capacity during hurricane emergencies.[27]

When developing the ordinance, the county analyzed the vacant lots in improved subdivisions and found that approximately 15,000 existed in unincorporated areas, amounting to a twenty-seven-year supply. The possibility of this open space being developed, combined with a thirty-five-hour evacuation rate, demonstrated that the county's evacuation capabilities would be overwhelmed.[28] Because the traditional zoning techniques and regulations posed significant constitutional problems when addressing the reduction of build-out of improved subdivisions,[29] the rate-of-growth regulation was determined to be the best means of addressing the constitutional issues.

The Monroe County's Dwelling Unit Allocation Rate of Growth Ordinance combined the permit allocation system and the land acquisition program. Less than half of the county's dwelling units per year were planned at a rate of 255. To qualify for the permit allocation system, developers must first

Figure 5.8A
Decision Points Matrix for Rate of Growth Ordinance (ROGO) for Monroe County, Florida

Issue	Alternatives	Decision
A. Purpose and Intent/Findings		
1. What is the purpose and intent of the ordinance (i.e., why is it necessary to regulate the rate/amount of growth)?	■ public facility constraints • water availability • sewer availability • traffic congestion • fire protection • police protection ■ public health and safety • water pollution • air pollution • septic tank failures ■ achieve orderly growth consistent with capital improvements program and service capabilities of County ■ achieve "balanced" growth (residential [housing] and nonresidential [jobs]) ■ environmental protection • endangered species • habitat protection • natural resources	■ to maintain a reasonable and safe hurricane evacuation clearance time ■ to prevent loss of life due to hurricanes

meet the requirements of the Monroe County Land Development Regulations. The applicants are then assigned scores and ranked based on a variety of criteria. The allocation is apportioned quarterly, by geographic area, and between affordable and market rate housing. Developers that do not receive a sufficient score to receive a building permit are automatically placed into the next quarter. The ordinance, authored by the Monroe County Planning Department, Robert Apgar, Wallace Roberts, and Todd and Freilich, Leitner, and Carlisle, received the 1994 Achievement Award from the National Association of Counties and a $7 million implementation grant from the Florida Communities Trust. It was recently upheld as constitutional by the Florida District Court.[30] (See Figure 5.8A.)

As local governments deal with the burdens associated with urbanization, it is vital that municipalities and counties be allowed to plan early in the expansion process to acquire and preserve transportation routes that will provide for future transportation service and act as an organizing base for the location of new developments in those growing areas of a community while at the same time encouraging growth to redirect partially back to eastern cities.[31] Palm Beach County, Florida, recognized that the monetary costs and planning requirements associated with the reservation of transportation corridors were overwhelming traditional taxation, condemnation, and police power techniques.[32]

A recent case from Florida, which I briefed and argued successfully before the Florida Supreme Court and which has advanced the cause of local government efforts to plan for future growth through the reservation of transportation corridors, is *Palm Beach County v. Wright*.[33] In reversing the court of appeals and holding that the county's use of the thoroughfare map was not facially unconstitutional, the Florida Supreme Court found that the county was properly exercising its police power, which substantially advanced a legitimate state interest. The court also welcomed the county's use of a thoroughfare map for coordination of land use and transportation planning needs, without which "the county's ability to plan for future growth would be seriously impeded. . . ."[34]

Palm Beach County began as a challenge to the thoroughfare map as a portion of the traffic circulation element of the Palm Beach County Comprehensive Plan. The thoroughfare map, as enacted pursuant to section 163.3177(6)(b), Florida Statute (1991), defined certain transportation corridors along specified roadways throughout Palm Beach County, and also designated other locations for the purpose of new future roadway construction. The purpose of the map was to protect identified transportation corridors from encroachment by other land use activities. The map required that any development be consistent with and provide for the unimpeded transportation right-of-way as shown on the thoroughfare map. No land use activity was permitted within any roadway designated on the thoroughfare map that would impede future construction of the roadway. All development approvals by the county were required to be consistent with the provisions of the Comprehensive Plan.[35]

The plaintiff owned land on the north side of an existing roadway within the county. The roadway was bordered on the south by a canal, so any future alignment of the right-of-way corridor would be measured northward from the then-existing southern property line of the roadway, onto the plaintiff's property. The plaintiff received a favorable summary judgment ruling from the trial court, finding that the traffic circulation element of the County Comprehensive Plan was unconstitutional and a taking in violation of the Fifth Amendment of the United States Constitution and article X, section 6, of the Florida Constitution. The Fourth District Court of Appeals affirmed the trial court's judgment, reasoning that the thoroughfare map was functionally indistinguishable from the reservation map that had been declared unconstitutional in *Joint Ventures.*[36]

The map of reservation in *Joint Ventures* was authorized by section 337.241(2), (3) of the Florida Statutes (1987), which allowed the Florida Department of Transportation to record a map that designated roadway corridors, and thereby prevent the issuance of any development permits for property that was in any way located within the traffic corridor right-of-way. This development moratorium was to occur for a period of five years, and could be extended for additional five-year periods, which had the practical effect of indefinitely prohibiting development by property owners along the proposed roads. The Florida Supreme Court found that this legislative procedure primarily sanctioned the Department of Transportation's attempts to depress land values in anticipation of eminent domain proceedings.[37] "Rather than supporting a 'regulatory' characterization, these circumstances expose the statutory scheme as a thinly veiled attempt to 'acquire' land by avoiding the legislatively mandated procedural and substantive protections of chapters 73 and 74."[38]

In the *Palm Beach* decision, however, the Florida Supreme Court found that there were substantial differences between the map of reservation in *Joint Ventures* and the thoroughfare map as presented in *Palm Beach County.*[39] The map of reservation that was struck down in *Joint Ventures* operated as a recorded easement, designating the precise width and location of future roadways. The map of reservation was not part of the future application of a comprehensive regulatory scheme: the recorded easement was only the exact width of the roadway and was not part of a transportation corridor. Furthermore, no development alternatives were involved (transfers of development rights were not permitted), and a variance for the affected property owner was limited only to a reduction of the right-of-way. The map of reservation precluded the issuance of all development permits for land within the recorded map area, and the *Palm Beach County* court noted that "the only purpose of that [map of reservation] statute was to freeze property so as to depress land values in anticipation of eminent domain proceedings."[40]

The argument I advanced completely distinguished the state's highway construction process from the county's land use approval process, which afforded constitutional as-applied relief. The thoroughfare map of the county limited development only to the extent necessary to ensure that property development occurred in a compatible manner with future land use. The thoroughfare map was not recorded, was allowed to be amended twice per year, and was part of a comprehensive system of regulations that were to be applied only in response to future development proposals. The proposed corridors were wider than the actual roadways, which created major benefits to landowners regarding use and density. The thoroughfare map procedure also allowed the application of those planning tools that adapt development to the required traffic corridors: clustering, upzoning, dedicating credits toward permits fees, transfer of development rights, and variances on the remainder of a property owner's land.[41]

The *Palm Beach County* court noted that the concurrency requirements of the thoroughfare map process, which allows development to proceed only if there are adequate public facilities to serve the property at the time of development, also served, in most cases, to benefit most of the property that would be subject to some development restrictions.[42] Those development projects that would be closest to new roads "are likely to benefit the most from construction of the roads even if a portion of the owner's property must be reserved for road construction."[43] The court also stressed that the plaintiff's challenge was only a facial attack against section 163.3177, Florida Statute, and as such the court's analysis and holding were limited to the facial constitutionality of the county's actions. The county's actions were a reasonable means of achieving a concededly valid public purpose. The court's analysis in this regard was aided by the earlier decision of *Tampa-Hillsborough County Expressway Authority v. A.G.W.S. Corp.*,[44] which held that landowners with property inside the boundaries of maps of reservation invalidated by *Joint Ventures* were not legally entitled to receive per se declarations of a taking.

Whether a map of reservation (proceeding with the analysis of *Joint Ventures*) or a thoroughfare map (after the holding in *Palm Beach County*) results in a taking of particular property would depend on whether the effect was to deny the owner of substantially all of the economically beneficial or productive use of the land.[45] The *Palm Beach County* court acknowledged that the thoroughfare map, as applied to certain property, may indeed result in a taking, but this determination would require analysis under the "ad hoc factual inquiry" established by a string of United States Supreme Court cases.[46] Takings in this manner could only occur on an individualized basis, as each property owner's interests will be affected in different ways through the use of a thoroughfare map. The Supreme Court has considered the distinction between facial and as-applied challenges on other occasions; and when the Court is presented with only a facial attack to a statute, a property owner must "run the gauntlet" before it can be determined whether an as-applied taking has occurred.[47]

The thoroughfare map is designed to be utilized as a long-range planning tool that identifies potential corridors for facilities that may be necessary beyond the needs identified at some future date. This map is also intended to give both property owners and public officials an understanding of the general location of potential future roads to meet traffic demands as the county expands. This planning process will allow land developers an adequate opportunity to plan their developments with proper road interfacing requirements.[48] When a right-of-way is needed by the county, dedication of all or a portion of that land designated under the thoroughfare map can be required as a valid exaction under the rational nexus and rough proportionality tests as expounded by the Supreme Court in *Dolan*.[49] As for the general use of the thoroughfare map, however, "there can be no question that the planning for future growth must include designation of the areas where roads are likely to be widened and future roads are to be built."[50]

I had also been working with Palm Beach for several years assisting in the development of a framework for growth management in Palm Beach County that builds upon the existing 1989 Comprehensive Plan and existing plan implementation mechanisms, but that recognizes the need for certain additional plan elements and implementation strategies. During the course of the project, significant and valuable input has been received from the Board of County Commissioners (Board) and, especially, the Land Use Advisory Board/Local Planning Agency (LUAB/LPA). Numerous public meetings, forums, and workshops were held, during which input was received from the general public and various interested parties and entities. This input contributed to the "Directions Statement" and "Overall Approach" ratified by the LUAB/LPA on May 5, 1995, and issued in written form as the "Proposal for a Growth Management Program: Working Draft" on May 15, 1995.

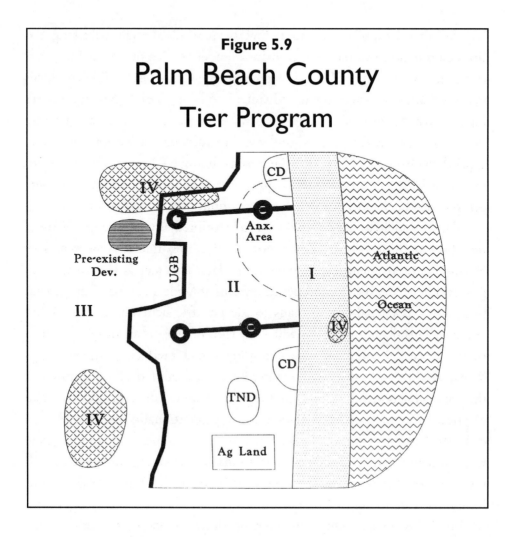

Figure 5.9

Palm Beach County
Tier Program

In addition to the "Overall Approach," I recommended that the implications resulting from one other factor be added to the equation—the adoption during the 1995 Florida legislative session of "The Bert J. Harris, Jr., Private Property Rights Protection Act" (hereinafter Property Rights Act), which would profoundly affect land use regulations adopted by local governments in Florida. At the same time that I was working on new plan elements, county staff would be reviewing and evaluating existing county implementation techniques to ensure that they reflected county policy, conform with the new Directions Statement and were compatible with the new growth management and economic development plan elements drafted by me. Several key aspects of the LUAB/LPA Overall Approach defined the proposed scope of consultant services (see Figure 5.9). These key elements included the following:

- the growth management strategy must be flexible;
- the growth management strategy should be based upon the mapped delineation of tiers, with distinct policies and implementation strategies applicable to each tier;
- the existing Urban Services Area boundary would remain as the limit for Tier II;
- the system would maintain environmental integrity;
- the growth management strategy would help to achieve and maintain a balance of land uses to meet future needs;
- the growth management strategy would ensure the timely and cost-effective provision of services and facilities; and
- the County should continue to rely upon existing innovative implementation techniques and programs.

The LUAB/LPA recommended the Overall Approach based upon the many planning and plan implementation accomplishments of the County achieved over the past several years, including, but not limited to:

- the Urban Service Area delineation;
- mixed-use development district (MXD);
- traditional neighborhood development district (NDD);
- purchase of development rights;
- transfer of development rights (TDR);
- concurrency;
- impact fees;
- neighborhood planning;
- geographic sector planning; and
- the identification of conservation areas and environmentally sensitive areas.

The LUAB/LPA-recommended Overall Approach also recognizes the need to develop certain short-term and long-term techniques to take an additional step in the direction of a sound, appropriate, and balanced growth management program for Palm Beach County that will serve the County's needs and implement the Board's policies for the next five to ten years.

The 1989 Comprehensive Plan, in its Land Use Element, enunciated a major goal of distributing population and economic growth with timely (phased) and cost-effective techniques of ensuring adequacy of public facilities to serve development and a quality of life that retains unique lifestyles. To achieve that goal, the plan included policies, directions, and techniques that emphasized:

1. infill development in urban areas;
2. direct development east to coastal cities;
3. linear open space and park systems;
4. development of an urban form;
5. meeting affordable and full-range housing needs;
6. using TDRs to achieve preservation of agricultural and environmentally sensitive lands;
7. promoting higher density and location of commercially viable development.

Thus, many of the techniques for good growth management, coordinated with full population and economic growth, had already been identified and, in many cases, integrated into authorized but not yet implemented programs. In August of 1993, I was retained to appear before the Board of County Commissioners to outline national and Florida approaches to growth management. These approaches emphasized "tier" and "phased" development, and establishing an urban form in terms of development "centers" or "corridors."[51] We explored intergovernmental coordination programs between counties and cities, including a complete analysis of concurrency management, the preservation of agricultural and environmentally sensitive land (with TDRs and bond acquisition programs), and the protection of development rights (vested rights, takings analysis).

Under the Overall Approach, the tier system would operate effectively with or without an annual population target. Timing and phasing in Tier II would allow for establishment of performance standards, and criteria for meeting the County's goals of limiting sprawl and encouraging infill with respect to development approvals and plan amendments. Priorities would be granted for developments within corridors, centers, traditional neighborhood developments (TNDs), mixed-use communities, contiguous development, and attractive, nonresidential, economic development. The utilization of a prioritized and coordinated capital improvements program would ensure that capital facility capacities would be directed to nonsprawl and Tier I development and to prioritized development in Tier II. Special waivers for concurrency and fees for economic development or affordable housing could be incorporated. (The addition of the tier system in promoting infill and economic development has

been fully demonstrated in the San Diego and Seattle metropolitan areas—water-based locations of similar size and population.[52])

Last, with respect to the new property rights legislation, the tier system would effectively be able to accommodate the new legislation best. The Property Rights Act describes "permanent" burdening of the use and value of property.[53] The suggested county program ensures an administrative vested rights determination, which can quickly and fairly assess whether any constitutional problems are presented.[54] Development—even if not capable of meeting full concurrency—could receive immediate partial development on a mandatory cluster basis. Such regulations would go a long way to ensure the development industry that the program will be fair and equitable. The timing and phasing of development will be based on priorities and concurrency that are fully sustainable and predicated upon the nonsprawl objectives of the plan. Full growth and development would be achieved or even enhanced because multiple markets would be developed—multifamily, corridors, centers, nonresidential economic development, TNDs, and coastal development—in place of the primary single-family sprawl. The development industry would be substantially enhanced economically.

The Boulder Regional Area and Grand Junction and Mesa County, Colorado: Concentrated Urban Growth

Many problems faced by local governments are regional in nature. Population growth, environmental preservation, land use forms, growth patterns, and the quality and quantity of public facilities and services often transcend local, neighborhood, or city boundaries. The decisions made by a jurisdiction on these issues often have extraterritorial effects. Such jurisdictional challenges, as well as the fluctuating growth cycles, have shaped growth patterns within Grand Junction and Mesa County. Unfortunately, during growth periods, utilities and roadways have been extended to serve the planning area without examining the long-term costs. Similarly, during economic downslides, relaxed development standards have led to deficient development and community resentment toward certain areas. These sprawling development patterns have created economic burdens and have caused the loss of large areas of agricultural and open space. Because of these problems, under my guidance in 1996, the City of Grand

Junction and Mesa County became partners in the management of urban growth in the Central Grand Valley, sharing the same goals for the future of the area.[55] The community as a whole realized the importance of working together, recognizing that the city and county, jointly, could better address environmental preservation, growth patterns, and public facilities and services.[56]

Grand Junction's planning process was guided by a steering committee comprised of residents of Grand Junction and the surrounding area. Early in the planning process, the committee recommended that the city and county jointly develop a preferred alternative for the entire urban areas. The initial City/County Steering Committee meetings were so successful that, at the committee's request, Grand Junction's City Council and Mesa's Board of County Commissioners authorized the two committees to develop the goals, policies, and strategies together for the joint planning area.

The city and county completed an alternatives analysis process to compare the consequences of different growth management strategies, and subsequently select future growth alternatives, that were consistent with community values and resources. The steering committee determined the composition of each alternative. The alternatives analysis focused on future land use patterns and their service impact, identifying the location of different types of growth within the community. Each alternative shared several characteristics, because they used existing land use patterns as a foundation. The analysis explored the advantages and disadvantages of each alternative by focusing on the distinctions among land uses, demands for services, public facility and service costs, and implementation strategies. The first, the current practices alternative, consisted of outward growth based on existing policies and practices where no substantial changes occurred in existing development approval practices. (See Figure 5.10.) The second alternative, the compact growth alternative, provided for infrastructure to guide the timing and location of growth; it was characterized by infill development, redevelopment, moderated outward growth, and support for a vital downtown core.[57] New urban growth—lots smaller than two acres—is limited to areas where water and street improvements were in place; and in nonurban, residential lots of two or more acres, parts of the community receive rural service levels (for instance, no sidewalks, minimal fire protection, and no sewer service). Private investment into blighted downtown areas is encouraged by incentives, whereas development of agricultural and open space is discouraged. (See Figure 5.11.) Finally, the "growth centers" alternative

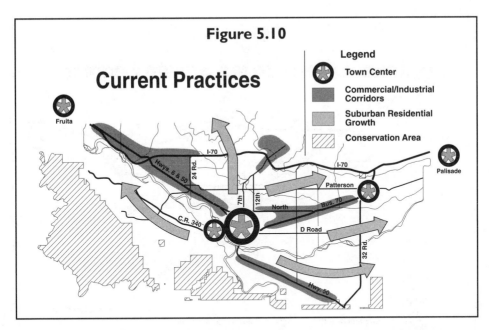

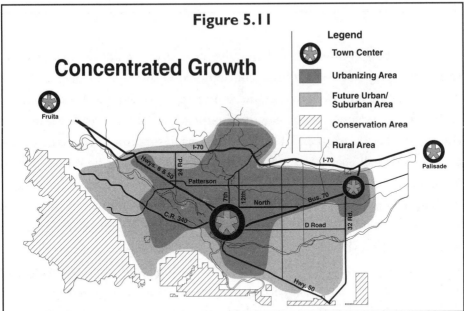

focused on development of several growth centers serving a variety of purposes. Major growth centers are mutually supportive and designated for general retail, travel-oriented services, entertainment, speciality retail, and office/industrial. Minor centers are located in residential areas, which include parks, schools, and neighborhood convenience services. (See Figure 5.12.)

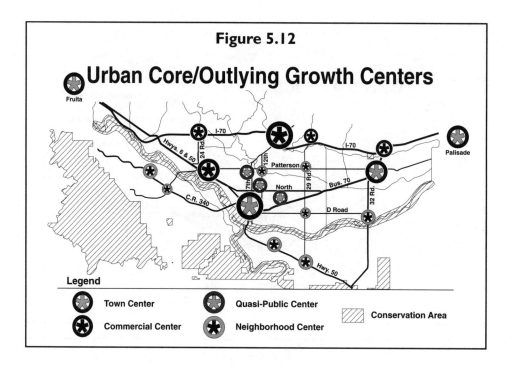

Figure 5.12
Urban Core/Outlying Growth Centers

The steering committees weighed the impacts of each of the plan alternatives and jointly selected a refined concentrated Growth Plan (the Plan). This Plan coordinated future land uses and zoning so that compatible uses adjoined each other. Land uses along the city's boundaries will be continued into the county in a logical manner.[58] The Plan also ensures improved adequate public services and facilities such as roads and schools, simplifying the review process for future developments because the same standards are adopted in the county.

The Plan is unique in its concentrated examination on urban revitalization and sustainability. The issues addressed under the concentrated urban growth plan would affect the Urbanizing Tier by timing and sequencing growth in the central city and preventing sprawl from encroaching onto the Urbanizing Tier and rural land. The plan reflects principles of concentric urban growth by strengthening the downtown focus, highlighting existing centers and their surrounding development including an urban open space network. Additionally, a UGB is to be defined as the outer limit of urban development within the Urban Planning Area. Enhancing existing neighborhoods by designing new roadways and maintaining the quality of life leads to continued density patterns in the Urban Area. Reinforcing existing community centers and providing open spaces throughout the Urban Area via neighborhood parks, natural open

spaces and greenbelts, trail networks, and designated floodplains improves the outward need to develop. The Plan disperses high-density housing located throughout the community rather than concentrated in a few small areas. Additionally, due to the growth and annexation in Grand Junction, Fruita, and Palisade, the cities are nearly contiguous with only an undeveloped buffer between the cities. The Plan gives specific design guidelines for the development of this buffer zone. The Plan's emphasis on urban growth addressing land use compatibility, compact development patterns, and adequate public facilities for residents and businesses provides the city and county the ability to preserve open land for years to come.

Boulder's interlocal agreement with Boulder County has helped manage growth outside the central city. In 1970, both the county and the city adopted a jointly sponsored comprehensive plan for the Boulder Valley area. While it is critical that the county participate because the city is in a holding period due to previous development, the City of Boulder continues to control growth management in that area. Boulder's approach to the urban growth boundary is a service area concept, which defines the part of the Boulder Valley planning area where Boulder either already provides services or will provide in the future. The plan is viewed as a contract between the City and County of Boulder, thereby carrying greater enforcement weight.[59]

In 1990, consistent with an ongoing update process, I examined the Subarea Planning Process of Boulder. It was recommended that the Boulder Planning Area be articulated into six to eight planning sectors (subcommunities) to determine service areas, design capacities, utilization levels, and current estimated deficits/surfeits for existing public facilities.[60] For each subcommunity, a carrying capacity for build-out land use could be stated in the term of Dwelling Unit Equivalents (DUE). Land use, population, and housing inventory input data should be recorded at the block level of detail and aggregated into transportation planning origin-destination zones. *Ramapo's* public facilities programming was emphasized in this level of planning and included virtually every system of facilities and services including parks and recreation, fire department, police department, libraries, water and sanitary systems, storm water management, municipal airports, transportation systems and thoroughfares, and public educational facilities. Thus, the Subcommunity Plans could become the foundation for the capital improvement programming process in Boulder as well as the basis for establishing fees for new development.

It was also suggested that the Subarea Plan should parallel the Subcommunity Plan with input data recorded at the block/parcel level, and individual structures and site improvements analyzed relative to land use intensity, height and bulk, quality of the build environment and sensitivity to environmental factors. Land use-to-use relationships should be carefully analyzed relative to the adequacy of on-site transitions articulated by: building, off-street parking, and landscape setbacks; visual and/or noise buffering techniques; solar and view access easements; and landscaping.

The most detailed level of planning within the hierarchy involves the area of significant growth in the Urbanizing Tier under the Neighborhood Plans. Delineated neighborhoods should be nested within Subareas and should involve very specific case studies or pilot projects. At the first step in the Subarea Planning Process, city staff needs to define and delineate Development Management Strategy Areas on an overlay that covers the entire Planning Area of the Boulder Valley Comprehensive Plan. These strategy areas will form a key basis for delineating Subareas. In this regard, the strategy area classifications should be delineated on the overlay, including preservation, conservation, conservation-infill, infill, infill-expansion, new development, and redevelopment.

A key land use impact measurement concept within the Subarea Planning Process is the DUE for stating carrying capacity for each Subarea. This approach applies projected unit traffic impacts, water and wastewater demand, and enrollment/patron generation rates to state per-new-acre impacts on public facilities for residential and nonresidential land uses within a common index. Each Subarea can therefore be assigned a build-out carrying capacity, stated as a range of DUEs. With shifts in land use mix, the remaining capacity to be absorbed can be monitored in a more consistent and direct manner.

Boulder's strategy was to reduce growth from in-migration by cutting back industrial search efforts, to protect a greenbelt surrounding the city, to preserve scenic easements, and to charge new development for the full cost of services. The strategy has been effective, as the city has successfully secured over 27,000 acres of greenbelt; this controls the rate of population by limiting building permits and defining urban growth boundaries within the county.[61] This impact of the growth control ordinance shows a population shift and there has been out-migration of young families and in-migration of established families.[62] The land outside the service area remains rural until the city and the county decide jointly to include additional property. The plan controls sprawl and protects

sensitive environmental areas and rural land uses; and its planning, by financing and providing urban services in a more rational way, creates a real edge between urban and rural development.[63]

Riverside, California

I was retained by Riverside to develop growth management strategies that contain urban sprawl, utilize impact fees for development financing, and increase city-county intergovernmental coordination. The growth management strategies consisted of various land use elements, including accommodating growth in accordance with community goals. The Land Use Element establishes a planned pattern for the development of the city for the next twenty years. The plan provides direction for developing individual properties according to the community's vision for its future. Following a plan, the city can establish programs to achieve its goals in a logical, incremental, and efficient manner. Similar to the *Ramapo* program, the basic blueprint for growth over the next twenty years is the program planning and timing according to construction of adequate public facilities.[64]

As with many of the regions that I represent, I proposed several land use patterns. Three General Plan alternatives were selected for a detailed analysis: the "Trends" alternative, the "Compact City" alternative, and the "Natural Areas" alternative.[65] When defining the alternatives, the planning committees considered levels of growth, location of new development, and policies related to community character. The committee reviewed nine projections of population and employment growth for the city in the year 2010. From the nine sets of projections, three were chosen for use in developing the alternatives for detailed study. Review of the three plan alternatives concluded that many impacts on the city are simply related to the fact that there will be more people in Riverside in 2010 than today and the demands for service will increase. After detailed analysis, the committee chose and combined desirable aspects from each of the plan alternatives and termed it "Quality City." It emphasized preservation of existing neighborhoods and agricultural areas from the Trends alternative, the intensification along transportation corridors and emphasis on downtown from the Compact City alternative, and the protection of environmentally sensitive areas from the Natural Areas alternative. Also, it reflected the concerns of Sphere of Influence residents by providing for development in their areas comparable to that presently planned for their communities by Riverside County government.

The "Quality City" scenario included five development intensity classes:

- rural/nonurban;
- semirural/low-intensity urban;
- moderate-intensity urban;
- high-intensity urban; and
- the downtown core.

The Rural/Nonurban class identifies land that is to be retained for the lowest intensities of development. Large residential lots, agriculture, and open space all characterize this type of development.

The Semirural/Low-Intensity Urban class is intended primarily for large-lot residential uses. It also encompasses some very limited types of commercial, institutional, and recreational uses, largely in support of the adjacent residential community. Residential development consists primarily of single-family lots of one-half acre or larger.

The Moderate-Intensity Urban class provides for the typical urban single-family residential densities, generally four to eight units per acre. Relatively low-density apartment projects and neighborhood shopping centers also are consistent with this category, as are neighborhood-scale institutional uses and neighborhood or community parks.

The High-Intensity Urban class provided for a full range of residential developments, including apartments. Commercial and industrial sites, such as regional shopping centers, professional and business offices, manufacturing facilities, and institutional uses are also consistent with this category.

The final class, the Downtown Core, is used in existing downtown areas and in areas planned for downtown expansion, provided the highest intensity of development in the General Plan area. A wide variety of uses, including high-density office, residential, government, cultural, visitor commercial, and institutional activities are compatible with this class.

Part of my work was the development of impact fees on all development to provide funds for acquiring wildlife habitats.[66] These impact fees will help promote the ability to purchase the Plan's conservation elements of air quality, water quantity and quality, natural resources, and open space elements. The impact fee process includes only facilities needed for new growth. It is unconstitutional to require development to pay for past deficiencies.[67] Thus the

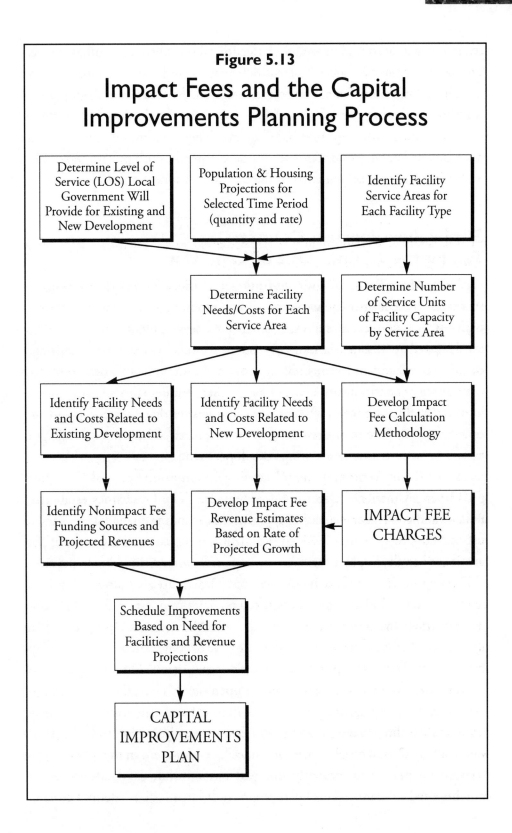

Figure 5.13

Impact Fees and the Capital Improvements Planning Process

community establishes its level of service for each facility, determines the percentage related to new growth versus deficiencies, and uses the impact fees on the former, but only general revenue sources on the latter. (See Figure 5.13.) Another interesting part of Riverside's plan is the development of plans for many sub-areas within the General Plan area. These community plans provide more detailed policies and standards for development, both private and public, within specifically mapped parts of the city and its sphere of influence.[68]

Simi Valley/Ventura County: Taking the County Out of Land Use

Federal and State "takings" law constitutional decisions have begun to recognize that cities and counties can work together to promote development in existing built-up areas and not in sprawling fringe area development. In 1991, a California appellate court ruled that city-county regional cooperation, requiring a compact development form, stressing growth within built-up cities "to protect the unique hill surrounded environment, enhance the quality of life, improve local air quality, reduce traffic demands and ensure that future demands for essential services are met," have long been recognized as legitimate public purposes and not a taking of the fringe developer's land.[69]

In 1969, the Ventura County Planning Commission adopted Guidelines for Orderly Urban Development (Guidelines).[70] The Guidelines established policies and criteria for evaluating applications for zoning changes from rural to urban land.[71] In 1976 and 1985, the Guidelines were revised, however, still promoting urban development within existing, incorporated cities due to the cities' ability to provide the full municipal services. The county also adopted Simi Valley City's General Plan, which designated the land in question for 1,110 units of residential development. However, in 1981, the county's Open Space Plan designated that same area as an "Urban Reserve overlay," encouraging developers to proceed with the appropriate city for development. The city and county, cooperatively, wanted to keep the land as open space. Thus, the city and county, through an intergovernmental strategy, rescinded the original area plan, under which the plaintiff, Long Beach Equities, had bought land (the 1,110 units) for residential development, forbade all development in the urban reserve overlay, downzoned the property, imposed a moratorium on the development, and imposed a growth-control plan to preclude large scale residential develop-

ment.[72] In a monumental case argued by Katherine Stone, of Freilich, Stone, Leitner & Carlisle, the California Court of Appeal held that the system was constitutional.[73]

It was Ventura County, California, and the Simi Valley area, which saw its population explode by five and one-half times since 1950,[74] under my guidance, that devised this intergovernmental growth management strategy, which worked with a less structured system to attain major goals and policies and to provide for planned growth on a countywide scale.[75]

Using a system of guidelines, the county clarified the relationship between the cities and the county with respect to urban planning, facilitated a better understanding regarding development standards and fees, and identified the appropriate governmental agencies responsible for making determinations on land use request. The major goals of the guidelines resembled and combined some of the alternative forms designed for Washoe County, Nevada:

1. to allow for cooperation between various levels of government (performance-based);
2. to allow urbanization while accommodating the goals of individual communities and conserving county resources (tier concept and policy considerations);
3. to facilitate efficient and effective delivery of community services (capital-driven expansion); and
4. to identify planning and service responsibilities of local governments (performance-based and capital-driven).

The California Appellate Court found that the guidelines advanced these goals.[76] The county developed policies—more specific description of how goals would be met—which were divided into two categories with the majority of the policies applicable within the city's sphere of influence and a smaller number of policies applicable to the more loosely defined area of interest.

Presently, the continued growth in Ventura County has created many new issues. New residents come to escape the turmoil of Los Angeles, to raise families, and to have a safer and better quality of life.[77] Many planners are expecting a surge in residential development and in commercial and industrial parks. However, their initiatives, which were upheld by the high courts of California, can stop unwanted, disorderly growth.

Currently, twenty-seven environmental groups have banded together to create a blueprint for protecting the state's natural environment, called

"Restoring the California Dream."[78] The groups fear that the state's expected population boom to fifty-one million by 2030 will trample the environment if planning for the future does not immediately take place.

The myriad terchniques of Smart Growth and curtailing urban sprawl that have been illuminated in this chapter reveal that we do not lack the tools to contain urban sprawl. We are more advanced in the nation (and in the world) than we have ever been. What is lacking is the political will to move ahead and achieve consensus. For this, the alternatives process that I have described works wonders. With coalesced groups of citizens we need proactive legislative leaders who are not "NIMTOOs"—not in my term of office. We decry the NIMBYs and the BANANAS (build absolutely nothing anywhere nor at any time) but we can achieve consensus. Will we have the leadership? Chapter 6 on Smart Growth is providing a number of answers.

Endnotes

1. My plan to revise Platte County, Missouri's comprehensive plan included key recommendations that the county government become more active and cooperate with cities in its boundaries. *See* Walton Whittaker, *County Plan Offered in Growth Era*, K.C. STAR, Oct. 19, 1969, at 14A.; *Urban Growth Can Be Orderly*, K.C. STAR, Oct. 23, 1969, at 4D.

2. Robert H. Freilich & S. Mark White, *The Interaction of Land Use Planning and Transportation Management*, 2 TRANSPORT POL'Y 101–15 (1994). Courts are also promoting county regulations; *see Wilkinson v. Board of County Commissioners of Pitkin County*, 872 P.2d 1269 (Co. Ct. App. 1993), *cert. denied*, (May 16, 1994) (the court held that county was allowed to regulate unincorporated land within the county to assist urban city infill through a growth management quota system—requiring new subdivision applications to compete for limited number of available new building rights allocated by the county each year—since the regulation achieved objectives enumerated in state statutes).

3. ARIZ. REV. STAT. ANN. § 9-461.11.

4. The agreements were worked out by James Neblett, the brilliant planning director for Mohave County, in cooperation with Lake Havasu City, Bullhead City, and Kingman; *see* FREILICH, LEITNER, CARLISLE & SHORTLIDGE, MOHAVE COUNTY GENERAL PLAN, Dec. 6, 1991, at 40.

5. For an historical view of the regional planning in Mohave County, *see* Terry D. Morgan, *Joint Planning in Arizona, in* STATE & REGIONAL COMPREHENSIVE PLANNING, 218 (Buchsbaum & Smith eds., ABA 1993).

6. WASH. REV. CODE § 36.70A *et seq.* (FREILICH, LEITNER, & CARLISLE, PIERCE COUNTY-TACOMA COUNTYWIDE PLANNING POLICIES, June 1996; FREILICH, LEITNER & CARLISLE, WASHOE COUNTY-RENO, NEVADA REGIONAL PLAN, November 1991). *See* NEV. REV. STAT. § 278.0272.

7. FREILICH, LEITNER & CARLISLE, TRUCKEE MEADOWS REGIONAL PLAN, Mar. 21, 1991.

8. Keith, *The Hawaii State Plan Revisited,* 7 U. HAW. L. REV. 29 (1985).

9. TRUCKEE MEADOWS REGIONAL PLAN, *supra* note 7.

10. *Id.*

11. FREILICH, LEITNER & CARLISLE, SUMMIT COUNTY, UTAH, SUMMIT COUNTY GENERAL PLAN, Dec. 28, 1992, at 1.

12. *Id.*

13. The Urban Growth Boundary and Tiers were designed to create an urban form with the following attributes:
- a compact and efficient development pattern with phased urbanizing areas;
- maintenance of the vitality of existing centers and nodes;
- maintenance of existing community and local identity;
- preservation of areas for rural use;
- creation of new centers and corridors with a mix of jobs and housing;
- definition of economic activity centers;
- phasing of urban and suburban development over time consistent with the availability of public services and facilities;
- protection of floodplain;
- creation of regional open space/greenbelt system;
- retention of most hillsides in nonurban use.

14. FLA STAT. at § 163.3177(6)(h) (West 1990); this coordination occurs between the local government, the adjacent cities/counties, the region, and the state.

15. *Id.* § 163.3167(2).

16. *Id.* § 163.3177 (West 1990).

17. *Id.* § 186.504(2)(a).

18. *Id.* § 163.3202(2)(g); *see* REPORT AND RECOMMENDATION ON PUBLIC FACILITIES ORDINANCE REVISIONS AND RELATED MATTERS, prepared by Freilich, Leitner, Carlisle & Shortlidge for Thomas G. Pelham (July 14, 1989); Pat Blanchat, *Workshop May Focus on Growth,* SARASOTA HERALD-TRIB., May 29, 1981, at B1 ("consultant Bob Freilich of Kansas City, who has been dubbed the father of growth control, will be there to discuss legally defensible ways to put a lid on the number of homes and condos that can be built in any one year. Freilich, who is doing a study for the county on the possibility of levying 'impact fees' on new residential construction to help pay for the expansion of public facilities made necessary by growth."); *see also The Florida Experience: Creating a State, Regional and Local Comprehensive Planning Process, in* STATE & REGIONAL COMPREHENSIVE PLANNING: IMPLEMENTING NEW METHODS FOR GROWTH MANAGEMENT 102, 107, 109, 110 (Buchsbaum & Smith eds., 1993).

19. *See* FREILICH AND LEITNER, GROWTH MANAGEMENT IMPLEMENTATION AND FINANCING PLAN, SARASOTA COUNTY (April, 1982); FREILICH & LEITNER, LEGAL BASIS FOR TIMING AND PHASING OF DEVELOPMENT, SARASOTA COUNTY (June 1982).

20. ERIC DAMIAN KELLY, MANAGING COMMUNITY GROWTH, 114 (1994) [hereinafter KELLY].

21. FLA. STAT. § 163.3180 *cited in* Richard Grosso, *Florida's Growth Management Act: How Far We Have Come, and How Far We Have Yet to Go,* 20 NOVA L. REV. 589, 658 (1996).

22. *See* EASTWARD HO! REPORT OF THE GOVERNOR'S COMMISSION FOR A SUSTAINABLE SOUTH FLORIDA (Oct. 1995); *see* Dawson, *The Best Laid Plans: The Rise and Fall of Growth Management in Florida,* 11 J. LAND USE & ENVTL. L. 325 (1996). *See* Tyrone Terry, *Hollywood*

Asks Environment Study to Justify North Beach Density Cap, THE MIAMI HERALD, May 19, 1977, at 2 (where the land firm had proposed building a 4,872-unit development. *See* FREILICH & LEITNER, LAND DEVELOPMENT ANALYSIS FOR THE NORTH BEACH, CITY OF HOLLYWOOD, FLA. (October 21, 1977); *Beach Development Study Will Cost City $100,000*, HOLLYWOOD SUN TATTLER (June 6, 1977); *Hollywood Approves Contract for N. Beach Planner*, SOUTH BROWARD-NORTH DADE SUN REPORTER, June 8, 1997, at 10; Jan Burge, *Hollywood to Make North Beach Study*, SUN REPORTER, May 21–22, 1977, at 4.

23. *See* FREILICH, LEITNER & CARLISLE; POST BUCKLEY SCHUH AND JERNIGAN, INC.; AND HALCYON, LTD., MIAMI BEACH SOUTH SHORE REVITALIZATION STRATEGY (June 1983); Michael Kranish, *Beach Blight May Yet Turn Bright*, MIAMI HERALD, June 28, 1983, at A1; Cynthia Bevans, *Renewal Zone Studied*, SUN RPTR., Nov. 11, 1982; Michael Kranish, *Beach Revives Rebuilding Plan Shelved in the '70s*, MIAMI HERALD, June 26, 1983, at 1B. (The South Beach Plan won the APA national and State of Florida awards.).

24. City of Hollywood v. Hollywood, Inc., 432 So. 2d 1332 (Fla. App. 4th Dist. 1983), *petition for review denied*, 441 So. 2d 632 (Fla. 1983). *See* Robert H. Freilich & Wayne M. Senville, *Takings, TDRs and Environmental Preservation: "Fairness" and the Hollywood North Beach Case*, LAND USE L., Sept. 1993, at 4–8.

25. MONROE COUNTY, FLORIDA, DWELLING UNIT ALLOCATION ORDINANCE, no. 016-1992.

26. Applicants must meet, among others, zoning, density, open space requirements. The eligible applicants are then assigned points and ranked based on various criteria including habitat value, voluntary density reductions, and impacts on endangered species. *See* SUMMARY OF SUBMISSION, MONROE COUNTY DWELLING UNIT ALLOCATION ORDINANCE.

27. Interview with Martin L. Leitner, Partner at Freilich, Leitner & Carlisle (Feb. 26, 1998) (due to the safety concern of evacuation during hurricane emergencies, a rate of growth system was allowed limiting the number of permits granted annually to keep the population sprawl at a minimum). The rate of growth system was developed in the early 1970s for Petaluma, California, where it established a limit of 500 new residential dwelling units per year. "The Petaluma program was simpler and far less interesting than the Ramapo program." *See* KELLY, *supra* note 20, at 33. However, "although [the Petaluma program was] less sophisticated than Ramapo's, [it] had an equal impact on planning practice." KELLY, at 34.

28. *Supra* note 25.

29. *Id.* (the 15,000 vacant lots may be considered vested by the courts).

30. *See* Burnham v. Monroe County, District Court for Monroe County (final judgment upholding constitutionality of rate of growth ordinance, 1998).

31. Steve Liewer, *Commission to Shift County Growth to East*, SUN-SENTINEL, Jan. 25, 1995, at B; *see* EASTWARD HO! REPORT OF THE GOVERNOR'S COMMISSION FOR A SUSTAINABLE SOUTH FLORIDA (Oct. 1995).

32. Robert H. Freilich & David W. Bushek, *Integrating Land-Use and Transportation Planning: The Case of* Palm Beach County v. Wright, 18, STATE & LOCAL LAW NEWS, Winter 1995, at 1; *see also* Robert H. Freilich & Stephen P. Chinn, *Transportation Corridors: Shaping and Financing Urbanization Through Integration of Eminent Domain, Zoning and Growth Management Techniques*, 55 UMKC L. REV. 153, 154 (1987).

33. 641 So. 2d 50 (Fla. 1994). The Florida Fourth Circuit District Court of Appeals, *Palm Beach County v. Wright*, 612 So. 2d 709 (Fla. 4th DCA 1993) had certified this issue for the Florida Supreme Court:

Is a county thoroughfare map designating corridors for future roadways, and which forbids land use activity that would impede future construction of a roadway, adopted incident to a comprehensive county land use plan enacted under the local government Comprehensive Planning and Land Development Regulations Act, facially unconstitutional under *Joint Ventures, Inc. v. Department of Transportation,* 563 So. 2d 622 (Fla. 1990).

34. *Palm Beach County,* 641 So. 2d at 54.

35. *Palm Beach County,* 612 So. 2d at 710.

36. Joint Ventures, Inc. v. Dept. of Transportation, 563 So. 2d 622, 623 (Fla. 1990).

37. *Id.* at 626.

38. *Id.* at 625. *See also, e.g.,* San Antonio River Authority v. Garrett Brothers, 528 S.W.2d 266 (Tex. Ct. App. 1975) (as prospective purchaser of land, local government may not prevent development that would increase costs of such future government acquisition).

39. 641 So. 2d, *supra* note 33, at 53–54.

40. *Id.* at 53.

41. *Id.* at 53–54.

42. *Golden v. Planning Bd. of Ramapo,* 30 N.Y.2d 359, 285 N.E.2d 291, 334 N.Y.S.2d 138, *appeal dismissed,* 409 U.S. 1033 (1972) was the basis for the adequate public facilities statutory requirement developed in Washington and Florida. *See also, e.g.,* MD. ANN. CODE, art. 66B, § 10.01 (1988), and N.H. REV. STAT. ANN. § 674:21–:22 (1990 Supp.), both authorizing timing and sequence provisions to plan for adequate public facilities.

43. 612 So. 2d, *supra* note 33, at 53.

44. 640 So. 2d 54 (Fla. 1994).

45. *See* Lucas v. South Carolina Coastal Council, 112 S. Ct. 2886, 2893 (1992). *See also* Concrete Pipe and Products of California, Inc. v. Construction Laborers Pension Trust for Southern California, 113 S. Ct. 2264, 2290 (1993), where Justice Souter commands that the relevant framework for regulatory takings analysis is whether the property taken is all, or only a portion of, the parcel in question. The test for regulatory takings requires the court to compare the value that has been taken from the property with the value that remains in the property, and one of the critical questions is determining how to define the unit of property the value of which is the denominator of the fraction. *Id.*

46. *See* Hodel v. Virginia Surface Mining & Reclamation Ass'n, 452 U.S. 264 (1981)

47. Yee v. City of Escondido, 122 U.S. 1522 (1992).

48. For further discussion regarding these tools, *see* Robert H. Freilich & S. Mark White, *Transportation Congestion and Growth Management: Comprehensive Approaches to Resolving America's Major Quality of Life Crisis,* 24 LOY. L.A. L. REV. 915 (1991).

49. *See* Dolan v. City of Tigard, 512 U.S. 374 (1994).

50. *Palm Beach County,* 641 So. 2d at 53.

51. *See* GROWTH MANAGEMENT PLANNING AND IMPLEMENTATION TECHNIQUES, August 12, 1993, which fully explained different approaches to urbanizing growth including: growth boundaries (Minneapolis/St. Paul, MN); phased growth (Ramapo, NY); transportation corridors (Montgomery County, MD, and San Diego, CA); centers and nodes (Baltimore County, MD); and tiered growth alternatives (Reno/Washoe County, NV).

52. *See* Freilich, Garvin & White, *Economic Development and Public Transit: Making the Most of the Washington Growth Management Act,* 16 U. PUGET SOUND L. REV. 949, 964–68 (1993).

53. *See* section 1(3)(e) of the Act.

54. *See* JAMES A KUSHNER, SUBDIVISION LAW AND GROWTH MANAGEMENT § 8.09(5) "Variance Administration" (Clark Bordman Callahan 1995).

55. FREILICH, LEITNER & CARLISLE, COMPREHENSIVE GROWTH PLAN, GRAND JUNCTION, COLORADO, Oct. 2, 1996, at I.7.

56. *Id.* at V.2.

57. *Id.* at exhibit IV.4.

58. *Id.* at V.2.

59. *See also* Boulder Builders Group v. City of Boulder, 759 P.2d 752 (Co. Ct. App. 1988) (City Growth Ordinance, which limits the number of building permits issued for new dwellings each year, was constitutional as it was not a matter of statewide concern and purely local).

60. FREILICH, LEITNER, CARLISLE & SHORTLIDGE, PHASED REPORT: EVALUATION OF DEVELOPMENT REGULATIONS AND REVIEW PROCESS FOR THE CITY OF BOULDER, COLORADO (April 9, 1990).

61. *Controlling Sprawl in Boulder: Benefits and Pitfalls*, LAND LINES, (Lincoln Institute of Land Policy) January 1998, Vol. 10, No. 1, Peter Pollock.

62. Freilich & Leitner, *supra* note 8; *see also* CITY OF BOULDER NEWSL., RESEARCH PERSPECTIVES, 1 (1992).

63. Peter Pollock, *Controlling Sprawl in Boulder: Benefits and Pitfalls*, 10 LAND LINES, (Lincoln Institute of Land Policy, January 1998) ("This approach owed much to the phased growth control ordinance pioneered in 1969 by the Township of Ramapo, New York.").

64. FREILICH, STONE, LEITNER & CARLISLE, CITY OF RIVERSIDE GENERAL PLAN 2010 (1989), at 214.

65. *Id.* at 102.

66. DOUGLAS R. PORTER, MANAGING GROWTH IN AMERICA'S COMMUNITIES 105; *see generally* MARK BALDASSARE, THE GROWTH DILEMMA 14 (1981).

67. Home Builders & Contractors Ass'n v. Board of County Commissioner, 446 So. 2d 140 (Fla. App. 1983); Marblehead v. City of San Clemente, 277 Cal. Rptr. 550 (Cal. App. 1991); Anema v. Transit Construction Authority, 788 P.2d 1261 (Colo. 1990).

68. *Supra* note 64.

69. Long Beach Equities, Inc. v. County of Ventura, 231 Cal. App. 3d 1016, 282 Cal. Rptr. 877 (1991); Freilich & Garvin, *Takings After* Lucas: *Growth Management Planning and Regulatory Implementation Will Work Better Than Before*, 22 STETSON L. REV. 409 (1993).

70. *Long Beach Equities*, at 1025.

71. *Id.*

72. *Id.* at 1026.

73. *Id.*

74. *See* Daryl Kelley, *California and the West: The Times Poll—Ventura County Backs Slow Growth*, L.A. TIMES, Oct. 19, 1997, at A3.

75. *Long Beach Equities, supra* note 69. The court went on to add that "ordinances which seek to preserve the surrounding environment and which consider open space and the density of development benefit both developers and the public by 'assuring careful and orderly development of residential property with provisions for open-space areas.'" *See also* Griffin Homes, Inc. v. Superior Court, 229 Cal. App. 3d 991, 1002, 280 Cal. Rptr. 792 (1991) (appellate court dismissed claims of a developer that failed to receive development permits in the annual allocation process); Building Industry Association of San Diego v. City of Oceanside, Nos.

N37638 and N37196 (San Diego Super. Ct., Aug. 6, 1991) (consolidated with *Del Oro Hills v. City of Oceanside*) (growth management ordinance is necessary for the public health, safety and welfare of the local population).

76. *Long Beach Equities, supra* note 69, at 886.

77. *See supra* note 71.

78. L.A. TIMES, Feb. 5, 1999, at A3.

CHAPTER SIX

Smart Growth in the States

Introduction

While traditional zoning and other local regulatory ordinances continue to be the primary method of controlling the development and use of land, a "quiet revolution" in land use controls has seen the retention of much of the broad, policy decision-making power by the states.[1] Important concepts have developed through state growth management systems that are beneficial to cities, counties, metropolitan areas, and states. Currently, there is an array of approaches utilized by states for controlling sprawl and unplanned development, which has come to be known as "Smart Growth."[2] State-sponsored growth management programs are generally provided for under state legislative enactments consisting of mandates for the preparation of local comprehensive plans and sometimes county or regional plans.[3] They typically encourage plan submittal to the state or agency for review or approval,[4] and compliance and cooperation are backed with system incentives, including encouragement to update plans periodically. Hawaii, Vermont, Florida, and Oregon were the first states to implement statewide planning,[5] and today numerous states have adopted some form of state legislation, through either growth management or Smart Growth land use strategies, that have helped to curtail urban sprawl.

This chapter explores the variety of state planning and Smart Growth legislation, most of them focusing on the use of "tiered" growth strategies stemming from the *Ramapo* case.[6] Such legislation coordinates local planning with state goals, and often involves joint city-county and regional cooperative planning. The Urbanizing Tier is perhaps the most critical area of importance for controlling sprawl, largely because the Ramapo system of timing and sequencing of adequate public facilities and services ultimately controls the pace and location of development in a given area. A common foundation shared by each state's legislation, and ultimately its growth management strategies, is the utilization of creative and flexible programs developed for controlling sprawl within the Urbanizing Tier stemming from the Ramapo system. As the reader will see, my Ramapo system truly laid the groundwork for modern Smart Growth systems.

Because *Ramapo* allowed municipalities to control the timing and sequencing of development, states have been able to take capital improvement program controls one step further by enacting fiscal policies that restrict state infrastructure funding to "smart growth" areas. What becomes apparent are both the complexity of land use issues that local governments deal with as financial resources are stretched tighter and the creative ways in which solutions have been found. As the reader will see, ingenuity and persistence in state legislation and fiscal policies have been the key to combatting sprawl in America over the past three decades.

Smart Growth in the States

Several states have enacted comprehensive smart growth management laws incorporating concurrency requirements and timed and sequenced growth.[7] Hawaii, for example, in 1961 became the first state to institute statewide land use control. The state legislature created the State Land Use Commission[8] which determines what lands will be developed classifying "urban," "agricultural," "conservation," or "rural" lands.[9] Considered one of the most sophisticated land use management systems in the country, Hawaii's plan consists of detailed development plans with common provision text, land use maps, and public facilities maps covering every inch of the Island of Oahu. County charters forbid even the "initiation" of a subdivision or zoning change unless it conforms to the development plan with adequate public facilities.

Colorado adopted new land use control legislation in 1970.[10] The Colorado Land Use Act[11] established a land use commission for the state that has the power to formulate a state land use planning program.[12] The Commission is empowered to establish guidelines classifying land use matters as either of statewide, regional, or local concern and that determine the proper roles and responsibilities of each level of government.[13] But even so, the basic policy behind the Act still recognizes " . . . that the decision making authority as to the

character and use of land shall be at the lowest level of government possible, consistent with the purposes of [the Act]."[14] In addition to the land use commission, fourteen state agencies have land use management responsibilities in either planning or regulation of development, which requires timed concurrency for infrastructure.[15]

The State of Maine, in 1969, adopted a statewide land use control scheme.[16] Under that provision, a state Land Use Regulation Commission[17] is empowered to classify the land of the state into four "land use guidance districts"—"protection," "management," "development," and "holding."[18] A developer must obtain a permit issued by the Commission before construction can begin on any new structure, building, or development.[19] The developer must comply with "land use guidance standards" formulated by the Commission as a prerequisite to gaining permit approval. The Maine legislation is limited, however, in that it applies only to unincorporated areas of the state.[20] A second land use-related Act was enacted in 1970—the Site Location Law of 1970.[21] That law is designed to ensure the environmental soundness of new governmental, commercial (including residential subdivisions) and industrial developments to be located anywhere within the state.[22] The Environmental Improvement Commission created by the Act reviews plans for any "development which may substantially affect the environment,"[23] and has veto power over any development that it finds may have an "adverse effect on the natural environment."[24] For industrial development or location of an industry to be approved, the developer must prove that there is adequate provision in the plans for fitting the project harmoniously into the existing natural environment as well as public facilities and that the project will not adversely affect existing uses, the land's scenic character, natural resources, or property values in the municipality or in adjoining municipalities.

The 1970 Vermont Land Use and Development Act[25] established a state environmental board and district environmental commissions to regulate land use and to establish comprehensive state capability, development, and land use plans. Under the Act, a permit must be obtained from the board prior to commencing construction of any development[26] or subdivision that involves ten or more acres of land.[27] It also applies to any commercial or industrial improvements on more than one acre of land within a municipality that does not have permanent zoning and subdivision laws; housing projects of more than ten units; and any construction improvements above 2,500 feet elevation—but these do not require the issuance of permits. Permits may not be issued if the proposed subdivision or development will cause "unreasonable soil erosion or reduction in the capacity of the land to hold water so that a dangerous or unhealthy condition may result."[28] Nor can they issue permits if the proposal would have an undue adverse impact on the scenic or natural beauty of the area, on the aesthetics of the area, historic sites, or on rare and irreplaceable natural areas.[29] Permits also may be issued only after a finding that the subdivision or development will not result in undue air or water pollution based upon

> . . . the elevation of land above sea level; and in relation to flood plains, the nature of soils and subsoils and their ability to adequately support waste disposal; the slope of the land and its effect on effluence; the availability of streams for disposal of effluents; and the applicable health and water resources department regulations.[30]

The Vermont Act also mandates that there be no unreasonable burdens on existing water supplies, on the ability of municipalities to provide educational or governmental services, or to proposed or existing highway systems.[31] The permit system is enforced by provisions providing that deeds cannot be recorded without an accompanying certificate from a commission that the conveyance and development of the property is in compliance with the permit requirements.[32]

Increased population growth, and the realization that Act 250 alone could not preserve the way of life Vermonters wanted, led to the passage of the Growth Management Act of 1998. Act 200, as it is known, significantly increases the planning obligations of municipalities, and regional and state commissioners and agencies. While Act 200 initially required that municipal plans be consistent with that Act's planning goals, a 1989 amendment deleted that mandatory feature. Nonetheless, municipal plans, which must take into account state legislative goals, are reviewed by regional planning commissions. Though consistency is not mandatory, failure to obtain regional approval subjects the municipality to affordable housing review by the state community development office. Approval also confers on the municipality the power to levy impact fees and makes it eligible to participate in a planning fund.

Only a few states have adopted a state comprehensive plan. Within this category, the representative states show that Hawaii was a state ahead of its times when that state's legislature adopted a state land use law in 1961 and a state

comprehensive plan in 1978.[33] Florida would be the next state to enact a state comprehensive plan in 1985.[34] New Jersey would follow with the release of a preliminary state plan in 1989, an interim state plan in 1991, and the New Jersey State Development and Redevelopment Plan in 1992.[35] While each of these three states has a state plan, each has taken a very different approach to planning, all however including the timing and sequencing of *Ramapo.*

Hawaii

The issues that spurred the government in Hawaii to adopt a state plan in 1961 included a desire to preserve rural, natural resource, and agricultural lands from rapid urban encroachment and a desire to promote economic development.[36] By 1975, the system had been in place for fifteen years, but urban encroachment was continuing to occur as well as agricultural and natural resource depletion.[37]

The Hawaii State Growth Management System authorizes the State Land Use Commission to establish the boundaries of four land use districts, and the Office of State Planning conducts a review of district boundaries every five years.[38] The four districts include an urban, a rural, an agricultural, and a conservation district. The state controls the conservation district, the local governments control the urban district, and the state and local governments split the control of land use in the remaining rural and agricultural districts.

The districts may be viewed as a combination of urban growth boundaries and tiered development. Each urban district has an urban growth boundary. Viewing the remaining districts as tiers is consistent because the land use within each district is controlled by different considerations based upon the particular characteristics of the land and an accompanying level of desire to encourage or discourage certain types of development. However, the districts lack the timing and sequencing quality of the traditional tier technique.

Joint control of the rural district involves control of about 1 percent of the land. The permitted uses in the rural district are generally low-density residential uses (that is, minimum lot size of one dwelling house per one-half acre), agricultural uses, and public facilities.[39] Public facility systems are supported by explicit objectives and goals including state and county cooperation in coordinating facility systems and capital improvement priorities, encouraging flexible design and development to promote efficient use of resources, and changing public demands. Special permits may be available for other uses in the rural district, based upon approval by the county if the application is for less than fifteen acres and by the Land Use Commission if the proposal involves more than fifteen acres.[40] Boundary amendments to the urban, rural, or agricultural districts may be approved by the county if the amendment involves fewer than fifteen acres.[41] All boundary amendments in the conservation district and amendments involving greater than fifteen acres in the other districts require approval by the state Land Use Commission.[42] Because the state defines the permitted uses and retains control of special uses for proposals over fifteen acres in three of the districts, the state assumes the majority of control of the land in Hawaii.

The Hawaii State Plan consists of the state's overall theme, goals, objectives, policies, priority guidelines, functional plans, the counties' general plans, and the state programs.[43] The need for a state planning system is outlined by the legislature as the need to improve the planning process in this state, to increase the effectiveness of government and private actions, to improve coordination among different agencies and levels of government, to provide for wise use of Hawaii's resources, and to guide the future development of the state.[44]

The Hawaii State Plan requires counties to adopt general plans that are consistent with the state plan.[45] State programs must also plan in conformance with the state plan.[46] This conformance mandate was softened in 1984 when the legislature defined conformance as a weighing of overall considerations and a determination that the action is consistent with overall theme and fulfills one or more of the goals, policies, or objectives.[47] The Office of State Planning conducts a review of major plans, programs, projects, and regulatory activities.[48] The counties are authorized to enforce land use restrictions.[49] I proposed to the Waikiki City Council a legislative package that would alter the basic concepts under which the tourist center had been developed by retaining open space through Transfer of Development Rights (TDRs) distributed to alternative centers located throughout the island of Oahu.[50]

New Jersey

In a significant attempt to manage growth on the state level, the New Jersey State Planning Commission was charged in 1985 by the state legislature with the task of producing a State Development and Redevelopment Plan.[51] I was retained by the Office of State Planning as chief legal consultant to conceptualize an overall growth management strategy that utilizes implementation tech-

niques that are both effective to the achievement of the plan's goals and objectives and legally defensible.

New Jersey is a small, densely populated state located between the two large metropolitan areas of New York and Philadelphia. A major shift in development location occurred between 1950 and 1985, when new development began in exurban and rural areas and resulted in the loss of over one-half of the farmland in the state.[52] In addition to the loss of agricultural land, many of the state's highway and wastewater treatment facilities operated over capacity.[53] It was in this context that the New Jersey Supreme Court issued the *Mt. Laurel* decisions in the early 1980s. The Court essentially required a state plan be maintained that could be used to assist in determining local government's affordable housing obligations.[54] Thus, the lack of affordable housing, the desire to protect agricultural and forest lands, and the deficits in highway and wastewater facilities were all primary issues that created a political environment that allowed the successful passage of the New Jersey State Planning Act in 1986.[55]

The Planning Act provided for the New Jersey State Plan to occur in three phases: a preliminary plan, an interim plan, and a final plan.[56] The preliminary plan was presented in 1989, an interim plan was adopted in 1991, and the final plan was adopted in June 1992.[57] Each phase of planning had a distinct purpose: The preliminary plan served as the initial plan for negotiation in the intergovernmental coordination efforts known as cross-acceptance.[58] The interim plan reflected the changes made to the plan during cross-acceptance.[59] The final plan was the plan that was implemented after approval by the State Planning Commission.[60]

The State Plan encourages local governments, counties, and regional entities to adopt comprehensive plans.[61] State, regional,[62] county, and local governments are all encouraged to provide adequate public facilities[63] and to plan those services according to the State Plan's goals and objectives.[64] Counties play a key integrating role in the cross-acceptance process.[65] The unique concept of cross-acceptance was developed in the New Jersey Plan; it is a process that facilitates different levels of government in the comparing of plans, the identification of areas of agreement and disagreement, and the resolution of conflicts, with the purpose of attaining compatibility between local, county, and state plans.[66] The State Planning Act outlines cross-acceptance as beginning with the State Planning Commission, which negotiates plan cross-acceptance with each county, after which each county planning board will negotiate plan cross-acceptance among local planning bodies within their jurisdiction.[67] Each of these negotiations results in a written report to the State Planning Commission, which identifies the degree of consistencies and the remaining inconsistencies between the preliminary plan and the county and municipal plans.[68] While the State Plan encourages planning and consistency among state, county, and regional plans, as well as consistency within each plan, the state provides no means of enforcement to ensure planning goals are met.[69]

After considering four alternative systems for managing growth,[70] the Commission concluded that *Ramapo's* "tier system" would provide the greatest flexibility in meeting the mandates of the State Planning Act.[71] The proposed plan incorporated a growth management system that identified seven differentiated functional planning tiers for which specific implementation strategies were recommended. The primary objectives of the plan were to reduce sprawl, to protect natural resources, to stimulate development in urban areas, and to channel growth into nodes within designated transportation corridors. Tiers One through Four were designated as Growth Areas, while the remaining Tiers Five and Six were designated as Limited Growth Areas.[72] The Growth Areas accommodate full economic activity and provide a full range of residential housing for all income levels. Limited Growth Areas reduce sprawl and preserve natural resource areas such as open space, agricultural lands, and ecologically significant areas. The timing and sequencing features of the tier system were appropriate for the New Jersey Plan because it incorporated key provisions of the State Planning Act:

1. identifying areas for growth, limited growth, agricultural, and open space conservation;
2. encouraging development and economic growth in locations that are well situated with respect to present or anticipated public service facilities; and
3. discouraging development where it may impair or destroy natural resources or environmental qualities.[73]

Though growth may occur in all tiers, the Plan recognizes that some of the communities should not grow unless these services have the capacity necessary to serve more growth. Additionally, the Plan recognizes that there will be growth pressures in rural communities that can be accommodated beneficially at appropriate densities or in compact forms at appropriate locations.

Areas included in Tier Four (the Urbanizing Tier) have experienced significant residential and commercial growth, which has exasperated traffic congestion and air quality. While Tier Four consists of the most attractive and affluent suburban municipalities in New Jersey, the communities are not fully developed and may consist of substantial open space. The rapid growth has caused many of these municipalities to face a number of critical issues including increased demands on public facilities and services, increased traffic congestion, anticipating what future needs will be concerning public facilities, services, and open space, as well as the need to develop a comprehensive plan. The proposed plan addressed these issues, establishing several policies.

To control growth within the Urbanizing Tier, the Plan suggested that the appropriate state departments, in cooperation with counties and municipalities, establish a coordinated and comprehensive approach to development. This comprehensive approach would promote stability and growth by establishing adequate levels of public investment in capital facilities and services, and prioritize the acquisition and development of existing open space for active and passive public recreational use with private and public funding. The Plan also suggested coordinating housing development at all levels to ensure that residential development is coordinated with public facilities and services to provide a range of housing choices while maintaining the community character. Finally, transportation facilities and service in the Urbanizing Tier should acknowledge the automobile as the dominant mode of transportation and encourage nontraditional service to reduce the number of trips in low-density areas.

Implementation strategies to achieve the goals and objectives of each tier were developed in April 1987. During the development of these strategies, concern arose about the methodology for development of the density standards recommended for the Limited Growth Areas and questioned whether they were legally defensible and reflected the national and New Jersey norms. Accordingly, the Office of State Planning requested that I conduct legal research and an analysis of the effectiveness of density standards proposed in the Implementation Report.

From 1987 through 1992, the planning process went through statutorily mandated preliminary, interim, and final plan stages upon its adoption in June 1992.[74] Under political pressure, following the statement by one of the Planning Commissioners that the growth management strategy brought "tiers to [his] eyes," the tiers were changed to "planning areas."[75] The 1992 Plan divided New

Jersey into five areas: two "growth areas" (metropolitan urban and outer suburban) and three tiers in "limited growth areas" (agricultural, environmentally sensitive, and urban fringe). These areas were designed to fulfill the mandate of encouraging development, redevelopment, and economic growth in areas that are situated near present or anticipated public services and facilities and were designed to discourage development where it might impair or destroy natural resources or environmental qualities.[76] The Plan also recommended a design system that linked communities into regional networks based upon the scale of their future development. This "region design system" was critical to ensuring that community character and identity were preserved during growth. The Plan's concept of "Communities of Place" reflected the need for a variety in the scale and location of communities. To achieve this diversity in housing, jobs, living environments, and other quality-of-life features demanded by the communities, cities must be large, urbanized, and attractive.[77] The Plan proposed that future growth be organized in and around existing and planned "central places" from which basic public and commercial services can be provided efficiently.

This tier technique is used to divide the entire state into five "planning areas." The planning areas possess specific characteristics and are assigned unique policy objectives. There is a metropolitan, a suburban, a fringe, a rural, and an environmentally sensitive planning area.[78] The planning areas are used to guide growth into appropriate locations and patterns within the state. Each planning area has two components: the centers and the environs. The centers are central places intended to receive projected growth while the environs are areas outside the development boundaries where conservation and protection policies are used. The State Plan identifies five levels of central places: urban centers, towns, regional centers, villages, and hamlets. There are several criteria for designating a community at one of these levels. Each level of community is defined by criteria such as density, population, employment base, and infrastructure. In general, urban centers are characterized by a population of greater than 40,000; towns will have a population between 1,000 and 10,000; villages, a population of less than 1,500; and hamlets, a population of between 25 and 250 persons. The planned regional centers are located along the major transportation corridors in the state, and use policies to organize growth and prevent sprawl.[79]

The Plan also utilized techniques to preserve agriculture and integrate planning for areas of critical state concern. Agricultural protection is accomplished

through policies established for the rural planning area, which contains most of the state's farmland. The policy intent is to encourage development in a form that is appropriate to and supports agriculture. In part, this is done "by promoting the location of goods and services essential to farming in convenient proximity to agricultural lands," and by supporting the "right to farm" within the rural planning area.[80]

The State Plan established policies to protect "areas of critical state concern." These policies assist in the coordination of planning for areas already established within the state, such as the New Jersey Pinelands, the Hackensack Meadowlands, and the coastal areas. Through cross-acceptance, other critical areas were selected for protection,[81] and the Plan allows for future designation of additional critical areas.[82]

The intergovernmental coordination to ensure consistency and compatibility among all levels of governmental plans was achieved through the cross-acceptance technique. Cross-acceptance is considered a negotiation phase where the different levels of governments and the public review and revise the state plan. The cross-acceptance process has three phases: the comparison phase, the negotiation phase, and the issue resolution phase. The comparison phase began with the release of the Preliminary State Development and Redevelopment Plan in 1989. The comparison consisted of cities and counties comparing the Preliminary Plan with their local plans and submitting reports and comments to the State Planning Commission. The negotiation phase occurred when representatives from the State Planning Commission met with city and county officials to discuss revisions to the Preliminary Plan, municipal plans, and county plans. The issue resolution phase consisted of final governmental and public review of the Interim Plan, which was followed by the adoption of the final State Development and Redevelopment Plan.[83] However, after a grandiose beginning, the plan has revealed the hard reality of state versus local political control. While the Plan does include statewide management, it remains short on implementation because it does not mandate that local plans be consistent, and state agencies are not compelled to use the Plan.

Last winter, in her boldest move yet, Governor Christine Todd Whitman announced one of the biggest land conservation campaigns in New Jersey state history. In her inaugural address, she announced plans to preserve about one million acres, about half of New Jersey's remaining open space.[84] To buy the land, Governor Whitman wants the legislature and the voters to approve a special ten-year fund that would provide about $170 million a year.[85] Part of this revenue will come from her proposed gasoline tax increase. This announcement is no new surprise, as many New Jersey counties already impose property taxes to preserve open space.

Washington

The Washington Growth Management Act (GMA) delineates several goals and issues including urban sprawl, transportation needs, and concurrency of public facilities and services.[86] It clarifies timetables that the municipal and county governments must follow in the submission of their comprehensive plans to the State Department of Community Development,[87] establishing county planning requirements and their relationship to local planning.[88] Involving all levels of government, it mandates planning by some cities and counties and by certain multicounty areas.[89] The multicounty area and counties required to plan must adopt countywide planning policies that serve as the framework for the county and city comprehensive plans. The state mandates specific elements in the comprehensive plans of cities and counties.[90] All counties are required to adopt development regulations that protect critical areas.[91] The GMA outlines consistency requirements for planning, including:

1. city and county plans must be consistent with state goals;
2. city and county plans must be internally consistent; and
3. city and county plans must be consistent with neighboring city and county plans.[92]

The two growth management techniques that are predominant in the Washington system are urban growth boundaries and concurrency management of transportation facilities. Counties that are required to plan must also delineate twenty-year urban growth areas (UGAs).[9] The cities propose the boundary of their UGA, the county consults with cities, and finally the county designates the boundary of the UGA.[94] Urban growth is encouraged within the UGA, and growth outside the boundary is allowed only if it is considered "not urban in nature."[95] The UGA is determined through population projections and is to provide adequate land to accommodate growth at urban densities for a twenty-year period as well as to provide a greenbelt and open space.

Similar to *Ramapo*, concurrency and timing for infrastructure is required. (See Figure 6-1.) This policy requires the cities or counties to identify funding

---

Figure 6.1

Washington 1990 Growth Management Act

1. Urban growth. Encourage development in urban areas where adequate public facilities and services exist or can be provided in an efficient manner. (§ 36.70A.020(1)).

2. Public facilities and services. Ensure that those public facilities and services necessary to support development shall be adequate to serve the development at the time the development is available for occupancy and use without decreasing current service levels below locally established minimum standards. (§ 36.70A.020(12)).

---

for transportation facilities, transportation facility deficits, and the future needs on a ten-year time frame.[96] Regional Transportation Planning Organizations (RTPOs) are then charged with the coordination of city and county transportation plans within a region.[97] The RTPO certifies the transportation portion of local comprehensive plans, develops and adopts a regional transportation plan, and identifies and plans for transportation improvements for corridors of regional significance.[98] Other regional entities are involved, including three regional planning boards that hear appeals concerning consistency or UGAs, and are authorized to reject a plan and require the submission of a new plan.[99] The State Department of Community Development reviews plans and development regulations for consistency and for required elements.[100] If a plan does not conform to the requirements, the regional planning board may recommend that the governor impose sanctions on the noncompliant cities or counties; the governor may initiate sanctions, such as temporary withholding of revenue collected by the state, which is normally passed on to the local government.[101]

The growth management system requires local governments to adopt and enforce ordinances that allow development only if the affected transportation facility will not decline below the predetermined level of services, unless those improvements or strategies for providing the facilities are made concurrent with the development. The legislature defines concurrency as improvements or strategies that are in place at the time of development or that a financial commitment is in place to complete the improvements or strategies within six years.[102] This timing and sequencing of concurrent facilities helps to control rapid growth and preserve Washington's sensitive environment.

Oregon

The issues that primarily motivated the Oregon legislature to enact a state growth management system included the desire to protect environmentally sensitive areas, such as forests and coastlands, to conserve natural resources, to provide public facilities and services, and to prevent further urban sprawl.[103] The Oregon system is based on nineteen state goals or policies that serve as legislative standards that state agencies, local governments, and a regional authority must comply with in their planning efforts.[104] The Oregon legislation established the state Land Conservation and Development Commission (LCDC), which adopts state goals,[105] reviews the local, regional, and state agency plans for consistency with state goals and for compliance with other planning and regulatory requirements,[106] and enforces the state planning requirements.[107] Another state agency, the Land Use Board of Appeals (LUBA) was established and granted exclusive jurisdiction over land use decisions made by state agencies, special districts, local governments, and the regional entity.[108]

All counties are required to coordinate planning with all other levels of government.[109] This role for the counties allows regional coordination of county, city, special districts, and state agency plans. A plan has met coordination requirements if "the needs of all levels of governments, semipublic and private agencies and the citizens of Oregon have been considered and accommodated as much as possible."[110] Special districts are not required to plan, but they are required to enter into a cooperative agreement with the county.[111] State agencies are required to plan for any program affecting land use in compliance with state goals and compatible with local comprehensive plans.[112] City, county, and state agency plans are required to be consistent with the state goals.[113]

Enforcement measures outlined in the Oregon Growth Management System allow LCDC or private parties to commence enforcement proceedings. A variety of situations may result in LCDC issuing an order to a local government,

a special district, or state agency to bring its plan, regulations, or decisions into compliance with the state goals or the applicable acknowledged plan and regulations. For instance, LCDC may issue an order of compliance if a local government's comprehensive plan or land use regulations does not meet the goals by the deadline, if the plan or regulation does not achieve compliance by the deadline, if a local government does not have a plan or land use regulations and is not taking action to meet a compliance schedule, if a local government makes decisions that violate its acknowledged plan and regulations, or if a local government fails to meet the periodic review requirements. The order by LCDC may limit the issuance of permits, place limits on development, or withhold state shared revenues until compliance is achieved.[114] The state requires a periodic review of plans[115] and authorizes LCDC to sanction local governments that do not meet the review requirements.[116]

The primary growth management techniques used in Oregon's growth management system are urban growth boundaries and intergovernmental coordination. The urban growth boundaries separate urban lands from agricultural, forest or other nonurban uses.[117] In connection with the urban growth boundary, several factors must be considered including the need for housing, employment opportunities, and orderly, timed, and sequenced provisions for public facilities and services. These *Ramapo* principles have contributed to Oregon's success in growth control.

California

The State of California uses an issue approach rather than a comprehensive approach to growth management. The predominant growth management issues in California are protection of environmentally sensitive areas, protection of air and water quality, and population increases. The state has passed many statutes regarding growth management, but the primary actors in growth management are the regional and local governments. The state requires all local governments to adopt a general plan that must include specified elements.[118] The mandatory elements of the general plan are:

1. a land use element;
2. a circulation element;
3. a housing element;
4. a conservation element; and
5. a safety element.[119]

The only portions of this planning mandate that the state enforces are the required affordable housing element and the traffic congestion element.[120]

Using *Ramapo's* linkage of development to infrastructure capacity, most cities in California have adequate public facility provisions.[121] Regional commissions work with localities to conform to the state policies. Some cities in California have expanded the adequate public facilities requirements that were set forth in *Ramapo*. For example, in 1987, Chula Vista, California, adopted threshold standards used in evaluating proposed development and its ability to service the infill of residents and development with public facilities capacity, including air quality and fiscal impacts.[122] Additionally, Carlsbad, California, established a three-tiered growth management program to link development to public facilities and services, including performance standards, provisions of facilities, and funding for facilities; the tiered approach targeted build-out areas around the city.[123]

Vermont

Prior to adopting a state growth management system, Vermont used a piecemeal development review process that occurred at the local level and resulted in development characterized by tourism, ski resorts, and second homes.[124] Five growth issues of primary concern were identified, including:

1. the decline of communities and the loss of community level control of growth management;
2. uneven distribution of growth;
3. a trend of low-income new service and industry jobs;
4. a deterioration of natural resources[125]—especially a decline in forestry and farming;[126]—and
5. an increased scarcity of affordable housing.[127]

The State of Vermont enacted twelve specific goals and four process goals[128] to guide development in the state.[129] The citizens of Vermont wanted to revive the traditional rural scene, which was characterized by concentrated settlement in villages and open countryside dotted with farms.[130]

The Vermont system mandated state agencies whose actions affect land use to prepare plans consistent with state goals and compatible with regional and approved municipal plans.[131] This included actions either sponsored by a state agency or funded by the agency. The state assigned the completion dates to agencies at early dates; thus, the compatibility requirement was not possible in their first round of planning. By 1993, many regional and local plans were to be completed and compatibility pursued. Compatibility of state agency plans may be difficult to achieve when resources are of statewide significance. A resource may be deemed to hold statewide significance if it "has value for more than one region, or when an agency has been directed by the Legislature to build at a specific location, as in the case of a correctional facility."[132]

Regional responsibilities are fulfilled by two entities, the Council of Regional Commissions and the Regional Planning Commissions. The Council of Regional Commissions reviews both state and regional plans and mediates conflicts between state, regional, and local plans.[133] Upon request, the Council also conducts formal review of Regional Planning Commissions decisions regarding confirmation of a local plan.[134] The Regional Planning Commissions review local plans for confirmation, determine local eligibility for incentives, review state capital expenditures for compatibility with regional plans, and prepare and adopt a regional plan.[135] The Regional Planning Commissions are composed of at least one member from each municipality in that region:[136] this ensures that local considerations will be integrated in the region's decision-making process. The growth management Act outlines required elements of the regional plan, which include: basic policies to guide development, a land use element, an energy element, a transportation element, a utility and facility element, a housing element, preservation policies, and a program outlining an implementation strategy.[137]

Local governments are encouraged to plan in a manner consistent with state goals and regional plans and are required to be a member of a regional commission.[138] If a local government chooses to plan, the state requires certain elements in the plan.[139] Incentives for local planning include: funding, exemption from state housing review, and assurance that state agency plans must be compatible with the local plan.[140] Thus, the Vermont system is characterized by incentives and greater regional responsibility. The regional role is unique in that it is accomplished with a local focus. Each of the twenty-seven-member communities has two representatives who serve as regional commissioners. This reflects "the commitment to a locally driven approach—to decision making at the most local level possible."[141]

The Vermont system is characterized by the growth management techniques of fiscal incentives and intergovernmental coordination. Fiscal incentives are used to enhance the desire for planning compliance at both the regional and local levels of government. The Vermont Planning and Development Act established a municipal and regional planning fund (the planning fund) to carry out the intent of the growth management system. Local governments may receive monies from the planning fund if they have a plan that is confirmed.[142] Disbursements from the planning fund to the Regional Planning Commissions are based upon considerations of the progress made in adopting a regional plan.[143] State aid applications by the Regional Planning Commissions from the agency of Development and Community Affairs is dependent on compliance with rules, regulations, and standards,[144] and the region must have been created according to the requirements in section 4341 of the Act.[145] The importance of intergovernmental coordination of planning was indicated when the legislature stated it as the first planning goal in the Vermont Planning and Development Act. The intent of the legislature was to establish a coordinated, comprehensive planning process and policy framework to guide decisions by municipalities, Regional Planning Commissions, and state agencies.[146]

The coordination of state, regional, and local planning is ensured by the mandatory interaction of each level of government during the planning process. Review and confirmation of local plans are conducted by the Regional Planning Commission and requires consistency with state goals and compatibility with other municipalities in the region as well as with the regional plan.[147] State agency plans must be compatible with local plans that have been confirmed. Regional Planning Commissions mandate membership of each municipality,[148] and regional plans must be compatible with approved municipal and adjoining regional plans.[149] This guarantees the interaction of all levels of government and satisfies the desire for coordination of the planning process.

Georgia

As in many other states, growth management issues in Georgia led to the appointment of a governor's commission to study and recommend solutions to the state's growth issues.[150] The commission identified three main issues that would lead to the current growth management system: the protection of natural resources, the provision of public facilities and services, and the support of economic development. The system in place in Georgia is characterized by its reliance on incentives to motivate planning and is implemented by a bottom-up planning approach.

Such incentives were implemented in an attempt to lessen the effects of the mass exodus Atlanta experienced when many of its residents moved outside of the I-285 loop that encircled the city. Atlanta's much-acclaimed spoke pattern rail system has enabled commuters to traverse, and in many cases bypass, the urban core, thus fueling suburan development and creating virtually unchecked sprawl. As a result, Atlanta's growth absorbed many communities on the distant outskirts of their town creating a textbook example of sprawl. In response, the Georia legislature created a transit superagency in April of 1999 which aimed at controlling sprawl-related transit problems and lessen the pollution and conjestion affecting the Atlanta area. The Georgia Regional Transportation Authority has the broad authority to veto major development projects and allocate resources to construct additional transportation facilitites as it sees fit. The situation in Atlanta serves as a lesson to the rest of the state of the importance of intergovernmental cooperation to formulate a regional comprehensive plan which anticipates growth patterns for the area as a whole.

In Georgia lawmakers have approved the creation of a new state agency aimed at conrolling air pollution, traffic, and urban sprawl in the fast-growing Atlanta region—essentially establishing a czar over urban sprawl. The bill establishing the Georgia Regional Transportation Authority, a top priority of Democratic Governor Roy Barnes, was signed after winning final approval from the legislature last spring. "Traffic and air quality will not improve tomorrow," Barnes said, "but if we push forward and insist on regional cooporation, I believe GRTA will provide the mechanism for fixing this problem." The agency would have the power to build and operate mass transportation in counties that violate federal clean-air standards. It would also have veto power over road projects by establishing "priority funding areas" such as transportaion corridors and centers in lieu of sprawl. It would also oversee city and county zoning for major developments such as shopping malls, arenas, office towers, and large subdivisions. Local governments refusing to cooperate would lose state funding. The action was promoted by concern over pollution and sprawl in Atlanta, where the population in the region has doubled in the last three decades to 3.1 million. Barnes made the transportation authority his top agenda item, saying traffic and pollution threaten not just metro Atlanta but also the wealth the area pumps into the state economy. The authority would initially have jurisdiction over thirteen counties in metro Atlanta that are in violation of federal pollution limits. State officials predict that more counties in the Augusta, Columbus, and Macon areas could be added to the list by the summer of 2000.[151]

Counties and cities are encouraged to prepare comprehensive plans that are consistent with state and regional standards. Cities and counties are required to become members of a Regional Planning Center.[152] The anticipated regional role in planning in Georgia includes regional review of local plans, preparation of a regional plan, mediation of local conflicts, provision of technical assistance to local governments, and impact analysis for developments of regional impact and regionally important resources.[153] Every county and all cities were required to negotiate and adopt a Service Delivery Strategy by July 1, 1999. Each strategy must identify all services presently provided in the county by cities, counties, and authorities.[154] Additionally, the strategy must assign which local government will be responsible for providing which service in what area of the county and a description of how all services will be funded. The primary growth management techniques used in the Georgia system include environmental and fiscal impact analysis and fiscal incentives. Like the *Ramapo* system, Georgia allows local governments to assess developers for their share of development and increased need for infrastructure.

Arizona

Similar to Georgia, the State of Arizona has experiencced unprecedented growth in recent times. Arizona has tripled in size in the last forty years and continues to grow at a rate three times faster than the rest of the nation.[155] Also, similar to Georgia, the governor selected a Growing Smarter Commission to study growth-related issues and recommend solutions to avoid population increase-related sprawl.[156] In addition, Arizona has had some success with calling legislative attention to the migratory growth trends that they are experiencing. In May of 1998 the legislature passed "The Growing Smarter Act" resolving to provide a program for the continuing evaluation of land use issues.[157] The resolution was defeated during referendum, but its mere inclusion on the November ballot represents the growing concern of the populous to take an active role of controlling sprawl in their communities.

While the State of Arizona has not adopted a statewide land use or growth management plan, it has enabled local governments to adopt comprehensive plans. The significant growth of the fastest-growing county in Arizona—Mohave County—necessitated legislation authorizing intergovernmental coordination in capital improvements schedules.[158] This rapid growth and lack of coordination between county and city planning efforts were permeated by the

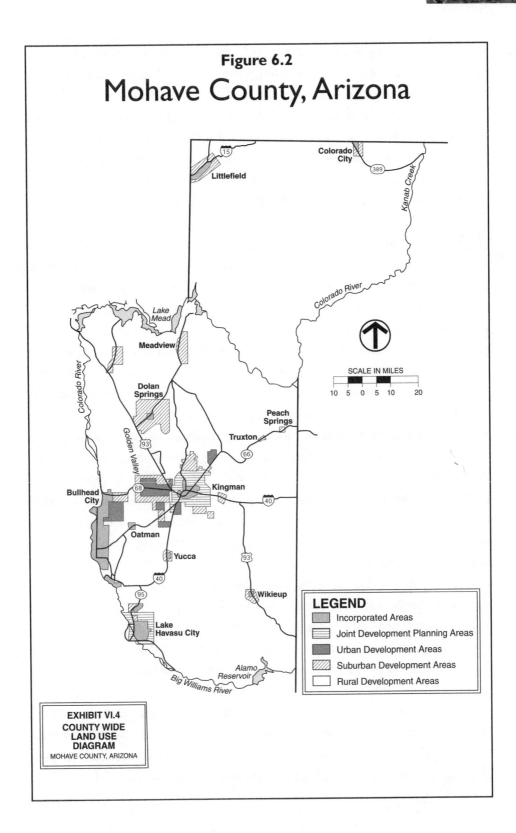

Figure 6.2

Mohave County, Arizona

LEGEND
- Incorporated Areas
- Joint Development Planning Areas
- Urban Development Areas
- Suburban Development Areas
- Rural Development Areas

EXHIBIT VI.4
COUNTY WIDE LAND USE DIAGRAM
MOHAVE COUNTY, ARIZONA

insufficient state legislation in the coordination of city-county mutual development. The county and neighboring cities of Lake Havasu City, Bullhead City, and Kingman soon established an agenda to develop cooperative solutions to similar issues.[159] From the agenda, the region was able to adopt special state legislation exclusively for the county that authorized intergovernmental agreements so that cities and Mohave County could jointly adopt a comprehensive plan.[160] This law also provided for joint development regulations[161] and policies for infrastructure financing.[162] *See* ARIZ. REV. STAT. ANN. § 11-952. (See Figure 6.2.)

More specifically, the law established an extraterritorial jurisdiction of twenty contiguous miles from the city boundary when entering into an intergovernmental agreement. Within the twenty-mile area, the agreement may be exercised either within a three-mile radius of the city or within a three-mile radius of an unincorporated area where there is expected annual population growth.[163] Additionally, the legislation authorized the adoption of a joint development plan that may include land use, conservation, recreation, transportation, economic development, and, most important, public services and facilities as elements. The adoption of a planning program, similar to that of *Ramapo*, which addresses "the timing and sequencing of public facilities and service to serve new and existing development and the staging of development in accordance with the availability of public facilities and services," provides broader power than what the city or county holds in its planning and zoning enabling acts.[164] It allows the region to agree on the timing of capital improvements needed to serve anticipated growth and to relate the timing of such growth to development inside city limits.

The legislation also allows the county to apply city development standards within the unincorporated areas or to establish different standards using the authority under the city's enabling act. This provision creates uniformity in construction and infrastructure standard encouraging future annexation. The county or cities may "borrow" the powers of the other when creating solutions to the provision of adequate public facilities and services. This unique legislation also recognizes the potential impacts of private development on public land with joint development planning areas. Designed especially for Mohave County and surrounding cities, the state law provides resolutions for intergovernmental coordination problems in regulations in Arizona.

Maryland

Maryland's population has increased by 22 percent over the last twenty years.[165] While the older central cities and urban areas have declined in population, much farmland and forest have been devoured by suburban development.[166] Abandoned urban areas and loss of open space created great concern for Maryland. In 1997, the legislature reacted, adopting a "Smart Growth" initiative.[167] Because transportation is a prevalent factor in controlling growth in Maryland, the new program has cited an emphasis on system maintenance to achieve greater mobility from highway and other modal systems. The legislation has provisions to encourage redevelopment of contaminated sites and tax incentives to create a better mix of housing and jobs.[168]

While Maryland is a home-rule state, where local governments have much control over land use decisions,[169] the state has given itself a new role in controlling urban sprawl. Maryland's Smart Growth initiative is designed to encourage compact development and direct capital facilities financing to local governments. Smart Growth Areas will be designated, including existing towns and areas within the Urbanized Tier. Smart Growth is unique in that it allows the state to make investments into efficient uses of land. Similar to the *Ramapo* system, if the state builds schools, roads, libraries, and sewage treatment plants, it is able to limit those investments to the "smartest" locations, areas capable of supporting growth.[170] The Smart Growth initiative allows the state the opportunity to influence, if not control, local land use decisions by directing transportation resources into priority and smart locations—those in urbanized areas where adequate public facilities are prevalent or can be easily provided.

Though Maryland's Smart Growth Program has been hailed as a beacon in the modern growth management maze, it certainly is not the final saving grace of orderly land use and environmental and open space areas. Smart Growth has brought the subtle issues of sprawl control into the light and revealed a landscape full of complicated growth and development decisions.[171] For example, Manchester's downtown main street has become a commuter arterial route, which has resulted in a lost sense of community and actual business.[172] The only way to revitalize the downtown is to get rid of the gridlocked commuter traffic, but this would require a bypass around the city.[173] The state is hesitant to grant funding for the project for fear of the peripheral growth that would follow.[174] This double-edged sword of planning is not easy to remedy. However, the positive side of these complex, sprawl-prevention problems is that Smart Growth "provides a basis for conflict, and then it provides for a process to sort it out."[175]

Prince George's County, adjacent to Washington, D.C., is developing its own smart growth initiative, which is compatible with the state's Smart Growth Program through the assistance of Freilich, Leitner, and Carlisle as principal consultants on developing a County Growth Management tier program.[176] The county's initiative divides the county into targeted growth areas, managed growth areas, and limited growth areas. It further divides the targeted growth areas into Metrorail/MARC areas, bus nodes, revitalization/redevelopment areas, and future transit areas. The Metrorail transit districts are areas within a half-mile of existing and funded-for construction of Metrorail stations. These are areas where there have been large investments in rail transit and where there are significant opportunities for residents and employees to use transit, thereby reducing reliance on automobile trips. The bus service nodes are areas within a quarter-mile of bus service. These are areas that are close to the intersection of two or more major bus routes. Revitalization areas are those where the county has already emphasized the need to direct resources and encourage development, redevelopment, and revitalization. They are areas that should receive priority for funding and special consideration to encourage future investment. The future transit areas are located where the county can plan to take advantage of relatively near-term transit improvements. It is important that development and these areas be planned and constructed to take advantage of the future facility's proximity.[177] The level of specificity helps to streamline efforts and resources to achieve best the goals of the initiative, such as promoting infill, fully utilizing existing facilities, controlling and lessening traffic congestion, and planning for future growth.

Colorado

In 1974, Colorado was one of the first states to adopt a statewide planning act, but it met political resistance that led to its repeal.[178] Nonetheless, Colorado has implemented a Growth Management Quota System (GMQS) regulation, under its Land Use Act, that provides for the regulation of population density, phased development of services and facilities, and land use regulations based on the impact upon the community or surrounding areas.[179] It establishes an annual quota system for new building permits based on a formula against which each development application is tested and scored. The applications are granted on the basis of their score; the high score is granted a permit first, and then the rest are granted in descending order until the annual growth management quota is filled. This elaborate system for phasing development was upheld in the 1994 case *Wilkinson v. Board of County Comm'rs of Pitkin County*.[180] In *Wilkinson*, the court upheld the denial of an application to develop land located near the city of Aspen. The land consisted of twenty-nine mining claims totaling approximately 184 acres that were patented in the 1980s and were located on Smuggler Mountain in unincorporated Pitkin County.[181] In 1985, the developers had acquired options to purchase the properties and thereafter acquired title to all the properties at issue. Their applications were denied because the mining lots were subject to subdivision regulations and subject to the GMQS process, which the developers did not follow. The county Planning and Zoning Commission determined that the land containing the developer's mining claims had merged into two single land parcels under common ownership and were subject to the subdivision regulations.

Additionally, Colorado's Land Use Act provides broad authority to local governments to plan for and regulate the use of land within their respective jurisdictions.[182] It provides local government with the extensive authority to plan for and regulate the use of land resulting in changes in population density based on the impact of development on surrounding areas.

South Carolina

As with several other states, South Carolina has a single legislative Act for community planning. It requires local governments with existing planning ordinances to comply with and conform to the Local Government Comprehensive Planning Enabling Act by 1999.[183] Local governments must establish a planning commission and a comprehensive plan. The plan must include at least seven different elements including population, economic development, natural resources, cultural resources, community facilities, housing, and land use. The community facilities element considers transportation networks, water supply, treatment and distribution, sewage and wastewater treatment, solid waste collection and disposal, fire protection, emergency medical services, and other necessary facilities and allows for *Ramapo*-type adequate public facility and timing and sequencing of development.[184] The enabling legislation provides that local governments may adopt regulations that provide for the harmonious development of the city and county.[185] It coordinates streets within subdivisions and other types of land development with other existing or planned streets. The legislation allows for the dedication or reservation of land for streets, school sites, recreation areas, and utilities easements and other public services and facilities.

Prior to the South Carolina statutory revision, Freilich, Leitner, and Carlisle helped develop growth management plans and regulations for the towns of Hilton Head and Kiawah Islands and Beaufort County. For the county, we specifically designed impact fees for drainage, fire protection, and schools.[186] The plans involved different challenges—in Hilton Head, it was to develop a transportation congestion management program for the island, which had only one major corridor into and out of the island.[187] In Kiawah, it was to develop a comprehensive town plan for *Ramapo*-type timing and sequencing of growth of the construction on pace with the major developer on the island, that had previously received zoning approval from Beaufort County before the town had been incorporated.[188] Both plans had significant impact on the goals, policies, and implementation provisions of the statute.

Florida

Florida has mandated consistency among plans at different government levels through intergovernmental coordination.[189] In the early 1960s, Florida experienced "major growth surges,"[190] but the concerns of unplanned growth did not surface until there was widespread wetland destruction and drinking water supply contamination later in the decade.[191] These mounting issues of diverse land with an explosive population ordered the Florida legislature to act and develop a comprehensive plan.[192] There were several predominant issues identified, including natural resources, sensitive area protection, and problems with adequate public facilities for the regions.[193] By the 1970s, the Florida legislature passed several laws to protect natural resources,[194] to mandate local comprehensive planning,[195] and to begin working toward the goal of a state comprehensive plan.[196] While the State Comprehensive Planning Act was passed in the 1970s,[197] the Florida State Plan was not passed until 1985.[198] In 1993, after several years of experience with the system, the state enacted major reforms to fine-tune and modify its growth management system.

The State Plan mandates local comprehensive planning,[199] local plan consistency with the regional and state plans,[200] county membership in a Regional

---

Figure 6.3

What Is "Concurrency"?

Definition. "Concurrency" means that the public facilities and services needed to maintain level of service standards adopted in a local comprehensive plan are available simultaneous to, or within a reasonable period of time after, development approval or construction.

- In Florida, public facilities must be "available when the impacts of development occur." Florida Administrative Code § 9J-5.003(19).

- In Washington, transportation facilities must be available within six years of development. WASH. REV. CODE § 36.70A.070(6)(e).

Planning Council,[201] and an adequate public facilities provision that is concurrent with development.[202] In addition to requiring local comprehensive plans, the state mandates specific plan elements.[203] These elements include:

1. capital improvements;
2. land use;
3. traffic circulation;[204]
4. sanitary sewer, solid waste, drainage, potable water, and natural groundwater aquifer recharge;
5. conservation;
6. recreation and open space;
7. housing;
8. implementation; and
9. intergovernmental coordination.[205]

Other requirements seek to enhance element compatibility within the plan and consistency among state, local, and regional plans.[206] This requirement was an innovative system of growth management through the integration of local capital improvements with the local land development regulatory process on a statewide, regional, and local basis similar to the *Ramapo* program.[207] The state requires internal consistency within the plan to ensure a lack of conflict among the various local comprehensive plan elements. The concurrency provisions are the "teeth" of the growth management system, requiring that every comprehensive plan include the availability of adequate public facilities when a development order is issued and that the requirement be enforced at the development order stage.[208] (See Figure 6.3.)

The predominant growth management techniques used through the Florida State Plan include *Ramapo's* concurrency management for adequate public facilities provision, impact analysis for development with regional impact, and projects proposed in critical concern areas. The Florida legislature has since decided the concurrency requirement is deemed satisfied "if the public facilities and services for a development are phased, or the development is phased, so that the public facilities and those related services which are deemed necessary by the local government to operate the facilities necessitated by that development are available concurrent with the impacts of the development."[209] While Florida's growth management efforts further the utilization of concurrency, they have failed to revitalize the older urban central cities. Florida's growth management techniques need to be timed and sequenced within the Urbanized Tier and with the appropriate planning basis.

While land use is generally local, Florida's legislature found that certain types of activities affect the state as a whole.[210] There are several regions in Florida that have developed effective programs based on mandatory conformance with the statewide comprehensive legislation. Growth management has been necessary, especially to southern Florida. The current plan addresses critical problems such as the restoration of the Everglades, Florida's future water supply, the loss of agricultural lands, and the need to preserve and restore Florida's environmental systems.[211] Florida's southeast coast is now implementing growth management techniques designed to provide a meaningful channel for growth in southeast Florida to lands other than those adjacent to the Everglades, thereby protecting the environment, encouraging more compact energy-efficient development patterns, and redirecting growth to the older coastal cities requiring revitalization and infill.[212]

Iowa

Most recently, I was invited to write growth management legislation for Iowa based on both a presentation I gave to the state's Commission on Urban Planning, Growth Management of Cities and Protection of Farmland, and the reputation of my firm's work in other Iowa cities and counties. The proposed legislation will be presented to the Iowa legislature during its 1999 general session. The legislation is needed because Iowa is currently witnessing endless urban sprawl as counties are being chopped up through random annexation. Cities are making agreements with other cities essentially to carve out large areas that they will not annex immediately, but claim the right to do so at an unspecified future point. The effect of these agreements has been the circumvention of any city-county cooperation for a comprehensive land use and growth management plan. Counties have essentially had to stand back as cities make these agreements, the ultimate effect of which is to make any county zoning authority hollow and fruitless.

At the center of this legislation, I incorporated my classic *Ramapo* techniques to set out a program of joint city-county planning and strategizing that delineates urban growth tiers and requires consistency among the need for growth and development and the timing and sequencing of adequate public facilities and services—concurrency requirements. The legislation aims at striking a balance between the need to preserve agricultural and environmentally sensitive areas while encouraging growth and development in an orderly, contiguous fashion.

The purposes of the city-county strategic development plan include:
- protection of nonreplaceable agriculturally and environmentally sensitive land;
- prevention of sprawl by encouraging infill and redevelopment of exisiting urban sites;
- giving local governments the authority to plan for urban development in an orderly and cooperative manner;
- identifying and protecting critical areas of local and statewide concern; and
- ensuring that development is concurrent with the availability of adequate public facilities.

Specifically, any city or county that forecasts even the slightest growth is required to write and adopt a strategic development plan. This plan integrates the planning functions of the local government, including concurrency requirements, and requires that once this joint plan is adopted, both city comprehensive plans and county zoning must conform to it. The plan must identify urban growth areas around each city and planned growth areas in the unincorporated part of the county, and localities must develop population projections for each of these areas for the next twenty years. The plan must also address adequate housing needs in conformance with its public facilities and services planning.

The legislation is based on smart growth fiscal and environmental preservation. The strategic development plan forbids extraurban development to use state monies in the form of grants or forgivable loans where the area is not governed by a joint city-county plan. Furthermore, agricultural preservation areas cannot receive tax increment financing, nor can such an area be included as part of a plan that does. And, the Act grants a city the authority to impose an increased property tax rate on vacant or underutilized land. The legislation asks Iowa State University to conduct land use inventories of the state. These inventories will be used to map and project areas of future growth and development and areas in need of agricultural preservation.

The legislation also provides for a moratorium on annexation until a joint city-county plan is created, adopted by both the city and county, and approved by the Board. The Board is given the authority to deny an annexation petition if it does not conform to the purposes of the Act. However, the annexation process as it currently exists was changed. Currently, a party seeking involuntary annexation must get approval first by the City Development Board and then by a City Development Committee, which consists of the five Board members and five local representatives. As amended, a party seeking involuntary annexation will only be required to get approval by the Board. The requirement of the petition's consistency with the Act is the additional burden that the annexing party must fulfill.

A state oversight board, the State Strategic Development Planning Council, was created. The Council includes members from major state departments such as Natural Resources, Economic Development, Transportation, Agriculture, and the Attorney General's office. The Council oversees planning by major agencies involved in large-scale development projects. This oversight ensures coordination and consistency between state level activities and local planning goals and requirements.

Tennessee

Tennessee has taken an interesting approach towards controlling its urban sprawl by requiring all counties and municipalities to prepare a recommended

growth plan by July 1, 2000, which shall be ratified within 120 days after receipt, by county legislative bodies and the governing body of each municipality within the county similar to the Pierce County-Tacoma Washington, process which I described in chapter five.[213] The recommended growth plan shall identify urban growth boundaries for each municipality as well as planned growth areas and rural areas within each county in an attempt to minimize and control urban sprawl. Tennessee is accomplishing such a task by using coordinating committees for every county and municipality that will propose an appropriate urban growth boundary, planned growth area, and rural area for their county or municipality.[214]

Deficiencies in Statewide Acts

Although many of the state plans discussed above were motivated by a necessity to deal with the problems of uncoordinated and haphazard growth, nearly all of those presently in effect place primary emphasis upon environmental problems, and very little emphasis upon urban problems. In addition, because many of the plans are limited to areas designated as "critical," the total amount of land controlled by the plans may be very small. The Florida Environmental Land and Water Management Act,[215] for example, limits the amount of the state's land that can be classified as an area of critical state concern to 5 percent at any particular time.[216] Limiting the use of the "area of critical state concern" classification to five percent of the state's land means that land use control in the remaining 95 percent of the state is subject to state influence only by means of the "development of regional impact" provisions of the Act. Likewise, the Maine land use legislation[217] limits the authority of the Maine Land Use Regulation Commission to unorganized and deorganized townships and mainland and island plantations—an area covering only 42 percent of the state's total land.[218] The Vermont Act[219] is limited in application because of the many exclusions provided by the Act itself. For example, the statute does not apply to construction of pipelines, power or telephone lines, or other "corridor" development, that is to extend more than five miles. In addition, construction for farming, logging or forestry purposes below 2,500 feet elevation is excluded, as are electric generation or transmission facilities certified by the state. As a result of limited application—common to most of the Acts discussed—it is difficult to envision positive, comprehensive planning in any of the states discussed.

One of the major problems discussed in earlier chapters—that of parochialism—is not solved by any of the provisions discussed. For example, under the Colorado Act,[230] aside from a land use planning program to be drawn up by the state Land Use Commission, the only provision for state control over local decisions contained in the Act is a cumbersome proceeding culminating in a personal review by the governor whenever local governments refuse to cooperate with the Land Use Commission.[221] Both the Maine and Vermont statutes are aimed primarily at regulating corporate developers of recreation, retirement, and second-home housing projects. Except where large new developments or subdivisions are concerned, there is no attempt to impose statewide or regional considerations upon the local governments. In addition, like some of the locally implemented growth control techniques discussed earlier, the effect of the state plans can be to exclude some from the boundaries of the state. Because metropolitanwide or regional problems do not stop at state boundaries, statewide development controls are no panacea for the problems resulting from traditional patterns of growth. Thus, the effect of a development-limiting statute such as Vermont's or Maine's may be to free other states to accommodate more than their "fair share" of regional growth patterns.

As has been stated before, the state plans presented here fail to deal "comprehensively" with the problems of modern urban America. Oriented toward environmental problems, or other concerns of relatively narrow scope, those plans fail to provide the affirmative, comprehensive regional-based planning necessary if the modern problems of uncoordinated, inefficient, and undesirable growth are to be solved. Even the Model Land Development Code[222] is premised upon the notion that land use regulations should be left to local decision makers except where such local regulations would "unreasonably restrict developments of regional benefit to be undertaken by public or quasi-public agencies."[223] In addition, the Model Code provides no role for regional agencies in the regulation of land development—state and local agencies occupy the entire field. From the discussion of problems and attempted solutions presented above, it is clear that something more is needed.

The nation's land use problems and the states' failure to reclaim some of their authority delegated early on to localities in the land use field points up the need for efficient and comprehensive planning at the state level.[224] It is clear that current state attempts to meet the needs of twentieth century America have largely failed. It appears that what is missing from state land use

schemes is a commitment to positive planning on a statewide or regional basis.

As a means of implementing affirmative statewide planning, it is suggested here that timing and sequential controls may provide the necessary vehicle. Only through a recognition of the significance of time as a planning tool can economically efficient, socially desirable, and environmentally sound planning be accomplished. With the added problems created by the energy crisis, the importance of efficient planning becomes even greater. No longer can states afford to wall themselves off from what are essentially areawide or national problems by enacting negative, exclusionary planning schemes motivated by parochial interests. It is suggested that through statewide or regional-based planning systems incorporating timed or phased development, states can affirmatively deal with the many problems facing them today.

Additionally, states that follow Maryland's Smart Growth Initiative will be able to influence and control local decisions on growth management, especially where funding for transportation occurs. Approximately a dozen states have highlighted the need for Smart Growth and the need to create a stronger role by the state.[225] New Jersey continually expresses the need to address sprawl issues and urban disinvestment, loss of farmland and open space, air pollution, and traffic congestion.[226] Smart Growth recognizes the role of development in maintaining and improving communities acknowledging the fiscal, environmental—and how to grow.[227] Each state and its communities can find its own individual formula; however, each will adopt common features of Smart Growth that will enhance a sense of community; protect investment in existing neighborhoods; provide a greater certainty in the development process; protect environmental quality; reward developers with profitable products, financing, and flexibility; decrease congestion by providing alternative modes of transportation; and make efficient use of public money.[228] Innovative plans and programs like this will allow states to have a larger role in growth management and the timing and sequencing of growth in the Urbanizing Tier.

Endnotes

1. DAVID L. CALLIES, ROBERT H. FREILICH & THOMAS E. ROBERTS, CASES AND MATERIALS ON LAND USE 675 (West 3 ed. 1999) [hereinafter CALLIES, FREILICH] & ROBERTS]; *see also* Dennis E. Gale, *Eight State-Sponsored Growth Management Programs—A Comparative Analysis,* 58 A.P.A. J. 425 (1992) [hereinafter Gale]; DOUGLAS R. PORTER, MANAGING GROWTH IN

America's Communities (Island Press, 1997); Peter Buchsbaum & Larry Smith, State and Regional Comprehensive Planning (ABA, 1993); James A. Kushner, Subdivision Law and Growth Management (Clark, Boardman, Callaghan, 1995, 1999 Supp.); F. Bosselman & D. Callies, The Quiet Revolution in Land Use Control (1971) [hereinafter Bosselman & Callies]; Cullingworth, The Political Culture of Planning: American Land Use Planning in Comparative Perspective (1993).

A1. Patricia E. Salkin, Smart Growth at Century's End, at 6.

A2. "Governor Celebrates the Passage of Growing Smarter," Agenda for Growing Smarter Press Conference, June 12, 1998.

A3. 1998 Ariz. HCR 2027 (May 20, 1998).

2. *See generally* Douglas R. Porter, Managing Growth in America's Communities 243, n.12 (1997) (current growth management statutes are: Fla. Omnibus Growth Management Act, 1985, H. B. 287; 1985 Fla. Laws ch. 85-55; Fla. State Comprehensive Planning Act (1985); Ga. Regional Transportation Act (1999); Md. Neighborhood Conservation and Smart Growth Act (Md. State Finance and Procurement Code Ann. § 5-7B-01 (1997)); Ma. Economic Growth, Resource Protection and Planning Act (1992); Me. Comprehensive Planning and Land Use Act (1988); N.J. State Planning Act (1986); N.J. State Acts 52:18; Or. Land Use Act, S. B. 100, 1973; Or. Rev. Stat. §§ 197.005-197.650, 215.055, 215.055, 215.515, 215.535, and 453.345; R.I. Comprehensive Planning and Land Use Regulation Act (1988); State Land Use and Development Bill, "Act 250," Vt. Stat. Ann. tit. 10, §§ 6001 *et. seq;* Growth Management Act, Vt. Stat. Ann. tit. 24 § 4350(e) (1998); and Wash. Growth Management Act (1990 & 1991 amend.)).

3. *See supra* note 1.

4. Oregon, Florida, Maine and Rhode Island require local plan preparation and state-level review. *See* Gale, *supra* note 1, at 426.

5. Callies, Freilich & Roberts, *supra* note 1, at 610 (Hawaii—1961; Vermont—1970; Florida—1972; and Oregon—1973).

6. *See* American Planning Association's Growing Smart Project, a periodical serving as a model of modern smart growth legislation.

7. Colorado Land Use Act, Colo. Rev. Stat. § 106-4-1 to -4-4 (1971); Haw. Rev. Stat. tit. 13, §§ 205-1 to -15 (1968); Me. Rev. Stat. Ann. tit. 12, §§ 681-689; Vt. Stat. Ann. tit. 10, §§ 6001-6091 (1973). *See generally* Patricia Salkin, Modernizing State Land Use Laws into the Twenty-First Century: An Inside View of Current Initiatives (Government Law Center, Albany Law School 1998).

8. Haw. Rev. Stat. tit. 13, § 205-1 to -15 (1968). *See also* Bosselman & Callies, *supra* note 1, at 5.

9. Haw. Rev. Stat., *supra* note 8, § 205-2 (Supp. 1972).

10. Colo. Rev. Stat. § 106-4-1 to -4-4 (Supp. 1971). *See also* The Council of State Governments, Land Use Policy and Program Analysis No. 3—Organization, Management and Financing of State Land Use Programs, at 31-41 (1974).

11. Colo. Rev. Stat., *supra* note 10.

12. *Id.* § 106-4-3(1)(a).

13. *Id.* § 106-4-3(1)(b).

14. *Id.*

15. *Id.*

16. Me. Rev. Stat. Ann. tit. 12, §§ 681-689 (Supp. 1972). *See also* The Council of State

GOVERNMENTS, *supra* note 10, at 54; Walter, *The Law of the Land; Development Legislation in Maine and Vermont,* 23 ME. L. REV. 315 (1971).

17. ME. REV. STAT. ANN. tit. 12, § 683.

18. *Id.* § 685-A.

19. *Id.* § 685-B.

20. *Id.* § 683.

21. ME. REV. STAT. ANN. tit. 38, §§ 481-488 (Supp. 1972).

22. *Id.* §§ 481, 482.2.

23. *Id.* § 482.2.

24. *Id.* § 483.

25. VT. STAT. ANN. tit. 10, §§ 6001-6091 (1973).

26. VT. STAT. ANN. tit. 10, § 6081.

27. *Id.* § 6001(3).

28. *Id.* § 6086(a)(4).

29. *Id.* § 6086(a)(1)-(10).

30. *Id.*

31. *Id.* § 6086(a)(3), (6), (5).

32. VT. STAT. ANN. tit. 24, § 4350(e). For a thorough discussion of the earliest Vermont legislation, *see* MELLONI & GOETZ, PLANNING IN GROWTH MANAGEMENT 160 (Buchsbaum & Smith eds. 1993). *See generally* BOSSELMAN & CALLIES, THE QUIET REVOLUTION IN LAND USE CONTROL, ch. 2 (1971); HEALY & ROSENBERG, LAND USE AND THE STATES, ch. 3 (1979); Daniels & Lapping, *Has Vermont's Land Use Control Program Failed? Evaluating Act 250,* 50 J. AM. PLAN. ASS'N 502 (1984). For discussion on an array of particular issues, *see* Williams and Rhy-Lincoln, *The Aesthetic Criterion in Vermont's Environmental Law,* 3 HOFSTRA PROP. L.J. 89 (1990); McKeon, *State Regulation of Subdivisions: Defining the Boundary Between State and Local Land Use Jurisdiction in Vermont, Maine, and Florida,* 19 B.C. ENVTL. AFF. L. REV. 385 (1991); Healey, Note, *Party Status and Standing Under Vermont's Land Use and Development Law,* 2 VT. L.. REV. 163 (1977); Jackson, Note, *Leaving the Scene: Aesthetic Considerations in Act 250,* 4 VT. L.. REV. 163 (1979); Kaplan, Note, *The Effects of Act 250 on Prime Farmland,* 6 VT. L.. REV. 467 (1981).

33. DAVID L. CALLIES, REGULATING PARADISE: LAND USE CONTROLS IN HAWAII 3, 12 (University of Honolulu Press 1984).

34. Thomas G. Pelham, *The Florida Experience: Creating a State, Regional, and Local Comprehensive Planning Process, in* STATE AND REGIONAL COMPREHENSIVE PLANNING: IMPLEMENTING NEW METHODS FOR GROWTH MANAGEMENT 94, 98 (Buchsbaum & Smith eds., A.B.A. 1993).

35. John W. Epling, *The New Jersey State Planning Process: An Experiment in Intergovernmental Negotiations, in* GROWTH MANAGEMENT: THE PLANNING CHALLENGE OF THE 1990S, 96, 101, 109 (Jay M. Stein ed., Sage Publications 1993) [hereinafter Epling].

36. BOSSELMAN & CALLIES, *supra* note 1, ch. 1; MANDELKER, ENVIRONMENTAL AND LAND USE CONTROLS LEGISLATION, ch. VII (1976); MYERS, ZONING HAWAII (1976); Callies, *Land Use Control in an Island State,* 2 THIRD WORLD PLAN. REV. 167 (1979); Mandelker & Kolis, *Whither Hawaii? Land Use Management in an Island State,* 1 U. HAW. L. REV. 48 (1979).

37. CALLIES, *supra* note 33, at 14. *See also* Carole Shifrin, *"Planned Growth" New Watchword,* K.C. STAR, Apr. 6, 1975, at 1 (at that time Hawaii's annual growth rate was 18 to 19 percent over a ten-year period).

38. HAW. REV. STAT. § 205-12 to -18 (1985 & Supp. 1992).

39. HAW. REV. STAT. § 205-5(c) (1985 & Supp. 1992).

40. HAW. REV. STAT. § 205-4 (1985 & Supp. 1992).

41. *Id.*

42. *Id.*

43. HAW. REV. STAT. § 226-52 (1985 & Supp. 1992).

44. HAW. REV. STAT. § 226-1 (1992).

45. HAW. REV. STAT. § 226-58 (1985 & Supp. 1992).

46. HAW. REV. STAT. § 226-59 (1985 & Supp. 1992).

47. David L. Callies, *Land-Use Planning in the Fiftieth State, in* STATE AND REGIONAL COMPREHENSIVE PLANNING: IMPLEMENTING NEW METHODS FOR GROWTH MANAGEMENT, 131 (Buchsbaum & Smith eds., A.B.A. 1993).

48. HAW. REV. STAT. § 226-53 (3) (1985 & Supp. 1992).

49. HAW. REV. STAT. § 205-12 (1985 & Supp. 1992).

50. *See* Douglas Carlson, *Waikiki "Studied to Death," Apply Plans—Consultant,* HONOLULU ADVERTISER, July 26, 1974, at 1; *Waikiki Planner Freilich to Arrive with Proposals,* HONOLULU ADVERTISER, Mar. 8, 1974, at A12. *See generally* CALLIES, *supra* note 33, at 6-7.

51. State Planning Act, N.J. STAT. ANN. 52:18A-196 (under the New Jersey State Planning Act, the State Planning Commission is charged with the task of developing a "coordinated, integrated and comprehensive plan for the growth, development, renewal, and conservation of the State and its regions"); *see also* CALLIES & FREILICH, *supra* note 1, at 588. For a comprehensive examination of the New Jersey State Planning Act of 1985, *see* PETER A. BUCHSBAUM & LARRY J. SMITH, STATE & REGIONAL COMPREHENSIVE PLANNING 176 (1993).

52. Recently, Governor Christine Todd Whitman proposed a seven-cent increase in that state's gasoline tax, which would raise $84 million a year to help underwrite an annual fund of $170 million to preserve one million acres of farmland—half of New Jersey's remaining undeveloped land—over the next decade. Additionally, it would raise $210 million a year to repair bridges and highways and buy new buses and trains. *See Bold Decisions in New Jersey,* N.Y. TIMES, May 20, 1998, at A24. Additionally, New Jersey citizens seem to agree that raising taxes is necessary and a good source of providing incentives to keep open space from being infringed by sprawl. *See* Robert Hanley, *To Preserve Open Space, More New Jerseyans Are Supporting New Local Taxes,* N.Y. TIMES, May 20, 1998, at A25.

53. Epling, *supra* note 35 at 97.

54. *Id.* at 98.

55. N.J. STAT. ANN. 52:18A-196.

56. Peter A. Buchsbaum, *The New Jersey Experience, in* STATE AND REGIONAL COMPREHENSIVE PLANNING: IMPLEMENTING NEW METHODS FOR GROWTH MANAGEMENT 179 (Buchsbaum & Smith eds., American Bar Association 1993) [hereinafter Buchsbaum].

57. JOHN M. DEGROVE & DEBORAH A. MINESS, THE NEW FRONTIER FOR LAND POLICY: PLANNING AND GROWTH MANAGEMENT IN THE STATES, 44, 48 (Lincoln Institute of Land Policy 1992) [hereinafter DeGrove & Miness].

58. N.J. STAT. ANN. § 52:18A-202.1f(1) (West 1993).

59. N.J. STAT. ANN. § 52:18A-202.1f(2) (West 1993).

60. N.J. STAT. ANN. § 52:18A-202.1f(3) (West 1993).

61. II THE PRELIMINARY STATE DEVELOPMENT & REDEVELOPMENT PLAN FOR THE STATE OF NEW JERSEY 6, Pol'y 3.2 & 3.3.

62. *See* BUCHSBAUM & SMITH, *supra* note 51, at 176.

63. *Id.*

64. *See supra* note 61, at 6, strategy 1.

65. *Supra* note 57, at 46.

66. N.J. STAT. ANN. § 52:18A-202 b. (West 1993); DEBORAH A. HOWE, URBAN GROWTH MANAGEMENT STUDY: REVIEW OF GROWTH MANAGEMENT STRATEGIES USED IN OTHER STATES 4 (Oregon Dep't of Land Conservation & Development 1991).

67. The county has the option of waiving the local negotiating responsibilities.

68. N.J. STAT. ANN. § 52:18A-202b. (West 1993).

69. *Supra* note 57, at 38.

70. The Commission studied four alternative systems for managing growth:

    1. The "Current New Jersey" system where growth is managed through uncoordinated plans and actions of 567 municipalities;

    2. A facility-driven system where growth is managed by local public service agencies with the objective of achieving efficiency in the delivery of public services;

    3. An "areas of critical concern" system in which growth is managed through agencies at all levels of government with the objective of protecting certain environment or natural resources; and

    4. A "tier" system where growth can be managed at multiple levels of government. *See supra* note 61, at 19.

71. The Preliminary State plan set clear objectives regarding land use, housing, economic development, transportation, natural resource conservation, agricultural and farmland retention, recreation, urban and suburban redevelopment, historic preservation, public facilities and services, and intergovernmental coordination. *See* N.J. STAT. ANN. § 52:18A-196.

72. For a summary of the standards, alternatives, and background of Tier 5 and 6, *see* FREILICH, LEITNER & CARLISLE, NEW JERSEY OFFICE OF STATE PLANNING, AGRICULTURAL PRESERVATION: DEVELOPMENT STANDARDS FOR LIMITED GROWTH AREAS, Jan. 27, 1988.

73. State Planning Act, N.J. STAT. ANN. § 52:18A-196, 1, 2, 5.

74. *See* Buchsbaum, *supra* note 56, at 178–80; *see also* CALLIES & FREILICH, *supra* note 1, at 57.

75. *See* THE NEW JERSEY STATE DEVELOPMENT AND REDEVELOPMENT PLAN: COMMUNITIES OF PLACE, at 5 (1992). *See also* PORTER, *supra* note 2, at 248.

76. N.J. STAT. ANN. 52:18A-196 *et seq.*

77. THE PRELIMINARY STATE DEVELOPMENT AND REDEVELOPMENT PLAN FOR THE STATE OF NEW JERSEY, at 21 (Nov. 1988).

78. COMMUNITIES OF PLACE: THE INTERIM STATE DEVELOPMENT AND REDEVELOPMENT PLAN FOR THE STATE OF NEW JERSEY 100–14 THE NEW JERSEY STATE PLANNING COMMISSION, (1991) [hereinafter COMMUNITIES OF PLACE 1991]; DEGROVE & MINESS, *supra* note 57, at 48.

79. COMMUNITIES OF PLACE 93–99 (1991), *supra* note 78.

80. *Id.* at 108–11.

81. These areas include the Delaware & Raritan Canal, the Delaware Watergap National Recreation Area, the Highlands, the Delaware River & Bayshore Area, the Great Swamp Watershed, and the Skylands. *Id.* at 85.

82. *Id.* at 84–92.

83. *Id.* at vii–viii.

84. Robert Hanley, *To Preserve Open Space, More New Jerseyans Are Supporting New Local Taxes,* N.Y. TIMES, May 20, 1998, at A25.

85. *Id.*

86. WASH. REV. CODE ANN. § 36.70A.020 (West 1991).

87. WASH. REV. CODE ANN. § 35.70A.106 (West Supp. 1993).

88. WASH. REV. CODE ANN. § 36.70A.210 (West Supp. 1993).

89. WASH. REV. CODE ANN. § 36.70A.040 (West 1991) (describes two categories of counties that are mandated to adopt comprehensive land use plans and development regulations and are also required to adopt countywide planning policies according to WASH. REV. CODE ANN. § 36.70A.210 (West 1991 & Supp. 1993).

Category 1: counties with a population of 50,000 or more and characterized by population increases of more than 10 percent in the prior ten years & all cities located within these counties must adopt comprehensive plans;

Category 2: counties which experienced population increases of more than 20 percent in the prior ten years & all cities located within these counties must adopt comprehensive plans);

WASH. REV. CODE ANN. § 36.70A.210(7) (West 1991) (multicounty regions that must develop planning policies; currently, this applies to the central Puget Sound Region, which encompasses King, Kitsap, Pierce, and Snohomish counties.).

90. WASH. REV. CODE ANN. § 36.70A.070 (West 1991) (mandated elements include: land use, housing, capital facilities, and transportation. County plans must also include a rural element).

WASH. REV. CODE ANN. § 36.70A.150 & 36.70A.060 (West 1991 & 1993 Supp) (other required elements include a conservation of agriculture, forests and mineral resources, and the identification of lands useful for public purposes such as utility corridors, landfills, sewage treatment facilities).

91. WASH. REV. CODE ANN. § 36.70A.060(2) (West 1991); Larry G. Smith, *Planning for Growth, Washington Style, in* STATE AND REGIONAL COMPREHENSIVE PLANNING: IMPLEMENTING NEW METHODS FOR GROWTH MANAGEMENT 145 (Buchsbaum & Smith eds., A.B.A. 1993).

92. WASH. REV. CODE ANN. § 36.70A.070, § 36.70A.100, § 36.77.010, § 36.81.121, and § 35.58.2795 (West 1991) (other consistency requirements are: state agency actions that relate to public facilities must be consistent with city and county plans; and the transportation element in plans must be consistent with the land use element and consistent with the six-year transportation plans of neighboring cities, counties, and multicounty areas).

Consistency is not defined in the statute; however, current interpretations of the Standard Planning Enabling Act show that zoning regulations must be in accordance with a comprehensive plan, which generally mandates that the goals, objectives, policies, and strategies of each document must be in agreement with and harmonious with the provisions of all other required documents.

93. WASH. REV. CODE ANN. § 36.70A.110 (West Supp. 1993).

94. Each city must be located within the UGA, but the UGA may encompass more than one city.

95. WASH. REV. CODE ANN. § 35.70A.110 (1) (West 1991).

96. WASH. REV. CODE ANN. § 36.70A.020(12) & § 36.70A.070(6) (West 1991); DEGROVE & MINESS, *supra* note 57, at 124.

97. WASH. REV. CODE ANN. § 47.80.030 (West Supp. 1993).

98. WASH. REV. CODE ANN. § 47.80.030 (West 1993).

99. WASH. REV. CODE ANN. § 36.70A.280 (West Supp. 1993).

100. WASH. REV. CODE ANN. § 36.70A.106 (West Supp. 1993).

101. WASH. REV. CODE ANN. § 36.70A.300 & § 36.70A.340 (West Supp. 1993).

102. WASH. REV. CODE ANN. § 36.70A.070(6) (West 1991).

103. Edward J. Sullivan, *Oregon Blazes a Trail, in* STATE AND REGIONAL COMPREHENSIVE PLANNING: IMPLEMENTING NEW METHODS FOR GROWTH MANAGEMENT, 55 (Buchsbaum & Smith eds., A.B.A. 1993); Deborah A. Howe, *Growth Management in Oregon, in* GROWTH MANAGEMENT: THE PLANNING CHALLENGE OF THE 1990S, 68–69 (Jay M. Stein ed., Sage Publications 1993).

104. REGIONAL URBAN GROWTH GOALS AND OBJECTIVES (Sept. 26, 1991).

105. OR. REV. STAT. § 197.040 (1991); *see also id.*

106. OR. REV. STAT. § 197.040(2)(d) (1991); REGIONAL FRAMEWORK PLAN—PORTLAND, OREGON, at 2 (Dec. 11, 1997).

107. Sullivan, *supra* note 103, at 53, 63, 68, 69.

108. OR. REV. STAT. § 197.810 & 197.825 (1991).

109. OR. REV. STAT. § 197.190 (1991).

110. OR. REV. STAT. § 197.015(5) (1991).

111. OR. REV. STAT. § 197.185(2) (1991).

112. OR. REV. STAT. § 197.180(1) (1991) (subsection (2) of this section outlines exceptions to the compatibility with local plan requirement).

113. Sullivan, *supra* note 103, at 53, 59.

114. *Id.* at 68–69.

115. 1991 OR. LAWS ch. 612.

116. Sullivan, *supra* note 103, at 63. The sanctions include "a mandate to apply the goals directly to land-use decisions, forfeiture of grant monies allocated to the periodic review, or other remedies provided by statute."

117. OR. REV. STAT. § 197.752 (1991).

118. CAL. GOV'T CODE § 65300 (West 1990).

119. CAL. GOV'T CODE § 65302 (West 1990).

120. William Fulton, *Sliced on the Cutting Edge: Growth Management and Growth Control in California, in* GROWTH MANAGEMENT: THE PLANNING CHALLENGE OF THE 1990S, 115, 123 (Jay M. Stein ed., Sage Publications 1993).

121. Madelyn Glickfeld & Ned Levine, REGIONAL GROWTH—LOCAL REACTION: THE ENACTMENT AND EFFECTS OF LOCAL GROWTH CONTROL AND MANAGEMENT MEASURES IN CALIFORNIA, (Lincoln Institute of Land Policy 1992).

122. For a summary of the various threshold standards, *see* PORTER, *supra* note 2, at 124-125.

123. *Id.* at 126-27.

124. DEGROVE & MINESS, *supra* note 57, at 70; Thomas R. Melloni & Robert I. Goetz, *Planning in Vermont, in* STATE AND REGIONAL COMPREHENSIVE PLANNING: IMPLEMENTING NEW METHODS FOR GROWTH MANAGEMENT 161 (Buchsbaum & Smith eds., A.B.A. 1993) [hereinafter Melloni & Goetz].

125. The environmental degradation of Vermont's natural resources was not a new problem. For example, the discharge of dairy wastes into streams, few sewage treatment plants, and the discharge of dyes into the rivers by textile mills were problems identified in the 1950s. THE

REPORT OF THE GOVERNOR'S COMMISSION ON VERMONT'S FUTURE: GUIDELINES FOR GROWTH (1988).

126. The number of farmers has declined dramatically during the past twenty years due to increased productivity, rising land values, low milk prices, and the federal whole herd buy-out program. Between 1986 and 1988, Vermont lost 10 percent of the dairy farms in the state. *Id.* at 14.

127. THE STATE AGENCY PLANNING IMPLEMENTATION COMMITTEE, SHAPING VERMONT'S FUTURE: THE CITIZEN'S GUIDE TO OPEN STATE AGENCY PLANNING, 2 (1991).

128. VT. STAT. ANN. tit. 24 § 4302 (1992); *see also id.*

129. Melloni & Goetz, *supra* note 124, at 163.

130. This desire to revive the traditional development pattern was consistently identified in several studies: VERMONT PLANNING COUNCIL REPORT, VISION AND CHOICE, (1968); GOVERNOR'S COMMISSION ON VERMONT'S FUTURE: GUIDELINES FOR GROWTH, (1988); and GOVERNOR'S COMMISSION ON THE ECONOMIC FUTURE OF VERMONT, PATHWAYS TO PROGRESS, (1989).

131. VT. STAT. ANN. tit. 3 § 4021 (1992).

Consistent with the state goals is defined by statute as: "[the plan] requires substantial progress toward attainment of the goals established in this section, unless the planning body determines that a particular goal is not relevant or attainable. . . . The determination of relevance or attainability shall be subject to review as part of a consistency determination under this chapter." VT. STAT. ANN. tit. 24 § 4302(f)(1) (1992) (a plan should be consistent with the Vermont Planning Goals, including both the Process Goals and the Specific Goals, SHAPING VERMONT'S FUTURE: THE CITIZEN'S GUIDE TO OPEN STATE AGENCY PLANNING, 5 [1991]).

Compatible with another plan means, "the plan in question, as implemented, will not significantly reduce the desired effect of the implementation of the other plan." The statute then sets out alternative means of reaching compatibility if it does reduce the desired effect of another plan. *Id.* § 4302(f)(2) (1992).

132. SHAPING VERMONT'S FUTURE, *supra* note 131, at 6.

133. Melloni & Goetz, *supra* note 124, at 167.

134. VT. STAT. ANN. tit. 24 § 4476 (1992).

135. VT. STAT. ANN. tit. 24 § 4350 (1992); Melloni & Goetz, *supra* note 124, at 164, 166; DEGROVE, & MINESS, *supra* note 57, at 75.

136. VT. STAT. ANN. tit. 24 §§ 4341 & 4342 (1992).

137. VT. STAT. ANN. tit. 24 § 4348a (1992).

138. VT. STAT. ANN. tit. 24 § 4341(a) (1992); Melloni & Goetz, *supra* note 124, at 164; DEGROVE & MINESS, *supra* note 57, at 74.

In 1987, prior to the enactment of the Growth Management Act, there were 246 towns and cities and 57 incorporated villages in Vermont. About 75 percent of the towns and 9 percent of the villages have town plans. Only a few of these plans are comprehensive. REPORT OF THE GOVERNOR'S COMMISSION ON VERMONT'S FUTURE: GUIDELINES FOR GROWTH, 18 (1988).

139. VT. STAT. ANN. tit. 24 § 4382 (1992) (required elements are: 1) a statement of objectives, policies, and programs to guide growth, 2) a land use plan, 3) a transportation plan, 4) a utility and facility plan, 5) preservation polices for irreplaceable natural areas, scenic and historic resources, 6) an educational facilities plan, 7) an implementation element, 8) an element showing the relationship of the plan to other plans, 9) an energy plan, and 10) a housing element).

140. Vt. Stat. Ann. tit. 24 § 4350 (1992); Melloni & Goetz, *supra* note 127, at 165.

141. Shaping Vermont's Future: The Citizen's Guide to Open State Agency Planning, 2 (1991).

142. Vt. Stat. Ann. tit. 24 § 4306(b)(4) (1992).

143. Vt. Stat. Ann. tit. 24 § 4306(b)(3) (1992).

144. Vt. Stat. Ann. tit. 24 § 4362(b) (1992).

145. Vt. Stat. Ann. tit. 24 § 4346(b) (1992).

146. Vt. Stat. Ann. tit. 24 § 4302(b)(1) (1992).

147. Vt. Stat. Ann. tit. 24 § 4382(a) (1992).

148. Vt. Stat. Ann. tit. 24 § 4342 (1992).

149. Vt. Stat. Ann. tit. 24 § 4345(a)(5) (1992).

150. DeGrove & Miness, *supra* note 57, at 103.

151. Russ Bynum, *Georgia Legislature Approves Anti-Sprawl Agency,* Associated Press Newswire, March 25, 1999.

152. Ga. Code. Ann. § 50-8-34-35.

153. DeGrove & Miness, *supra* note 57, at 108; Gale, *supra* note 1, at 426–27.

154. *See* James V. Burgess, Jr., *Governmental Reform in Georgia,* Envl. and Urb. Issues 1 (Spring 1997), at 1.

155. Patricia E. Salkin, Smart Growth at Century's End, at 6.

156. "Governor Celebrates the Passage of Growing Smarter," Agenda for Growing Smarter Press Conference, June 12, 1998.

157. 1998 Ariz. HCR 2027 (May 20, 1998).

158. Ariz. Rev. Stat. Ann. § 9-461.11(a). *See* Freilich, Leitner, Carlisle & Shortlidge, Mohave County, Arizona, General Plan—Baseline Analysis, 40 (Dec. 6, 1991).

159. *See* Mohave County, Arizona, General Plan, *supra* note 158, at 40; for a historical view of the regional planning in Mohave County, *see* Terry D. Morgan, *Joint Planning in Arizona, in* State & Regional Comprehensive Planning, 216 (Buchsbaum & Smith eds., A.B.A. 1993) [hereinafter Morgan].

160. *See* Morgan, *supra* note 159, at 218.

161. *See* Robert H. Freilich & Brenda Nichols, *Public Private Partnerships in Joint Development: The Legal and Financial Anatomy of Large Scale Urban Development Projects,* 1 Mun. Fin. J. 5 (1986).

162. *See* Robert H. Freilich & David W. Bushek, Exactions, Impact Fees and Dedications, Shaping Land Use Development and Funding Infrastructure in the *Dolan* Era (Freilich & Bushek eds., A.B.A. 1995).

163. Ariz. Rev. Stat. Ann. § 9-461.11(G).

164. *Id.*

165. Much of Maryland's heavy population lies within heavily traveled transportation corridors, near major passenger and freight railroads and interstate highways that cover its length on the east coast. *See* Hon. David L. Winstead, Secretary of Transportation-Maryland, *Smart Growth, Smart Transportation: A New Program to Manage Growth in Maryland,* Presentation to U.S. German-Marshall Workshop on Sustainable Transportation in Metropolitan Areas (Oct. 29–30, 1997), Berlin, Germany [hereinafter Winstead].

166. Maryland Office of Planning, Populations Projections for Maryland Subdivisions, July 1997.

167. *See* Md. Code Ann., ch. 759 (1997).

168. Maryann Froehlich, *Smart Growth: Why Local Governments Are Taking a New Approach to Managing Growth in Their Communities*, PUBLIC MGMT., May 1998, at 5 [hereinafter Froehlich].

169. Under the Smart Growth initiative, localities still have the power to direct growth as they wish. *Id.* at 7.

170. Winstead, *supra* note 165, at 3.

171. Governance, January 1999, at 20.

172. *Id.*

173. *Id.*

174. *Id.* at 19.

175. *Id.* at 22.

176. *See* JOHN FUNK & TOM TYSON, WHITE PAPER, MANAGING GROWTH IN THE 21ST CENTURY, A SMART GROWTH INITIATIVE IN PRINCE GEORGE'S COUNTY, June 1998.

177. *See* Robert H. Freilich & Michael J. Lauer, Memorandum, Prince George's County Proposed Tier and Development Process, December 1, 1998.

178. Porter, *supra* note 2, at 244.

179. COLO. REV. STAT. §§ 29-20-104(1)(e)(f)(g).

180. 872 P.2d 1269 (Colo. Ct. App. 1994).

181. *Wilkinson,* 872 P.2d 1269.

182. COLO. REV. STAT. § 29-20-104(1).

183. South Carolina Local Government Comprehensive Planning Enabling Act of 1994.

184. S.C. CODE ANN., art. 3, § 6-29-510(D)(5).

185. S.C. CODE ANN. § 6-29-1130.

186 FREILICH, LEITNER, CARLISLE & JORDAN, Jones & Goulding, REPORT ON CALCULATION METHODOLOGIES FOR DEVELOPMENT OF SCHOOLS AND FIRE PROTECTION IMPACT FEES, Beaufort County, South Carolina, Aug. 25, 1995.

187. A five-year rate of growth ordinance was adopted regulating the issuance of development approvals until the permanent transportation corridor overlay regulations were approved. *See* FREILICH, LEITNER & CARLISLE, RATE OF GROWTH AND IMPACT DOCUMENTATION, TOWN OF HILTON HEAD ISLAND ZONING ORDINANCE, art. VII, Jan. 4, 1988; Land Management Ordinance, Corridor Overlay Zoning District, June 21, 1994.

188. FREILICH, LEITNER & CARLISLE, TOWN OF KIAWAH ISLAND DEVELOPMENT REGULATIONS, July 13, 1995.

189. FLA. STAT. at § 163.3177(6)(h) (West 1990 & Supp. 1993). This coordination occurs between the local government, the adjacent cities/counties, the region, and the state.

190. In 1960 the population of Florida was 4.5 million, by 1970 it was 6.8 million, by 1980 it grew to 9.5 million, and in 1990 it was 12.9 million. *See* DEGROVE & MINESS, *supra* note 57.

191. *Id.* at 8 (an end to "Florida's love affair with growth" occurred as people began feeling the negative impacts of unplanned growth).

192. Craig A. Robertson, *Concurrency and Its Relation to Growth Management,* 20 NOVA L. REV. 891 (1996); *see also* ERIC DAMIAN KELLY, MANAGING COMMUNITY GROWTH 113 (1994) (Florida grew from the twentieth among states in population in 1950 to eighth in 1976) [hereinafter Kelly]; Vanessa Steinberg-Prieto, *The Growth Management Pendulum: The Ecological Clock Is Ticking for Florida and Other States,* 20 NOVA L. REV. 987, 990 (1996) (the shortage of space has not caused the overpopulation; however, the use of the same land over and over has

caused the overdevelopment of specific areas) [hereinafter Steinberg-Prieto]; Robert H. Freilich served on the Elm's Committee in 1972.

193. DEGROVE & MINESS, *supra* note 57, at 14.

194. The Environmental Land and Water Management Act of 1972, FLA. STAT. ch. 380, the Water Resources Act, FLA. STAT. ch. 373, and the Land Conservation Act, FLA. STAT. ch. 259.

195. FLA. STAT. ch. 163 (1990).

196. The State Comprehensive Planning Act, FLA. STAT. ch. 23 (1990).

197. *Id.*

198. FLA. STAT. ANN. ch. 187 (West 1987 & Supp. 1996); David M. Layman, *Concurrency and Moratoria,* 71 FLA. B.J. 49 (Jan. 1997).

199. FLA. STAT. at § 163.3167(2) (West 1990).

200. *Id.* at § 163.3177 (West 1990).

201. *Id.* at § 186.504(2)(a).

202. *Id.* at § 163.3202(2)(g); Thomas G. Pelham, *The Florida Experience: Creating a State, Regional and Local Comprehensive Planning Process, in* STATE & REGIONAL COMPREHENSIVE PLANNING: IMPLEMENTING NEW METHODS FOR GROWTH MANAGEMENT, 102, 107, 109, 110 (Buchsbaum & Smith eds., 1993).

203. FLA. STAT. ANN. at § 163.3177 (West 1990 & Supp. 1993).

204. *Id.* at § 163.3177(6)(j) (these changes were intended to enhance the coordination between the transportation and land use planning elements).

205. *Id.* at § 163.3177.

206. *Id.* at § 163.3177(10)(a) (the Florida legislature defined when "local comprehensive plans are consistent with the state comprehensive plans and the appropriate regional policy plan," as when "the local plan is compatible with and furthers such plans. The term, 'compatible with' means that the local plan is not in conflict with the state comprehensive plan or appropriate regional policy plan. The term, 'furthers' means to take action in the direction of realizing goals or policies of the state or regional plan").

207. David M. Layman, *Concurrency and Moratoria,* 71 FLA. B.J. 49 (Jan. 1997); *see also* THOMAS G. PELHAM, 19:973 ADEQUATE PUBLIC FACILITIES REQUIREMENTS: REFLECTIONS ON FLORIDA'S CONCURRENCY SYSTEM FOR MANAGING GROWTH 974 (1992).

208. FLA. STAT. § 163.3180 *cited in* Richard Grosso, *Florida's Growth Management Act: How Far We Have Come, and How Far We Have Yet to Go,* 20 NOVA L. REV. 589, 592-93 (1996) [hereinafter Grosso]; *see also* David L. Powell, *Recent Changes in Concurrency,* 68 FLA. B.J. 67 (1994) quoting Letter from Thomas G. Pelham, Secretary, Department of Community Affairs, to Senator Gewn Margolis, North Miami Beach 1 (Mar. 7, 1988), quoted in Department of Community Affairs, *The Evolution and Requirements of the CMS Rule,* Technical Memo 4 (Aug. 1991) *cited in* Steinberg-Prieto, *supra* note 192, at 987, 994, n.74. *See also* Pelham, *supra* note 202, at 978 (1992).

209. *Id.* at § 163.3177(10)(h) (the 1993 Act increased the flexibility of the concurrency requirement for transportation facilities by allowing an areawide level of service averaging in "a compact geographic area with an existing network of roads where multiple, viable alternative travel paths or modes are available for common trips.").

210. KELLY, *supra* note 192, at 114.

211. FLA. STAT. § 163.3180 *cited in* Grosso, *supra* note 208, at 658.

212. *See* EASTWARD HO! REPORT OF THE GOVERNOR'S COMMISSION FOR A SUSTAINABLE

South Florida (Oct. 1995); *see* Dawson, *The Best Laid Plans: The Rise and Fall of Growth Management in Florida,* 11 J. Land Use & Envtl., 325 (1996).

213. Tennessee Public Act 1101 (1998).

214. *Id.*

215. Fla. Stat. Ann. § 380.012 to .10 (1973)

216. *Id.* § 380.05(17).

217. Me. Rev. Stat. Ann. tit. 12, §§ 681-689 (1972).

218. *Id.* §§ 683-685C (1972). *See also* 2 Env't Rep. 321 (1971–72).

219. Vt. Stat. Ann. tit. 10, §§ 6001-6091 (1971).

220. Colo. Rev. Stat. § 106-4-1 to -4-4 (1971).

221. *Id.* § 106-4-3(2)(a).

222. A.L.I. Model Land Dev. Code (Tent. Draft No. 3, 1971). *See also* Babcock, *Comments on the Model Land Development Code,* 1972 Urb. L. Ann. 59.

223. A.L.I. Model Land Dev. Code § 7-402.

224. Despite the need for national land use policies, the Court again and again reinforces the sovereign power of the states, which in the end will allow each locality to examine individual issues necessary for smart growth. *See New State Ice Co. v. Liebmann,* 285 U.S. 262, 311 (1931); Justice Brandeis in his dissent wrote: "There must be power in the States and the Nation to remould, through experimentation, our economic practices and institutions to meet changing social and economic needs. . . .To stay experimentation in things social and economic is a grave responsibility. Denial of the right to experiment may be fraught with serious consequences to the nation. It is one of the happy incidents of the federal system that a single courageous State may, if its citizens choose, serve as a laboratory; and try novel social and economic experiments without risk to the rest of the country." Also, Justice Harlan in *Roth v. United States,* 354 U.S. 476, 505 (1956) stated: "It has often been said that one of the great strengths of our federal system is that we have, in the forty-eight states, forty-eight experimental laboratories. 'State statutory law reflects predominately this capacity of a legislature to introduce novel techniques of social control. The federal system has the immense advantage of providing forty-eight separate centers for such experimentation.'" *See also* Henry M. Hart, *The Relations Between State and Federal Law,* 54 Colum. L. Rev. 489, 493 (1954). Justice Black next noted in *Ferguson v. Skrupa,* 372 U.S. 726, 730 (1962): "Legislative bodies have broad scope to experiment with economic problems, and the Court does not sit to 'subject the State to an intolerable supervision hostile to the basic principle of our Government and wholly beyond the protection which the general clause of the Fourteenth Amendment was intended to secure.'" *citing Sproles v. Binford,* 286 U.S. 374, 388 (1932).

225. Froehlich, *supra* note 168, at 9.

226. Governor Whitman of New Jersey has announced plans to encourage central city redevelopment, farmland protection, preservation of open space and green space, and guidelines for new development. Froehlich, *supra* note 168, at 7.

227. *Id.* at 9.

228. *Id.*

CHAPTER SEVEN

Specific Tier Strategies in Urbanized Areas

The Urbanized Area and the Promotion of Urban Infill

Land Planning and Development

As suburban migration occurs, policies initiated in suburbia have a tremendous impact upon the central city that migration left behind.[1] Exclusionary techniques designed to keep "undesirables" from moving into predominantly middle-class suburban areas have the effect of placing a heavy burden upon other areas of the region, including the central city. Through restrictive zoning ordinances—minimum lot size or floor area requirements, exclusive single-family limitations, stringent building codes, and other practices[2]—the cost of suburban housing is raised to a level too high for low- and moderate-income buyers to afford. Discriminatory public housing site selection policies prevalent in suburbia[3] effectively prevent blacks and other minorities from moving into suburban areas and keep central urban areas racially segregated. In addition, discriminatory lending and selling practices have ensured that suburban residential areas can maintain their status as havens for the white middle class.[4] The effect of such policies on the central cities has been devastating. Economic and racial separation between city and suburb has drained the central city of many of its resources. Housing left behind by "white flight" tends to be older, in worse condition, and in less desirable neighborhoods than its counterparts in suburbia.[5] As a result, financial institutions and even residents have "disinvested" urban housing stock until vast areas of our central cities have become abandoned wastelands where crime, pollution, poverty, and psychological deterioration are everyday occurrences.[6]

As the city has declined, the out-migration to suburbia has continued, pushed by the ever-increasing deterioration and unlivable conditions in the city.[7] Once residential dispersion began, it was quickly followed by the out-migration of industry to suburbia where land was plentiful and cheap, and a resident workforce was readily available.[8] This loss of industry and jobs to suburbia left central urban areas without enough jobs for the relatively poor, unskilled labor left behind, and with an insufficient tax base to provide municipal services for those still living there. In addition, as a result of increasing population on the fringe, and because of apportionment practices in many states, suburbia has been able to gain control of municipal policies and essentially to block policy programs initiated in central urban areas.[9] Thus, attempts to expand governmental jurisdiction to a base large enough to deal effectively with regional problems have been consistently circumscribed by the power of the electorate.

Redeveloping cities need to devise strategies and implement policies to address a web of entangled and mutually reinforcing dilemmas, while simultaneously building upon their unique strengths. The critical issues adversely affecting these locales include an eroded economy and middle-class exodus. Many Tier I municipalities have experienced sizable population losses, which were not simply the result of decreases in household size or an aging population. Middle- and upper-income groups have left the central city for newer places. Older urban and suburban jurisdictions are the concentrated centers for the least affluent segments of a state's population. These municipalities are often expected to provide a vast array of services for a disproportionate share of the state's impoverished population. Fiscal distress is the imbalance between the financial demands placed on municipal services and the resources available to pay for those services. The loss of commercial ratables and the inability to attract new ones has led to increased tax burdens on residential property owners who remain in the central city. These residents are often expected to pay more for municipal services at the same time that those services are diminishing in quality.

A deteriorating environment has also become a critical issue to the central city. Nineteenth century settlement patterns evolved without adequate design consideration. Private disinvestment and public fiscal distress have led to neglect and abandonment of an already unattractive physical setting. In many

urban areas, the physical deterioration has become painfully obvious. In extreme cases, the municipalities become the landlords of last resort through the tax foreclosure process. In lesser instances, deferred maintenance of buildings and infrastructure leaves its unmistakable signs. The combination of an eroded economy, middle-class exodus, fiscal distress, and loss in quality public services, as well as the deteriorated physical environment, contribute to and reinforce a negative image. Potential and incumbent residents lower their expectations. The business community avoids unattractive investment. Firms that can exercise choice opt for alternative locations. Added to these ills is the lack of an effective planning capability. Piecemeal intervention and crisis management on the municipal level exacerbate these difficulties. Where planning has occurred, it has not been action-oriented. Planning, decision making, and implementation have too frequently been disconnected activities. The lack of a planning capability has at times inadvertently permitted political strife to interfere with necessary redevelopment activity.

Urban revitalization, whether downtown redevelopment, urban renewal, historic preservation, housing code enforcement, or infill, requires a basic understanding of many complex tools and techniques involving both the private and public sectors.[10] The revitalization of cities requires the utilization of an entirely different approach to development. To ensure urban revitalization, the central city must take steps and utilize the techniques that will encourage development and redevelopment. One of the basic techniques for urban revitalization involves the government's power of eminent domain.[11] It involves condemnation of land and interests in property to enable the assembly of parcels requiring a public use or purpose to allow the taking of private property, with just compensation paid to the property owner.[12]

Other techniques including tax increment financing will help to determine the level of subsidy required to equalize suburban with inner-city development costs.[13] Incentives and bonuses in the size of development can be granted in exchange for amenity packages of open spaces and cultural features.[14] The public and private sector can be linked together in partnership on large-scale projects in which each side brings important assets into the union.[15] Intergovernmental agreements can provide a useful tool in creating cooperative initiatives in the prevention of sprawl. Also, under the Regional General Welfare Doctrine, local governments in the central city can seek judicial injunctions to find a cooperative understanding from other tiers within the region when other areas zone unreasonably, affecting the entire region and the central city.[16] The world of redevelopment has come a long way from the early days of urban renewal.[17]

Creating urban infill requires Tier I authorities to select these various alternatives. They each have significant effects on preventing the loss of open space and urban sprawl.[18] The central area objectives focus on attracting the most intensive and varied land uses, including office/administrative, financial, residential, and entertainment. The objectives for the remaining older communities stress conservation of social/environmental characteristics and deteriorating neighborhoods' rehabilitation.

Bonus and Incentive Zoning

A community may offer economic incentives to developers by relaxing various restrictions in the zoning requirements applicable to the land in exchange for the development of desired types of projects or amenities within projects.[19] Bonus and incentive zoning has been most frequently used in downtown areas for the purpose of encouraging attractive buildings with adequate facilities.[20] The technique is based upon a trade between the city and the developer. The city allows the developer to build more profitably by including more rentable floor area in its project than the prevailing zoning otherwise permits. In return, the developer provides either a public amenity or open space at its own expense, or pays money in lieu of the dedication that will enable the city to finance the purchase of a public improvement, or provide for low- and moderate-income housing.[21] These techniques can be most effective as growth control techniques when specifically utilized for this purpose.

A number of cities have enacted comprehensive ordinances detailing the trades each city is willing to make, in exchange for a theater, off-street parking, a public plaza, multiple entrances, or access to rapid transit. Each amenity, or combination, allows a certain density increase, through increasing the floor area ratio. Thus, increased density, which is generally considered undesirable, is offset by an increase in public amenities directly related to the density or by public facilities such as theaters or observation decks that the municipality has found to be so desirable as to be willing to accept the problems inherent in additional population.[22] In the town of Clarkstown, for example, the community allowed landowners to build at a higher density than was allowed in the zone if they would agree to sequence the development over a specific period of time. As a result, the community was able to ensure more effectively that growth would proceed in accordance with the provision of proper facilities, adequate schools, recreational facilities, open space, and streets.[23] It can also provide a highly effective means of ensuring that the community provides an adequate supply of low- and moderate-income housing, thus establishing a more balanced and stable community. Bonus and incentive zoning is a sophisticated form of barter, designed as a means of achieving both developer profit and municipal amenity.

The most common incentive offered is increased floor area ratio (FAR). The FAR is the ratio that the floor area within the building bears to the lot area of the zoning lot containing the building. In New York City, where a builder is willing to reserve the lower floors of a building for retail shops at reasonable rents, he or she is given a bonus in the form of permission to erect a larger building with a greater amount of rentable floor space.[24] The scheme is not based on a comprehensive plan for the entire downtown area; instead, specific incentive plans have been developed that only apply to certain areas deemed to be of special character (for instance, New York theater district, Fifth Avenue, and Lincoln Square district). San Francisco, California, also employs a plan based on the same techniques. However, in San Francisco, the scheme is based on a comprehensive plan for the entire downtown area. In the San Francisco plan, the planning department plays a much greater role, with the power to interpret the ordinances and establish direct contact with the architect concerning the amount of bonus space that may be achieved.

Bonus or incentive zoning provides a flexible means of dealing with the dilemmas of cities. By allowing for a lot-by-lot analysis of development within a specific area, it becomes possible to promote the most beneficial use of that tract within the context of the surrounding area. It also provides some incentive making development within these areas more desirable and feasible, minimizing many of the vital problems of the urban fringe are minimized.

Historic Preservation

Historic preservation measures are generally intended to enhance the quality of life by preserving the character and desirable aesthetic features of a city that are grounded in historic, architectural, and culturally significant structures, districts, and neighborhoods. A 1996 survey of growth management and statewide comprehensive land use planning Acts in Delaware, Florida, Georgia, Hawaii,

Maine, Maryland, New Hampshire, New Jersey, Oregon, Rhode Island, Vermont, and Washington found that all included historic preservation as a goal or a required planning element.[25]

An historic preservation program should be incorporated in the early creation phases of the comprehensive plan. Similarly, the objectives and strategies of the historic preservation programs should be integrated with all land development strategies.[26] The element of the comprehensive plan for the central city that includes development of transportation corridors should work hand-in-hand with the historic preservation portion of the plan by concentrating high-density development at locations that do not impede or interfere with historic and cultural preservation objectives.

Bonus and incentive zoning may be used for preservation of historic resources and structures. For example, the owner of an historic structure could qualify for bonuses and incentives such as "additional use opportunities," including home occupations, residential conversions, and guest-house uses. Additionally, the owner of an historic structure could possibly apply for special exceptions allowing modification of lot size, lot dimension, or enlargement of nonconforming uses if the owner agrees to preserve the structure in its historic condition.

Housing Development

Tier I authorities should establish a coordinated and comprehensive approach to housing redevelopment to encourage both new construction and rehabilitated housing for all income groups and tenure types. Counties and municipalities, with financial and technical assistance from the state, should plan a comprehensive housing program that will encourage the provision of a wide range of housing choices at reasonable cost. State departments involved in the permitting of any aspect of housing redevelopment, along with counties and municipalities, should streamline the permitting process and thereby reduce unnecessary and costly delays to redevelopment. Municipalities should establish and maintain a vigorous code enforcement program to ensure the preservation of the existing housing stock. Municipal property maintenance codes should be based on a model property maintenance code promulgated by the state. Code enforcement should be connected to housing rehabilitation, with funding programs to provide both regulatory disincentives and financial incentives to maintain and improve the existing housing stock.

Flexible Housing Codes

A flexible housing code can provide the city with an approach to the problem of urban blight and continuing abandonment. Specialized housing courts will help in alleviating the problem of enforcing a single standard housing code in all areas of the city without judges who are knowledgeable about repeat offenders and the condition of the housing or neighborhood.[27] Consideration should be given to revising the housing code to make it more flexible and to establish differential standards to limit repairs to economically affordable limits in the worst areas of the city.[28] The flexible housing code differs from the single standard housing code, which provides only one set of maintenance standards for the entire community.[29] Using the flexible housing code, the local governing body designates areas for "protection," "rehabilitation," and "demolition," corresponding to what is frequently termed the "good," "gray" and "worst" areas of the community.[30]

Cities should formulate code standards to cover the "worst" areas, the "gray" areas, and the "good" areas that pose a difficult problem, since any single standard code that is designed to provide effective minimum standards in the "worst" areas will necessarily prove inadequate in realizing the "protection" or "rehabilitation" potential of the code. A standard designed for "protection" or "rehabilitation" would be at best only partially enforceable in the "worst" areas.[31] Too strong a standard in the worst areas may lead to a finding of a regulatory economic taking.[32]

The city and state should provide financial and technical assistance for the improvement and maintenance of public housing that serves the least advantaged segments of the housing market in Tier I. City officials and citizens should work together to develop affordable housing that will enable residents from all economic segments to live in a clean, safe, and healthy environment.[33] A housing element in a local plan can provide these necessities where an expanding population includes low-income and minority families. A housing element can encourage the central city to reduce housing costs with design, regulatory, and financial tools. Potential home buyers and developers of low-income housing can receive financial assistance through proposed tax credits, density bonus incentives, and subsidies. Such an element is required if the city is requiring Community Development Block Grants from the federal government.[34]

The state and central city, with additional federal assistance, should provide financial incentives to encourage the development and rehabilitation of low- and moderate-income housing in Tier I. Such incentives should include land leasing, land write-downs, tax abatements, infrastructure improvements, subsidized financing, and regulatory flexibility including such devices as density bonuses. These various mechanisms will create a desire and demand to move into downtown development.

Tax Abatement and Tax Increment Financing

Tax-abated redevelopment provides an incentive for private entities to develop within a deteriorating area by freezing the assessed value of the project area at its predevelopment assessment, thus permitting the developer to pay only those taxes at the frozen assessed valuation even while property values increase.[35] The abatement exists only for a set statutory period, subsequent to which the owners pay tax on the full assessed value. Tax abatement usually requires a state constitutional amendment to avoid the problem of uniformity of taxation requirements (because the tax is not paid on the differential between the frozen and fair market values).[36] Only a few states, such as Missouri and New York, utilize tax abatement. Under the New York scheme, qualifying property owners pay a "'mini tax' which is calculated not on the assessed value of the new improvement but by applying the current tax rate to the assessed value of the property in the year before construction began." The full exemption lasts for two years and then is phased out.[37] Missouri's tax abatement is accomplished with a constitutional provision and a statutory procedure delegating condemnation and redevelopment powers to private redevelopment corporations.[38]

Many tax increment finance statutes require a showing of "blight" in the area as the triggering device for redevelopment.[39] The Washington statute emphasizes substandard housing conditions as a trigger for blight including substantial physical dilapidation, deterioration, age, or obsolescence of buildings, unsanitary and unsafe conditions, inadequate ventilation, danger to person and property, and detriment to public health, safety, morals, and welfare.[40] If a city offers this incentive to downtown developers, urban revitalization can be guaranteed.

Enterprise Zoning

The central city should designate and support commercial enterprise zones. The states have considerable experience with enterprise zones as approximately thrity-seven states have adopted enterprise zone legislation. A 1987 study found

that they had created 113,600 new jobs and retained 67,400 existing jobs.[41] This program would be modeled after existing Urban Enterprise Zones, extending those benefits to developers by creating new tax and financial incentives for production within targeted areas. Municipalities should review and amend their land use ordinances and plans to ensure a reasonable balance among various land uses so that lands zoned for industrial and commercial use do not exceed reasonable expectations of demand for such uses and so that adequate lands are available to satisfy the anticipated demand for residential housing. The state should require municipalities to devise a community development strategy that targets housing and economic development programs to designated neighborhoods and weaves these policies with community services, economic development and job training, education, and public safety efforts.[42] In 1993, sparked by the Rodney King verdict riots in Los Angeles, Congress adopted President Clinton's program and created nine empowerment zones and ninety-five enterprise "communities." Tax incentives amounting to $2.5 billion were provided in the form of wage credits that entitles an employer to take credits equal to 20 percent of the first $15,000 of each employee's wages. The zones were granted the power to use tax exempt bonds to finance businesses.[43]

Displacement

Municipalities engaged in redevelopment should make reasonable efforts to minimize displacement effects that may be attributed to those redevelopment activities, whether publicly or privately funded. Central cities need to be aware of the problems of gentrification and condominium conversion. Gentrification is the process of middle-class influx into lower-income areas. Housing is rehabilitated, rents go up, and low-income residents are displaced.[44] One form of the displacement occurs when rental apartments are converted to condominiums requiring the tenant to purchase the unit or leave. Conversion gives financial incentives to both the developer and the buyer where the developer realizes an immediate profit as opposed to the long-term amortization of principal through rental payments and the buyer receives equity and tax deductions.[47] Many cities are adopting regulations requiring replacement funds when low-income housing is demolished.[46]

Displacement occurs because tenants do not have sufficient capital, equity, or credit to purchase the condominium. Typically, low-income apartments are converted to high-price condominiums. State and local assistance for those displaced by gentrification has taken a number of paths.[47] Such relocation assistance has come in both financial and nonfinancial forms. The financial protection primarily involves subsidy for moving expenses. In some cities, assistance payments for replacement housing also have been made available. One state court has invalidated a municipal requirement that condominium developers extend such benefits.[48] Nonfinancial protections include extending tenants' leases to give them additional time to search for new housing, and rendering relocation advisory assistance services.[49] A number of states have enacted legislation similar to the URA to protect citizens displaced by gentrification. The authorities in the central city must be aware of the programs available to tenants that may be displaced to help in the revitalization of the urban area and to keep citizens from moving into the Urbanizing Tier.

Downtown neighborhood revitalization will contribute to advancing urban infill and promotion of sufficient housing. It involves the improvement in older housing, loft housing in older unused manufacturing or warehouse facilities,[50] and the promotion of a neighborhood's better overall physical, social, and economic environment.[51] It has been taking place in more central city areas in recent years and will continue to spread. The main causes of its recent intensification are higher capital costs of new construction, which encourage renovating older structures; an increase in downtown office complexes, creating greater demands for nearby housing units from households with relatively high incomes; and demographic shifts toward smaller households, which are more suited for in-city living—especially two-worker professional households with no children.[52]

Transportation and Economic Development

Traffic congestion has emerged as the newest urban crisis for the land use planning, engineering, and legal professions most recently moved out into the Urbanizing Tier. The U.S. Department of Transportation released a national policy statement in 1990 identifying problems associated with automobile congestion and encouraging governmental reliance on user charges and transportation trust funds. In 1987, over 65 percent of peak hour travel on urban interstates occurred under heavily congested conditions. Highway travel annually consumes over two billion hours in lost economic production. Rapid growth of the nation's major metropolitan areas has overwhelmed the capacity of federal, state, and local government to utilize traditional techniques of taxa-

tion, eminent domain, and regulation to provide adequate public facilities, particularly in transportation.[53] The United States is not alone in facing planning problems caused by traffic and related transportation issues.

The relationship between traffic congestion and economic growth and development is welldocumented. New roadways are a major stimulant of new development. Construction of roadways in outlying urban areas for the past generation has fostered urban sprawl, inefficient growth patterns, and enormous economic, housing, and environmental costs. Congestion is a major factor in the perceived quality of life in a city. It contributes to neighborhood deterioration, psychological discomfort, increasing response times for police, fire, and medical services, and reductions in economic productivity and mobility.

Major contributors to traffic congestion include land use patterns, funding systems, and the structural framework of the transportation network. Traffic congestion is primarily a function of the supply of transportation facilities and the demand for those facilities. Efforts to increase the amount or efficiency of transportation facilities depend upon an adequate and reliable source of funding. Supply-oriented or "structural" techniques to regulate traffic congestion in the United States tend to rely on increases in roadway capacity and, to a lesser extent, mass transit. Federal funding for mass transit and other traffic systems management programs has declined dramatically in recent years. Structural solutions, such as freeway construction and recent innovations such as high-occupancy vehicle lanes and ramp metering, are increasingly seen as ineffective when used in isolation. Accordingly, land use controls and other regulatory devices, such as transportation demand management (TDM) and growth management controlled land use patterns of transportation corridors, centers, and compact development encouraging infill, are often used to regulate or reduce the demands placed upon the transportation circulation network. Defining the appropriate balance between structural mechanisms and demand-oriented and land use mechanisms to regulate traffic congestion should flow from a coordinated, comprehensive plan.

Local city authority, along with the state, should establish adequate levels of public investment in transportation facilities and services to meet current and projected needs. Transportation facilities and services in the central city need to be employed as redevelopment tools by improving travel to, from, and within the city as well as reinforcing centers of economic activity and employment growth. Ensuring that transportation planning is effectively accomplished with respect to municipal, county, regional, and statewide plans, and accounting for existing and anticipated land uses, traffic demands, and regional concerns will help in revitalization. Transportation planning should consider the redevelopment objectives with respect to Tier I among its goals. Tier I municipalities should ensure that the area is sufficiently linked with major highway and public transportation corridors throughout the region and the state by emphasizing a comprehensive transportation strategy. The state should ensure that Tier I receives priority funding to maintain and improve public transportation services. A higher priority in funding in this regard should be given to Urban Centers. Parking management strategies should be encouraged in the use of public transportation in Tier I. In particular, access to commuter rail services and bus routes should be enhanced wherever feasible through the use of adequate parking facilities at station sites.

In the United States, many governmental entities have begun a cooperative effort and dismiss their roles as public servants or regulators of private land, and often share in the profits generated by development on land.[54] Traditionally, the public sector was involved in development, if at all, through the urban renewal process. The city's role was to eliminate blight and deterioration in central cities and to utilize grant and incentive funds to stimulate the process of distributing land to redevelopers.[55] The government did not seek to obtain profits from development projects other than through normal property and sales taxes applied later to the property. Government played the role of planner, regulator, and facilitator.[56] For a unique zoning technique upheld by the courts to restore blighted single-family neighborhoods from the incursions of boarding houses and rooming houses, Kansas City, Missouri, passed a zoning ordinance wiping out all uses other than single-family, even if vested or valid nonconformimg uses, by providing compensation to the ousted building owners. Public purpose was found in the restoration of the single-family neighborhood.[57] Housing values went up extraordinarily. In Champaign, Illinois, I helped devise the solution to preserve a largely single-family eighty-eight-square-block "in-town" neighborhood by limiting two-family or boarding houses to four blocks (representing their estimated demand). Neighborhood values shot up.

Private/Public Partnerships

The federal programs, ISTEA and TEA-21, discussed in chapter ten, are significant measures that help promote the transportation corridor, a key to keep-

ing growth in the central city. Public-private development can be utilized in the construction of these transportation corridors. While jurisdiction for regulating development typically resides with the local government, it may use joint development to alleviate the actual or perceived risks associated with undertaking development in the corridor and to obtain financial benefits related to construction and operation of transit systems and other public facilities.

For transportation corridors, the term "joint development" refers to the development of real estate that is integrated with a transportation corridor center or transit facility/station. It may include transportation corridor center development and may also include transit development such as an office tower built in the air rights over a transit terminal or a retail facility directly linked to a transit terminal by a pedestrian walkway. Regardless of the form it takes, joint development is a pairing of public and private resources to achieve a project that will benefit both sectors. Joint development also includes a value capture connotation in which the public sector attempts to recoup some of the real estate-related monetary benefits that result from public investments. Revenues derived from joint development can be used by the public sector to:

1. offset the original transportation corridor center development and capital costs;
2. guarantee provision of desired public amenities; and
3. finance a portion of the transit investment and/or help to pay for ongoing operating costs of the transit system.

Joint development approaches typically include techniques that capitalize on real property assets acquired in the course of transportation corridor development. Examples include those involving property taxes or assessments and excess land acquisition such as land and air rights leasing,[58] negotiated private sector investments in land and capital costs,[59] connection fees for direction tie-ins to transit stations,[60] and concessions at transit stations.[61] Some states include a proportionality requirement in joint development deals.

The zoning and land use controls adopted by the local government must be carefully considered in the joint development process. The approval of the local government may be required for construction and development. Joint development legislation may also require that the services provided pursuant to the agreement be consistent with the use and zoning of land adjacent to the right-of-way. At the same time, general-purpose units of local government (such as cities or counties) may be authorized and empowered to do many things that are unavailable to the transit agency. Cities may be authorized to do a number of things, including:

- develop and adopt comprehensive plans to guide their growth and development;
- enact zoning regulations;
- undertake redevelopment and designate reinvestment zones;
- utilize tax increment financing; and
- approve special assessment benefit districts, among other powers.

Cities, through zoning approval processes and/or subdivision regulations, can exact various contributions from development adjacent to transit stations, including easements, access points, improvements, connections, and even fees that would aid in transit station development and related joint development. The exercise of these powers in coordination with the transit agency's station development policy can materially benefit both the agency and the local government unit. The transit agency and local governments, through cooperative agreements, can aggregate all of the essential governmental powers and authorities for successful large-scale joint development.[62]

Agencies in California and Oregon have used transit-oriented development to provide housing along transit lines. For example, the Santa Clara Transit Authority has used joint development authority along its rail systems. The agency uses long-term seventy-five-year ground leases to construct high-density, multifamily residential housing known as "Trandominiums" on park-and-ride districts adjacent to the city's light-rail line. This approach, commenced in 1990, involves the lease of land to private developers that enter into a long-term ground lease, construct projects, and pay rental to the district for the term of the lease. The district owns ten large park-and-ride lots consisting of 101 acres of land. Using its ownership rights, the district has entered into three joint public-private projects for the development of both affordable housing and day care.

The district hopes to accomplish three major objectives through its joint development projects. First, it seeks a continuing source of revenue to defray operating and other expenses. Second, the development will attract new transit riders through the development of high-density, multifamily housing at the park-and-ride lots. Third, the developments will create a sense of place and community near the park-and-ride lots, incorporating them into the surrounding community and "make them something more than sterile expanses

of asphalt that emptied out at the end of the day." The joint development will reduce traffic congestion, improve air quality, create live-travel options for transit-dependent groups, and promote infill and preservation of natural resources.[63]

In other instances, agencies have been instrumental in encouraging the adoption of land use policies supportive of transit-oriented development. For example, in Sacramento County, California, the transit-oriented development policies have been described as the "cornerstone" of the county's General Plan. These policies include restrictions on the uses permitted around transit stations, revisions in density restrictions, and the use of design amenities to encourage transit ridership. Snohomish County, Washington, recently authorized park-and-ride lots and transit centers in all of its land use districts, excluding its mineral conservation and waterfront beach zoning districts. Parking lots are permitted in the multifamily residential district, freeway service, neighborhood business, planned community business, community business, general commercial, industrial park, business park, light industrial, and heavy industrial districts, and are permitted as a conditional use in all other districts. Park-and-pool lots are also permitted in those commercial districts as well as in residential zoning districts by conditional use.[64]

The information from the nine agencies engaged in joint development projects that responded to the survey shows a wide variety of projects throughout the country. Since 1978, approximately 6,371 dwelling units, 2.6 million square feet of floor space of office use, 1.5 million square feet of floor space of commercial or retail use, and 1.7 million square feet of floor space of industrial or institutional use have been added in joint development projects by the agencies that provided information. Additionally, public-private partnerships are currently paving the way in reviving urban parks. Success depends on both good planning and sound park design, as well as continued public-private support for and involvement in park programming and management.[65]

Today, government entities at all levels are finding new and innovative ways to expand their financial and economic horizons through participation in, and in some instances even initiation of, private sector development. This newer approach expands the public sector role to include any of the following:

- risk sharing;
- participation in loan commitments and mortgages on the site;
- sharing operating as well as capital costs;

- participation in sale/leaseback arrangements;
- assisting the private sector by reducing administrative red tape and regulation problems;
- encouraging cooperation among the state and regional authorities, counties, and special districts;
- creating special redevelopment authorities; and
- directly participating in development ownership activities.

In fact, the preservation of historic properties and culturally significant sites in the central city is a unique way that the public and private sectors can join to preserve the area's history and culture for future generations. Regions can implement proposals into their plan to encourage adaptive reuse of underused or abandoned historic structures, thereby giving them a second life for housing, commercial buildings, or even government offices.[66] It advocates incentive systems that encourage preservation of cultural and historical sites, including density bonuses, transfer of development rights, and tax benefits.

The role of the private sector has expanded to include developer participation in the planning, design, financing, and ultimate marketing of the project. The private sector, through impact fees and exactions, directly funds the financing, design, construction, ownership, and operation of the public facilities that serve the site such as roads, schools, fire, police, sewer, water, and drainage.[67] Private and public participation will go a long way in urban renewal by providing the necessary capital and resources for redevelopment.

Transit-Oriented Development

While suburban sprawl continues,[68] professional planners believe that there is deep-seated dissatisfaction with twentieth century urban sprawl and have championed a return to mixed-use villages and centers that promote pedestrian and transit travel. The so-called "new urbanists"[69] are challenging cities and developers to employ concepts known as "transit-oriented development" (TOD) and "pedestrian-oriented development" (POD) as alternatives to urban sprawl that can be utilized within the Urbanizing Tier as well as in Tier III.[70] This form of development has five major characteristics. First, a TOD has sufficient density to encourage the use of public transit. Second, a TOD locates residences, jobs, and retail destinations close to public transit facilities. Third, a TOD consists of mixed uses, with retail and employment locations within walking distance of residential areas. Fourth, the TOD is built on a grid trans-

portation network, which is not divided into the arterial-collector-local road classification system found in most suburban areas. Finally, most TODs contain urban design guidelines and design features to encourage a more pedestrian orientation, which theoretically encourages its residences to eschew the automobile in favor of more communal forms of transportation.[71]

Transit-oriented development is designed to accomplish several key public objectives. First and foremost, a TOD is designed to encourage residents and workers to utilize public transit rather than the automobile as a primary means of transportation. A second purpose, related to the first, is the minimization of congestion on surrounding roadways. Finally, a TOD is designed to increase pedestrian utilization of streets, sidewalks, and other transportation facilities. TODs, as a form of neotraditional development, are not just an attempt to encourage greater utilization of public transit. TODs also reflect a new approach to suburban development that encourages a greater variety of uses and architectural design than the monotonous, single-use suburban subdivision—the "new suburbia" that has been described as the "packaged villages that are becoming the barracks of the new generation."[72] In fact, the prototype of most neotraditional ordinances—or traditional neighborhood development (TND) ordinances—is the older, urban neighborhood with its mixed uses, narrow gridiron streets, and higher densities.[73]

TOD presents both a challenge and an opportunity for the transit agency. While transit agencies typically lack jurisdiction over land-use-permitting decisions, they can work with local governments within the Urbanizing Tier to encourage transit-supportive land use patterns. In addition, they can form partnerships with the private sector to fulfill the mandates of TOD regulations.

Transportation Corridors

The transportation corridor is a geographic and functional area equivalent to a Tier III area. Transportation corridors are the rapidly urbanizing areas in most communities.[74] As such, they provide an excellent framework for the application of established precepts of growth management and the sound integration of multidisciplinary and intergovernmental planning. Transportation facilities are the most effective and significant growth and land use determinant. If creatively harnessed, such facilities can serve as the centerpiece for a well-conceived regional growth management system. They provide a perspective that is broader than the one from which the problem of explosive population growth is traditionally viewed—the local government. Transportation corridors are, by nature, regional. The focus is the development of a comprehensive plan that allows for the coordination of local, regional, and state planning objectives to ensure the rational and orderly development of a regional corridor, the backbone of which is a specified transportation facility and critical economic development.[75]

The encouragement of high-density development within the corridor is a key element of the overall transportation corridor concept. By promoting high-density development adjacent to transportation facilities within the corridor, the use of mass transportation and multimodal transportation facilities is encouraged and a sufficient client base is established to help make the massive expenditures required to construct high speed or rapid transit more feasible. High speed and mass transit reduce the dependency of the automobile as a source of travel, effectively reducing energy needs and despoliation of the environment.

> As the situs of high density development, the corridor becomes the focus for the state's developmental activity where major commercial, office, industrial and high density residential development occurs, assuring that employment and a proper mix of housing is available within the state. By encouraging high density residential development of property immediately adjacent to transportation facilities, the unique transportation needs of the elderly and the handicapped are more easily met. By the promotion of high density development within the corridor through joint development and other governmental techniques such as transfer of development rights and bonus and incentive zoning, the public sector is more easily able to protect environmentally sensitive and critical land, protect agricultural lands and historically, architecturally and archaeologically significant sites and structures, and provide for open space to break urban sprawl and maintain an urban-rural balance within the state.[76]

Endnotes

1. DOUGLAS S. MASSEY AND NANCY A. DENTON, AMERICAN APARTHEID: SEGREGATION AND THE MAKING OF THE UNDERCLASS (Harvard 1993); MYRON ORFIELD, METROPOLITICS: A REGIONAL AGENDA FOR COMMUNITY AND STABILITY (Brookings Inst. 1997).

2. Ford, *The Boundaries of Race: Political Geography in Legal Analysis,* 107 HARV. L. REV. 1841 (1994); CHARLES M. HAAR, SUBURBS UNDER SIEGE (Harvard 1995); S. MARK WHITE, AFFORDABLE HOUSING: PROACTIVE AND REACTIVE PLANNING STRATEGIES, PLANNING ADVISORY SERVICE REPORT NO. 441 (1992); DEP'T OF HUD, NOT IN MY BACK YARD: REMOVING BARRIERS TO AFFORDABLE HOUSING (1991); Patricia Salkin, *Barriers to Affordable Housing: Are Land Use Controls the Scapegoat?* LAND USE L. & ZONING DIG. 3 (April 1993); DAVID RUSK, CITIES WITHOUT SUBURBS 2d ed. (Woodrow Wilson Center Press, 1995) at 34; Jane Gross, *Poor Without Cars Find Trek to Work Is Now a Job,* N.Y. TIMES, Nov. 18, 1999, at A-1; ANTHONY DOWNS, NEW VISIONS FOR METROPOLITAN AMERICA 169–82 (Brookings Inst. 1994). *See also* Freilich & Bass, *Exclusionary Zoning: Suggested Litigation Approaches,* 3 URB. LAW. 344 (1974).

3. *See, e.g.,* Walker v. U.S. Dep't of HUD, 734 F. Supp. 1231 (N.D. Tex. 1989); Walker v. City of Mesquite, 169 F.3d 973 (5th Cir. 1999); James v. Valtierra, 402 U.S. 137 (1971); United States v. City of Blackjack, 508 F.2d 1179 (8th Cir. 1974); Gautreaux v. Chicago Housing Authority, 503 F.2d 930 (7th Cir. 1974); Shannon v. HUD, 436 F. 809 (3d Cir. 1970); Britton v. Town of Chester, 595 A.2d 492 (N.H. 1991).

4. *See* Macey & Miller, *The Community Reinvestment Act: An Economic Analysis,* 79 VA. L. REV. 349 (1993) (compelling banks to reinvest in redlined areas); Clayton v. Village of Oak Park, 453 N.E.2d 937 (Ill. 1983) (maintaining racial balance through insurance guarantees); NATIONAL COMMISSION ON URBAN PROBLEMS (THE DOUGLAS COMMISSION), BUILDING THE AMERICAN CITY, at 100 (1968); Searing, *Discrimination in Home Finance,* 48 N.D.L. 1113 U.L. REV. 72 (1973); Stegman, *Low-Income Ownership: Exploitation and Opportunity,* 50 J. URB. L. 371 (1973); Comment, *Exploiting the Home-Buying Poor: A Case Study of Abuse of the National Housing Act,* 17 ST. LOUIS U. L.J. 525 (1972).

5. THE DOUGLAS COMMISSION, *id.,* at 77–78.

6. *See, e.g.,* WILLIAM J. WILSON, THE TRULY DISADVANTAGED: THE INNER CITY, THE UNDERCLASS AND PUBLIC POLICY (Chicago 1987); DAVID RUSK, CITIES WITHOUT SUBURBS, 2d ed. (Wash. 1995); CENTER FOR COMMUNITY CHANGE, NATIONAL URBAN LEAGUE, THE NATIONAL SURVEY OF HOUSING ABANDONMENT (1971); G. STERNLIEB & R. BURCHELL, RESIDENTIAL ABANDONMENT—THE TENEMENT LANDLORD REVISITED (1973); *Project, Abandonment of Residential Property in an Urban Context,* 23 DEPAUL L. REV. 1186 (1974); Comment, *Property, Abandonment in Detroit,* 20 WAYNE L. REV. 845 (1974); Note, *Building Abandonment in New York City,* 16 N.Y.L. F. 798 (1970).

7. For a summary of urban growth patterns, *see generally* J. Thomas Black, *The Pros and Cons of the Current Pattern of Growth and Development in Metropolitan Areas, in* CREATING MORE LIVABLE METROPOLITAN AREAS, URBAN LAND INSTITUTE (1997). *See generally* John D. Kasarda, Stephen J. Appold, Stuart H. Sweeney & Elaine Sieff, *Central-City and Suburban Migration Patterns: Is a Turnaround on the Horizon?* 8 HOUSING POL'Y DEBATE 307 (1997).

8. *See* U.S. COMM'N ON CIVIL RIGHTS, ABOVE PROPERTY RIGHTS, at 9 (1972). *See generally* Margery Austin Turner, *Achieving a New Urban Diversity: What Have We Learned?* 8 HOUSING POL'Y DEBATE 295 (1997).

9. *See, e.g.*, Holliman, *Invisible Boundaries and Political Responsibility, A Proposal for Revision of California Annexation Law,* 3 Pac. L.J. 533 (1972); Comment, *Annexation Elections and the Right to Vote,* 20 UCLA L. Rev. 1093 (1973).

10. *See generally* Alexander Garvin, *Urban Parks and Open Spaces: Enhancing the Urban Realm, in* Creating More Livable Metropolitan Areas, Urban Land Institute (1997).

11. David L. Callies, Robert H. Freilich & Thomas E. Roberts, Cases and Materials on Land Use 486 (West 2d ed. 1994) [hereinafter Callies & Freilich].

12. *See* Hawaii Housing Authority v. Midkiff, 467 U.S. 229, 104 S. Ct. 2321, 81 L. Ed. 2d 186 (1984) (the Supreme Court held that the power of eminent domain is conterminous with the police power and may extend to any conceivable public purpose); Berman v. Parker, 348 U.S. 26, 75 S. Ct. 98, 99 L. Ed. 27 (1954) (the Court held that a planning commission was authorized to lease or sell the balance of the land acquired by condemnation to private parties who would develop the property); New York City Housing Authority v. Muller, 1 N.E.2d 153 (N.Y. 1936) (condemnation of slums for the purpose of constructing government-subsidized low-income housing was a public purpose).

13. Hayes & Godec, *Enhanced Sales Tax Incentive Programs (EATS),* 22 Urb. Law. 143 (1990); Winter, *Tax Incremental Financing: A Potential Redevelopment Mechanism,* 18 Ford Urb. L.J. 655 (1991); Davies, *Business Improvement Districts (BIDS),* 52 Wash. U. J. Urb. & Contemp. L. (1997).

14. John Costonis, Icons and Aliens: Law, Aesthetics and Environmental Change (1989); Weinstein, *Bonus and Incentive Zoning,* 2 Zoning & Land Use Controls, chap. 8 (Rohan ed., 1994).

15. Judith Wegner, *Utopian Visions, Cooperation Without Conflicts in Public-Private Ventures,* 31 Santa Clara L. Rev. 313 (1991); Michael S. Bernick & Amy E. Freilich, *Transit Villages and Transit-Based Development: How Government Can Work with the Private Sector to Make It Happen,* 30 Urb. Law. 1 (1998); Robert H. Freilich & Brenda Nichols, *Public-Private Partnerships in Joint Development: The Legal and Financial Anatomy of Large-Scale Urban Development Projects,* 7 Mun. Fin. J. 5 (1986).

16. David Callies, Robert Freilich & Thomas Roberts, Cases and Materials on Land Use 485 (West 3d ed. 1999); Britton v. Town of Chester, 595 A.2d 492 (N.H. 1991); S.A.V.E. v. City of Bothell, 576 P.2d 401 (Wash. 1978); Briffault, *Our Localism: Part I, The Structure of Local Government Law,* 90 Colum. L. Rev. 1 (1990); Steven G. Kopel & Dwight H. Merrian, Regional General Welfare: The End of a Trend? 1985 Inst. on Planning, Zoning & Em. Dom. (Southwestern Legal Found.).

17. Robert H. Freilich & Brenda L. Nichols, *Public-Private Partnerships in Joint Development: The Legal and Financial Anatomy of Large-Scale Urban Development Projects,* 7 Mun. Fin. J. 1 (Winter 1986) [hereinafter Freilich & Nichols].

18. South Florida's Eastward Ho! encourages urban infill at the appropriate densities and intensities, separates urban and rural uses, and discourages urban sprawl development patterns while preserving public open spaces and planning for buffer-type land uses and rural development consistent with their respective character along and outside the urban boundary. John M. DeGrove, *Sustainable Communities: The Future Direction for Managing Growth in Florida,* II ALI-ABA Course of Study Materials, Land Institute: Planning, Regulation, Litigation, Eminent Domain and Compensation, Aug. 14–16, 1997.

19. Callies & Freilich, *supra* note 11, at 506.

20. *Id.*

21. *Id.*

22. *See generally* CALLIES & FREILICH, *supra* note 11, at 506; Freilich, *Awakening the Sleeping Giant: New Trends and Development in Environmental and Land Use Controls,* 1974 INST. ON PLAN., ZON. & EMINENT DOMAIN 1, 45. *See* Dean Wegner's discussion of ways in which "new coinage might be minted" by local government. Wegner, *Utopian Visions: Cooperation Without Conflicts in Public/Private Ventures,* 31 SANTA CLARA L. REV. 313 (1991).

23. Josephs v. Town of Clarkstown, 198 N.Y.S.2d 695 (App. Div. 2d Dep't 1960).

24. This unusual system is discussed in Fonoroff, *Special Districts: A Departure from the Concept of Uniform Controls, in* THE NEW ZONING (Marcus & Groves eds., 1970) and explained in Elliott & Marcus, *From* Euclid *to* Ramapo: *New Directions in Land Development Controls,* 1 HOFSTRA L. REV. 56, 62 (1973).

25. David Listokin, *Growth Management and Historic Preservation: Best Practices for Synthesis,* 29 URB. LAW. 2 (Spring 1997) citing NEW JERSEY OFFICE OF STATE PLANNING, STATEWIDE PLANNING FOR DEVELOPMENT AND REDEVELOPMENT IN THE UNITED STATES (1996).

26. Robert H. Freilich & Terri A. Muren, Growth Management and Historic Preservation, a study I prepared for the City of Atlanta, March 1988.

27. For further discussion of housing courts, *see* Scott, *Housing Courts and Housing Justice: An Overview,* 17 URB. L. ANN. 3 (1979); and HOUSING JUSTICE IN THE UNITED STATES: RECOMMENDATION FOR CHANGE AND INNOVATION IN OUR COURTS (Scott ed., A.B.A. 1981); Ramsey & Zolna, *A Piece in the Puzzle of Providing Adequate Housing: Court Effectiveness in Code Enforcement,* 18 FORD. URB. L.J. 605 (1991).

28. *See* Salsich, *Housing and the States,* 2 URB. LAW. 40 (1970).

29. *See* Landman, *Flexible Housing Code—The Mystique of the Single Standard: A Critical Analysis and Comparison of Model and Selected Housing Codes Leading to the Development of a Proposed Model Flexible Housing Code,* 18 HOWARD L.J. 251, 255 (1974).

30. Note, *Municipal Housing Codes,* 69 HARV. L. REV. 1115 (1956).

31. *See Municipal Housing Codes, supra* note 30, at 1117. However, a housing code that creates differing requirements for disparate areas runs some risk of violating the Equal Protection Clause. The classification of a city into housing code zones may be upheld as reasonably related to the ultimate legislative purposes of health, safety, and slum prevention. Equal protection is not denied when different methods are employed to obtain validly differentiated objectives. *See* Brennan v. Milwaukee, 60 N.W.2d 704 (Wis. 1953).

32. City of St. Louis v. Brune, 515 S.W.2d 471 (Mo. 1974); Block v. Hirsch, 256 U.S. 135, 156 (1921) (such regulations may amount to a taking without due process of law); *contra,* Moore v. City of Detroit, 406 N.W.2d 488 (Mich. App. 1987) (no violation of substantial due process, equal protection, or taking).

33. *See generally* Diane R. Suchman, *Urban Change and Infill Housing Development, in* CREATING MORE LIVABLE METROPOLITAN AREAS (Urban Land Institute 1997).

34. The Cranston-Gonzales National Affordable Housing Act, signed into law in 1990, requires local governments to prepare a Comprehensive Housing Affordability Strategy as a condition to receiving federal aid for affordable housing. 42 U.S.C.A. § 12702 *et seq.* (Nov. 28, 1990).

35. *See* Zoeckler, *The Tax Abatement Program for Historic Properties in Georgia,* 28 GA. ST. BAR J. 129 (1992); Menezes & Morgan, *Michigan's Industrial Property Tax Abatement Law: Fortuity or Futility?,* 7 COOLEY L. REV. 139 (1990). For a discussion of the major subcategories of tax-related assistance, *see* Malloy, *The Political Economy of Co-Financing America's Urban*

Renaissance, 40 VAND. L. REV. 67 (1987). "Tax increment financing is a value capture technique premised upon the assumption that a development or redevelopment project in a particular area will result in both increased property values and an increased tax assessment base. The 'tax increment' is the difference between the amount of taxes raised from the project area and that generated prior to development or redevelopment. In tax increment financing, the tax base of the project area is frozen at predevelopment value. The tax above the frozen base is actually paid, but the proceeds go into a special fund that can be used to pay for site acquisition or improvement and may constitute a stream of revenue for bond retirement." Freilich & Nichols, *Public Private Partnerships in Joint Development: The Legal and Financial Anatomy of Large-Scale Urban Development Projects,* 7 MUN. FIN. J. 5 (1986). The developer receives the subsidy at the beginning of the project with tax increment financing if bonding is used rather than at the end with tax abatement. Tax increment financing has become the technique of choice over tax abatement because the full tax is paid although diverted to the redevelopment area through a trust fund and therefore can be used to bond projects.

36. *See* Annbar Associates v. West Side Redevelopment Corp., 397 S.W.2d 635 (Mo.1965).

37. *See* D.S. Alamo Associates v. Commissioner of Finance, 525 N.Y.S.2d 823, 824 (1988), where the court allowed a tax abatement for the entire thirty-two-story mixed-use condominium, which included office space, against the city's contention that only the residential space qualified for preferential tax treatment.

38. *See* ANN. MO. STAT. ch. 353 (West 1999).

39. For readings on tax increment finance and redevelopment, *see* Young, *The Tax Increment Allocation Redevelopment Act: The "Blighted" Statute,* 15 S. ILL. U. L.J. 145 (1990); Bucholtz, *Tax-Exempt Redevelopment Financing in Florida,* 20 STETSON L. REV. 667 (1991); Hayes & Godec, *Taxation Innovations: Enhanced Sales Tax Incentive Programs,* 22 URB. LAW. 143 (1990).

40. WASH. REV. CODE ANN. § 35.81.010 (West 1999). *See State v. Miami Beach Redevelopment Agency,* 392 So 875 (Fla. 1980), which illustrates the use of tax increment finance bonds in severely blighted area. Tax increment financing legislation has been enacted in at least thirty-eight states. For a list of those states and their citations see Winter, *Tax Increment Financing: A Potential Redevelopment Financing Mechanism for New York Municipalities,* 18 FORDHAM URB. L.J. 655, 656, n.9 (1991); Comment, *Tax Increment Financing for Redevelopment in Missouri—Beauty and the Beast,* 54 UMKC L. REV. 77 (1985).

41. Williams, *The Enterprise Zone Concept at the Federal Level: Are Proposed Tax Incentives the Needed Ingredient?,* 9 VA. TAX REV. 711, 721–22 (1990); Tschirgi, *Aiming the Tax Code at the Distressed Areas: An Examination and Analysis of Current Enterprise Zone Proposals,* 43 FLA. L. REV. 991, 1030 (1991).

42. Wolf, *An Essay in Re-Plan, American Enterprise Zones in Practice,* 21 URB. LAW. 29 (1989).

43. *See* DAVID CALLIES, ROBERT FREILICH & THOMAS ROBERTS, CASES AND MATERIALS ON LAND USE 561 (West 3d ed. 1999).

44. *See generally* McGee, *Afro-American Resistance to Gentrification and the Demise of Integrationist Ideology in the United States,* 23 URB. LAW. 25 (1991).

45. LONGHINI & LAUBER, CONDOMINIUM CONVERSION REGULATIONS: PROTECTING TENANTS (1979).

46. *See* Sintra, Inc. v. City of Seattle, 829 P.2d 765 (Wash 1995) (demolition fee for low-income housing replacement); Commercial Builders v. City of Sacramento, 941 F.2d 872 (9th Cir. 1992) (fee to housing trust fund).

47. *See* Lauber, *Let's Put Some Limits on Condo Conversions,* PLANNING, Sept. 1977, at 25.

48. Rockville Grosvenor, Inc. v. Montgomery County, 422 A.2d 353 (Md. 1980).

49. *See* Dubin, *From Junkyards to Gentrification: Explicating a Right to Protective Zoning in Low-Income Communities of Color,* 77 MINN. L. REV. 739–801 (1993).

50. *See* DAVID DOLLIER, HOW SMART GROWTH CAN STOP SPRAWL (Essential Books 1998) at 47: "*Re-envisioning Downtown Development.* Part of the challenge is seeing the potential of downtowns in new ways and then devising new strategies—zoning, redevelopment, and planning—to achieve them." For example, in Providence, R.I., Downcity was a dilapidated and forlorn classic American business district. Dvany, Plater-Zyborg's (DPZ) insight was that the fine, old infrastructure of buildings was perfectly suited to other uses: The old office buildings and department stores could be converted into apartments and loft space for young people, taking advantage of the Rhode Island School of Design. JAMES H. KUNSTLER, HOME FROM NOWHERE 155–60 (1996).

51. For a complete discussion of California's Relocation Act, *see Beatty v. Imperial Irrigation District,* 231 Cal. Reptr. 128 (Cal. App. 1986); and for discussion of a variety of downtown housing strategies, *see* California, The Marks-Foran Residential Rehabilitation Act, Health & Safety Code § 37910 *et seq.*

52. CALLIES & FREILICH, *supra* note 11, at 529.

53. *See* R. FREILICH & E. STUHLER, THE LAND USE AWAKENING, ZONING LAW IN THE SEVENTIES 5 (1981); Freilich, *Managing Energy Conservation Under Planned Growth, in* ENERGY & LAND USE, 453, 454–56 (1981).

54. *See* Freilich & Nichols, *supra* note 17.

55. For the seminal case, *see Berman v. Parker,* 348 U.S. 26 (1954) (upholding the acquisition of property through eminent domain for urban renewal).

56. *See* Merrill, *The Economics of Public Use,* 72 CORN. L. REV. 61 (1986).

57. *See* City of Kansas City, Mo. v. Kindle, 446 S.W.2d 807 (Mo. 1969); *see also In* re Coleman Highlands, 401 S.W.2d 385 (Mo. 1966), in which the compensation could be paid.

58. Land and air rights leasing involves negotiation of a long-term lease agreement for real property that is originally purchased by the transit agency for transit purposes such as station sites and parking areas or is owned by a public agency. In these cases, a plan is developed whereby the transit facility requirements can be met within the structure of a larger project, creating space for incremental commercial uses. In most cases, the station facilities are wholly integrated in the development project, and ancillary facilities, such as parking and entranceways, are shared. These arrangements are typically structured as long-term leases, and the transit agency and/or other public agency can expect to gain contributions to station capital costs as well as long-term lease revenues. Lease revenues can be derived from a base rental value and/or as a percentage of project income, making the public agency a true equity partner in the development. Most states limit the duration of leasehold interests that may be granted pursuant to a public-private development. *See* Michael S. Bernick & Amy E. Freilich, *Transit Villages and Transit-Based Development: The Rules Are Becoming More Flexible,* 30 URB. LAW. 1 (Winter 1998).

59. A negotiated investment is an agreement between a developer and a public agency or agencies, through which the developer agrees to contribute property and/or capital costs to a transit improvement in exchange for some concession that will benefit his development. These types of agreements can range from total integration of the transit station and ancillary facilities within the development project to agreements to provide access facilities or other public amenity improvements that enhance the transit facility. In certain instances, local governments

can utilize zoning and building permit authorities to bargain with developers to pay for transit-related improvements. *See* Bernick & Freilich, *id.*

60. Connection fees can be charged to owners/developers of both existing and future buildings for being physically connected to a station facility. Traditionally, these fees have included:

    1. lump sum payments to cover capital costs of knock-out panels, entrance areas, and so on, plus a fee to cover the intrinsic value of the connection;

    2. an annual contribution to the operating costs of the station facility;

    3. in lieu of dedication of property for station areas or easements; and

    4. architectural and operational enhancements to the facility.

Connection fee agreements are best utilized with either subway or elevated stations where direct access to mezzanine levels creates additional prime rentable areas at the upper or lower levels of buildings. The enhanced value of these areas thus becomes the basis for connection fees and capital investments on the part of the developer. *See Russ Building Partnership v. City and County of San Francisco,* 750 P.2d 324 (Cal. 1988).

61. Concessions involve the generation of revenues through the sale or lease of portions of their station facilities for concessions. Concessions may include mechanical or "vending" equipment ranging from automatic teller banking machines to food dispensers to pay telephones. Alternatively, concessions may include space set aside within the station site for retail stands and kiosks or roving vendors permitted to sell from floating locations. Major retail stall-form concessions dictate specific design requirements and accommodations in station areas. These can include supplemental provisions for electrical/water needs and additional space requirements. Freestanding kiosk-type outlets can reduce the structural accommodation requirements. *See* Bernick & Freilich, *id.*

62. *See* Freilich & Nichols, *supra* note 17; *see also* Robert H. Freilich & S. Mark White, *Transportation Congestion and Growth Management: Comprehensive Approaches to Resolving America's Major Quality of Life Crisis,* 24 LOY. L.A. L. REV. 915 (June 1991).

63. *See* Bernick & Freilich, *id.*

64. *Id.*

65. Martin J. Rosen, *Reviving Urban Parks,* URB. LAND, at 54, 55 (Nov. 1997).

66. *See* PIERCE COUNTY'S COMPREHENSIVE PLAN, at i-8.

67. For insightful analyses, *see* Babcock, *The City as Entrepreneur: Fiscal Wisdom or Folly,* 29 SANTA CLARA L. REV. 931 (1989), and Wegner, *Utopian Visions: Cooperation Without Conflicts in Public/Private Ventures,* 31 SANTA CLARA L. REV. 313 (1991).

68. For a description of how urban sprawl has overwhelmed the capacity of the nation's major metropolitan area transportation systems, *see* Freilich, *Managing Energy Conservation Under Planned Growth,* ENERGY AND LAND USE 453, 454–56 (Rutgers U. Press 1981); JOEL GARREAU, EDGE CITY: LIFE ON THE NEW FRONTIER (Doubleday 1991); ALAN DURNING, THE CITY AND THE CAR 24 (Northwest Environment Watch, 1996).

69. The term "new urbanism" has been in use for many years, originally referring to the trend *away* from traditional village-oriented development. C. TUNNARD, THE CITY OF MAN (1953) at 362–85; *see* THE NEW URBAN NEWS, Sept./Oct. 1998, at 3. *The New Urban News* is a periodical devoted to the new urbanism, smart growth, livable communities, traditional neighborhood development, and walkable neighborhoods as the answer to suburban sprawl.

70. P. CALTHORPE, THE NEXT AMERICAN METROPOLIS: ECOLOGY, COMMUNITY, AND THE AMERICAN DREAM (1990); P. KATZ, THE NEW URBANISM: TOWARD AN ARCHITECTURE OF COMMUNITY (1994).

71. Substantial data resulted from a study conducted by Freilich, Leitner & Carlisle for the Transportation Research Board. S. MARK WHITE, THE ZONING AND REAL ESTATE IMPLICATIONS OF TRANSIT-ORIENTED DEVELOPMENT, TCRP J-5, Topic 3-03 (1999).

72. DOUGLAS KELBAUGH, TOWN AND NEIGHBORHOOD REGIONAL DESIGN (Univ. of Wash. Press 1997); RICHARD MOE & CARTER WILKIE, CHANGING PLACES: REBUILDING COMMUNITY IN THE AGE OF SPRAWL (Henry Holt & Co. 1997); Reid v. Architectural Board of Review, 192 N.E.2d 74, 80 (Ohio App. 1963) (Corrigan, J., dissenting).

73. Marlon G. Boarnet & Nicholas S. Compin, *Transit-Oriented Development in San Diego County: The Irreverential Implementation of a Planning Idea,* 65 J. AM. PLAN. ASS'N 80 (1999); Daniel R. Mandelker, *Environmental Policy: The Next Generation,* 61 TOWN PLANNING REV. 107 (1993).

74. CALLIES & FREILICH, *supra* note 11, at 587.

75. Robert H. Freilich, Elizabeth Garvin & S. Mark White, *Economic Development and Public Transit: Making the Most of the Washington Growth Management Act,* 16 PUGET SOUND L. REV. 16 (1993).

76. Freilich & Chinn, *Transportation Corridors: Shaping and Financing Urbanization Through Integration of Eminent Domain, Zoning and Growth Management Techniques,* 55 UMKC L. REV. 153 (1987); *see also* Freilich & White, *Transportation Congestion and Growth Management: Comprehensive Approaches to Resolving America's Major Quality of Life Crisis,* 24 LOY. L.A. L. REV. 915 (1991).

CHAPTER EIGHT

Promoting Agricultural and Rural Preservation

The impact of urbanization on agricultural land has created a major agricultural crisis we now face through the loss of prime farmland and open space throughout the United States.[1] The growing interest in environmental protection, energy conservation, inner-city revitalization, local government fiscal solvency, and orderly growth in the Urbanizing Tier coalesces with agricultural concerns.[2] It is this final tier of land that timed and sequenced growth management will protect.[3] The loss of valuable agricultural land in the United States has been, and continues to be, staggering in its proportions. Urban sprawl eats up two acres a minute, three million acres a year.[4]

The reasons for conversion in regions and states coincide with national patterns that suggest that the land market and skyrocketing land values are the chief inducement to conversion and the chief obstacle to preservation.[5] The high market value of farmland in urban areas exerts powerful pressure on farm owners to sell their land for nonagricultural development.[6] Those who resist the temptation to sell are often still faced with soaring property tax assessments, higher taxes associated with increased governmental costs, special assessments for urban-level improvements and services from which they derive little real benefit unless their land is converted to urban use, adjacent urban uses that conflict with the agricultural activity, higher costs and lower net farm income relative to the value of their real estate, despite attempts to use newer techniques. In the face of these pressures, many farmers are "forced" to sell their land to developers.

The preservation of the final tier should play an important role in the overall planning and growth management program for the entire region.[7] It is the area in which urban growth should not be directed or encouraged—in which growth-supporting public facilities should not be provided, but in which provision may be made for accommodation of rural population. If adequate provisions (sufficient land) are made available elsewhere for the projected growth and development in the region, then it is more reasonable to impose development limitation regulations on rural, environmental, and prime agricultural land; and it is more likely that such regulations will be effective and legally valid. Thus, in terms of policy and strategy development, it is imperative to consider the planning and growth management approaches in other geographic areas and other plan elements to evaluate accurately the merits of the existing rural, open space, environmental, and agricultural land preservation approaches.[8]

Local authorities in this tier should explicitly recognize the importance of agriculture. Farmland is a unique and valuable resource that is difficult to renew once it is converted to other uses. Development needs to be prudently managed in these areas to ensure the continuing viability of the agriculture industry well into the future. Many agricultural areas are likely to be affected by several critical issues over the next two decades. The changing composition of agriculture is a significant issue. Retaining sufficient farmland to sustain a viable agricultural economy is necessary because farmland is under considerable pressure. Healthy soil, adequate water supplies, and contiguous lands are essential to sustaining farmland productivity, but they are also the prime attributes for large sprawling subdivisions. Sustainable farm practices can ensure fertile soils. But adequate water supplies and contiguous lands require prudent land development practices.

Nationally, the direction of agricultural land preservation strategies is to integrate differential assessment programs with other land use planning techniques, including zoning, subdivision controls, special districts and agricultural preserves, acquisition of land or development rights, and growth management systems. The latter is of particular importance in metropolitan areas in which substantial growth is occurring and in which shifts in land use and population indicate a steady centripetal migration that consumes rural and agricultural land while at the same time leaving depressed and abandoned areas behind. This pattern can and does occur solely through internal migration even where there is no "real" growth in population. Where there is real growth, the shift may be accelerated. This trend is occurring nationally, as well as locally, in regions and counties and presents a substantial threat to preservation programs. However, many plans are effective. Summit County, Utah, incorporated various techniques into its general plan, to ensure that all property owners have a reasonable use of their land within a reasonable period of time, including conservation easements, preferential tax assessments, cluster housing, planned unit developments, transfer of development rights, purchase of property, open space, and greenbelt designations.[9]

In some areas of America, the market value of farmland for nonagricultural development purposes far exceeds its value for agricultural uses. This disparity leads to a pattern of sprawling land development, undermining farmland contiguity and at times causing competition for water usage. As farmlands become interspersed by residential and commercial developments, nuisance conflicts proliferate. Farms experience troubling trespass, theft, and vandalism from neighbors, which ultimately results in a loss of farmland profitability. Also, the ability of agriculture to remain economically viable over time is largely dependent on the governmental environment within which it operates. This relates to the several levels of government that establish programs and policies that can encourage and stimulate or discourage and hamper agricultural operations—beyond those actions that relate primarily to land use. Without full consideration being given to agricultural endeavors (nonland) needs or the impact of general regulatory (cost-related) actions, agriculture can be seriously threatened even though a land base may be reasonably secured.

The marginal profitability of some farm operations has resulted in some farmers relying on nonagricultural sources of income. As these pressures persist, farmers depend more heavily on their frequently rising land values as collateral for loans for both farm and nonfarm expenses, and for retirement income. The need for loans and off-farm income are just two symptoms of eroding agricultural profitability. In more extreme cases, farmers began to sell land parcels in an effort to liquidate their equity. This activity, when multiplied throughout a region, leads to heightened land use conflicts, nuisance complaints with neighbors, and, ultimately, further loss in farmland profitability. Prudent land management techniques are necessary to reverse this spiral.

Much of an area's intensive, high-value agriculture is maintained by the availability and application of an adequate supply of irrigation water. In addition, some field crops rely on irrigation as well. Short-term rainfall deficits at a critical growing period, or an extended drought can result in complete crop loss. To enable agriculture, particularly high-value operations, to continue, adequate and reliable water supplies are necessary. In addition to the effects of water on farming, the effects of farming on water are important. Watershed lands and aquifer recharge areas, which provide drinking water supplies, are sensitive resources that need protection even in agricultural areas. Farm operations, as any land use, contribute to the deterioration of water quality by nutrient and sediment loading, and by applications of chemical fertilizers and pesticides. Further study and enhanced management practices can identify and alleviate water-quality concerns caused by agricultural operations. Biological systems that are diverse, stable, self-regulating, sustaining, purifying, and beneficially associated with agriculture are a natural legacy requiring protection for future generations.

Channeling development out of and away from the agricultural land and open space is critical.[10] Timing and sequencing within the Urbanizing Tier is a significant part in the undertaking of agricultural preservation, as well as the promotion of urban infill in Tier I. While the federal government has only recently played a role in the preservation of agricultural land, integrating the concepts of the Urbanizing Tier into state plans will create high standards.[11] States have enacted agricultural preservation laws that create higher density within the urban growth boundaries restricting the leapfrog effects into the open space and agricultural land. New state constitutional approaches have emerged—a state substantive due process theory—that applies a regional general welfare standard, required when local and county governments act—since they have been delegated power by the state and must use that power to broaden regional rather than local or parochial interests.[12] Local governments must consider the impacts of their land use measures on the region, whether they affect affordable housing or other exclusionary measures.[13]

Rural Land Planning and Development

Regions and counties should promote a diverse and efficient land development pattern that directs development and preserves the rural character by managing growth according to carrying capacity analysis and retains large, contiguous, and economically viable areas of productive, high soil quality farmland that is

buffered from incompatible uses.[14] The combination of methods used to attain these land development patterns should maintain a fair value of the land. State and local authorities should establish and maintain planning capability to formulate and implement farmland retention programs throughout agricultural areas in the state. This improved planning capability should be encouraged through personnel sharing and the provision of financial and technical assistance. Intensity and use of development and nonpoint source pollution control measures in the rural development areas so that on-site wastewater treatment facilities, either individually or in combination with other development, are effective in protecting surface and ground water from pollution should be managed. Ironically, water usage in the United States is declining in every area except for rural subdivision sprawl.[15]

Regions should ensure that development in the rural development areas will have safe and adequate on-site portable water sources that can be used without adversely affecting surface and groundwater quality and quantity. Tier III authorities should manage the use, intensity, and location of development in the rural development areas and in exsisting small towns to preserve and enhance their rural and small town character. The factors that comprise rural character in a specified area should be regionally and locally determined.[16]

They should also manage the use, intensity, and location of development in rural development areas to protect and preserve large, contiguous tracts of farmland and large, contiguous tracts of natural land in an undisturbed condition particularly to support wildlife movement which is rapidly losing ground to the suburbs.[17] Municipalities should manage development in rural development areas so that traffic generated by existing and future development in the rural development areas will not exceed the capacity of the local components of the existing rural road network to provide safe, efficient, and convenient traffic movements during peak traffic periods.[18] When these programs are applied to farmlands, priority should be given to farmland in Tier III.

Agricultural Zoning

In the early years of zoning, the orientation was almost entirely urban and zoning for agriculture was rare. As a consequence of urban sprawl and the resulting pressure upon rural land, however, agricultural zoning has become more common. By zoning land exclusively for agricultural uses, subdivisions are prevented from consuming valuable agricultural land, and a holding zone is created to contain and restrict urban expansion.[19] The need for such zoning is pointed up by the realities of sprawl. As the community begins to expand outward, commercial and residential development cause property values to spiral upward as more and more acres of land are sold to speculators. The result is scattered development, premature conversion of rural land to urban use, and a definite loss of agricultural productive potential. For exclusive agricultural zoning to be valid, the land must actually be capable of being used for meaningful agricultural activity. If land that is not agricultural is zoned exclusively agricultural, the landowner may be deprived of all reasonable use of his or her land and, therefore, any reasonable return on investment-backed expectation—thus the ordinance might result in a taking of this property without just compensation.[20]

Preservation of prime agricultural lands is of increasing importance. Agricultural lands not only provide visible open spaces, but they provide necessary food supplies for an ever-increasing population and form an important part of the economy of many states. Exclusive agricultural zoning is one technique for preserving such land. By zoning exclusively agricultural, residential development of any significant density is forced to go elsewhere. In addition, by utilizing some type of tax abatement or preferential assessment policy, a municipality can delay the premature conversion of farmland into residential subdivisions.

Other regulatory techniques include population quotas,[21] flexible zoning, and impact zoning. Flexible zoning may provide for the utilization of extremely small lot zoning coupled with planned unit development (PUD),[22] clustering,[23] or averaging density. For example, Pennsylvania has adopted a "growing greener" approach to subdivision design that is yielding extraordinary results.[24] Essentially, developers first identify primary and secondary conservation areas on a subdivision parcel, and whatever remains is a potential development area. Houses are located within this potential devleopment area—density is determined by the zoning district, then the developer connects the dots by aligning streets between the houses and away from conservation areas.[25]

In impact zoning, zoning approvals would be assigned based upon contiguity with village centers, prime soils, economic productivity, and environmental sensitivity. Exclusive agricultural use zones or agricultural districts have been upheld in numerous situations as a valid regulatory technique.[26] In agricultural districts, all incompatible nonagricultural uses are excluded. Criteria for designation of land as an "agricultural district" often include analysis of soil type, productivity, and location.

Protecting small-town main streets from peripheral, big box development can also be readily accomplished. Rutland, Vermont; Santa Monica and Pasadena, California; and several cities in Iowa are excellent case studies on the techniques that communities have used to resist "big box" sprawl on the perimeters of small towns.[27]

Taxation Techniques

The pressure of rising property taxes often "forces" farmers to sell their land to developers. One of the major attempts to ease the crunch of paying taxes at the higher market rates on farmland, which is rising, has been to assess agricultural land at its current or farm use value rather than at its fair market value, which often includes a substantial element of development value. So-called "differential assessment" laws are now fairly widespread, but have had limited success, particularly where they operate independently of other agricultural land preservation techniques and planning programs.

An alternative to differential assessment is a deferred tax. A deferred tax would only be levied if the owner changes the use of the land to one not qualified under law, restrictive agreements between the landowner and the governmental entity, or exemptions from applicable tax rates.[28] Although tax alternatives and favorable value assessment reduce the tax pressures, they cannot stop urban sprawl since development pressures still exist on the land. The capital gains from land development still far outweigh the property tax incentive to keep the land undeveloped. To be effective, taxation techniques must be integrated with other agricultural land preservation strategies.

To prevent the premature urbanization of agricultural land, many states have adopted preferential tax treatment policies to induce farmers to keep land for agricultural purposes.[29] An example of such legislation is the California Land Conservation Act, also known as the "Williamson Act."[30] The Act authorizes the establishment on the local level of "agricultural preserves"—by contract or by agreement, land within these preserves is restricted to agricultural and other compatible uses. Between the individual landowners and the municipality or county, the contract restricts the land to agricultural and other compatible use for a minimum period of ten years.[31] The Act has resulted in a reduction in the assessed valuation of such land because assessments are based upon the income-generating value of the land rather than upon its potential uses.

Most states have some form of preferential taxation, while several others have it under serious consideration. The four methods by which this is accomplished are:

1. preferential assessments—where property is taxed on the basis of its actual use;
2. deferred taxation—the difference between the market value of the property and its actual use is deferred until the property is developed; and
3. restricted use—the land must be subject to a land use restriction as a condition precedent to use-value assessment.
4 single land use tax which forces development into closer built-up areas and preserves farmland.[32]

LESA

In order to effectively inventory which agricultural lands should be protected, a soil analysis is needed to determine the proper land to be cultivated. This has led to the land evaluation and site assessment (LESA) system. Created by the United States Soil Conservation Service in 1981, LESA helps elected officials, citizens, farmers, soil conservationists, and planners objectively rate a tract's soil potential for agriculture and for social and economic factors including location, access to market, and adjacent land use.[33] LESA is a two-part system that can be used as part of an agricultural preservation program helping implement the federal Farmland Protection Policy Act,[34] to choose the farm units to be included in the agricultural land protection programs, as well as to help in determining the minimum parcel size for farm subdivisions in agricultural districts. LESA enables the planning of sewer, water, and transportation projects or the creation of agricultural districts, and the assessment and review of environmental impacts.[35] LESA can also be used to determine the lands to be included in a transfer or purchase of development rights programs.

Also related to soil conservation and agricultural preservation is the concept of sustainability. It has emerged as a viable theory in the preservation of the final tier.[36] It is the practice of implementing sustainable tools and applications so that humans and the environment, including wildlife and their ecosystems, can survive and be sustained indefinitely into the future.[37] It is believed that sustainability can be accomplished by strengthening environmental laws and decreasing human consumption and waste.[38]

Currently, Florida is working for the sustainability of South Florida. In

March 1994, the Governor's Commission on a Sustainable South Florida was established.[39] Over the last several years, the Commission has recommended compact development to reduce conversion of agricultural land and helped shape joint development programs creating new directions for Florida's growth management system. In its initial report, an implementation strategy called for an Eastward Ho! initiative that focused on redevelopment of the traditional urban corridor to help sustain growth.[40]

Right to Farm Laws

Most states have "right to farm" statutes.[41] The statutes can be broken into three separate groups. The "right to farm" for *general* agricultural operations provides that a farming operation cannot be declared a nuisance if it was not a nuisance at the time it began operation.[42] The second type of statute serves to protect specific types of agricultural activities: cultivation of land, production of agricultural crops, raising of poultry, egg production, milk, fruit, livestock (including hog feeding lots), and other horticultural crops.[43] The third type of statute protects farmers and food companies from suit over food safety.[44]

These laws are quite effective when metropolitan areas begin to encroach on outlying farm communities. They prevent "cappuccino cowboys" (urbanites who want a rural lifestyle with an urban income) from thereafter rethinking their decisions when airborne pesticides, odors, dusty roads, slow-moving farm machines on roads, roosters crowing at crack of dawn, and noise of machines and tractors disturb their "rural tranquility."[45] Without these laws common law nuisance suits against farm operations might well succeed.[46] Protecting farms from suits for nuisance does not, however, effectively confront the underlying problem of the incompatibility of the uses. What is needed is the creation of exclusive agricultural districts prohibiting all residential use within the district,[47] combined with enforcement of environmental laws regulating hog and cattle waste, pesticides, and chemical surface water drift.[48]

Recently feedlots have come under increasing pressure from government and individuals. The odor and sewage waste, especially from hog farms (concentrated Animal Feeding Operations–CAFOs) where farms with over 17,000 animals (unusual) feed waste into large lagoons which may hold as much as thirty million gallons of liquid animal waste (equivalent to a daily sewage runoff of a city of 300,000 people). The waste is then chemically broken down, spread on-site or injected into the soil with the effect of reducing air quality in the area, emitting high and possibly even dangerous levels of hydrogen sulfide, ammonia, and methane gas into the air. Leaks in lagoons are responsible for numerous incidents of water contamination.

Since most agricultural states have Right to Farm Laws and agricultural exemptions from zoning, the CAFOs have been allowed to operate as an agricultural use[49] subject in a few cases to limited health codes.[50]

The Clinton administration has propsed legislation that would require livestock farms to develop plans to store animal waste as a condition of remaining in business. The strategy was developed by the Environmental Protection Agency and the Department of Agriculture and is aimed at reducing the pollution which runs off livestock farms and CAFOs into surrounding rivers and streams. the largest livestock facilities would have to be in compliance by 2003 and the smaller ones by 2008.[51]

Better smart growth and agricultural district and tier planning are essential, especially in the light that a recent decision of the Iowa Supreme Court (with a petition to the U.S. Supreme Court denied) has held that a Right to Farm Law constitutes a taking of the adjoining property owner's rights. The Court held that the state cannot regulate property so as to insulate users from private nuisance claims without providing for just compensation.[52]

Transfer of Development Rights

The Transfer of Development Rights (TDR) concept provides for planning on an areawide basis by allowing landowners in restricted areas (or "sending areas") to transfer densities and other development rights to landowners in areas appropriate for higher densities (or "receiving areas"). I developed an innovative TDR system for Hollywood, Florida, that preserved the last remaining stretch (3.5 miles) of unspoiled beach between Miami and Palm Beach on Florida's Gold Coast.[53] A TDR system can be used to support transit-oriented development by designating areas around transit stops as receiving areas for TDRs. The TDR system may also have the secondary effect of channeling development into transportation corridors by restricting development outside transit centers. The usual purpose of TDRs is to ameliorate the harshness of zoning restrictions. TDRs give planners an alternative to purchasing the land outright or abandoning any attempt to enforce carrying capacity by allowing the market to furnish "fair compensation" for rights relinquished through zoning restrictions. The transit agency can use TDRs to encourage transit-supportive development by working with general-purpose local governments to design transit station areas as receiving areas and encouraging development restrictions in peripheral areas.[54]

This method of providing for orderly, controlled growth is somewhat similar to the marketable interest in traditional mineral rights, except that it is usually implemented in densely occupied urban areas. It is a process in which the transferor site conveys to the transferee site all or a portion of its unused potential zoning capacity that would otherwise lay fallow.[55] To initiate the process, each political subdivision draws up a master plan that specifies the percentage of land in each planning district to be developed, then designates where such specific types must occur. Upon completion of the plan, developmental rights are assigned to all landowners within each district for two categories of development—commercial and residential. The number of rights in each category, assigned to each landowner, would be proportioned to the percentage of his or her property within the plan with all rights transferable or salable by the owner without selling the land.

TDRs are also extremely effective for preserving agricultural land. Montgomery County, Maryland, combined TDRs with zoning ordinance. In the agricultural preservation area development is limited to one dwelling unit per twenty-five acres. Owners recapture their losses from low density by selling one development right per five acres to corridor and center receiving areas. This sophisticated program was upheld against a taking challenge in *Dufour v. Montgomery County Council,* No. 56954 (Circuit Court, 1983), discussed in 3 LAND USE LAW 19 (1983).

The actual aspect of the plan that controls development is the requirement that a developer must possess all the rights required for a designated use before any building commences. The obstacle is that, at the start of the plan, no single developer owns enough rights to build on the whole property. The developer must buy the additional rights on an open market from other landowners within the plan. The actual number of rights required is determined by the local planning body and/or the legislative body in each political subdivision. The number of rights required would be based upon ecological and population concerns; in other words, the less sprawling the development, the fewer rights would be required.

Once a landowner sells or transfers the rights for development to another landowner, the land becomes open space at absolutely no cost to the local government. The owner is permanently barred from ever building commercial or residential developments on that land, with the same restraint applying to the landowner's heirs or transferees. There is also a provision whereby an individual can petition for an increase in the density of the plan. If the petition is successful, additional rights will be allocated to all owners of rights within the plan on a pro rata basis, resulting in a new negotiation of rights.[56]

To ensure that the necessities for a balanced community are included, agricultural and certain outdoor recreational developments do not require rights, nor do lands for public schools, libraries, hospitals, or police or fire stations. Since these uses are exempt from the developmental right requirement, the cost to the government and taxpayer would be greatly reduced. Another element that will tend to decrease taxpayer expenditures is the fact that the subdivision is entitled to all rights assigned to property owned by state and local government. This would help to pay for capital costs for several years. It should also be noted that all governmental units are exempt from the developmental rights requirement so that they could, therefore, sell their rights at any time.

The transfer of development rights is not an ordinary part of the bundle of rights that accompany land ownership. State governments must enact specific legislation to enable a local government to legalize the sending of a building right from one parcel to another.[57]

Land Banking

As it has become increasingly apparent that conventional methods have not been completely successful in controlling unplanned growth in urban areas, the concept of land banking as a more effective means of controlling such growth has recently received greater attention in this country.[58] In essence, this concept calls for the establishment of land banks for the purpose of acquiring lands in urban areas where expansion is expected to prepare it for development and to ensure it is developed at the most advantageous time for the community as a whole.[59] The land banks are governmental units that could either purchase agricultural land in fee simple title and lease the land back to the farmers or purchase only the development rights to the land.[60] Through the actual ownership of land, a land bank obtains many advantages over more traditional planning devices. By giving public officials a more personal interest in the property and

its regulation, it helps promote sounder planning practices. It also allows for more unrestricted comprehensive land use plans than would ordinarily be possible. A land bank can achieve a flexibility in its regulations that is superior to any other planning method because it controls the land being sold and the land being acquired.[61] Land banking and spatial management of land is new to American land use planning though it has long been a dominant feature in other countries. A noted example is the British Greenbelt program which for a half-century has limited the growth of cities to preserve open space and agricultural land and prevent urban sprawl.[62]

The Clinton administration has begun to take a powerful stance toward land banking. Vice President Gore announced in September of 1998 the latest federal farmland protection program grants providing matching funds of more than $17 million to purchase conservation easements in nineteen states. Similarly, in New Jersey, Governor Whitman placed on the November 1998 ballot $1 billion for protection of one million acres of New Jersey's best farmland. In Maryland, Governor Glendening's Rural Legacy Initiative added $29 million to the state's farmland protection land bank program in 1998, and California Governor Pete Wilson signed a new 1999 state budget that includes $13.7 million for the Agriculture Land Stewardship program, a nearly sevenfold increase since 1995.[63]

Perhaps the most advanced program of local government is Jacksonville's "The Preservation Project." As the largest city in the nation (841 square miles) and larger than six states, The Preservation Project plans to take ten to twenty square miles of land out of development during the next five years. The $312.8 million plan leverages local, state, and federal funding as well as private donations and federal income tax donations.[64]

To achieve this flexibility, a public land bank needs the power to purchase property and to condemn land. The land bank should be granted the power to hold the land for indefinite periods of time. It must also be financially able to pursue its policies. To ensure adequate financing capabilities, the land bank needs the power to borrow money, to issue bonds, and to obtain government aid. These powers should be granted to the land bank when it is created.

In 1980 I was retained by King County (Seattle), Washington, to devise regulations to support a $100 million purchase of development rights to preserve farmland. The regulations were adopted, substantial amounts of land were purchased, and the program is considered a great success.[65]

The legality of the use of eminent domain by a public land bank has been questioned. The requirement that private property be taken only for public use is the primary limitation on the power of eminent domain. However, the Supreme Court has never reversed a state court where it held that a condemnation was for a public use, nor has it ever declared a federal taking invalid because it was not for a public use.[66] Both state and federal courts have declared that if the purposes of the project as a whole are beneficial to the community, and the use of the condemned property had a reasonable relation to these purposes, then the taking is for a public use.[67]

The prevention of urban sprawl and the control of unplanned growth are considered public purposes, and land banking is a reasonable means of fulfilling such purposes.[68] Because land banking is in pursuance of a comprehensive plan, it is much more likely to be upheld by the courts than other planning controls, which often are piecemeal and sporadic efforts.[69] Effectively instituted, the land bank serves to minimize or eliminate urban sprawl, redevelop the inner city, reduce the cost of urban land, curb public land speculation, and provide for public uses.[70]

Developmental Easements

Development easements give local governments a nonpossessory, less-than-fee interest in a subject land. Such easements may either be positive in that certain rights are granted in using the land, or negative in that they prevent the landowner from using his or her land in certain ways. The purpose of development easements is to preserve vital open space from intensive, uncontrolled development—sprawl.

There are many advantages to acquiring easements to the land rather than purchasing the entire fee.[71] Land encumbered by an easement remains with the landowner. The expense of maintaining the land also remains with the owner. The easement may also serve as an inexpensive interim measure to prevent development on land that the municipality or state may eventually want to purchase for parks or recreation.[72]

Granting an easement rather than selling the entire fee can also be of benefit to the landowner, who is able to remain on the land and, in most instances, is able to make some use of it. There are also tax advantages: Making a gift of the easement qualifies it as a deduction from taxable income equal to the fair

Figure 8.1
Installment Purchase vs. Developer Sale
A Hypothetical Comparison

	Installment Purchase	Outright Purchase
Cost of 50 acres	$3,000 per =$150,000	$15,000 per =$750,000
Split of transfer tax	0	-$4,625
Ag. Transfer Tax 5%	0	-$37,500
Capital Gains Tax	0	-$247,000
Poten. 170(h) deduc.	+$200,000	0
Subtotal:	**$350,000**	**$459,375**
Other Potential Costs or Savings:		
Replacement Housing	0	-$150,000
Retained Farm Value	+$150,000	0
Real Value	**$500,000**	**$309,375**
Per Acre	**$10,000**	**$6,188**

---

market value of the property rights donated. Also, usually such land receives preferential property tax treatment in that the owner is taxed only on the present value of the property subject to the easement. This assessment takes into account the development potential of the land and the present uses permitted on the land, and usually results in substantial tax savings for the landowner.[73] Granting an easement may be the only way a landowner can retain his or her land profitably and thereby resist the property tax pressures and the promises of profits if the land is sold for development. Combined with clustering lots on the nonvaluable soils, retaining the farmhouse and operating profit from the farm, and TDR programs for highly valuable soils, the farmer can actually come out far ahead of selling the land for development on large lot tracts. See Figures 8.1, 8.2, and 8.3 demonstrating the greater value of retention over sale. Figure 8.1 is Howard County, Maryland's program. Figures 8.2 and 8.3 show how TDRs and cluster work into the equation so successfully.

In Howard County, Maryland, just such a program designed by Freilich, Leitner & Carlisle with Uri Avin, Planning Director, has been tremendously

Figure 8.2

Farm Retention vs. Sale
A Hypothetical Comparison

	Retention	Sale
Cost of 50 acres	$3,000 per =$150,000	$15,000 per =$750,000
TDR or Cluster Value	$50,000	0
Capital Gains Tax (18%)	0	-$135,000
Poten. 170(h) deduc.	+$200,000	0
Subtotal:	**$400,000**	**$615,000**
Other Potential Costs or Savings:		
Replacement Housing	0	-$150,000
Retained House Value	+$150,000	0
Retained Farm Value	+$150,000	0
Real Value	**$700,000**	**$465,000**
Per Acre	**$14,000**	**$9,300**

Figure 8.3

Farm Retention vs. Sale

50-acre parcel with house, purchased for $3,000 per acre
Zoned 1 unit/acre; sale at $15,000 per acre

	Retention	Sale
Gains		
Land Sale		$750,000
Retained House Value	$150,000	
Retained Farm Value	$150,000	
IRC § 170(h) deduction	120,000	
TDR's (1 per 5 acres)(10 units)	150,000	
Clustering (10 units)(5 acres	150,000	
Subtotal:	**$720,000**	**$750,000**
Losses		
Capital Gain	$55,000	-$135,000
Replacement Housing		-$150,000
Net Gain	**$775,000**	**$465,000**
Per Acre	$15,500	$9,300

And You Have Your Farm!

successful.[74] See Figure 8.1 for a detailed comparison of the benefits of retaining the land with Smart Growth techniques over selling the land.[75] Similarly, a cluster program for preserving the agricultural land in Pershing County, Nevada, has been dramatically successful. The Plan combines clustering of lots and development easements in a highly innovative program developed by Freilich, Leitner & Carlisle.[76]

Environmental Controls

Permanent environmental growth controls can legally be applied if they are utilized properly within the final tier. One major area where such controls have been upheld is in the regulation of floodplains.[77] To meet the requirements of substantive due process, the legislation relating to floodplain control must be designed to accomplish an end that the enacting authority has the right to achieve, be reasonably calculated to achieve the legitimate end, and be reasonable in relation to that end.[78] Reasonable purposes that are legitimate exercises of the police power are the prevention of the following:

- health problems and loss of life;
- damage to land contiguous to the floodplains;
- excess governmental expenditures on flood control projects and relief;
- crippling disruptions of the local economy; and
- the onset of urban blight.

Short-term moratoria can also be used to restrict development during an environmentally critical period in the community's development. Dade County, Florida, for example, has adopted a short-term moratorium on sewer hookups and building permits. Additionally, Fairfax County, Virginia, also has used a sewer moratorium as one phase of a plan that would have allowed it to cope effectively with the environmental problems that directly follow from rapid development and population growth. The Virginia State Water Authority sets capacity sewage rates for the state through regulation. To implement this regulation, the Fairfax County, in 1973, enacted a provision whereby the issuance of a building permit is conditioned upon the prior acquisition of a sewer hookup.[79]

To ensure that short-term environmental moratoria are valid, they must be temporary, reasonable, and unburdensome on the individual. Each community has the responsibility to provide needed services and facilities so that community growth can proceed; yet there is a definite need for them to proceed in a manner that will not be harmful to the environment. The short-term environmental moratorium is an effective means of ensuring this. However, the validity of one that extends indefinitely is highly questionable—even more so if there is no affirmative effort to provide the facilities and services that the community has an obligation to provide.

Vice President Al Gore has developed his own environmental program for Smart Growth. He is a firm supporter of the federal Conservation and Reinvestment Act of 1999 introduced into both the House and Senate. The bills would restore the Land and Water Conservation Fund, which would match federal grants with local and state land conservation bond issues.[80] He wants to limit sprawl and contain traffic congestion as part of what he calls his "Livability Agenda."[81] During the 1998 congressional campaign, Vice President Gore barnstormed the country focusing on environmental land conservation, farmland preservation, and the spending of highway dollars to serve existing built-up acres instead of sprawl.[82]

Democrats aren't the only ones interested in Smart Growth. In two northern Virginia counties upstart Republican candidates rode to victory by calling Democrats soft on growth. Environmental land conservation measures did exceedingly well, particularly in New Jersey, where Republican Governor Christine Whitman obtained a 68 percent favorable vote on a $1 billion bond issue to preserve at least half of the two million acres of farmland, forests, and environmentally sensitive lands, through outright purchase of fee simple, development easements and TDRs.[83]

Endnotes

1. Charles Benbrook, *The World Must Eat*, WALL ST. J., Dec. 4, 1996, at A19 ("[t]he millions of cropland acres converted each year from agricultural to housing, roads, and other development, much of it highly productive land near population centers, will be replaced . . . as farmers move up hillsides, cut forests and try to grow crops in deserts and wetlands"). *See generally* SCHNIDMAN, SMILEY & WOODBURY, RETENTION OF LAND OF AGRICULTURE: POLICY, PRACTICE AND POTENTIAL IN NEW ENGLAND (1990); DANIELS & BOWERS, HOLDING OUR GROUND: PROTECTING AMERICA'S FARMS AND FARMLAND (1997).

2. *See* American Political Network, *U.S. Farmland Shrinks from 1992 to 1997*, 7 GREENWIRE Feb. 4, 1999, at 9 (the amount of farmland acreage declined from about 946 million in 1992 to approximately 932 million in 1997); *see generally The Economic Value of Open Space Conser-*

vation, LAND LINES 9 (Mar. 1998) ("communities are recognizing that conservation of open space can benefit their economic health").

3. *See generally* FREILICH, LEITNER & CARLISLE, NEW JERSEY OFFICE OF STATE PLANNING: AGRICULTURAL PRESERVATION: DEVELOPMENT STANDARDS FOR LIMITED GROWTH AREAS (Jan. 27, 1998).

4. *Id.* note 2.

5. *See generally* FREILICH & LEITNER, A PROPOSED AGRICULTURAL LANDS PRESERVATION STRATEGY FOR KING COUNTY, WASHINGTON, at 1 (Nov. 1979).

6. *See* Daniels & Bowens, *Holding Our Ground, Protecting America's Farms and Farmlands* (Island Press, 1997); Miller & Wright, *Preservation of Agricultural Land and Open Space,* 32 URB. LAW. 821 (1991); Freilich & Davis, *Saving the Land: The Utilization of Modern Technologies of Growth Management to Preserve Rural and Agricultural America,* 13 URB. LAW. 27 (1981).

7. *See* Nico Calavita, *Vale of Tiers: San Diego's Much-Lauded Growth Management System May Not Be as Good as It Looks,* PLANNING, 18, 21 (American Planning Ass'n, 1997) (describing my five-tier program and the failure of the city to approve my proposed environment, agriculture, and rural tier until 1990. "One of its redeeming features [of the protection of the urban reserve] was that almost half of the future urbanizing area was to remain open space, thus becoming the first step toward resurrecting Freilich's proposal for a Citywide Environmental Tier.").

8. *See* THOMAS M. POWER, LOST LANDSCAPES AND FAILED ECONOMIES: THE SEARCH FOR A VALUE OF PLACE (Washington, D.C., Island Press, 1996) (describes how to deal with development pressures on rural towns, from mining and tourism); JIM HOWE, ED MCMAHON & LUTHER PROBST, BALANCING NATURE AND COMMERCE IN GATEWAY COMMUNITIES (Washington, D.C., Island Press, 1997) (examines case studies of such towns adjacent to national forests).

9. *See* FREILICH, LEITNER & CARLISLE, LAND USE ELEMENT—SUMMIT COUNTY GENERAL PLAN, SNYDERVILLE BASIN (Dec. 28, 1992).

10. *See* Mark Arax, *Sprawl Threatens Central Valley,* L.A. TIMES, Oct. 26, 1995 at A3, (state could lose $5.3 billion a year if farm belt cities do not stem urban expansion and use controlled growth to preserve farmland).

11. *See* DAVID L. CALLIES, ROBERT H. FREILICH & THOMAS E. ROBERTS, CASES AND MATERIALS ON LAND USE at 656 (West 3d ed. 1999) [hereinafter CALLIES, FREILCIH & ROBERTS] (the U.S. Department of Agriculture has developed a policy that supports its major role as an advocate of retaining land to produce food, fiber, and timber. The Council of Environmental Quality oversees the efforts of other federal agencies in preparing environmental impact statements required by the National Environmental Protection Policy Act. The Environmental Protection Agency (EPA) has internal policies to protect environmentally significant agricultural land from irreversible conversion.).

12. *See* S.A.V.E. a Valuable Environment v. City of Bothell, 576 P.2d 401 (Wash. 1978); Committee for Sensible Land Use v. Garfield Township, 335 N.W.2d 216 (Mich. App. 1983); WILLIAMS, ADV. COMM'N ON INTERGOVERNMENTAL REL., STATE CONSTITUTIONAL LAW, M-159S (October 1990).

13. *See* Southern Burlington County NAACP v. Township of Mount Laurel, 336 A.2d 713 (N.J. 1975); Berenson v. Town of New Castle, 341 N.E.2d 236 (N.Y. 1975); Surrick v. Zoning Hearing Bd., 382 A.2d 105 (Pa. 1977); Associated Home Builders v. City of Livermore, 557 P.2d 473 (Cal. 1976).

14. *See* the Rath-Hoyt proposed Smart Growth Economic Competitiveness Act, Bill No. S. 1367/A, 87th Cong. (1969); Memorandum in Support of the Legislation, New York State Assembly, March 26, 1999 (the bill provides for "preservation of agricultural land and other open space resources" on a local and regional mandatory-plan basis).

15. RANDALL ARENDT, RURAL BY DESIGN: MAINTAINING SMALL TOWN CHARACTER (Cambridge, Mass., Lincoln Land Institute, American Planning Ass'n 1994).

16. Brent Freeze, *Urban Sprawl: Wildlife Is Losing Ground to the Suburbs*, K.C. STAR, May 9, 1999, at C-1, col. 1.

17. *See* FREILICH, LEITNER & CARLISLE, NEW JERSEY STATE PLAN, *id.* at note 3.

18. William K. Stevens, *Expectations Aside, Water Use in U.S. Is Showing Decline*, N.Y. TIMES, Nov. 10, 1998, at A-1 ("The amount of rural household use has risen 58% since 1980.").

19. *See* TOM DANIELS & DEBORAH BOWERS, HOLDING OUR GROUND, PROTECTING AMERICA'S FARMS AND FARMLAND, 105 (Island Press 1997) [hereinafter DANIELS & BOWERS]; FREILICH, 1974 INST. ON PLAN., ZON. AND EMINENT DOMAIN, DEVELOPMENT TIMING, MORATORIA, AND CONTROLLING GROWTH, 147, 205.

20. *See, e.g.,* Gisler v. County of Madera, 38 Cal. App. 3d 303, 112 Cal. Rptr. 919 (1974); State *ex rel.* Randell v. Snohomish, 488 P.2d 511 (1971).

21. Population quotas have always been valid. *See* Schenck v. City of Hudson, 114 F.3d 590 (6th Cir. 1996); Wilkinson v. Board of County Comm'rs of Pitkin County, 872 P.2d 1269 (Colo. Ct. App. 1993); Village of Belle Terre v. Boras, 416 U.S. 1, (1974) (holding that a prohibition against all multifamily dwellings, which essentially permanently prevented the population of the village from increasing, was reasonable and within the zone of public welfare—such dwellings contributed to urban problems such as traffic congestion.); Guilano v. Town of Edgartown, 531 F. Supp. 1076 (Mass. Dist. Ct. 1982) (town examined many factors, similar to Ramapo, when it granted permits including "the impact on schools, other public facilities, traffic and pedestrian travel, the availability of water and sewer, recreational facilities, open spaces and agricultural resources, traffic hazards. . . ."); City of Boca Raton v. Boca Villas Corporation, 371 So. 2d 154 (Fla. Dist. Ct. App. 1979) (permanent cap on total population build-out versus annual population quotas was held ultra vires); Sturges v. Town of Chilmark, 402 N.E.2d 1346 (Mass. 1980); *but see* Rancourt v. Town of Barnstead, 523 A.2d 55 (N.H. 1986) (population restrictions must have an appropriate plan to assure adequate forethought).

22. ANN SORENSON, RICHARD GREEN, AND KAREN RUSS, FARMING ON THE EDGE (American Farmland Trust 1997); U.S. ADV. COMM'N ON INTERGOVERNMENTAL REL., ACIR STATE LEGISLATIVE PROGRAM, 1970 CUMULATIVE SUPP. 31-36-00 at 5 (1969); Comment, *Planned Unit Development*, 35 MO. L. REV. 27 (1970), *cited in* Robert H. Freilich & Linda Kirts Davis, *Saving the Land: The Utilization of Modern Techniques of Growth Management to Reserve Rural and Agricultural America*, 13 URB. LAW. 27, n.68 (1981) [hereinafter Freilich & Davis].

23. ZONING FOR FARMING: A GUIDEBOOK FOR PENNSYLVANIA MUNICIPALITIES ON HOW TO PROTECT VALUABLE AGRICULTURAL LANDS (Harrisburg Center for Rural Pennsylvania 1995); TOM DANIELS & DEBORAH POWERS, HOLDING OUR GROUND: PROTECTING AMERICA'S FARMS AND FARMLANDS, MODEL ZONING ORDINANCE APPENDIX (Island Press 1997). *See also* Dykman, Book Review, 12 UCLA L. REV. 991 (1965), *cited in* Freilich & Davis, *supra* note 22, n.69.

24. Randall Arendt, *Connecting the Dots*, PLANNING, Aug. 1998, at 20–23.

25. Julie Marx.

26. *See* Wilcox v. Zoning Bd. of Appeals of City of Yonkers, 17 N.Y.2d 249, 2128 N.E.3d 633, 270 N.Y.S.2d 569 (1966); N.Y. AGRIC. & MKTS. LAW §§ 300–07 (McKinney 1972 & Supp. 1975); Siegil, *Illinois Zoning: On the Verge of a New Era*, 25 DEPAUL L. REV. 616 (1977); Tomain, *Land Use Controls in Iowa*, 27 DRAKE L. REV. 254 (1978), *cited in* Freilich & Davis, *supra* note 22, n.70, at 40.

27. *See* CONSTANCE E. BEAUMONT, BETTER MODELS FOR SUPERSTORES: ALTERNATIVES TO BIG BOX SPRAWL (National Trust for Historic Preservation 1977).

28. Freilich & Davis, *supra* note 15, at 41.

29. *See* Alden & Schockro, *Preferential Assessment of Agricultural Lands: Preservation or Discrimination?*, 42 S. CAL. L. REV. 59 (1969).

30. CAL. GOVT. CODE §§ 51200 to -295 (West Supp. 1974).

31. CAL. GOVT. CODE § 51244 (West Supp. 1974).

32. Thomas A. Gihring, *Incentive Property Taxation: A Potential Tool for Growth Management*, 65 J. A.P.A. 62 (1999).

33. Frederick R. Steiner, Introduction, A DECADE WITH LESA: THE EVOLUTION OF LAND EVALUATION AND SITE ASSESSMENT, at 13 (1991).

34. The Farmland Protection Policy Act (FPPA) is a part of the Food and Agriculture Act of 1981, 7 U.S.C.A. § 4201 *et seq.* For a review of the Act, *see* Johnson & Fogelman, *The Farmland Protection Policy Act: Stillbirth of a Policy?* 1986 ILL. L. REV. 563.

35. Lloyd E. Wright, *The Development and Status of LESA, in* A DECADE WITH LESA, at 36 (1991).

36. "A report by the President's Commission on Sustainable Development appears to endorse the New Urbanist philosophy of contained development." *See* 11 CALIFORNIA PLANNING & DEVELOPMENT REPORT (April 1996).

37. For an interesting analysis of sustainability, *see A Constitutionally Valid Justification for the Enactment of No-Growth Ordinances: Integrating Concepts of Population Stabilization and Sustainability*, 19 HARV. L. REV. 93 (1997).

38. In the Farms for the Future Act of 1990, 7 U.S.C.A § 42d, Congress authorized the Secretary of Agriculture to make federal loan guarantees and interest rate assistance to lending institutions in states with state-operated agriculture and environmental lands preservation funds, 7 U.S.C.A. § 1465. *See* CAMPBELL-MOHN, BREEN & FUTRELL, ENVIRONMENTAL LAW: FROM RESOURCES TO RECOVERY 323 (1993).

39. John M. DeGrove, Land Use Institute, *Sustainable Communities: The Future Direction for Managing Growth in Florida*, ALI-ABA COURSE OF STUDY MATERIALS, (Aug. 14–16, 1997) [hereinafter DeGrove, *Sustainable Communities*].

40. *Id.* (Eastward Ho! is a voluntary incentive-based strategy that provides a channel for sustainable growth through use of joint development partnerships).

41. *See* ARIZ. REV. STAT. § 3-112 and IOWA CODE ANN. §§ 176B.11; CAMPBELL-MOHN, BREEN & FUTRELL, ENVIRONMENTAL LAW: FROM RESOURCES TO RECOVERY 323, n.160 (1993); CALLIES, FREILICH & ROBERTS, CASES AND MATERIALS ON LAND USE, chap. 7D, "Preservation of Agricultural Land and Open Space" 653, 662 (West 3d ed. 1999).

42. *Id.,* CALLIES, FREILICH & ROBERTS at 662.

43. MD. CODE, CTS. & JUD. PROC. § 5-308(a).

44. Melody Petersen, *Farmers' Right to Sue Grows, Raising Debate on Food Safety,* N.Y. TIMES, June 1, 1999, at A-1, col. 1.

45. *See* Bove v. Donner-Hanna Coke Corp., 258 N.Y.S. 229 (App. Div. 4th Dep't 1932)

(location of industrial or farm sites pursuant to a comprehensive plan prevents nearby residents who "came to the nuisance" from bringing nuisance suits); *see also* Spur Industries, Inc. v. Del E. Webb Dev. Co., 494 P.2d 700 (Ariz. 1972).

46. *See Pendoley v. Ferreira,* 187 N.E.2d 142 (Mass. 1963), where odoriferous hog farm started in rural area was subsequently invaded by a nearby subdivision and the court held that the farmer was conducting a nuisance and ordered him to liquidate the business.

47. *See* John Nolon, *The Stable Door Is Open: New York's Statutes to Protect Farmland,* 67 N.Y. ST. BAR J. 36 (1995); ESSETS & MCDONALD, INCENTIVES: AGRICULTURAL DISTRICT-ING IN THE PROTECTION OF FARMLAND, A REFERENCE GUIDEBOOK FOR STATE AND LOCAL GOVERNMENTS 76 (NALS 1981); for an overview of the use of Right to Farm Laws *see* Thompson, *Defining and Protecting the Right to Farm,* 5 ZONING & PLAN. LAW REPORT 57, 65 (1982).

48. *See* BLOMQUIST, APPLYING PESTICIDES: TOWARDS RECONCEPTUALIZING LIABILITY TO NEIGHBORS FOR CROP, LIVESTOCK AND PERSONAL DAMAGES FROM AGRICULTURAL CHEMICAL DRIFT.

49. Premium Standard Farms v. Lincoln Township of Putnam County, 946 S.W.2d 234 (MO. 1997); Board of Supervisors v. Val Adco, 504 N.W.2d 267 (Minn. 1993); Kuehl v. Cass County, 555 N.W.2d 686 (Iowa 1996).

50. *See* Blue Earth County Pork Producers, Inc. v. County of Blue Earth, 558 N.W.2d 25 (Minn. 1997); Burns, *Eight Million Little Pigs—A Cautionary Tale: Statutory and Regulatory Responses to Concentrated Hog Farming,* 31 WAKE FOREST L. REV. 851 (1996). For a comprehensive review of other regulatory and statutory reform alternatives, *see* Organ & Perry, *Controlling Externalities Associated with Concentrated Animal Feeding Operations: The Continuing Viability of Zoning and Common Law Nuisance,* 3 MO. ENVTL L. & POL'Y REV. 183 (1996).

51. Goodman and Warrick, *U.S. Plans Rules to Curb Livestock Waste Pollution,* WASH. POST, at A-1 (Sept. 14, 1998).

52. Bormann v. Board of Supervisors In and For Kossuth County, 584 N.W.2d 309 (Iowa 1998), *cert. denied,* 199 S. Ct 1096 (1999).

53. *See* City of Hollywood v. Hollywood, Inc., 432 So. 2d 1332 (Fla. App. 1983); Robert H. Freilich & Dwayne Senville, *Takings, TDRs and Environmental Preservation: "Fairness" and the Hollywood North Beach Case,* 35 LAND USE LAW 4 (June 1983).

54. *See* Michael S. Bernick & Amy E. Freilich, *Transit Villages and Transit-Based Development: The Rules Are becoming More Flexible—How Government Can Work with the Private Sector to Make It Happen,* 30 URB. LAW. 1 (1998).

55. DANIELS & BOWERS, *supra* note 19, at 171; Suitum v. Tahoe Regional Planning Agency, 117 S. Ct. 1659 (1997) (upholding TDRs for Environmentally Sensitive Lands but remanding for determination whether just compensation is required); Julian Juergensmyer, James Nichols & Brian D. Leebrick, *Transferable Development Rights and Alternatives After* Suitum, 20 URB. LAW. 441 (1997); *see also* Carmichael, *Transferable Development Rights as a Basis for Land Use Control,* 2 FLA. ST. U. L. REV. 35 (1974); Costonis, *Development Rights Transfer: An Exploratory Essay,* 83 YALE L.J. 75 (1973); Rose, *Transfer of Development Rights: A Preview of an Evolving Concept,* 3 R.G. L.J. 330 (1975); Rose, *Proposal for the Separation and Marketability of Development Rights as a Technique to Preserve Open Space,* 51 J. URB. LAW. L. 461 (1974).

56. For an up-to-date report on TDRs *see* Julian Juergensmyer, James Nichols & Brian D. Leebrick, *Transferable Development Rights and Alternatives After* Suitum, 30 URB. LAW. 441 (1998).

57. DANIELS & BOWERS, *supra* note 19, at 172.

58. *See, e.g.,* Schnidman, Smiley & Woodbury, *Retention of Land for Agriculture,* LINCOLN INST. OF LAND & POL'Y (1990) at 14-15, 18-19; Note, *Judicial Review of Land Bank Dispositions,* 41 U. CHI. L. REV. 377 (1974); Note, *Public Land Banking: A New Praxis for Urban Growth,* 23 CASE W. RES. L. REV. 897 (1972).

59. For a detailed report on efforts state-by-state to purchase open space through land banking and charitable deductions or gifts of open space, *see* Patricia A. Salkin, *Smart Growth at Century's End: The State of the States,* 31 URB. LAW. 3, Summer 1999; *see also Open Space Under Assault,* N.Y. TIMES, Nov. 23, 1997, at 1, 11 (describing the Nature Conservancy's purchase of open space land across the nation).

60. Freilich & Davis, *supra* note 22, at 41.

61. U.S. NATIONAL RESOURCES PLANNING BOARD, PUBLIC LAND ACQUISITION PART II: URBAN LANDS, at 2 (1941).

62. *See* DANIEL R. MANDELKER, GREEN BELTS AND URBAN GROWTH (1962); U. GAIL EASLEY, STAYING INSIDE THE LINES: URBAN GROWTH BOUNDARIES (Am. Plan. Ass'n Planning Advisory Report No. 440, 1992).

63. *See* Ralph Grossi, AM. FARMLAND, Fall 1998, at 2.

64. Mayor John A. Delaney, *Preserving Our Cities,* 22 STATE & LOCAL LAW NEWS 9, No. 3 (Spring 1999).

65. For a description of the program *see* Ruth Eckdish Knapp, *Small Is Fruitful: A Hands-On Approach to Farmland Preservation,* PLANNING, (Am. Plan. Ass'n, June 1999), at 9, 10.

66. Marquis, *Constitutional and Statutory Authority to Condemn,* 43 IOWA L. REV. 189 (1958).

67. Berman v. Parker, 348 U.S. 26 (1954); Redevelopment Agency of San Francisco v. Hayes, 266 P.2d 105, *cert. denied,* 348 U.S. 897 (1954).

68. Reub v. Oklahoma City, 435 P.2d 139 (Okla. 1967); *see also Public Land Banking, supra* note 31.

69. Mandelker, *The Comprehensive Planning Requirement in Urban Renewal,* 116 U. PA. L. REV. 25, 28 (1967).

70. *Public Land Banking, supra* note 31, at 899.

71. Jordahl, *Conservation and Scenic Easements: An Experience Resume,* 39 LAND ECON. 343, at 354 (1963).

72. CITIZENS ADVISORY COMMITTEE ON ENVIRONMENTAL QUALITY, COMMUNITY ACTION FOR ENVIRONMENTAL QUALITY, at 16 (1970).

73. Comment, *Easements to Preserve Open Space Lands,* 1 ECOLOGY L. REV. 728, 737 (1971).

74. *Id.*

75. Howard County, Maryland, General Plan (adopted July 2, 1990) at 38–48, "Agricultural Land Preservation Program."

76. Unified Development Code, Nov. 4, 1998 (Agricultural Districts and Preservation § 17.05.2B—including agricultural preservation districts, clustering, right to farm, agricul;tural service establishments, densities, agricultural preservation easement, and tax credits).

77. *See* Jon Christensen, *California Floods Changes Thinking on Need to Tame Rivers,* N.Y. TIMES, Feb. 4, 1997 at B10 (environmentally approved levees are being set back from river channels to give rivers room to move and develop that will reduce upstream and downstream flooding).

78. Hines, Howe, & Montgomery, *Suggestions for a Model Floodplain Zoning Ordinance,* 5 LAND & WATER L. REV. 321, at 328 (1970).

79. *See* TASK FORCE ON COMPREHENSIVE PLANNING AND LAND USE CONTROL, PROPOSAL FOR IMPLEMENTING AN IMPROVED PLANNING AND LAND USE CONTROL SYSTEM IN FAIRFAX COUNTY, FINAL REPORT (June 11, 1973).

80. Editorial, *Restore Federal Funds for Wildlife,* K.C. STAR, at K-2, col. 1 (June 27, 1999).

81. Katherine Q. Seelye, *The Unbuttoning of Al Gore: Act I,* N.Y. TIMES, at A-20, col. 1 (June 15, 1999).

82. Richard Lacayo, *The Brawl Over Sprawl,* TIME, at 45, col. 3 (March 22, 1999).

83. Neil R. Pierce, Washington Post Writers Group, *Sprawl Control and Smart Growth Become Key Issues,* K.C. STAR, D-8, col. 2 (Nov. 24, 1998).

The New Federal Policies

Controlling sprawl by redirecting growth will benefit built-up areas; benefit the environment by preserving agriculture, resources, and open space; aid in reducing energy consumption and reduce the costs of service to suburbanites by limiting the area over which services must be extended (by using non-sprawl corridors, centers, and contiguous development and neotraditional communities); and aid in the fiscal solvency of local governments. To battle the problems of sprawl effectively, the federal government must assist states, regions, and local governments in the implementation of effective smart growth programs.

For decades the federal government has encouraged urban sprawl,[1] whether inadvertently or purposefully, through its guaranteed loan programs, tax breaks for homeowners, federal highway systems, and other federal agency initiatives. As discussed in chapter two, much of the federal government's traditional fiscal involvement in regional and local planning has been criticized as being inadequate, perpetuating a lack of resources in urban areas and subsidization of suburban sprawl, based on data from 1970 to 1990.[2] However, the circumstances of the central cities have greatly improved since the 1990 census. Noteworthy examples of successful cities now abound.[3] The federal government can provide guidance and strong incentives to the states in solving these problems, taking into account the new federalism, which strengthens the ability of the federal government to produce effective solutions on the local level.[4] The new initiatives of the Clinton administration directly address the problems of the six crises that have afflicted the country from the beginning of urban sprawl.[5] Still, the United States is the only major Western nation that has failed to adopt an explicit national urban growth policy.[6] All of this is beginning to change, however, with the new all-encompassing Livability Agenda of the federal government affecting interdepartmental cooperation at all levels.[7]

The federal government has recently recognized the problem through governmental initiatives designed specifically for urban revitalization and preserving open space, agricultural lands, and environmentally sensitive areas. National studies on the problem have encouraged urban planning and the development of new growth controls. Other indications of heightened government awareness are requirements for urban or environmental impact analysis, executive orders to protect the land, and departmental policy statements such as the U.S. Department of Agriculture *Statement of Land Use Policy* directing USDA agencies to avoid proposing or assisting actions that could reduce the amount of land available for food and fiber production.

On September 2, 1998, the entire approach of the federal government changed. Vice President Gore's remarks to the Brookings Institution declared war on the problem of urban sprawl:

> How then can the federal government encourage and strengthen smarter, more livable sustainable growth? Again, smart growth is about local and community decisions . . . but I believe there is nevertheless an important role for federal support of local energies. . . . We can get our own house in order by reexamining federal policies that may have been well intentioned but have encouraged the wrong kind of growth and runaway sprawl.[8]

The administration has followed that speech by announcing a $1 billion initiative to stem urban sprawl in the fiscal year 2000 federal budget. The Clinton-Gore Livability Agenda proposes, among other things, to:

- preserve green spaces that promote clean air and clean water and provide pedestrian-friendly communities;
- ease traffic congestion by improving road planning, strengthening existing transportation systems, and expanding use of alternative transportation;
- restore a sense of community by encouraging better local planning in the placement of adequate public facilities and schools;
- promote collaboration among neighboring communities and cities, schools, and rural areas, to develop regional growth strategies and address urban sprawl.[9]

The Environmental Protection Agency is following the executive branch's initiative in enacting a program that will use statutory authority to combat sprawl. EPA Region 1 Administrator John Devillars said urban sprawl is "degrading our environment, it's fiscally inefficient and it's undermining our social fabric. . . . Action to curb it is long overdue."[10] The program consists of additional funding for brownfields revitalization[11] and makes $2.5 million available for smart growth projects at the local level. A brownfield is an abandoned urban industrial site with environmental problems. The Government Affairs Office estimates that 450,000 brownfield sites existed as of 1995. In 1976 in the Superfund Act, the federal government made current and even future buyers and lenders liable for cleaning up detected pollution.[12] Under the new administration, Congress responded by passing the Lender Liability Act of 1996, which limits the scope of lender liability to make financing more readily available[13] and has also made tax credit incentives available.[14] EPA plans to oppose projects that contribute to sprawl while requiring mitigation measures where necessary.

The need to revive the central city and offer enhanced livable conditions continues to be addressed by the federal government.[15] In 1990, the Low-Income Housing Preservation and Resident Homeownership Act and the Cranston-Gonzalez National Affordable Housing Act have sought to fund and preserve affordable housing to low-income families and to minimize the involuntary displacement of tenants.[16] The Cranston-Gonzales Act requires local governments to prepare a Comprehensive Housing Affordability Strategy (CHAS) as a condition of receiving federal funds for affordable housing.[17] The CHAS must include an analysis of the effect of existing land use regulations such as growth limits and impact fees on housing prices. However, the Act does not require the elimination of regulatory barriers as a condition of receiving federal aid for affordable housing.[18] This situation may change as a result of actions taken by the Advisory Commission on Regulatory Barriers to Affordable Housing established by Jack Kemp, Secretary of the United States Department of Housing and Urban Development (HUD), in 1990.[19] The Commission's responsibility is to advise the secretary on the effect of land use regulations and other forms of local legislation on housing prices.[20] Unfortunately, the report rather indiscriminately lumped every regulatory planning implementation tool in the same category. The types of legislation subject to review include "zoning, impact fees, subdivision ordinances, codes and standards, rent control, permitting and processing, and federal and local environmental regulations."[21] Fortunately, much of this has changed since the advent of the Clinton administration in 1992. For the first time since the 1960s' War on Poverty and the Model Cities Acts, the government is shifting to production of housing, not destruction of planning, as its tool, and to greater emphasis on housing and economic development in urbanized areas.[22]

First, Congress addressed the problem of displacement[23] under the Uniform Relocation Assistance and Real Property Acquisition Policies Act of 1970 (URA).[24] HUD allows local governments to borrow against their HUD funds set aside for water, sewers, and streets—and invest the loans into revenue-making establishments.[25] This section 108 program allows subsidy and feasibility to reduce the costly part of projects in urbanized areas.[26] These federal initiatives promote the revitalization of the central city and the reduction of migration out into the Urbanizing Tier, increasing affordable housing, home ownership, economic development, and quality of life.

Federal enterprise zone legislation has been adopted as a way to revitalize the central city. In past years, due to the federal deficit, federal budgetary decisions were unlikely to increase public funds that would be spent on the cities.[27] Enterprise zones can be a way to encourage businesses to relocate back into impoverished urban areas. The states have considerable experience with enterprise zones—approximately thirty-seven states have enterprise zone legislation.[28] A 1987 study found the program had created 113,600 new jobs, retained 67,400 existing jobs, and provided a capital investment of $8.8 billion.[29] After the 1992 Los Angeles riots, the Bush administration responded with a plan that would have vastly expanded the nation's enterprise zone programs in the inner cities.[30] Congress eventually approved a scaled-down version of the plan, which was then vetoed by President Bush because of his fear of tax increases.

Ironically, at the same time that Congress is trying to incentive jobs in inner cities with enterprise zones, it has failed to stem the leakage of jobs to suburbia lured by massive sales and real property tax increment financing for corporate, industrial, retail, office, and even residential development. A bill has now been introduced by Representative David Minge of Minnesota that would levy a surtax on companies outside of enterprise zones that receive state and local government tax escapes.[31]

President Clinton proposed expanding the enterprise zone concept to cre-

ate ten new "Empowerment Zones," offering large-scale federal tax breaks to business, as well as 100 new "Empowerment Communities," enhancing access to social and community services.[32] Under the initial plan, these communities would receive $4.1 billion in tax credits. In 1993, Congress responded with a scaled-down version of Clinton's program. Nine "empowerment" zones were created: five to be located in large urban centers, one in a medium city, and three in rural areas.[33] Tax incentives amounting to $2.5 billion were provided in the form of wage credits that entitled an employer to take credits equal to 20 percent of the first $15,000 of each employee's wages, with a maximum of $3,000.[34] The legislation also provided $720 million for social service grants for child care, education, and job training. Finally, the zones were granted the power to use tax-exempt bonds to finance businesses. The areas were to be selected by the secretaries of HUD and Agriculture. In addition to the empowerment zones, ninety-five "enterprise communities" were created that receive the tax-exempt bond powers of the empowerment zones and $280 million for social service grants.[35]

Earlier federal programs have also helped in the revitalization of urban areas. In 1974, Congress created the Community Development Block Grant (CDBG) program, controlled by local authorities with minimal federal review.[36] The Urban Development Action Grant (UDAG) program started in 1978, which used federal funds to leverage private investment and thereby make specific projects financially feasible, attracted the participation of developers and lenders.[37]

The federal government's promotion of transportation has exhaustively continued throughout the last several decades. Transportation is, in many ways, the most important segment of a community's infrastructure and has a profound influence on its land use patterns and rate of growth. Not only is the transportation network a shaper of urban form, but a region's land use patterns influence the transportation modes used for work and nonwork interurban travel. The issue of the appropriate level at which land use controls should be exercised—local or regional—has been raised in nearly every major land use court decision in the United States.[38] Since the advent of the Federal Aid Highway legislation of 1954, the automobile has become the predominant form of transportation in the nation's urban areas.[39] Highways in urban areas have fostered urban sprawl,[40] characterized by low-density, single-use suburban development, which has hastened the decline in public transit as a mode of interurban travel.[41] This phenomenon has increased the spatial separation of jobs and residences, encouraged development in areas not served by public transit, and created a pattern of development in our suburban areas that ensures almost exclusive reliance on the automobile as the primary means of travel to work and shopping.[42]

Interurban highway travel has proven very inefficient[43] despite its relative popularity. Other unintended consequences of highway travel include automobile fatalities, dependence on imported oil and energy, and environmental and economic impacts.[44] These negative impacts have prompted changes in federal legislation designed to encourage shifts in urban travel from the automobile to public transit,[45] such as the Intermodal Surface Transportation Efficiency Act (ISTEA),[46] the Transportation Equity Act for the 21st Century, known as TEA-21,[47] and the Clean Air Act Amendments of 1990.[48] The Clean Air Act, which was adopted in 1963, was amended in 1990 to help achieve reductions in urban sprawl by promoting other alternatives to single-occupancy vehicles.[49] While the 1990 Amendments to the Clean Air Act focused primarily on the improvement of air quality through the reduction in motor vehicle use, ISTEA and TEA-21 require comprehensive transportation planning and call for increased funding for transit.[50] ISTEA and TEA-21 expand the role of local governments through the planning process.[51] Both Acts encourage the use of transportation system management (TSM), capital improvements, transportation demand management (TDM), and land use controls. "Transit supportive existing land use policies" are one consideration in the issuance of a grant or loan for the construction or expansion of fixed guideway systems under ISTEA and TEA-21.[52] This consideration requires states to enact plans and programs to achieve transportation and land use controls utilizing state growth management legislation and expanding the role of regional planning through Metropolitan Planning Organizations (MPOs) to coordinate local government initiatives in a regional context.

The Transportation Equity Act for the 21st Century, or TEA-21, provides for the further upgrade of the nation's highways and mass transit systems.[53] The funding for mass transit will finance everything from subways, light rail, and ferry boats. With several types of provisions, motorists will have the ability to utilize mass transit, which will foster the discouragement of new interstate routes because of the inevitable build-up around transit corridors. TEA-21 and other transportation proposals will focus growth in higher densities around

transit-based developments, causing migration back into the central city and prevention of sprawl. These transit-based developments are getting additional help from the federal government. The Federal Transportation Authority is promoting transit-based development including flexible property rights, transit grants for joint development purposes, and funding for rail systems.[54] Additionally, in order to keep large sections of forest land from being developed, the federal government has proposed an eighteen-month moratorium on road-building into sections of forest land.[55] Thus, the government's promotion of nonconstruction in environmentally sensitive areas and open space, as well as construction around transit-oriented developments, will help control rapid, haphazard development.

Other detrimental environmental impacts related to sprawl have prompted the federal government to take action. Upon a recent announcement that the wild Pacific salmon are nearly extinct, the federal government put urban areas on notice that states and regions must develop their own plans for recovery or the federal government will come in and regulate.[56] Many areas are responding by limiting growth and seeking support from commercial and industrial developments.

In the preservation of agricultural land, the federal government has expanded its role. The United States Department of Agriculture has developed policies that support its role as an advocate of retaining land to produce food, fiber, and timber.[57] The Council of Environmental Quality (CEQ) oversees the efforts of other federal agencies in preparing environmental impact statements required by the National Environmental Protection Policy Act.[58] The CEQ requires federal agencies to determine the effects of a proposed project on unique agricultural land to incorporate the findings into environmental impact statements.[59] Over the last twenty years, the Environmental Protection Agency (EPA) has implemented an internal policy to protect environmentally significant agricultural land from irreversible conversion. The EPA has also offered to provide technical assistance to states and local governments that want to factor agricultural land considerations into environmental planning efforts.[60] In the Farms for the Future Act of 1990, Congress authorized the Secretary of Agriculture to make federal loan guarantees and interest rate assistance available to lending institutions in states with state-operated preservation funds.[61] Despite the United States's unparalleled abundance of agricultural resources, disappearing farmland has caused the federal government to apply, finally, a

1981 law that required it to examine alternatives to proposed highways, airports, and other public projects that consume prime farmland.[62] Additionally, in the 1996 farm bill, Congress authorized spending $35 million over the next six years to promote state and local programs that pay farmers not to sell to developers.

The federal government has also promoted other environmental solutions. The Clinton administration recently proposed a strategy for protecting waterways from manure pollution through tighter regulations.[63] The regulations will resemble the tight EPA pollution limits under the Clean Air Act imposing strict pollution-control permits on all large farms by 2003.[64] Additionally, the National Flood Insurance Act[65] provides a new incentive for floodplain zoning. Areas that develop adequate land use regulations for floodplains can obtain insurance from private companies subsidized by the federal government. Existing residences and small businesses may be insured at subsidized rates, but new improvements must obtain coverage at full actuarial rates. Existing structures cannot obtain the subsidized rates if they are in violation of any state or local zoning laws that are "intended to discourage or otherwise restrict land development or occupancy in flood prone areas."[66]

One of the primary regional problems facing municipal governments, as a result of the tremendous growth on the urban-rural fringe and the exclusionary policies that have been initiated, are the increasing economic and racial separation between suburbia and the central city. Typically, the suburbs exist as predominantly white, middle-class residential areas where low- and moderate-income housing is nearly nonexistent. One method that has been utilized in an attempt to provide for a broadening economic and racial mix in developing areas is the regional low-income housing allocation, or "fair-share" plan promulgated by the federal government.[67] Although many of these plans differ in specific requirements, or implementation provisions, their overall goals are similar—to provide open-occupancy, low- and moderate-income housing units in areas where such housing has "traditionally not been provided."

In a series of cases involving the Dallas metropolitan area, the Dallas Housing Authority and HUD were found responsible for racial segregation in low-income public housing by selecting sites for lower income housing predominantly. In *Walker v. HUD*, 734 F. Supp. 1231, 1244 (N.D. Tex. 1989) (*WalkerI*), the court ordered the use of sites in integrated suburban areas. In *Walker v. Dallas Housing Authority and U.S. Dep't of HUD*, 734 F. Supp. 1289

(N.D. Tex. 1989) (*Walker III*), the court issued an order requiring the authority to disperse housing units to other parts of the city and suburbs by entering into consent agreements with the suburbs. But by 1999 there was such success in blacks of low and moderate income in moving to the suburbs under HUD's section 8 housing subsidy program, that an order to the authority by HUD to build in the suburbs was rejected by the 5th Circuit Court of Appeals.[68] A different result was obtained in the City of Yonkers, New York, where the courts ordered the building of 118 new homes in white neighborhoods for blacks and Hispanics.[69]

To implement a "fair-share" plan, there must be some regional jurisdictional base—the aim of such plans is to provide a "fair share" of low- and moderate-income housing for the region. Many innovative approaches on the local level have been attempted. For example, the Massachusetts Housing Appeals Law allows a state board to override local zoning that does not provide for a representative proportion of low-income housing.[70] Under that law, developers of low-income housing can apply to the local government for a "comprehensive permit" in lieu of all other permits. If that permit is denied, the developer can appeal to the Housing Appeals Committee, which has the power to vacate the denial and direct the issuance of a permit if the denial was not "reasonable and consistent with local needs." The Miami Valley Regional Planning Commission, of Dayton, Ohio, devised a plan to disperse, in four years, 14,000 units of federally subsidized housing throughout the metropolitan area on a "fair-share" basis, computed on the basis of both community needs and capacities—in other words, a plan "to build low and moderate income housing, including public housing, in white suburbs."[71]

The vehicle for effective regional housing was provided by the power of A-95 review—this sanction requires that municipal proposals for federal assistance for public facilities first be evaluated by regional planning bodies for their necessity and regional impact.[72] Armed with the A-95 review power, the Miami Valley Regional Planning Commission is enabled to exert considerable leverage in persuading municipalities to comply with fair-share requirements since these municipalities often cannot construct sewers and other facilities without federal aid. Another example of an expanded jurisdictional base capable of implementing such a program was provided by the New York State Urban Development Corporation (UDC), established in 1969.[73] There, a state government-controlled corporation was created to fill the void between

government interests and actions, and those of private enterprise. Until its dissolution, UDC had the authority to undertake four types of projects:
- residential projects consisting of low- and moderate-income housing;
- industrial projects;
- civic projects and land improvement projects.

It was empowered to acquire land by purchase or condemnation, to override local zoning and building codes, and to build, sell, manage, or lease any of its projects.[74]

The statistics as of 1990 were gloomy,[75] but in the great housing boom of the '90s, much of this has been reversed. When President Clinton took office in 1993, 42 percent of blacks and 39 percent of Latinos owned their own homes. By spring of 1999, those figures had jumped to 46.9 percent of blacks and 46.2 percent of Latinos.[76] Moreover, under Clinton, bank regulators have breathed the first real life into enforcement of the Community Reinvestment Act, a twenty-year-old statute meant to combat redlining by requiring banks to serve their low-income communities.[77] Between 1993 and 1997, home loans grew by 72 percent to blacks and by 45 percent to Latinos.[78] It also is notable that every major city in the U.S. is showing a positive growth of residents in the downtown, a trend projected to increase further to 2010.[79]

Federal policies and legislation have come a long way in providing guidance and procedure to local growth problems. The federal government has begun to change its policies toward growth management—a step in the right direction. The federal government's encroachment into the state's domain is always controversial. State and county governments often find federal policy conflicting with the economic viability of their regions. In fact, in Utah, state and local officials are opposed to the federal government setting aside large tracts as wilderness, believing that mining, ranching, recreation, and other uses of the land are in Utah's economic interest.[80] Now it appears that state officials may have been right all along. Letting livestock graze helps banks, streams, and lakes.[81] The federal approach is still fragmented and contains inconsistencies. Until a national coordinated and consolidated growth policy comes into existence, the central city, the suburbs, and the agricultural/rural areas must look to tools that will allow each to succeed in battling sprawl. Nevertheless, the climate is improving. More cities are seeing the population bleed become stemmed, crime rates going down, and revitalization occurring.[82]

Endnotes

1. *See* SPRAWL: THE DARK SIDE OF THE AMERICAN DREAM at 1 (Sierra Club, Sept. 25, 1998).

2. Shelby D. Green, *The Search for a National Land Use Policy: For the Cities' Sake*, 26 FORDHAM URB. L.J. 69 (1998). "In the early 1970s, it seemed likely that Congress would pass national land use legislation. Several Senate and House bills aimed at establishing a national land use policy that would require comprehensive land use planning by state and local governments, as well as coordination between them. Unfortunately, the proposed legislation failed to win the approval of Congress. And now, nearly three decades later, little has changed. In fact, land use regulation remains a patchwork of discrete state and federal laws and policies on use and development. Sometimes these policies are at odds with each other and respond largely to economic forces and private interests. Some of the resulting land use and development patterns have been destructive to the vitality of cities, the environment, and the ecology."

3. *See Smart Cities: What Your Hometown Can Learn from Six Success Stories*, U.S. NEWS & WORLD REPORT, June 8, 1998; *An Urban Improvement, but Not Quite Fat City*, N.Y. TIMES, June 19, 1998, at A16 (report of Secretary of HUD Cuomo to U.S. Conference of Mayors provides ample evidence that the country's economic growth has significantly improved conditions in cities of all sizes); GOVERNING, June 1998, at 29.

4. *See* Robert H. Freilich et al., *The New Federalism: American Urban Policy in the '80s: Trends and Directions in Urban, State and Local Government Law*, 15 URB. LAW. 159 (1983).

5. The crises include the following:

    1) the deterioration of central cities, first-ring suburbs, and closer-in neighborhoods, resulting in depopulation and abandonment of housing and the employment base;

    2) spiraling suburban sprawl, creating massive infrastructure, as well as energy, costs;

    3) loss of prime agricultural lands;

    4) environmental crises and threats to open space, air and water quality, environmentally sensitive lands, and natural resources;

    5) transportation congestion and resultant loss of quality of life; and

    6) inflating cost of housing and its effect on affordable housing.

See Robert H. Freilich, Elizabeth A. Garvin & S. Mark White, *Economic Development and Public Transit: Making the Most of the Washington Growth Act*, 16 PUGET SOUND L. REV. 949, 950 (1993); *see also* Robert H. Freilich & Eric O. Stuhler, THE LAND USE AWAKENING, ZONING LAW IN THE '70s 32–33 (1981); Robert H. Freilich & Linda Kirts Davis, *Saving the Land: The Utilization of Modern Techniques of Growth Management to Preserve Rural and Agricultural America*, 13 URB. LAW. 27 (1981) [hereinafter Freilich & Davis].

6. Freilich & Davis, *supra* note 5, at 37; *see* Green, *supra* note 2.

7. *See* Margaret Kriz, *The Politics of Sprawl*, NAT'L L.J., Feb. 6, 1999.

8. Vice President Al Gore, Remarks to the Brookings Institution (Sept. 2, 1998).

9. Vice President Al Gore, Remarks on the Clinton-Gore Livability Agenda: Building Livable Communities for the 21st Century, Smart Growth Network (Jan. 11, 1999).

10. *EPA to Take on Problem of Sprawl Using Legal Authority, Regional Chief Says*, DAILY ENVTL. REP., Feb. 4, 1999, at A 3-4.

11. Tara B. Koch, *Betting on Brownfields—Does Florida's Brownfields Redevelopment Act Transform Liability Into Opportunity?* 28 STETSON L. REV. 171 (1998); Paul Kibel, *The Urban Nexus: Open Space, Brownfields and Justice, 25* B.C. ENVTL. AFF. L. REV. 589 (1998); TODD S.

DAVIS & KEVIN D. MARGOLIS, BROWNFIELDS: A COMPREHENSIVE GUIDE TO REDEVELOPING CONTAMINATED PROPERTY (Section of Environment, Energy, and Resources, ABA 1997).

12. *See* United States v. Fleet Factors Corp., 901 F.2d 1150 (11th Cir. 1990) (lender liable if it has significantly participated in company management).

13. 42 U.S.C.A § 9601(20)(E).

14. Stephanie B. Goldberg, *Let's Make a Deal: Cooperation, Not Litigation*, A.B.A. J. (March 1997); Andrea Wortzel, *Greening the Inner Cities: Can Federal Tax Incentives Solve the Brownfields Problem?* 29 URB. LAW. 309 (1997).

15. Elisabeth Rosenthal, *U.S. to Pay New York Hospitals Not to Train Doctors, Easing Glut*, N.Y. TIMES, Feb. 18, 1997, at 1 (the federal government, in an attempt to move doctors to other central cities, will pay New York hospitals subsidies not to train residents).

16. *See* LOW-INCOME HOUSING PRESERVATION AND RESIDENT HOMEOWNERSHIP ACT OF 1990, 12 U.S.C. § 17141; CRANSTON-GONZALEZ NATIONAL AFFORDABLE HOUSING ACT, Pub. L. No. 101-625, 104 Stat. 4079; *see* Green, *supra* note 2.

17. *See* DAVID L. CALLIES, ROBERT H. FREILICH & THOMAS E. ROBERTS, CASES AND MATERIALS ON LAND USE 586 (West 3d ed. 1999) [hereinafter CALLIES, FREILICH & ROBERTS]. *See also* 42 U.S.C.A. § 12702 *et seq.*, Pub. L. No. 101–625, 104 Stat. 4079 (Nov. 28, 1990).

18. CALLIES, FREILICH, & ROBERTS, *supra* note 17, at 586.

19. Report, "Not In My Backyard: Removing Barriers to Affordable Housing," Advisory Comm'n on Regulatory Barriers to Affordable Housing (1991).

20. *Id.* at 2-14 n.4.

21. CALLIES, FREILICH & ROBERTS, *supra* note 17, *citing* the Commission's report, entitled "Not In My Back Yard: Removing Barriers to Affordable Housing" [hereinafter NIMBY], issued in 1991, blasts local government for creating excessive regulatory burdens through zoning ordinances and environmental laws that raise the cost of an average new house by 25 to 35 percent. Unfortunately, the report's conclusion is based primarily on scattered interviews with members of the development community rather than on empirical research. One expert addressing nexus issues concluded that local land use controls were not a statistically significant factor in regard to housing costs, but this is mentioned only briefly in a footnote. *See* NIMBY, at 2–14 n.4 (*citing* GLICKFELD & LEVINE, THE RELATIONSHIP BETWEEN LOCAL GROWTH CONTROLS AND THE PRODUCTION OF AFFORDABLE HOUSING: A CALIFORNIA CASE STUDY (Feb. 14, 1991)). In addition, the report acknowledges that housing finance and tax policies have played a significant role in rising housing costs, and that "poverty is the primary reason that affordability problems exist." *Id.* at 5-1.

22. Even the ultraconservative Heritage Foundation has reported: "Recently the issue of 'urban sprawl' received top billing at a White House event at which President Clinton and Vice President Gore announced their Livable Communities Initiative, which, it was promised, would reduce traffic congestion, promote cleaner air, preserve open spaces, and retard urban sprawl. To achieve these objectives, Clinton and Gore propose to provide the suburbs with additional funds for mass transit and loans to buy land for parks and greenbelts. Their initiative would assign to the Department of Housing and Urban Development the responsibility for encouraging and financing 'smart growth' strategies to encourage 'compact development' and regional cooperation." Wendell Cox, *The President's New Sprawl Initiative: A Program in Search of a Problem*, HERITAGE FOUNDATION BACKGROUNDER, March 18, 1999, No. 1263.

23. CALLIES, FREILICH & ROBERTS, *supra* note 17, at 586, citing the housing phenomenon that occurs when a household is forced to move from its residence by conditions that

1) affect the dwelling or its immediate surrounding area;

2) are beyond the household's reasonable ability to control or prevent;

3) occur despite the household's having met all previously-imposed conditions of occupancy; and

4) make continued occupancy by that household impossible, hazardous, or unaffordable.

24. 42 U.S.C.A. §§ 4601–4655 (1982).

25. Tim W. Ferguson & Josephine Lee, *Corporate Welfare*, FORBES, April 20, 1998, at 42.

26. *Id.* (property clearance, assembling adequate square footage for people, goods, and cars, and the expense of building in a congested space tend to make urban redevelopment economically infeasible).

27. CALLIES, FREILICH & ROBERTS, *supra* note 17, at 561.

28. David L. Callies & Gail M. Tamashiro, *Enterprise Zones: The Redevelopment Sweepstakes Begin,* 15 URB. LAW. 231 (1983); Michael Allan Wolf, *An "Essay in Re-Plan": American Enterprise Zones in Practice,* 21 URB. LAW. 29 (1989).

29. *See* Williams, *The Enterprise Zone Concept at the Federal Level: Are Proposed Tax Incentives the Needed Ingredient?,* 9 VA.TAX REV. 711, 721–22 (1990). Others dispute these figures. *See* Tschirgi, *Aiming the Tax Code at the Distressed Areas: An Examination and Analysis of Current Enterprise Zone Proposals,* 43 FLA. L. REV. 991, 1030 (1991).

30. Marilyn Marks Rubin & Edward J. Trawinski, *New Jersey's Enterprise Zones: A Program That Works,* 23 URB. LAW. 461 (1991); Wolf, *Enterprise Zones: State Realities and Federal Prospects,* 327 PLI/REAL 611 (1989).

31. Ralph Nader, *Socialism for the Rich,* N.Y. TIMES, May 15, 1999, at A27.

32. Aprill, *Caution: Enterprise Zones,* 66 S. CAL. L. REV. 1341 (1993).

33. *Id.* note 32.

34. CALLIES, FREILICH & ROBERTS, *supra* note 17, at 561.

35. *See id.* at 520, *citing* "Critics, like former HUD Secretary Kemp, label the program a 'hoax.'" McGinley, *Some Advocates of Enterprise Zone Concept Find Little Cheer in Democrats' Legislation,* WALL ST. J., August 9, 1993, at A14. Kemp prefers capital gains tax relief to wage credits. Supporters say the program is a critical pilot for an unproven concept and a first step to urban relief. With the amount of financial support likely to be low, it is better, some suggest, to focus on a few communities than to dilute the effect of the incentives by spreading them across the country. *Conversely, see* Michael Allan Wolf, *An "Essay in Re-Plan": American Enterprise Zones in Practice,* 21 URB. LAW. 29 (1989); Marilyn Marks Rubin & Edward J. Trawinski, *New Jersey's Urban Enterprise Zones: A Program That Works,* 23 URB. LAW. 461 (1991).

36. CALLIES, FREILICH & ROBERTS, *supra* note 17, at 561, *citing* Salsich, *A Decent Home for Every American: Can the 1949 Goal Be Met?* 71 N.C. L. REV. 1619, 1622 (1993). Though funding comes and goes, CDBGs have proven popular with local government officials. *See* Pierce & Guskind, *Reagan Budget Cutters Eye Community Block Grant Program on Its 10th Birthday,* NAT'L L.J., Jan. 5, 1985, at 12–15; Pierce, *The GOP Senators' Pork in a Poke,* NAT'L L.J., Apr. 24, 1993. Criticism of CDBGs often comes from advocacy groups for those who are supposed to be the primary beneficiaries of the grants: low- and moderate-income persons. Since CDBGs "allowed local authorities to pursue locally developed priorities . . ., the Act subordinated the needs of the poor, who were usually politically powerless, to the desires of local political leaders." Boger, *Race and the American City: The Kerner Commission in Retrospect—An Introduction,* 71 N.C. L. REV. 1289, 1308, n.97 (1993). Though local citizen input is required through notice and hearings, some view it as a meaningless formality. Congress has responded

to some complaints. Legislation now requires that 70 percent of CDBG funds be used for the benefit of persons of low or moderate income. 42 U.S.C.A. § 5301(c). CDBG grants are permitted for twenty-five distinct activities with affordable housing a prime target. Recent legislation also permits grants for economic development characterized as "microenterprises," consisting of businesses with five or fewer employees. *See* Salsich, *supra* note 36, at 1644–45.

37. *See* Zox & Ain, *HUD'S UDAG Program: A Potent Source of Capital for Developers,* NAT'L L.J., June 25, 1984, at 32, 33. UDAG was terminated in 1989. For coverage of UDAGs and other governmental programs, *see* DAYE ET AL., HOUSING AND COMMUNITY DEVELOPMENT: CASES AND MATERIALS (2d ed. 1989).

38. *See, e.g.,* Village of Euclid v. Amber Realty Co., 272 U.S. 365, 389-90 (1926); Associated Home Builders v. City of Livermore, 18 Cal. 3d 582, 604, 557 P.2d 473, 486, 135 Cal. Rptr. 41, 54 (1976); Southern Burlington County NAACP v. Township of Mt. Laurel (Mount Laurel II), 92 N.J. 158, 238, 456 A.2d 290, 430 (1983); Golden v. Planning Bd. of Ramapo, 30 N.Y.2d 359, 383, 285 N.E.2d 291, 304–05, 334 N.Y.S.2d 138, 158 (1972).

39. Carlson, *Surface Transportation Policy Project, in* AT ROADS' END: TRANSPORTATION AND LAND USE CHOICES FOR COMMUNITIES 6 (1995). Transit now accounts for only 5.12 percent of work trips in this country as opposed to 12.6 percent in 1960, while the modal share of the automobile increased from 69.5 percent to 88 percent over the same time period. 1995 U.S. DEP'T OF TRANSP., NATIONAL TRANSPORTATION STATISTICS, at 231.

40. The Federal Highway Act providing preferential federal highway expenditures, promoted use of large tracts of land as well as providing the routes to which suburbia and the central city could be connected. DAVID BOLLIER, HOW SMART GROWTH CAN STOP SPRAWL, 8–9 (Essential Books, 1998).

41. LINCOLN INSTITUTE OF LAND POLICY, THE BROOKINGS INSTITUTION & NATIONAL TRUST FOR HISTORIC PRESERVATION, ALTERNATIVES TO SPRAWL (1995) at 6–8; Davis & Seskin, *Impacts of Urban Form on Travel Behavior,* 29 URB. LAW. 215 (1997).

42. *See* Robert H. Freilich & Bruce G. Peshoff, *The Social Costs of Sprawl,* 29 URB. LAW. 183 (1997); Burchell, *The Economic and Fiscal Costs of Sprawl,* 29 URB. LAW. 159 (1997).

43. While a typical highway lane can accommodate only 2,400 persons per hour, a busway can carry up to 9,400 persons per hour, and a light rail system can handle over 22,000 persons per hour. MUNICIPALITY OF METROPOLITAN SEATTLE, DRAFT ENVIRONMENTAL IMPACT STATEMENT, REGIONAL TRANSIT SYSTEM PLAN (October 1992) at xvi.

44. Motor vehicle accidents are the leading cause of death for Americans until they reach their mid-thirties. 1997 U.S. DEP'T OF TRANSP., BUREAU OF TRANSPORTATION STATISTICS, TRANSPORTATION IN THE UNITED STATES: A REVIEW. Imported oil as a share of national consumption has increased from 27 percent in 1985 to 44.5 percent in 1995. Transportation accounts for two-thirds of U.S. oil consumption, with highway vehicles accounting for the largest share. *Id.* Approximately 40 percent of manmade hydrocarbon and nitrogen oxide (NOX) emissions, as well as two-thirds of carbon monoxide (CO) emissions are generated by automobile travel. M. BERNICK & R. CERVERO, TRANSIT VILLAGES IN THE 21ST CENTURY 44 (1997). Automobiles also generate airborne particulate (pm-10) water pollution from highway construction and drainage, and noise impacts. *Id.,* BUREAU OF TRANSPORTATION STATISTICS.

45. The Federal Aid Highway Act of 1962 established that federal funds for urban highways be based upon a "continuing, comprehensive transportation planning process carried out cooperatively by states and local communities" (the so-called "3C" process). 23 C.F.R. § 450.100; Robert H. Freilich & S. Mark White, *Transportation Congestion and Growth Management:*

Comprehensive Approaches to Resolving America's Major Quality of Life Crisis, 24 Loy. L.A. L. Rev. 915, 923.

46. Pub. L. No. 102-240, 105 Stat. 1914 (Dec. 18, 1991). ISTEA provides new standards and procedures for transportation planning and investment. The centerpiece of the legislation is the U.S.C. Title 23 programs involving new investment in highways, public transit, and transportation planning. Title I, Part A, §§ 1001-1109, 105 Stat. 1915-2064. Funds allocated for the NHS may be spent on innovative projects as well as new highway construction, § 1006(d), to be codified at 23 U.S.C. § 103(i), including FTA transit projects not on the NHS but within the same transportation corridor and that improve the level of service on NHS highways. The Metropolitan Planning Organization (MPO) and the state long-term transportation plan must take into consideration a number of planning criteria that include congestion relief, effect on land use and development, transportation management and congestion monitoring systems, and methods to expand, enhance, and increase use of transit services. ISTEA § 1024(a) (codified at 23 U.S.C. § 134(f)) and § 1025 (codified at 23 U.S.C. § 135(c)).

47. Pub. L. No. 105-78 (June 19, 1998); *see* Eric D. Kelly, *Beyond Regulation: Implementing Comprehensive Plans in the New Millennium,* 51 Land Use Law & Zoning Dig. No. 5, at 7 (May 1999).

48. Pub. L. No. 101-549, 104 Stat. 2399. Section 108 of the Clean Air Act Amendments of 1990 require the Environmental Protection Agency (EPA) to publish, in consultation with the Secretary of Transportation, guidance on maintaining a "continuous transportation–air quality planning process," including alternative planning and control activities, plan review, funding and other implementation alternatives, and methods to ensure public participation. § 108(e). This process is to be coordinated with the surface transportation planning process created under ISTEA. Transportation control measures to be included in EPA guidance include, among other things, public transit. § 108(f)(1)(A). The EPA is authorized to disapprove highway projects for failure to submit a SIP or to conform the SIP to applicable law. In lieu of highway money, the secretary may approve specific TDM and TSM measures. 42 U.S.C. § 7509(b)(2). These include public transit, HOV roads, employer-based trip reduction plans, and other transportation control measures listed in the statute are excluded from these sanctions. The relationship between transit and land use must also be recognized in air quality planning in some states. *See, e.g.,* 9 Va. Admin. Code § 5-15-140 (transportation plans in serious, severe, or extreme ozone nonattainment areas and serious carbon monoxide nonattainment areas must allow for modeling of transit ridership and show that there is reasonable relationship between expected land use and the transportation system).

49. *Id.,* note 48.

50. *See* Robert H. Freilich & S. Mark White, *The Interaction of Land Use Planning and Transportation Management,* Transp. Pol'y, 1994, at 101. *See also* Edith Netter & Jay Wickersham, *Driving to Extremes: Planning to Minimize the Air Pollution Impact of Cars and Trucks, (Parts I & II),* 16 Zon. & Plan. L. Rep. 145 (Sept. & Oct. 1993).

51. For a summary of the effects of ISTEA and the Clean Air Act Amendments, *see* Gloria Jeff, *ISTEA and the Clean Air Act Amendments: Implications for State and Local Planning, in* Modernizing State Planning Statutes: The Growing Smart Working Papers 125 (APA vol. 1).

52. ISTEA 23 U.S.C. § 101-140, TEA-21, Pub. L. No. 105-78 (June 19, 1998).

53. Robert D. McFadden, *A Transport Bill May Give Workers Some Free Rides,* N.Y. Times, Mar. 13, 1998, at A1 (the Senate bill entitled "The Transportation Equity Act for the 21st Cen-

tury," or TEA-21, consisted of $214 billion to upgrade highways and help construct mass transit systems, $171 billion on highway construction programs through 2003, $2 billion on transportation safety programs, and $41.3 billion on mass transit raising overall federal transportation spending by 40 percent). *See also* David Hess, *Senate OKs $214 Billion Compromise Transportation Finance Bill*, K.C. STAR, Mar. 13, 1998, at A8; Allison Mitchell, *House Support Public Works at Record Price*, N.Y. TIMES, April 2, 1998, at A1.

54. Michael S. Bernick & Amy E. Freilich, *Transit Villages and Transit-Based Development: The Rules Are Becoming More Flexible; How Government Can Work with the Private Sector to Make It Happen*, 30 URB. LAW. 1 (1998) (the Federal Common Grant Rule provides certain previously restricted land may be transferred in joint development projects for mass transportation purposes; the Federal Transit Act and the FTA Master Agreement have been modified to allow for more flexibility in joint development projects). For a view that transit-focused development has made little progress because it encounters neighborhood resistance and little effective governmental leadership at either the regional or local government level, *see* Douglas R. Porter, *Focused Development: A Progress Report*, 64 J. AM. PLAN. ASS'N 475, 485 (1998).

55. Timothy Egan, *Get Used to New West, Land Managers Tell the Old West*, N.Y. TIMES, Feb. 12, 1998, at A10.

56. Timothy Egan, *Bid to Save Fish Puts West on Notice*, N.Y. TIMES, Feb. 26, 1998.

57. TOM DANIELS & DEBORAH BOWERS, HOLDING OUR GROUND: PROTECTING AMERICA'S FARMS AND FARMLANDS (Island Press 1997).

58. FRANK SCHINDMAN, AGRICULTURAL LAND PRESERVATION, THE EVOLVING FEDERAL ROLE IN LAND USE REGULATION AND LITIGATION 100 (1984).

59. CAMPBELL-MOHN, BREEN & FUTRELL, ENVIRONMENTAL LAW: FROM RESOURCES TO RECOVERY 323 (1993).

60. *Id.*; *see also* Schnidman, AGRICULTURAL LAND PRESERVATION: THE EVOLVING FEDERAL ROLE IN LAND USE REGULATION & LITIGATION 100 (1984).

61. 7 U.S.C.A. §§ 4201, 1465; *see also* CAMPBELL-MOHN, BREEN & FRUTRELL, ENVIRONMENTAL LAW: FROM RESOURCES TO RECOVERY 323 (1993).

62. Barnaby J. Feder, *Towns Are Slowing Invasion of Farms by Bulldozers*, N.Y. TIMES, Mar. 20, 1997, at Business 1.

63. John H. Cushman, Jr., *Pollution Control Plan Views Factory Farms as Factories*, N.Y. TIMES, Mar. 6, 1998, at A-1.

64. Goodman & Warrick, *U.S. Plans to Curb Livestock Waste Pollution*, WASH. POST, at A-1 (Sept. 14, 1998).

65. 42 U.S.C. § 4011 *et seq.* (1970).

66. *Id.* at § 4023.

67. *See* 24 C.F.R. § 200.700 (1998), listing eleven site dispersal requirements for HUD assisted housing. These were adopted after the decision in *Shannon v. U.S. Dept. of HUD*, 436 F.2d 809, 821 (3d Cir. 1970); *see, e.g.*, D. LISTOKIN, FAIR SHARE HOUSING DISTRIBUTION: WILL IT OPEN UP THE SUBURBS TO APARTMENT DEVELOPMENT, 299–319 (D. Listokin ed., 1974); Kleven, *Inclusionary Ordinances—Policy and Legal Issues in Requiring Private Developers to Build Low Cost Housing*, 21 UCLA L. REV. 1432 (1974); Note, *Required Low-Income Housing in Residential Developments: Constitutional Challenges to a Community Imposed Quota*, 116 ARIZ. L. REV. 439 (1974). *See also* Heyman, *Legal Assaults on Municipal Land Use Regulation*, 5 URB. LAW. 1 (1973); *Jones v. Meade*, 510 F.2d 961 (2d Cir. 1975).

68. *Walker v. City of Mesquite*, 169 F.3d 973 (5th Cir. 1999), holding that strict scrutiny

is applicable to any race-conscious remedy and that there was insufficient evidence to use race-conscious site selection to remedy the effects of past discrimination.

69. Berger, *Pact Will Provide Minority Housing: A Yonkers Settlement to Buy and Build Houses in White Areas,* N.Y. TIMES, Dec. 2, 1998 at A-25. *See also Spallone v. United States,* 493 U.S. 265 (1990), where the Supreme Court ordered contempt fines until the housing was built.

70. MASS. GEN. LAWS ANN. ch. 408, §§ 20–23 (1969). *See also* Board of App. v. Housing App. Comm., 294 N.E.2d 393 (Mass. 1973).

71. Craig, *The Dayton Area's "Fair Share" Housing Plan Enters the Implementation Phase,* 6 CITY 50 (1972). *See also* Bertsch & Chager, *A Regional Housing Plan: The Miami Valley Regional Planning Commission Experience,* PLANNERS NOTEBOOK, at 2–5 (No. 1, Apr. 1971).

72. *See, e.g.,* Myhra, *A-95 Review and the Urban Planning Process,* 50 J. URB. L. 449 (1973). A-95 has since been repealed.

73. N.Y. Unconsol. Laws §§ 6251-6285, ch. 174, §1 (McKinney 1969) (New York State Urban Development Corporation Act).

74. Moore, *Politics, Planning and Power in New York State—The Path from Theory to Reality,* 37 J. AM. INST. PLANNERS 66 (Mar. 1971). *See also* Brandon, *Integrating Recreation and Open Space Facilities into Urban Development Projects,* 24 SYRACUSE L. REV. 929 (1973).

75. For every American who moved to a city from 1970 to 1990, four moved to a suburb. In 1990, 14 percent of city census tracts were classified as high poverty, more than double the figure of 1970. The statistics, at least as of 1990, were gloomy; but, a decade later, reality has changed. HUD's 1990 State of the Cities Report.

76. Ronald Brownstein, *Behind the Boom in Minority Home Ownership,* L.A. TIMES SYNDICATE, K.C. STAR, June 13, 1999 at K-1.

77. COMMUNITY REINVESTMENT ACT OF 1977, 12 U.S.C.A. § 2901 *et seq.* The Act was significantly strengthened in 1989. *See* Macey and Miller, *The Community Reinvestment Act: An Economic Analysis,* 79 VA. L. REV. 349 (1993).

78. *Id.,* note 73.

79. Haya El Nasser, *Downtown Increasingly Becoming Hometown,* USA TODAY, Sept. 25, 1998 at 3A, col. 3.

80. John H. Cushman, Jr., *Defining Road in Utah's Wilderness,* N.Y. TIMES, Jan. 28, 1997, at A9 (state and local officials are documenting thousands of "little-known" trails as established roads to curtail the federal government's designations. The Federal Land Policy and Management Act of 1976 and the Wilderness Act of 1964 preclude establishing wilderness designations except in roadless areas).

81. Perry Knize, *Winning the War in the West,* ATLANTIC, July 1999, at 54.

82. Brendan Koerner, *Cities That Make It,* U.S. NEWS & WORLD REPORT, June 28, 1998, at 26. An interesting statistic, however, is emerging: Large cities are now growing; small and medium cities are rapidly declining. Richard Wolf, *Small, Midsize Cities Not Sharing in Strong U.S. Economy,* USA TODAY, June 11, 1999, at 10A.

CHAPTER TEN

Conclusion

In combating sprawl, it is not necessary to give up the American dream; it must only be slightly revised.[1] Growth can be orderly through timing and sequencing; and, with adequate comprehensive planning, the population's housing needs can be met without infringing upon agricultural and rural land. The process of growth does not have to be characterized by urban sprawl and leapfrog development. It is not necessary to acquiesce quietly to a process for urbanization that magnifies the environmental and energy crises; relegates the central cities and existing first- and second-ring suburbs to a constant struggle with racial barriers, housing abandonment, and fiscal inefficiencies; and devours agricultural open space and environmentally sensitive lands at alarming rates.[2]

The nation's attitude over the last several decades has changed—not only in the federal government's realization of the problem, but also in citizens' interest in conservation, preservation, rehabilitation, and fiscal growth.[3] The courts are responsive to workable and responsible growth management. Within the framework of comprehensive regional planning, the expansion of the police power provides a means for utilizing the various tools, strategies, and techniques of land use regulations in a fair and beneficial manner. The "best" combination of land use devices for any locality will depend upon the identified regional needs, problems, and objectives, as well as the community's resources and legislative flexibility. The key factors are legitimate and nondiscriminatory goals, consideration of regional factors, careful preparation of and adherence to a comprehensive plan, the will to control urban sprawl for the benefit of urban renewal, timed and sequenced growth within the Urbanizing Tier, and the preservation of agricultural and environmentally sensitive land.

Furthermore, citizens must realize the advantages of utilizing these techniques. First, that creating zoning for multiple-use development as well as single-family detached housing provides worthwhile taxpayer savings and multiple markets for developers. Second, that as infill of urban centers is promoted, equity is added to both new and old developments and far greater economic development is achieved. Third, that twice as much land can be made available for open space if building design and location conform to rational plans that emphasize the aesthetic, biological, and economic values of people-oriented communities and preserved open space.[4]

Municipalities have learned lessons as smart growth systems have evolved from Ramapo to the present day. First, it is better for local planning entities to use smart growth systems because people prefer the freedom, flexibility, and incentives of such systems to the rigid restraints of police power regulations—that is, rather than just a stick, people prefer to have a carrot and a bendable wand. The key to solving most problems is to assert economic interests, because by finding economic solutions through incentives and better design and form, everybody benefits.[5]

Second, the lessons learned through consensus-building concepts like those in Washoe-Reno County, Nevada, should be extended to encompass statewide legislation and federal urban growth policy initiatives. True consensus will require input from all the players in the smart growth game to achieve the most efficient shared vision.

Third, we have reached the point in the evolution of smart growth systems where virtually all of the tools and techniques have been identified. Increasingly, they have been put to use in flexible and creative combinations to achieve astounding success. Now, we simply need the political will to utilize and implement these tools and techniques further to create communities with a true sense of place.[6]

Thus, the missing link preventing the widespread use of smart growth systems is the political will to act and to reconcile competing interests and concepts of private property rights. State-level takings legislation is not the answer.[7] What *is* the answer is more evolved and advanced smart growth systems involving and encouraging the widest array of public participation platforms to gather information and input for a truly complete shared vision. While such a notion always looks good on paper and in theory, people still often regard government-guided efforts at land use planning as socialistic. But these people fail to see planning for what it is: simply the use of human intelligence with a sense of forethought, not a Stalinist five-year plan. They fail to recognize that

their system of personal planning, from their children's college to their own retirement and estate planning, as well as business America's vast "corporate planning departments" and the government's military and foreign "intelligence" planning, is based on this very same fundamental concept.

To recapture this fading political will to act will require not only citizen participation in local elections and a greater realization of balancing the community's needs in lieu of NIMBY (Not In My Back Yard syndrome) but also responsible voting to avoid electing NIMTOO public officials—Not In My Term Of Office lame ducks. Citizens do not want to carry a huge burden, but neither do they want to feel as if they could not possibly make a difference. Joint responsibility and cooperative action between public and private smart growth players will be necessary to capture a shared ideology offering benefits to all politically willing actors.[8]

Smart growth systems of action give credence to the notion of intergenerational equity. We can no longer afford to allow developers to build blindly where land is cheapest. We can no longer afford to allow the development sector to be pitted against preservationists. We can no longer isolate ourselves after the Columbine (Littleton, Colorado) High School massacre, in gated subdivisions with Beefeater guards at the walls.[9] Smart growth systems are all about promoting environmental values and concerns while allowing private investors to achieve their bottom line.

I believe that an equilibrium point exists for each individual neigborhood, city, county, and region. And that equilibrium point can only be reached when each of these is able to work cooperatively to reverse the five crises necessitating a smart growth system,[10] namely by:

- dealing with inappropriate design, decline, and blight in existing built-up areas;[11]
- promoting development that works with, not against, nature's systems and fosters sustainable environmental quality;[12]
- designing communities to lower individual energy consumption by creating "softer" transportation routes and methods with pedestrian-friendly activities and mixed-use centers;[13]
- demanding concurrency of adequate public facilities and infrastructure with development to alleviate our massive infrastructure deficiencies;[14] and
- promoting agricultural, environmental, rural, and open space preservation.[15]

The future is bright for the twenty-first century, however. Smart growth is exciting stuff! Planners, lawyers, environmentalists, city managers, nonprofit organizations, governmental councils and boards, and, most important, average citizens must recognize their roles in the smart growth process. For, we are not only shaping and designing the future, we are creating livable, peaceful space that is continuously moving toward its equilibrium point through smart growth systems. Thus, it is time for everyone to jump on the smart growth bandwagon. While its tune may not be in perfect harmony to all ears yet, if we give it our enduring attention and persistence, smart growth systems will continue to evolve until they find their own harmonious equilibrium point.

Endnotes

1. ROBERT H. FREILICH, TO SPRAWL OR NOT TO SPRAWL: NATIONAL PERSPECTIVES ON KANSAS CITY (Western Historical Manuscript Society, Kansas City, Mo., 1977).

2. SPRAWL: THE DARK SIDE OF THE AMERICAN DREAM, Sierra Club, May 26, 1999. (The report points out that an astounding 70 percent of prime or unique farmland is now in the path of rapid development.) Kansas City, Mo., was listed as being the number one city in the nation in population density loss. The five worst sprawling cities in America were not Los Angeles, New York, Chicago, or Denver, but Atlanta, St. Louis, Washington, D.C., Cincinnati, and Kansas City.

3. Timothy Egan, *Dreams of Fields: The New Politics of Urban Sprawl,* N.Y. TIMES, Week in Review, November 14, 1998.

4. PETER KATZ, THE NEW URBANISM: TOWARD AN ARCHITECTURE OF COMMUNITY (McGraw-Hill, 1996).

5. PHILLIP LANGDON, A BETTER PLACE TO LIVE: RESHAPING THE AMERICAN SUBURB (Univ. of Mass. Press, 1994) (an excellent work on urban and suburban design and an argument for a new union).

6. LUCY R. LIPPARD, THE LURE OF THE LOCAL: SENSE OF PLACE IN A MULTICENTERED SOCIETY (New Press, 1977).

7. For an excellent article on the need for uniform federal takings legislation, *see* John J Delaney & Duane J. Desiderio, *Who Will Clean Up the "Ripeness Mess"? A Call for Reform So Takings Plaintiffs Can Enter the Federal Courthouse,* 31 URB. LAW. 195–256 (with Professor Daniel Mandelker's testimony before the Subcommittee on Courts and Intellectual Property, House Judiciary Committee), on H.R. 1534, the Private Property Rights Implementation Act of 1977. For an opposite view, *see* Glenn P. Sugaurelli, *"Takings" Bills Threaten People, Property, Zoning and the Environment,* 31 URB. LAW. 177 (1999).

8. MYRON ORFIELD, METROPOLITICS: A REGIONAL AGENDA FOR COMMUNITY AND STABILITY (Brookings Institution, 1997).

9. BLAKELY & SNYDER, FORTRESS AMERICA AND WALLED COMMUNITIES IN THE UNITED STATES (Brookings Institute, 1997) (a sociological examination of Americans retreating form

communities into gated subdivisions with like-minded people, the affluent, the retired, and the fearful).

10. DAVID RUSK, CITIES WITHOUT SUBURBS (Woodrow Wilson Center Press, 2d ed. 1995) (how urban disinvestment and suburban sprawl can be eliminated).

11. JANE JACOBS, THE DEATH AND LIFE OF GREAT AMERICAN CITIES (Vintage Books, 1961) (the monumental classic in the dynamics of city design to ensure vibrant life, diversity, and community).

12. PETER CALTHORPE, THE NEXT AMERICAN METROPOLIS: ECOLOGY, COMMUNITY, AND THE AMERICAN DREAM (Princeton Architectural Press, 1993).

13. DAVID L. GREENE, TRANSPORTATION AND ENERGY (Eno Transportation Foundation, 1997) (an excellent presentation of arguments for a combination of alternative strategies to change people's behaviors, including land use reforms, transportation demand management, technological R&D, alternative fuels and vehicles, efficiency in building corridors and centers).

14. DOUGLAS R. PORTER, MANAGING GROWTH IN AMERICA'S COMMUNITIES (Island Press, 1997); Martin Leitner & Susan Schoettle, *A Survey of State Impact Fee Enabling Legislation,* 25 URB. LAW. 491 (1993); Franklin James, *Evaluation of Local Impact Fees as a Source of Infrastructure Finance,* 11 MUN. FIN. J. 407 (1990).

15. Douglas P. Wheeler, *Ecosystem Management: An Organizing Principle for Land Use, in* DIAMOND & NOONAN, LAND USE IN AMERICA (Island Press, 1996); DAVID BOLLIER, HOW SMART GROWTH CAN STOP SPRAWL (Essential Books, 1998) (describing at pp. 20–24 the vast environmental harm engendered by sprawl).

Table of Cases

Jurgenson v. County Court, Union County, 600 P.2d 1241 (Or. 1979), 166 n.223

Just v. Marinette County, 56 Wis.2d 7, 201 N.W.2d 761 (1972), 70, 97 n.163

J.W. Jones Companies v. City of San Diego, 157 Cal.App.3d 745, 203 Cal.Rptr. 580 (Ct. App. 1984), 159 nn.79–81, 159 n.83, 157 nn.85–86, 158 n.102

K

Kaiser Aetna v. United States, 444 U.S. 164 (1979), 96 n.155

Kansas City, Mo., City of v. Kindle, 446 S.W.2d 807 (Mo. 1969), 275 n.57

Katobimar Realty Company v. Webster, 118 A.2d 824 (N.J. 1955), 87 n.19

Kennedy Park Homes Ass'n v. City of Lackawanna, 436 F.2d 108 (2d Cir. 1070), *cert. denied*, 401 U.S. 1010 (1971), 34 n.23

Keystone Bituminous Coal Ass'n v. De Benedictis, 480 U.S. 470 (1987), 75, 96 n.155, 97 n.171, 97 nn.173–74, 100 n.190

Kit-Mar Builders, Appeal of, 439 Pa. 466, 268 A.2d 765 (Pa. 1970), 87 n.18, 87 n.22

Kuehl v. Cass County, 555 N.W.2d 686 (Iowa 1996), 300 n.49

Kunzler v. Hoffman, 48 N.J. 277, 225 A.2d 321 (1966), 104 n.230

L

Lake Country Estates, Inc. v. Tahoe Reg. Plan. Agency, 440 U.S. 391 (1979), 13 n.40

Lake Illyria Corp. v. Town of Gardiner, 352 N.Y.S.2d 54 (A.D. 1974), 94 n.118

Larsen v. County of Washington, 387 N.W.2d 902 (Minn. Ct. App. 1986), 93 n.117

Lionshead Lake, Inc. v. Wayne Township, 89 A.2d 693 (N.J. 1952), 87 n.20

Long Beach Equities, Inc. v. County of Ventura, 231 Cal. App.3d 1016, 282 Cal. Rptr. 877 (Ct. App. 1991), 93 n.117, 101 n.205, 206 nn.69-73, 206 nn.75–76

Loretto v. Teleprompter Manhattan Corp., 458 U.S. 419 (1982), 97 n.168

Lucas v. South Carolina Coastal Council, 112 S. Ct. 2886 (1992), 77, 93 n.113, 96 n.155, 205 n.45

Lynch v. Household Fin. Corp., 405 U.S. 538 (1972), 13 n.40

M

Mahaley v. Cuyahoga Metropolitan Housing Authority, 500 F.2d 1087 (6th Cir. 1974), 34 n.25

Marblehead v. City of San Clemente, 277 Cal. Rptr. 550 (Cal. App. 1991), 158, 206 n.67

Marcus Associates, Inc. v. Town of Huntington, 393 N.Y.S.2d 727 (1977), 13 n.47

Maryland National Capital Park & Planning Commission v. Rosenberg, 307 A.2d 504 (Md. 1973), 64

Matter of Rubin v. McAlevey, 54 Misc.2d 338, 282 N.Y.S.2d 564 (1967), *aff'd*, 29 A.D.2d 874, 288 N.Y.S.2d 519 (A.D.2d 1968), 46, 88 n.31, 99 n.185

Matter of Russo v. New York State Department of Environmental Conservation, 55 A.D.2d 935, 391 N.Y.S.2d 11 (1977), 88 n.31

Metropolitan Housing Dev. Corp. v. Village of Arlington Heights, 616 F.2d (7th Cir. 1980), 154 n.35

Metropolitan Housing Development Corp. v. Village of Arlington Heights, 558 F.2d 1283 (7th Cir. 1973), 35 n.28

Monell v. Dept. of Soc. Ser. of the City of New York, 436 U.S. 658 (1978), 13 n.40

Monterey, City of v. Del Monte Dunes at Monterey, Ltd., 119 S.Ct. 1624, 1999, S.W. 320798 (1999), *aff'g* 95 F.3d 1422 (1997), 74

Index